LLLAM

D0618970

Land Law

Land Law

Issues, debates, policy

Edited by
Louise Tee

WILLAN
PUBLISHING

Published by

Willan Publishing
Culmcott House
Mill Street, Uffculme
Cullompton, Devon
EX15 3AT, UK
Tel: +44(0)1884 840337
Fax: +44(0)1884 840251
e-mail: info@willanpublishing.co.uk

Published simultaneously in the USA and Canada by

Willan Publishing
c/o ISBS, 5824 N.E. Hassalo St
Portland, Oregon 97213-3644, USA
Tel: +001(0)503 287 3093
Fax: +001(0)503 280 8832

First published 2002

ISBN 1-903240-76-X (paper)
ISBN 1-903240-77-8 (cased)

British Library Cataloguing-in-Publication Data

A catalogue record for this book is available from the British Library.

Typeset by PDQ Typesetting, Newcastle-under-Lyme, Staffordshire
Printed by T. J. International, Padstow, Cornwall

Contents

Table of Cases

Table of Statutes

Introduction

Land law is concerned in a general sense with how people own, occupy and use land. But the 'land' of lawyers includes structures and buildings, and so this extends the reach of land law far beyond any field called Blackacre. Land law embraces not only the commercial relationships which connect businesses to their premises and farmers to their farms, but also the most intimate and private of legal relationships which connect people to their homes. The multifarious purposes which land serves are all potentially relevant to how people buy, sell or use land; all is the stuff of land law. So it is not surprising that the subject is complex and wide-ranging.

This is a particularly exciting time for land law, with continued development played out against the backdrop of an ever-changing society. A typical response to movement is legislative activism – and for land law, two initiatives are especially important, the Human Rights Act 1998 and the Land Registration Act 2002. The full impact of these two statutes will no doubt become apparent over time and, at the moment, any discussion is necessarily speculative. An expectation prevails that both Acts will produce fundamental shifts in the land law of the coming decades, and their presence, informs consideration of all areas of the law.

This book hopes to reveal the fascination of land law. Seven land lawyers with individual approaches and styles have each taken a major topic and have explored its ideas and concepts. A knowledge of the basic law is assumed, so that the chapters can concentrate on the policies and principles which underlie the subject, but which are so often masked by an emphasis on nuts and bolts. The contributions are all very different, reflecting the perceptions and interests of the respective authors. But even so it is possible to identify various themes that emerge and re-emerge throughout the book. These themes represent the current issues relevant to land law today. More often than not, the themes amount to tensions within the law, as differing or opposing objectives compete for priority. It is the attempt to find the appropriate balance which gives land law much of its critical interest, and fuels academic debate.[1]

---

[1] Of course, many of these themes are relevant in other areas of the law as well. See Herring's Introduction in his *Family Law Issues, Debates, Policy* (2001, Willan) which identifies several of these key issues in the context of family law.

Certainty or fairness

A pervasive theme involves the tension between the need for certainty in the law and the quest for fair outcomes in individual cases. This tension is not new; indeed, it is as old as equity itself, which came into being as a means of tempering the certainties of the common law with discretion. Obviously, the ideal would be a law in which both certainty and fairness coincided in all cases but, realistically, this is rarely achievable. Certainty is desirable so that people can arrange their affairs with confidence in the legal effect of their actions. It promotes transactional efficiency and a general feeling that the law is a reliable friend and tool. But there comes a point when certainty may come with too high a price-tag. Then the courts, or at least individual judges, may refuse to buy and instead resort to stratagems to produce a fairer result.[2] Or the statutory provision designed to achieve certainty may come with a let-out clause – just in case – which the courts then seize upon with enthusiasm.[3] Either way, the clarity of the law is compromised, but justice for an individual is achieved. Likewise, when an equitable jurisdiction becomes too uncertain and discretionary for judicial comfort, the court will try to impose a restraining hand of principle – as, for example, happened in *Lloyd's Bank plc* v. *Rosset*.[4] It is almost as if some self-righting mechanism underlies land law, working to restore to equilibrium any area that has strayed too far from the consensual mean.

The tension between certainty and fairness is only too apparent in the legislation and case law that Mika Oldham considers in her chapter on mortgages. Another example is provided by the new Land Registration Act, which tries to steer a careful path between the conflicting demands. Roger Smith discusses the implications in his chapter. How successful the Act will be remains to be seen. It has tried to shift the land registration system in the direction of certainty and, if its provisions are strictly applied, many arrangements made by ordinary people will be denied protection against third parties. Its rigorous contraction of overriding interests will leave many neighbours, for example, vulnerable to the loss of rights that they had sensibly negotiated with each other, but without legal advice. If the harsh imperative of the statute seems unpalatable to a judge in the future, then who knows how a court will react?

---

[2] As happened, for example, in the classic case of *Ives (ER) Investment Ltd* v. *High* [1967] 2 QB 379.
[3] See *Yaxley* v. *Gotts* (1999) 2 FLR 941.
[4] [1991] 1 AC 107.

Contract or status

Another theme concerns the important question of how much respect the law should give to individual autonomy. Should land law strive to give effect to the intentions of individuals, or should it impose legal consequences upon people because of their 'status' and regardless of what they themselves wanted? The question involves both issues on a 'macro' level – as evinced by Kevin Gray looking at the responsibilities of citizenship – and on a 'micro' level, looking at specific areas of jurisprudence. Thus Anna Lawson considers easements of necessity, which involve issues nicely encapsulating this problem. Stuart Bridge draws attention to the contract/status tension when discussing *Street* v. *Mountford*.[5] In that case, the Court of Appeal gave effect to the express intentions of the parties that the agreement into which they had entered amounted to a mere licence to occupy. In Stuart Bridge's words, the House of Lords, by contrast, took a 'paternalistic and interventionist' approach. Status reasserted itself over contract. The parties' intentions were overridden by policy considerations. In other words, individual freedom was restricted – Mr Street could not do what he wanted to do – because the court thought that, for the greater good, people should not be able to contract out of the Rent Acts.

The contract/status issue is also apparent within constructive trusts, and is relevant to the 'problem' of homesharing, which I discuss in the chapter on trusts. The debate continues as to whether the law should impose property transfers or some sort of joint ownership upon couples who have shared a home together, but have not shared the title. For couples who marry, status trumps contract, and in divorce proceedings the courts have wide powers to distribute property as they think fit; the desires or intentions of the parties are of minor relevance. This is generally considered acceptable – marriage is a status that people choose to acquire and which carries with it certain obligations and consequences which are well known and understood. But the issue of whether a couple should be subjected to legal consequences merely because they have enjoyed a close emotional relationship is far more difficult. Society is then imposing a normative justice upon those very people who may have deliberately eschewed such a norm. At its heart, one can see a basic conflict between law, as the representative of society, trying to impose certain standards of behaviour upon individuals, or trying to redress perceived unfairness, and law, as the protector of individual freedoms, trying to facilitate personal autonomy. Obviously, this same conflict is played out in many other legal spheres, but it achieves a special resonance in land law because so often the subject-matter of the dispute is a person's home or business premises.

---

5   [1958] AC 809.

The public/private divide

This same tension can be analysed in a slightly different way, as a question about the extent to which the state should interfere in the private lives of individuals. Traditionally, private property has been seen as a bulwark against overweening state ambition. This interpretation may evoke a wry laugh when one thinks of the statutory inroads into private life over the last century. But the 'home is one's castle' mentality still survives in attenuated form, and it is still an issue which attracts the attention of civil rights activists. Paradoxically, human rights can push both ways. So the imperative of human rights can be to restrict the powers of landowners – as Kevin Gray shows. But human rights can also restrict the interference of the state into private lives and ordering. Kevin Gray explores issues surrounding human rights and land law. Obviously, with the 1998 Act, this is a newly vigorous area, and already a few claimants in areas as diverse as adverse possession,[6] overreaching[7] and overriding interests[8] have attempted, with varying degrees of success, to argue that pre-existing orthodoxies must be revisited to take account of the Convention rights incorporated by the Act. There is scope for the ambitious litigant, because in some areas land law has, historically, adopted a robust attitude to the preservation of individual rights. Thus, in adverse possession, the paper owner has had to 'use it or lose it'. So far, the courts have proved reluctant to be too radical with regard to mainstream principles but, with increasing confidence, this might change.

Kevin Gray shows that the relevance of human rights or values in land law is not new, but rather that the law of property has always involved a range of value judgments about the proper entitlement of individuals. What is new is merely the express legislative requirement to consider these fundamental principles, though even here there is a relevant legislative precedent for the UK in the Government of Ireland Act 1920. Gray focuses on the key issue of when a landowner should be compensated for the restrictions or takings imposed by the state. He shows how random the present system is, and explores the philosophical bases that underlie decisions about compensation. Rival views as to the appropriate balancing of individual and community interests – indeed, of citizenship itself – shape the jurisprudence in this increasingly contentious area.

---

6   *Pye (JA) (Oxford) Ltd* v. *Graham* [2001] 2 WLR 1293.
7   *Birmingham Midshires Mortgate Services Ltd* v. *Sabherwal* (1999) 80 P & CR 256.
8   *Parochial Church Council of Aston Cantlow & Wilmcote* v. *Wallbank* [2001[3 All ER 393.

Balancing estates and interests

A tension exists at the very heart of land law, with the differing needs of proprietors of estates on the one hand, and the owners of third-party interests over those estates on the other. A persistent mantra throughout the last two hundred years has been that land should be freely alienable. This objective inspired the reforms of 1925, and also has been operative in the drafting of the new Land Registration Act. The commercial imperative has resulted in, for example, overreaching, which protects purchasers from inconvenient family interests. Even so-called 'commercial' third-party interests, such as easements or restrictive covenants, can cause problems to purchasers. For easy conveyancing, third-party rights should be limited and readily identifiable, and subject to clear rules as to priorities and enforceability. But another equally fervent ambition, the promotion of full beneficial user of land, requires the encouragement and protection of third-party rights. Anna Lawson refers to this in her chapter on easements. She points out that the public interest in ensuring full use of land has led judges to insist that the list of rights which are capable of existing as easements is not closed. And of course that immediately makes conveyancing more uncertain and more difficult.

This tension sometimes appears as a conflict between commercial convenience and domestic protection, when a purchaser-mortgagee may be affected by third-party interests in the family home. Then the issue can be described, in Lord Denning MR's words, as a struggle between 'monied might' and 'social justice'.[9] This particular tussle has now evolved into questions about the protection that should be offered to guarantors and family members, as so recently considered by the House of Lords in *Royal Bank of Scotland plc v. Etridge (No 2)*.[10] Mika Oldham subjects the case to careful consideration.

The distinction between proprietary and personal interests

The very nature of third-party rights is also contentious. Proprietary interests form the traditional building blocks of land law. They are the interests that attach to land and that may be enforced against purchasers. Martin Dixon explores the nature of such interests, and shows how difficult it is to delineate them with any precision, or define them with any certainty. He concludes that, ultimately, whether or not an interest is 'proprietary' is becoming increasingly irrelevant, and that of far more

---

[9]   *Williams & Glyn's Bank v. Boland* (CA) [1979] 1 Ch 312 at 333.
[10] [2001] 3 WLR 1021.

significance is whether or not an interest is registrable. The logical corollary of this is that we can more clearly focus on deciding which interests we wish to be enforceable against third parties – for economic or social policy reasons – and we can then legislate accordingly. Indeed, it is arguable that this is already happening with the provisions in the Land Registration Act which enable 'mere equities' to be protected on the register.[11] Roger Smith also touches on this issue in his chapter on registered land, and considers the relevance of proprietary status in the future. Elsewhere,[12] I have argued that the categorisation of an interest as proprietary is not especially helpful in relation to registered land, and that occupiers whose occupation is both actual and apparent should be able to enforce against third parties any interests they have in the land, other than those requiring personal skill and confidence. Roger Smith takes issue with this. He argues that if one is going to widen the ambit of enforceable interests, then logically the scope of minor interests should be expanded correspondingly, and that this would result in the virtual disappearance of the proprietary/personal divide in registered land. He concludes that the disadvantages would outweigh the advantages. However, there is a clear logic in confining the suggested expansion to the rights of occupiers, and not extending it to minor interests. Generally, monetary compensation for the loss of a right is adequate for a non-occupier but is grossly inadequate for an occupier, when the right may well involve his or her home or business. The argument about the extent to which occupiers *should* be protected is especially relevant now, in the light of the Land Registration Act. The Law Commission has adopted a robust, restrictive approach.

The theme of the increasingly elusive nature of proprietary rights emerges in other chapters as well. The difficulty of identifying rights at all is a pervasive theme in Kevin Gray's contribution, while Stuart Bridge, in his chapter on leaseholds, shows how the distinction between proprietary and non-proprietary right has been ignored in *Bruton* v. *London & Quadrant Housing Trust*.[13] As ever, the more one examines apparent bright-line distinctions, the more one realises how illusory or unhelpful they are.

Conclusion

Obviously, these themes are disparate and freely overlap. Indeed, a question such as the role of constructive trusts can be interpreted as an

---

[11] Land Registration Act 2002, S. 114.
[12] 'The rights of every person in actual occupation: an enquiry into Section 70 (1) (g) of the Land Registration Act 1925', [1998] CLJ 328.
[13] [2001] 1 AC 406.

illustration of several, if not all, of the tensions mentioned above. This is because all these themes that have been identified provide different, but not mutually exclusive, ways of analysing the law. The question of how to achieve a balance between competing demands is, in essence, an aspect of the fundamental and crucial question – what policy or policies should inform land law? This, of course, is in itself a subset of the even bigger question, what is the purpose of law?

And it is vital for any intelligent appreciation of land law to bear these fundamental questions in mind. The subject-matter of this law directly impinges upon the domestic and working lives of people; it is important to get it right. But it is difficult. Not only are there conflicting interests and objectives. There are also people. People enter into arrangements that do not easily slot into recognised legal categories; people fail adequately to protect rights, through ignorance or indolence or negligence. So land law, whether it likes it or not, has to deal with all this chaos that people continually create, while still trying to provide a reliable framework for conveyancers and lawyers generally. It is no wonder that the law involves fundamental questions. It is no wonder that the subject is so full of fascination. Read, think – and enjoy.

1

Proprietary and non-proprietary rights in modern land law

Martin Dixon

Land law is about proprietary rights in land.[1] Surely, this is a truth universally acknowledged by all. Conversely, as we also know, land law is not centrally concerned with non-proprietary rights (personal rights) as these are more the province of the law of obligations, especially the law of contract. This, apparently, is not a mystery for the physical manifestation of land[2] is immovable, durable and indispensable and only a primitive legal system (which of course English common law is not![3]) would countenance rules that did not fully protect 'ownership' of such a precious asset.[4] Indeed, such is the grip held by the distinction between proprietary and non-proprietary rights on the jurisprudence of land law that virtually every text, student or otherwise, is laid on this foundation. It is the creed recited by teachers in lectures and students in examinations and it is an intellectual sin to deny it. Needless to say, it is not the purpose of this chapter to encourage heresy and sin: at least not mortally. Nevertheless, there is much in the distinction between proprietary and non-proprietary rights as it applies in today's system of land law that is perplexing and this is in addition to the lingering lack of clarity about

---

[1] The concept of a proprietary right, being a right to assert ownership of 'a thing' against the whole world, is not unique to land law; neither is the concept of a 'proprietary claim', being the right to recover 'the thing' itself (and not 'merely' its value) from whosoever possesses it. See, for example, the purpose behind proprietary claims in the law of trusts as in *Foskett* v. *McKeown* [2000] 3 All ER 97 and, generally, Birks, 'Before we begin: five keys to land law' in Bright and Dewar, *Land Law: Themes and Perspectives* (1998, Oxford University Press).

[2] Of course, the definition of 'land' for the purposes of land law includes the physical substance and tangible and intangible rights therein: see Law of Property Act 1925 (hereafter LPA) s. 205 (1) (ix).

[3] As always, this description arrogantly includes Wales.

[4] This was, of course, a powerful reality when land was the foundation of wealth, power and status.

what it really means for a right to be classified as 'proprietary' and an almost accepted lack of certainty about whether a number of emerging or marginal rights to use or enjoy land really are proprietary at all. This chapter will explore some of these difficulties, not primarily from a jurisprudential standpoint[5] but, rather, via an examination of the mechanics of modern land law.

The distinction in principle

The conceptual distinction between proprietary and non-proprietary rights is well known to the common law, both within and without land law. In essence, a proprietary right is regarded as a right enforceable against 'a thing' rather than the person who has in some way acted in relation to 'the thing'. It is an assertion of a right of ownership or use over the thing itself (sometimes called the *res*). In consequence, a proprietary claim entitles the claimant to recover the *res* itself or to use it, rather than be limited to recovery of its value or a sum for loss of use.[6] As well as in land law, proprietary claims arise, *inter alia*, in the law of trusts, marine law and bankruptcy. Necessarily, a proprietary claim is particularly useful where the person against whom suit is made is unable to satisfy the claimant personally as to the value of the *res* so that recovery or use of 'the thing' is the only available substantive remedy. A good example arises in insolvency where assertion of ownership of the *res* against the current possessor through a proprietary claim ensures that the *res* does not fall into the hands of the 'merely' personal creditors of the bankrupt.[7] Of course, the distinction is not unique to legal systems founded on the common law and civilian lawyers whose legal scholarship is based on the Roman model might express the distinction in terms of rights *in rem* and rights *in personam* or, in loose translation, as the distinction between 'real' rights and 'personal' rights. A pedantic English land lawyer, however, might prefer to stick with 'proprietary' and 'non-proprietary' on the ground that the match between proprietary rights and rights *in rem* (and therefore between non-proprietary rights and rights *in personam*) is not perfect. As is well known, a leasehold estate is a proprietary right albeit historically a right *in personam*.[8]

---

5   Of the many such analyses, see Harris, *Property and Justice* (1996); Penner, *The Idea of Property in Law* (1997); Gray and Gray, 'The idea of property in land', in Bright and Dewar, *Land Law: Themes and Perspectives* (1998, Oxford University Press), n. 1.

6   'Limited' is pejorative. It implies that a non-proprietary claim against a person is in some way inferior to a proprietary claim. Whether this is true, however, must depend on the circumstances in which the claim is made.

7   For a complicated and controversial example, see *FC Jones & Sons* v. *Jones* [1996] 3 WLR 703.

8   It is tempting to think this is mere pedantry and perhaps it is. However, as explained below, recent case law has opened up the possibility that the true *in personam* character of a lease could have consequences. See below, fn. 25.

Following this conceptual approach, proprietary rights in land – traditionally regarded as the central subject-matter of land law – are said to be rights that are enforceable against the land itself. For example, a claimant to a right of way by easement need not take his or her remedy in money from the person who has denied the right, but may obtain a remedy effectively authorising continued use of the right of way.[9] The right vindicated by the remedy fixes on the land, rather than operating personally against the person denying the right. Importantly, however, if the conception of a proprietary right in land is to have real meaning, it must go beyond the simple assertion that the claimant has a right to use the land itself. If that were all, we would mean nothing more than that a claimant with a proprietary right is entitled to a specific *type* of remedy: use of the land rather than money for a denial of the right. The other vital element is that the proprietary right is enforceable against the land even if the immediate defendant had no part in the creation of the right and often if he or she had no awareness of the existence of the right and hence no *mens rea* in relation to its violation. In our simple example, the proprietary easement is in principle enforceable against the land burdened by it, no matter that the owner of the estate in the burdened land has no personal legal connection to the claimant by contract or otherwise. The easement is not personal, but proprietary, and the absence of a contractual (or other) link between claimant and defendant is immaterial. This duality – that a proprietary right generates a remedy against the land and that this operates in principle irrespective of the identity of the person currently possessing that land[10] – seems to be at the heart of the concept of proprietary rights in land.

Identifying proprietary rights in land

It is axiomatic that not all rights arising in connection with the use and enjoyment of land are proprietary. It would be absurd if they were. Imagine purchasing a freehold estate that was in principle subject to every current legal obligation affecting the land. It takes only a moment's reflection to appreciate that if all rights affecting land were able to take effect against the land itself rather than personally against the individuals who created them, the land would quickly become inalienable and economically stagnant. Hence, it is vital that there exists a category of

---

[9] *Nicholls* v. *Ely Beet Sugar Factory Ltd* [1936] Ch 343.
[10] I have avoided 'owns' here, not only because 'ownership' of the land is unknown even in modern land law (a person owns an estate, the Crown owns the land), but also because as a matter of principle a proprietary right is enforceable against the land irrespective of who currently occupies or possesses it. It is no excuse from liability that the occupier is an adverse possessor.

rights affecting land whose essential quality is that they are enforceable only against the person who has created them or, in special cases, against the current owner of the burdened land because of some rule independent of land law. These are non-proprietary rights. Such rights also have names (*licence* is a traditional example) and they play a vital role in the system of modern land law. Despite being negatively defined as rights affecting an estate in the land that are *not* proprietary, they promote the beneficial use of land and aid the development of the system of land law. Although we would not want all these rights to be proprietary – they would 'clog' the title – land would be considerably less useful without them. For example, we need a concept that allows us, among many other things, to have the right to enter or cross another's land for a limited purpose without committing a trespass, to place an advertisement on another's land in return for a fee (a billboard) or to purchase the use of another's land for a limited purpose, such as hiring the land as a venue for a meeting. Moreover, over time, rights that were non-proprietary in origin might become so useful for the economic or social exploitation of land that they 'harden' into proprietary rights, often through judicial recognition. The restrictive covenant, once a creature of pure contract binding only between the original parties, is a venerable example.[11] In truth, then, proprietary and non-proprietary rights have an almost symbiotic relationship. The one is the counter-category of the other and they exist in harmony with an osmotic wall between them.

In theory there is no limit to the number of non-proprietary rights that can exist over land,[12] but the familiar example of the purchase of a cinema ticket provides a suitable illustration. The purchaser of the ticket acquires no proprietary claim over the land but rather enjoys a contractual right to enter and view the film. Should the owner of the cinema sell the land before the contractual right to view can be exercised, the viewer has no proprietary claim against the new owner to enter and view. Failing an agreement between vendor and purchaser of the cinema as to the continuing validity of existing tickets, the ticket holder's remedy lies in contract against the original owner – he or she who issued the ticket and made the contract. This is not controversial, but why *exactly* is this right non-proprietary? First, we should not make the mistake of believing that this contractual licence is a non-proprietary right *simply* because the main purpose of the right granted is to see a film rather than to use the land *per se*. The main purpose of a *profit à prendre*, such as the profit of estovers, is to take something from the land (wood) and the rationale of a covenant restrictive of use (e.g. prohibiting trade or business) might be to protect a commercial interest, but both are proprietary. The substance of

---

[11] *Tulk* v. *Moxhay* (1848) 2 Ph 774.

[12] Given thats many non-proprietary rights are the creations of contract, their substance is as variable as the terms of a contract. *Quaere* whether there is a limit to the number of proprietary rights.

proprietary rights is not limited only to those activities intimately connected to the land *as land*. Secondly, in the same vein, a contractual licence, even to see a film, may in appropriate circumstances be enforced against the promisor (licensor) by obtaining a decree of specific performance or injunction,[13] but this does not make the licence proprietary simply because the remedy *apparently* lies against the land itself.[14] As we have seen above, the availability of a remedy apparently operating against the land *per se* is not at the centre of the distinction between proprietary and non-proprietary rights. Furthermore, lest we be tempted, it is hardly sufficient to say that this contractual licence is non-proprietary because of its 'inherent nature'. That empty mantra merely begs a host of questions. The essential question still remains: how do we distinguish proprietary rights like easements from non-proprietary rights like the contractual licence enjoyed by a visitor to the cinema?

Let us consider a number of possibilities. Given the exalted status proprietary rights enjoy within the jurisprudence of land law, the first possibility is that there might actually be a list of them. Such a *numerus clausus* is not a new idea,[15] and if we really do need a sharp line between rights in property and rights in contract, a list is as good a tool as any, and better than most. It has the estimable quality of being clear. Secondly, should we decide against the prescriptive list approach, perhaps there might be an *a priori* definition of a proprietary right, something we can turn to in order to measure up contenders. Certainly, a Martian arriving on the Clapham spaceship might reasonably believe that the great and sophisticated English common law could have managed to define what is meant by a 'proprietary right' or at the very least have developed a practical method of identifying such rights. Thirdly, if even this is not possible – and often definitions can be tricky in practical situations[16] – perhaps we can identify proprietary rights by focusing on their attributes, or at least what we believe their attributes are in modern land law.

---

13 *Verrall* v. *Great Yarmouth B.C.* [1981] QB 202.

14 In reality, the remedy lies against the person, but merely is manifested by ensuring that that person permits the other to use the land. In other words, only the promisor could be liable to specific performance and only if he or she retained the land over which the licence by contract was given. As said by Lord Wilberforce in *National Provincial Bank* v. *Ainsworth* '[t]he fact that a contractual right can be specifically performed, or its breach prevented by injunction, does not mean that the right is any less of a personal character . . . what is relevant is the nature of the right, not the remedy which exists for its enforcement.' [1965] AC 1175 at 1253.

15 See, for example, Rudden, 'Economic theory versus property law: the *numerus clausus* problem' in Eekelaar and Bell, *Oxford Essays in Jurisprudence*, (3rd Series, 1987).

16 Consider whether any meaningful definition of the 'duty of care' is possible in the law of tort given the novel situations in which claimants allege liability to have arisen.

Making a list

First, let us think about a list of proprietary rights. Although rather mechanical, this approach to differentiating between proprietary and non-proprietary rights has much to commend it. A *numerus clausus* might lack theoretical coherency,[17] but it would bring certainty. There would be no more searching for, or seeking to avoid,[18] binding precedent when faced with a novel situation and, although we would be left with the problem of determining why and when new rights could be added, would this be too large a price to pay?[19] We might even be able to remove rights from the list when they had become outmoded or otiose.[20] This, however, has not been the way of the common law, or indeed of the legislature. The former has a preference for piecemeal and gradual change as a way of responding to fluctuating social and economic conditions[21] and a search of the statute book brings only partial answers. For example, while s. 205 (1) (ix) LPA provides a statutory definition of what amounts to 'land', this is not equivalent to, nor intended to be, a list of proprietary interests in land.[22] Neither is the categorisation of certain rights as 'legal' or 'equitable' in s. 1 of the same Act. This often overlooked section tells us simply which rights, having already been accepted as proprietary, may further qualify as 'legal' or 'equitable' in nature. Even if we alight on s. 70 (1) of the Land Registration Act 1925, we find both that it is open-ended[23] and that a number of rights included in the definition of 'overriding interests'

---

[17] Of course it might not, for there is nothing to prevent such a list being theoretically coherent. The point is, rather, that the list may be drawn up by reference to criteria other than, or in addition to, the yardstick of theory.

[18] As in *Errington* v. *Errington* [1952] 1 KB 290 where Lord Denning in the Court of Appeal ignored binding House of Lords authority *in King* v. *David Allen & Sons, Billposting Ltd* [1916] 2 AC 54 that a licence was not proprietary.

[19] 'Why' new rights could be regarded as potentially proprietary, and become so by addition to the list is, of course, the serious issue. Without such a conception, there is no inherent merit in the list other than the simple fact of its existence.

[20] Instead, it seems that the Human Rights Act 1998 can be used to remove the proprietary effect of rights, see *Parochial Church Council of Aston Cantlow & Wilmcote* v. *Wallbank* [2001] 3 All ER 393 and the emasculation of the ancient proprietary obligation of chancel repair liability.

[21] As already noted, leases have changed character in the feudal past, restrictive covenants followed in the wake of the industrial revolution and, more recently, contractual licences have been both vested and divested of proprietary status, again for social reasons.

[22] It is descriptive of 'land' (in its tangible and intangible senses), but uses generic terms in its descriptions. Thus we know that 'incorporeal hereditaments' are proprietary, but what qualifies as one?

[23] For example, the infamous s. 70 (1) (g) in theory can make any proprietary right 'overriding', but assumes that we will know whether a right is already proprietary or not.

traditionally might not be regarded as proprietary at all.[24] Of course, one could attempt to generate a list from the case law and, although it would contain all the usual suspects, there would be a number of rights affecting that land that could be included or excluded on a provisional basis only. We know about freeholds, easements, rentcharges, restrictive covenants, mortgages and many others, but what of rights generated by estoppels, licences coupled with an equity, the right to set aside a proprietary transaction (e.g. a mortgage) because of undue influence? Indeed, it seems that the status of even leaseholds is not entirely free of doubt.[25] Unfortunately, this is more than simple uncertainty about what to include in a list of 'proprietary rights' and what to consign to the dimly understood realms of contract law. If that were all, some competent authority could simply decide what to include and what not.[26] Rather, it is the tip of a much subtler problem: namely, that English land law is apt to regard the nature of a right as dependent on the factual background in which it arises. At its highest (or possibly worse), this means that what appears to be the same substantive right might be proprietary or not, depending on the circumstances in which it arises.

This fact is not usually apparent in the everyday operation of our modern system of land law, not least because the relative security of

---

[24] For example, 'public rights' and 'customary rights' within s. 70 (1) (a) and local land charges within s. 70 (1) (i). It is true that to fall within s. 70 (1) of the Land Registration Act 1925 (hereafter LRA) the rights must first 'subsist with reference to land', but that means that the rights must relate to property, not necessarily that all are proprietary. Note that Russell LJ in the Court of Appeal in *National Provincial Bank Ltd* v. *Hastings Car Mart* [1964] Ch 665 at 696 appears to disagree by asserting that s. 70 'in all its parts is dealing with rights in reference to land which have the quality of being capable of enduring through different ownerships of land, according to normal conceptions of title to real property'. It might be thought that this is not borne out by reading the entirety of LRA s.70(1), although undoubtedly it applies to s. 70 (1) (g) (at least if we take a narrow view of the proprietary character of 'mere equities': see *Blacklocks* v. *J.B. Developments (Godalming) Ltd* [1982] Ch 183; *Collings* v. *Lee* [2001] 2 All ER 332; Tee, 'The rights of every person in actual occupation: an enquiry into Section 70 (1) (g) of the Land Registration Act 1925' [1998] CLJ 328). In any event, s. 70 (1) also suffers from the problem encountered elsewhere: that it uses generic descriptions of rights and assumes that we already know what an 'easement' or a 'lease' is. The same 'problem' is replicated in schedules 1 and 3 of the Land Registration Act 2002, the intended replacement for S.70(1) LRA 1925.

[25] *Bruton* v. *London & Quadrant Housing Trust* [2000] 1 AC 406 where the House of Lords contemplates the existence of a 'non-proprietary lease'.

[26] This is not far fetched. Some might argue that the Law Commission has decided, despite considerable academic and judicial uncertainty, to include 'estoppels' within the category of proprietary rights: see Law Commission Report No. 271, *Land Registration for the Twenty-First Century* (2001) para. 5.29 *et seq*. This is now to be the law: see section 116 Land Registration Act 2002 that also determines that 'mere equities' can bind successors in title to the land they affect. In so far as some of these are not already proprietary (see fn. 24 above), this also confounds existing notions of the importance of the distinction between proprietary and non-proprietary rights. See also text below accompanying fn. 70.

relying on title registration hides many conceptual deficiencies.[27] Nevertheless, the ability of the same substantive rights to take on a different character according to the circumstances in which they arise is one compelling reason why a *numerus clausus* of proprietary rights has never been compiled in statute or elsewhere. Moreover, in case it is thought this is too bold an assertion, a simple example will illustrate the problem. Let us assume our list of proprietary rights includes 'easements and leases'. All well and good, but what are 'easements and leases'? These descriptive terms are themselves labels for substantive concepts and by including them in a list we are doing no more than postponing our definitional problem to a secondary level. We still need to know when a right can be regarded as 'an easement' or 'a lease' and this is where the context becomes important. For example, it is clear from the case law that a right to park a car on neighbour's land may, in differing circumstances, be either an easement (proprietary) or a licence (personal). The essence of the right is the same (to park a car), but the context invests the right with a different quality.[28] Perhaps this is unproblematic in practice, and certainly it is realistic, but what if 'the context' that can alter the character of a right consists not only of its factual backdrop, but can also comprise other, less solid considerations? A right to possess exclusively the property can amount to a 'lease'[29] and this is on our list. But, the right to occupy non-exclusively is not a lease and the court can determine 'exclusiveness' by reference to the state of mind of the parties even if contrary to their words (i.e. 'pretences'[30]) and even because of social issues surrounding the arrangements (e.g. acts of charity[31]). Consequently, essentially the same substantive right can be either proprietary or non-proprietary and to have 'easements' and 'leases' on our list does not actually take the matter much further. With a list, *if* a disputed right falls into one of the categories of

---

[27] For example, if the registration statute says something is binding, either automatically or on registration, then in most practical cases we have no cause to examine its underlying character. Alas, this emphasis on the practical rather than the theoretical is less helpful where the relevant registration rule is generic rather than specific, as with LRA 1925, s. 70 (1) (g) and the equivalent paragraph of schedules 1 and 3 to the LRA 2002 that assume that something must already be proprietary to be included. Neither does it help with rights not specifically mentioned by registration schema, as with estoppels, although for the future s. 116 LRA 2002 at least tells us that they are to be regarded as proprietary.

[28] *Batchelor* v. *Marlow*, Lawtel 28 June 2001, Court of Appeal, the right to park in context was not an easement; *K-Sultana Saeed* v. *Plustrade Ltd.* (2001) RTR 452, Chancery Division, the right in context was an easement. Note the baffling decision on appeal in *Plustrade* where the Court of Appeal appears to decide that the disputed proprietary character of the right to park was irrelevant.

[29] Assuming such possession is not referable to some other clear legal relationship (*Street* v. *Mountford* [1985] AC 809) such as that the possessor is the recipient of the largesse of a charitable trust, *Gray* v. *Taylor* [1998] 1 WLR 1093 or a service occupier, *Norris* v. *Checksfield* [1991] 1 WLR 1241.

[30] *Antoniades* v. *Villiers* [1990] 1 AC 417.

[31] *Gray* v. *Taylor* [1998] 1 WLR 1093.

proprietary right, then we have an answer, but there is still enough flexibility in the meaning of the term on the list to render any perceived certainty merely an illusion.

Abstract definition

Lest it be thought that the need to identify proprietary rights with some precision is just an academic fetish, we should remember that the most commonly cited a priori definition of what constitutes 'a proprietary right' is provided by the judgment in a case that, had it been decided otherwise, would have changed fundamentally the law relating to co-ownership and mortgage lending. *National Provincial Bank* v. *Ainsworth*[32] revolved around the alleged right of a wife to remain in occupation of the matrimonial home even though she owned no part of it, either at law or by equitable co-ownership. This quaintly named 'deserted wife's equity' was enforceable against the husband personally, but would not, indeed could not, bind a purchaser unless it was proprietary.[33] In the leading speech, Lord Wilberforce both reiterates the orthodoxy that it is only proprietary rights that are capable of binding purchasers of land and then goes on to consider whether this 'equity'[34] has such a character. Accordingly, '[b]efore a right or interest can be admitted into the character of property, or of a right affecting property, it must be definable, identifiable by third parties, capable in its nature of assumption by third parties and have some degree of permanence or stability.'[35]

It should surprise no one that this attempted definition of a proprietary right has come in for some sharp academic criticism.[36] Not only are academics difficult to please and usually able to find some flaw in the most well constructed analysis, it is true that Lord Wilberforce's definition is very leaky. Given that one important reason why we need to identify proprietary rights is to ascertain whether a disputed right (like a 'deserted wife's equity') is capable of binding a new owner of the land, it is evidently circular to say that a right is proprietary if it is capable of binding a third party ('capable in its nature of assumption by third parties'). Of course it is: but why? It cannot be that it is proprietary because it binds third parties, and that it binds third parties because it is proprietary! Moreover, it is not as if the other elements of Lord Wilberforce's definition add a great deal. Many rights are 'definable',

---

[32] [1965] AC 1175.

[33] See now matrimonial home rights under the Family Law Act 1996, Part IV.

[34] Not to be confused with an 'equitable interest' under a trust of land which as an equitable form of ownership is proprietary and capable in appropriate circumstances of binding purchasers.

[35] *National Provincial Bank* v. *Ainsworth* [1965] AC 1175 at 1247–1248. The claimed right failed this test.

[36] See, in particular, Gray and Gray in *Themes op. cit.* above fn. 5.

but not proprietary: a contractual licence is definable as to its terms, extent and attributes, but it is not 'real property'. Many rights affecting land are 'identifiable' by third parties, but the substance of many of these, such as the 'deserted wife's equity' itself and the rather obvious advertising hoarding attached to the side of my house, do not spring from proprietary rights. Conversely, is it true that all proprietary rights enjoy the characteristics that Lord Wilberforce alleges? In what sense is an equitable share of ownership established through constructive trust 'identifiable by third parties' and if it is, why has case law gone so far to protect the purchaser of land that is burdened by such an interest?[37] Similarly, is it true that the rights of a person in the process of acquiring title by adverse possession enjoy 'some degree of permanence or stability'[38] and what of leases that can be determined by immediate notice on either side?[39] Once more, how is it that an easement can be said to be 'definable' when so much turns on the context in which the alleged easement arises? Of course, there might be answers to some of these apparent inconsistencies, but it is not the purpose of this chapter systematically to pick holes in Lord Wilberforce's definition and then attempt to fill them in. The point is that Lord Wilberforce's definition raises as many questions as it answers and it fails the key test. When faced with an alleged new proprietary right – can we determine conclusively its proprietary status by applying the *Ainsworth* test? Patently we cannot.

Perhaps, however, we should pause a little before we consign Lord Wilberforce's dictum to the juridical shredder. It is unlikely that the learned judge set down his ideas simply for the fun of it. Certainly, there is an attempt – albeit flawed – to provide a template for the future and possibly there is something here that is useful. We cannot know, but it is doubtful that Lord Wilberforce meant to be prescriptive in the sense that all proprietary rights must meet all his criteria and that all non-proprietary rights had none of them. The latter interpretation would indeed be absurd, and so we might think is the former. Perhaps what we have is an attempt to capture the essence of *why* we need a measure of clarity in our conception of 'proprietary rights'. Logically flawed it may be, but in the real world proprietary rights *will* bind third parties and they need to be definable in order to measure (and value) their impact on the land over which they exist. How much more or less valuable is a title affected by an easement of way, but not affected by a licence given to store equipment? In other words, Lord Wilberforce's 'definition' actually expresses a few

---

[37] See *City of London Building Society* v. *Flegg* [1988] AC 54; *State Bank of India* v. *Sood* [1997] Ch 276; *Equity & Law home Loans Ltd* v. *Prestidge* [1992] 1 WLR 137.

[38] Lest we think that possession is not proprietary, see Hill, 'The proprietary character of possession' in E. Cooke (ed.), *Modern Studies in Property Law. Vol. 1.* Hart Publishing (2001)

[39] The point is not met by saying that while they exist they are permanent and stable. The point is we do not know how long they are going to exist for.

policy truths rather than presents a checklist of essential elements of proprietary status. Thus, those rights which are proprietary (however assessed) *should* be clearly definable and ascertainable by third parties, both as to the benefits they give and the burdens they impose because this will be reflected in the price paid for the estate or the use made of the land. Similarly, we might think that anything that is not measurable, not definable or not marketable, *should not* endure for the benefit and burden of the prize economic asset that is land. Of course, this does not mean that such immeasurable, indefinable or non-marketable rights always will be non-proprietary (and vice versa) because there is more to land law than conceptual clarity. But, Lord Wilberforce's dictum captures why it is necessary to be able to draw the distinction between proprietary and non-proprietary rights in the first place.

Using external criteria

Instead of concentrating on some schema or formula for identifying proprietary rights and then deductively identifying which specific rights are proprietary, might it be possible to concentrate on the known attributes of proprietary rights and use these to reason inductively? To put it differently, by taking known attributes of rights that are clearly proprietary and by asking which other rights share these attributes, it may be possible to assess the status of disputed rights. Necessarily, this requires a degree of certainty about what the attributes of proprietary rights are and therein may lie a problem. In addition, while this is a pragmatic approach, it may suffer from the lack of a 'key criterion'. That is, there is a danger that the attributes of proprietary rights may be so general they can be seen in many other types of right which are clearly non-proprietary and, *if* this is true, all we are left with is a list of attributes which are necessary for proprietary status but are not sufficient. Nevertheless, despite these concerns, let us see whether there is anything to learn from examining three further criteria, all of which appear to play an important role in the concept of proprietary status.

(a) Formality of creation

It is a feature of rights affecting land that, with some well-known exceptions, they must be created with some degree of formality. This formality is often justified by the need to have certainty and predictability when dealing with rights that both affect a valuable economic asset and that can endure through changes in ownership of that asset.[40]

---

[40] Much has been written on this. For a classic exposition see, Fuller, 'Consideration and form' (1941) Col LR 799. For a modern appraisal and useful references see Critchley, 'Taking formalities seriously' in Bright and Dewar, *Land Law: Themes and Perspectives* (1998, Oxford University Press).

Consequently, there is a direct link between the rules that govern the creation of rights in land and aspects of their proprietary character: the fact of their proprietary character requires their existence to be as certain as possible, hence they are created with formality. A number of statutory provisions contain the formality rules applicable to the creation of rights in land and, although not all are as clear as we might hope, generally they disallow the creation of a right in land by merely oral disposition. Accordingly, the Law of Property (Miscellaneous Provisions) Act 1989 lays down the formal requirements for the existence of a deed and also ensures that no disposition of a right in land can be effective unless it is in writing and conforms to the requirements of s. 2 of that Act. These provisions are supplemented by the rather more difficult ss. 52 and 53 LPA 1925 relating to the creation of leases and of trusts in land. As is obvious from all these statutory provisions, some kind of written instrument is usually crucial.[41]

At first blush, this 'external' criterion – the need for formality – seems rather promising as a way of distinguishing between proprietary and non-proprietary rights. We can say with some conviction that a 'deed' as defined in the 1989 Act is generally required for the creation of a proprietary right that is 'legal' in character,[42] and that a written document is generally required for a proprietary right that is 'equitable' in character. It might then follow, by inductive reasoning, that any alleged right not created using the required formality will not be proprietary. We should be able to say, for example, that an alleged right of way could not exist as an easement if it were created orally between two neighbours. It would be a mere licence. In this way, formality indirectly might allow us to distinguish between proprietary and non-proprietary rights.

Unfortunately, however, all is not plain sailing when it comes to using formality as the touchstone of proprietary character. The need for formality is procedural: it says nothing about the substance of the right but instead focuses on the manner of its creation. So, as in the easement example, there is no doubt that it is possible to have a right that is in substance identical to a proprietary right (for example, an orally granted right of way), but which is not proprietary because of the manner of its creation. Of itself, the existence of identical substantive rights, one proprietary and one not according to the manner of their creation, is not necessarily a 'bad thing'. If landowners are slapdash in the way they deal with their land, failing to observe what are really quite simple formality rules, should not their creations be denied the status of proprietary rights?

---

[41] Noting, of course, the exception of proprietary estoppel, short leases, prescriptive easements.

[42] See also LPA 1925 s. 1 identifying which proprietary rights are capable of existing as legal estates or interests. Note also for land of registered title the need substantively to register certain matters before they can take effect as a legal estate or interest.

Moreover, if such proprietary rights are created 'properly', they may be more obvious to a prospective purchaser of the land who would not then be stuck with binding rights of whose existence he or she was unaware. Consequently, the fact that formality rules can result in a different status being accorded under the law to the same substantive right (proprietary or non-proprietary according to the manner of creation) has advantages. However, English land law is not always concerned with such dry arguments, being intimately concerned with real life, and so has shied away from insisting on strict adherence to formality requirements, especially where the substance of the right given in a non-formal way is so clearly 'proprietary' in substance. Thus, English land law has developed two large doctrines whereby rights that are clearly proprietary may be created without any formality at all: first, resulting and constructive trusts, especially in the law of co-ownership; and, secondly, the law of proprietary estoppel.[43] Both these doctrines make it difficult to see formality as the key to distinguishing between proprietary and non-proprietary rights.

This is not the time to examine in detail the mysteries of these two sets of rules, rather the point is that they loom large in the everyday operation of land law and provide a handy lifejacket for those claimants unable to rely on rights created in compliance with the known formality requirements. In recent years, the constructive trust as it operates in the law of co-ownership has mushroomed into a near remedy of discretion, seemingly supplanting the concept of resulting trust and breaking free from the strictures that limited the doctrine in its first form.[44] The consequences of this are well known, with both purchasers from the legal owner and the equitable owner being buffeted by move and counter-move in the battle for control over the legal title.[45] Clearly, not all this uncertainty stems from the fact that these proprietary rights can arise without formality, but some of it does. Likewise, it illustrates that although it is unsafe to equate proprietary status with 'formality' absent a link between formality and proprietary status, there is a risk of uncertainty when third parties deal with land affected by these 'silent' proprietary rights. The sword is double-edged, leading to an explosion of litigation that is continuing to the present day.[46] The same is true of the ubiquitous doctrine of proprietary estoppel, except on a grander scale.

---

[43] In addition, there are the well-known exceptions to the need for formality. For example, rights acquired through adverse possession, easements by prescription and short-term leases.

[44] Contrast *Lloyds Bank* v. *Rosset* [1991] 1 AC 107 with *Midland Bank* v. *Cooke* [1995] 4 All ER 562 and see [1997] Conv. 66.

[45] See cases cited above at fn. 37 and *Williams & Glyn's Bank* v. *Boland* [1981] AC 487.

[46] Recently manifest in cases of alleged undue influence, the latest attempt by co-owners to avoid an otherwise paramount mortgage. This litigation is likely to continue in the form of negligence claims against solicitors who advise clients considering surrendering their proprietry rights to mortgages: see *RBS* v. *Etridge* 2001.

Although the resulting/constructive trust concepts allows an escape from formality, there is at least some certainty about their outcome: the claimant will have a proprietary right in the land behind a 'trust of land' governed by the Trusts of Land and Appointment of Trustees Act 1996. In contrast, a successful claim to estoppel may lead to any remedy, proprietary or otherwise. For example, the claimant might rely on estoppel to establish a lease over land, an easement or even a freehold. On the other hand, the claimant may be awarded a licence, an injunction or a monetary remedy. Until the court 'crystallises the remedy' we do not know if the outcome will be a proprietary right or not.[47] This uncertainty may be bad enough, but it is nothing compared to the problems generated by the more aggressive and current view of proprietary estoppel. According to this view, 'estoppel' is not an informal process that may, or may not, lead the award of a proprietary right in favour of the claimant. An 'estoppel' (that is, the inchoate right that a successful claimant enjoys pre-crystallisation) itself is proprietary. It – the uncrystallised estoppel – enjoys all the advantages that appear to accrue to proprietary rights and can (for example) bind a purchaser of land. Indeed, as much has now been accepted by the judiciary (*Lloyd* v. *Dugdale*, November 2001) and is confirmed by s.116 of the Land Registration Act 2002. It takes only a moment's reflection to appreciate that this is a new departure for the concept of proprietary rights in land. Not only is this proprietary right created without any formality (although that is not unique), it now seems that the right is inherently fluid, indeed inherently indeterminate pending the decision of the court. This is some distance from what we might think is at the core of the concept of proprietary rights in land. If we then realise that there is little agreement about the necessary conditions for a successful estoppel,[48] and certainly no predictability about when a claimant will be successful, it becomes apparent that any attempt to tie 'proprietary' status to formality is not going to be entirely successful.

(b) Durability through changes in the ownership of land

We have seen above that attempts to use the 'durability' or 'bindingness' of rights as the touchstone of their proprietary nature have generated criticism because of the circularity of the argument. That debate will not be repeated here. However, it may prove illuminating to consider for a moment what is meant by 'durability' and whether the way 'durability' works in practice can be used as a torch in the search for a meaningful way of distinguishing between proprietary and non-proprietary rights.

---

47 In *Campbell* v. *Griffin*, Court of Appeal, 27 July 2001, the result of a successful estoppel claim was an award of £35,000 in lieu of a proprietary right see also *Jennings* v. *Rice*, February 2002.

48 Save the deliberately vague need for an assurance, coupled with detrimental reliance.

'Durability' has two aspects: first, that the ability to enforce the alleged proprietary right passes with ownership of the land benefited by the right and, secondly, that the obligation to permit the right passes with the land burdened by the right. A simple example from the law of easements is where the owner *for the time being* of the dominant tenement (not being the original grantee of the right) is able to enjoy the easement over the servient tenement, even though the servient tenement has passed from the hands of the original grantor of the right. However, we need to be precise about the idea of durability in relation to proprietary rights. Strictly speaking, proprietary rights are those rights that are *capable* of enduring through changes in the ownership of the estate to which they relate. There is nothing 'automatic' about it. Whether *in fact* a proprietary right is durable in this sense depends on other factors. Consequently, the link between proprietary status and durability is not as simple as it first appears.

Prior to the 1925 property legislation, *if* a right was proprietary, then its durability would be determined (at least as to the burden) by its legal or equitable status, which in turn depended on a raft of other factors unrelated to its 'inherent' attributes (including as now the manner of its creation). Thus, we had the now largely defunct rule that 'legal rights bound the whole world' and equitable rights bound the whole world except for the populous category known as the bona fide purchaser for value of a legal estate without notice of the equitable right ('equity's darling'). These principles have now been replaced in the main by the provisions of the Land Charges Act 1972 and the Land Registration Acts 1925–2002 but the concept is the same: namely, that a proprietary right is durable in practice only if it conforms to a further set of rules.[49] For example, in respect of land of unregistered title, an equitable proprietary right qualifying as a land charge will be void against a purchaser if unregistered[50] or, if incapable of registration, will be void against a purchaser of a legal estate who has no notice of it.[51] In respect of land of registered title, a proprietary right not qualifying as an overriding interest and not protected as a minor interest by an entry in the charges section of the register will also be void against a purchaser.[52] The conclusion is obvious: that something that is apparently proprietary may not actually be durable in practice. We cannot rely on 'durability' to provide the answer to our search for a firm distinction between proprietary and non-proprietary rights.

[49] For example, is it within the definition of an overriding interest; is it a registerable disposition; is it a protected minor interest under the LRA 1925 or their equivalents under the LRA 2002?

[50] Land Charges Act 1972 (hereafter LCA), s. 4, and *Midland Bank Trust Co.* v. *Green* [1981] AC 513.

[51] Illustrated by *Caunce* v. *Caunce* [1969] 1 WLR 286. It is now clear such a purchaser as in *Caunce* would have notice; see *Kingsnorth Finance Co* v. *Tizzard* [1986] 1 WLR 783.

[52] LRA, 1925 55.3, 20, 23. See equivalent provisions under LRA 2002.

In fact, the problem is more complicated than this. We might accept that durability alone cannot safely be used to identify a proprietary right because there are some circumstances in which an avowedly proprietary rights is not durable, but can we be confident that something that both affects the use or enjoyment of land and is durable is always proprietary? Alas, no. First, following the entry into force of the Contracts (Rights of Third Parties) Act 1999, it is now possible to ensure that the benefit of a contract can endure for persons not originally parties to it. Admittedly, the original parties to (say) a contractual licence will have to construct their contract with care if they are to utilise the 'passing provisions' of the Act, and it may well be that the Act will be little used in the practice of land law. But if the Act does find favour with property professionals, it could have a profound impact on the way we think about rights affecting land.[53] Secondly, it remains possible for avowedly personal rights and non-protected proprietary rights[54] to be effective against a purchaser of land through the mechanism of the personal constructive trust. Simply put, this occurs when the purchaser of land has agreed to take that land subject to the right and thereby gains some advantage, such as a paying a lower purchase price.[55] The right (proprietary or not, protected or not) is then enforceable against the purchaser personally because it would be unconscionable for him or her to deny it. Although this doctrine has been subject to academic criticism,[56] it remains embedded in the case law and is largely responsible for the Denning-era confusion over whether certain types of licence were, or were not, interests in land.[57] Thirdly, even modern statute law has divorced durability from proprietary status. Thus, under the Landlord and Tenant (Covenants) Act 1995, the benefits and burdens of all qualifying leasehold covenants will 'run' with the land even if they are non-proprietary in the sense of being substantively personal to the original parties.[58] This occurs automatically by force of

---

[53] For contracts entered into on or after 11 May 2000. As well as passing the benefit of contractual licences, the Act could usefully be used in the law of freehold and leasehold covenants. In theory, it could be used in any case where the durability of the right was not clearly established by its proprietary status. See Burrows and Harpum, 'The Contracts (Rights of Third Parties) Act 1999 and its implications for property transactions', *Blundell Lecturers 2000*.

[54] That is, proprietary rights that are durable only through compliance with registration principle where such compliance is absent.

[55] *Ashburn Anstallt* v. *Arnold* [1989] Ch 1. and confirmed in *Lloyd* v. *Dugdale* (2001) Constructive trust here is used in a different sense from that dealing with the acquisition of an equitable share in another's land.

[56] Bright [2000] Conv. 388 written before *Lloyd* v. *Dugdale*.

[57] The purchaser *appeared* to be 'bound' by the right, thus making it appear the right was proprietary. In fact, the purchaser took the land personally subject to the right. A perfect example of why durability and proprietary status should not be conflated.

[58] For leases granted on or after 1 January 1996. See Landlord and Tenant (Covenants) Act 1955, (hereafter LTCA), ss. 2 and 3.

statute and the covenants will 'run' even if, in the old terminology, they do not 'touch and concern the land'.[59] Fourthly, there are some incongruities surrounding the 'benefit' of a proprietary right and its durability. For example, why is it necessary for the 'benefit' of the indisputably proprietary restrictive covenant to be annexed to the land either expressly or by statute?[60] Given the proprietary character of the right, should not the benefit pass without the need for such complexities, as it does in the law easements? Likewise, it seems that in some circumstances it may be possible to sever the ability to enjoy the benefit of a proprietary right from the land to which it once accrued. For example, in *Bettison* v. *Langton,* the House of Lords held that it was possible to sever a right of pasturage (grazing) from the land that it benefited; hence the owner of the benefited land could sell the land to one person and the benefit of the right to another.[61]

All these are powerful examples. Certainly they typify the pragmatism of English law and, no doubt, they have been developed piecemeal by the judiciary in response to specific circumstances or are found in specific statutes designed to remedy specific problems. Nevertheless they illustrate clearly that there is no necessary correlation between the proprietary character of a right and its durability through changes in ownership of the land. Durability, it seems, is a possible consequence of proprietary status, not a litmus test of its existence.

(c) Is the right registerable?

We all know that the Land Registration Acts 1925–2002 and the LCA 1972 regulate the effects of proprietary rights in land, especially on the occasion of a transfer of the title. Among other things, these statutes contain the additional rules required to make conceptual 'durability' a practical reality. Consequently, it is possible that we might find in the provisions of these statutes some assistance in our search for a sharp(ish) line of distinction between proprietary and non-proprietary rights.

Once again, the outlook is promising as many provisions of these registration statutes either expressly or impliedly identify proprietary

---

[59] The parties can remove this durability provided that the covenant is 'expressed to be personal' (LTCA, s. 3 (6)). It seems it will not be enough to trigger this exclusion 'merely' that the covenant is personal in substance. For the consequences of dismantling the proprietary/non-proprietary distinction in relation to leasehold covenants falling within the 1995 Act, see *BHP Petroleums Great Britain LH* v. *Chesterfield Properties Ltd,* Lawtel 6/3/2001.

[60] See, for example, the arguments around LPA 1923 s.78 and *Federated Homes* v. *Mill Lodge Properties* [1980] 1 WLR 594. See also *Whitgift Homes* v. Stocks (2001).

[61] [2001] UKHL 24 (transcript). The burden – the obligation to allow the grazing – fell on other land. The position is thus similar to that of *profits à prendre* which may also exist 'in gross'.

rights. For example, under the LRA 1925,[62] only legal estates in freehold and certain legal leaseholds may be registered with their own title number; only proprietary rights may qualify as overriding interests under s. 70 (1) (g) when coupled with actual occupation; the Registrar will refuse to enter a notice in the charges section of the register in order to 'protect' a clearly personal right or matter; and, under the LCA 1972, several of the classes of land charge are defined by reference to avowedly proprietary rights. But, of course, this is a simple picture and the truth is that the land registration statutes were never intended to provide a roll call of proprietary rights in land. Their purpose was, and is, to identify and record the many and varied types of right or matter that may affect a title, be they proprietary or not. Thus, some categories of overriding interest in LRA 1925, s. 70 (1) are certainly not proprietary in the sense discussed here but are instead in the nature of public rights or rights of general utility.[63] Likewise, the existing provisions concerning restrictions and inhibitions (two ways of protecting a person's concerns about land of registered title) can cover a whole range of matters, some certainly not proprietary in nature.[64] A similar pattern exists with respect to land of unregistered title, where the classes of land charge are not restricted to proprietary rights – the classic example being the Class F land charge.[65] More examples exist, but the point need not be laboured. Registration is not meant to be, nor does it operate as, a handy touchstone for determining the proprietary status of rights affecting land. We cannot conclude that just because something falls within the remit of these statutes that it must necessarily be proprietary.

Indeed, we can go further and point out that there are matters outside these statutes that clearly *are* proprietary. An obvious example is leasehold covenants that for historical and practical reasons have their own body of common and statute law. But we might also think on interests behind trusts of land and a whole host of minor rights concerning land of unregistered title that are non-registerable.[66] What also of the role of estoppels in both registered and unregistered conveyancing? How can the systems deal with these informally created rights, uncertain in scope

---

[62] In reality, most of the 'nuts and bolts' are found in the Land Registration Rules but for ease of explanation this chapter will confine itself to the governing provisions of the Registration Acts.

[63] See text above accompanying fn. 24 and note Schedules 1 and 3 LRA 2002.

[64] For example, bankruptcy order (inhibition) and requirement of compliance with Charities Act 1993 (restriction). This is likely to continue under the new 'restrictions' of the LRA 2002.

[65] The modern equivalent of the non-proprietary 'deserted wife's equity': see text above accompanying fn. 33.

[66] For example, pre-1926 equitable easements, pre-1926 restrictive covenants, leasehold covenants in an equitable lease not concerning the land subject to the lease, equitable co-ownership rights that are not overreached, equitable estoppels.

and highly dependent on judicial discretion?[67] For sure, this is not headline news, but it further reminds us to take care when using registration statutes to identify our proprietary rights.

A re-evaluation

The preceding analysis has attempted to demonstrate that while English land law clings determinedly to the distinction between proprietary and non-proprietary rights, it has not so readily provided us with a mechanism for making this distinction in practice. An inquiring mind might wonder: why? If it is so important, then we might expect there to be some core concept or clear definition or reliable process we could use. Of course, as indicated above, it is not difficult to identify a substantial body of rights that are clearly proprietary (at least in theory[68]) and a substantial body of rights that clearly are not and, in truth, that is enough to make the system of land law work on a daily basis without too much difficulty. Perhaps, however, this position of relative comfort has made us blind to a much more interesting truth: namely, that the distinction between proprietary and non-proprietary rights *as a concept* is gradually becoming irrelevant.

This contention is not as revolutionary as might first appear. As soon as registration replaced the legal/equitable distinction as the primary means for determining the effect of rights over land when the title to that land was transferred, it became possible – perhaps inevitable – that older concepts would become less useful. Whereas in the pre-registration era, the effect of a right on a purchaser depended principally on its 'inherent' character as proprietary or non-proprietary in conjunction with its legal or equitable status, in the current registration era the effect of a right on a purchaser depends primarily on where it falls within the statutory registration schema. In what little remains of land of unregistered title, legal rights bind the whole world (a throwback to the old ways), but the majority of equitable rights depend on registration as land charges or are overreached and the statute defines what is a land charge and what may be overreached. In land of registered title, a right is either a registerable title or disposition, an overriding interest or a minor interest (or

---

[67] In unregistered land, *Ives v. High* [1967] 2 QB 379 suggests that such rights are reliant on the doctrine of notice. In registered land, they may fall within LRA, s. 70 (1) (g) if coupled with actual occupation. Note the Law Commission's proposal to allow substantive registration or overriding status for estoppels, now effective because of *Lloyd* v. *Dugdale* (2001) and s.116 LRA 2002.

[68] See above (text above accompanying fn. 28) the argument that there are so many 'second level' definitional problems in (say) distinguishing between a lease and a licence that to say one is proprietary and the other is not hardly takes the matter further.

equivalent under the LRA 2002) and once again it is the statute that defines the categories. There is, in consequence, no conceptual reason why non-proprietary rights could not be accorded the same effect as proprietary ones. It is no longer a matter of principle, but a matter of practicalities. Those rights that are necessary or desirable for the proper economic or social exploitation of land can be made effective within the registration system, irrespective of (even in ignorance of) their proprietary or non-proprietary character. Before the registration era, this was not possible; now we have registration it is possible simply by manipulating statutory categories. For example, it is possible (*quaere* desirable?) to add a new provision to s. 70 (1) (g) LRA 1925 and Schedules 1 and 3 of the LRA 2002, to the effect that 'contractual licences for 15 years or more shall be overriding interests'? The fact they are inherently non-proprietary is no bar.

Moreover, this is no mere theory. As indicated above, the registration statutes already embrace rights which are determinedly non-proprietary because this is thought the most beneficial way of dealing with their effect on land. Likewise, the status of leasehold covenants and the role of third parties in relation to contracts (even land contracts!) has been altered by statute with no fear that this could compromise the 'essential' distinction between proprietary and non-proprietary rights. Even the common law seems able to distance itself from the old certainties. The decision in *Bruton* v. *London & Quadrant Housing Trust*[69] signifies, no more and no less, that leases are not always proprietary in nature, *when they do not need to be*. This may cause a certain chilling of the academic blood, but it seems to be consistent with the decline in importance of the proprietary character of leases generally and other land concepts.[70] And then what of the burgeoning law of proprietary estoppel? Something has been said of this already, but it now seems that the debate between those who saw estoppel 'merely' as a process possibly leading to the creation of proprietary rights and those who regarded the estoppel itself as a 'new' form of proprietary right has reached a conclusion. The case law now favours the proprietary character of estoppel (*Lloyd* v. *Dugdale* 2001) the mind of the Law Commission was made up and s. 116 LRA 2002 provides the final confirmation. Perhaps, however, it was actually a pointless argument. It could be argued that the issue was not really whether 'an estoppel' was proprietary itself or could occasionally lead to a proprietary

---

[69] [2000] 1 AC 406.

[70] The contractualisation – and consequent 'de-propertising' – of leases has been well charted, as has the gradual shift away from regarding mortgages as creatures of property, but rather more as creatures of contract (although, see recently, *Jones* v. *Morgan*, Court of Appeal, 28 June 2001, TLR 24 July 2001, in which the proprietary character of a mortgage triumphs over freedom of contract).

right. Rather, it is whether a person who purchases land over which an estoppel claim exists can be required to honour that estoppel claim. This is, in essence, a matter of policy in its broadest sense[71] and to think about it in terms of the distinction between 'proprietary' and 'non-proprietary' rights misses the point. It might even be the case that the argument over the proprietary nature (or not) of estoppel has obscured due consideration of its real role and purpose within the system of land law.

And, then, what of the future? The Law Commission's long-awaited final report on land registration has been digested and there is a new registration statute expected to enter force (at least in part) in mid 2003. The LRA 2002 is a mighty work but it seems, at least to this author, to leave behind the whole issue of the distinction between proprietary and non-proprietary rights. We could even go so far as to say that the irrelevance of the distinction is inherent in the scheme for land registration found in the new Act. More is to be registered, there will be fewer 'off-register' transactions, and paper conveyancing with its emphasis on formality will fade away. With it will go a large part of the foundation for thinking in terms of proprietary and non-proprietary rights. Adverse possession, long the ultimate expression of feudal conceptions of property and property rights, will be transformed (or rather castrated). Any pre-registration conceptions of property that still linger in our system are to be swept away in favour of a modern, effective and electronic register. Of course, we can still talk in our lectures and in our essays about 'proprietary' rights; we will still be able to identify many. But it will not govern the operation of our modern system of land law and, indeed, perhaps it has not really been governing it for many years past.

Further Reading

Birks, 'Before we begin: five keys to land law' in Bright and Dewar, *Land Law: Themes and Perspectives* (1998, Oxford University Press).
Burrows and Harpum, 'The Contracts (Rights of Third Parties) Act 1999 and its implications for property transactions' in *Blundell Lecturers 2000*.
Fuller, 'Consideration and form', (1941) 41 Col LR 799.
Gray and Gray, 'The idea of property in land' in Bright and Dewar, *Land Law: Themes and Perspectives* (1998, Oxford University Press).
Harris, *Property and Justice* (1996).
National Provincial Bank v. *Ainsworth* [1965] AC 1175.

---

[71] For example, involving considerations of fairness to the claimant and the purchaser, considerations of alienability, considerations relating to the need to preserve the integrity of formality requirements.

2

The role of registration in modern land law

Roger Smith

Our system of registration of title has roots dating back to 1857, though very few titles were registered until 1897 when compulsory registration was first introduced. For many years, the governing legislation was the Land Registration Act 1925 (hereafter LRA), based on the Land Transfer Acts 1875 and 1897. The 1925 Act has proved, like so much of the 1925 legislation, remarkably durable. There have been amendments, relating particularly to leases, compulsory first registration and some aspects of rectification and indemnity, but until 2002 these have left the fundamental principles unscathed. Louise Tee got the sense of this most effectively in the title of her article on the Law Commission report leading to the Land Registration Act 1997: 'Gently reforming land registration.'[1] Much more radical ideas have, however, emerged from the Law Commission's more recent proposals in Law Com No. 254. In 2001, the Land Registration Bill 2001 was introduced into Parliament and a final Law Commission report[2] was published. The report employs the telling subtitle 'A conveyancing revolution'. At the time proofs were corrected, the Land Registration Act 2002 (hereafter '2002 Act') received the Royal Assent. We now have legislation in place that will not only effect a fundamental rewriting of the law, but also develop and amend many basic principles.

It is in the light of this reform that it is appropriate to assess the significance of land registration in modern land law. Why is it important? How does it fit with traditional property principles? How should it fit in

---

[1] [1996] CLJ 241.
[2] *Land Registration for the Twenty-First Century: A Conveyancing Revolution*, Law Com No. 271. Unusually, the Bill was introduced some three weeks in advance of the publication of the report recommending it! This material has been incorporated into this chapter at the last minute.

the modern teaching of the subject? One thing is clear from modern developments: it is no longer satisfactory to bolt land registration on to the end of the land law syllabus as a recent development standing apart from the mainstream of the subject. Peter Sparkes[3] is surely correct in arguing that land registration has to be central to the exposition of land law today. Not only are some 90% of titles already registered, but every new conveyance, mortgage and lease (over 21 years) requires registration.[4]

Yet experience of the law demonstrates it is difficult completely to expunge older principles. The building blocks of legal analysis frequently possess an enduring quality and pervade new as well as old structures. To view land registration as existing in a legal vacuum, a world of its own, is as equally objectionable as attempting to force it within the old principles. A further feature is that it would be profoundly disturbing to have radically different rules operating according to where the property is located.[5] In other words, there is an argument that differences should be kept to a minimum while registered and unregistered land each applies to large numbers of titles. As so often in legal analysis there are competing pressures, but I should make my personal standpoint clear. As to the last point (criticism of different rules for different locations), it was valid while there were really large numbers of both registered and unregistered titles. But as the number of unregistered titles drops below 10%, it becomes increasingly difficult to support. It is thought that virtually all land (save that which is never transferred) will be registered by 2009.[6] So at least soon there will be no justification for holding back the development of principles for registered land. Indeed, the Law Commission has already proclaimed that 'it is now highly desirable that land registration in England and Wales should develop according to principles that reflect both the nature and the potential of land registration' rather than merely 'translate [unregistered land] principles into a registered format'.[7] Yet the great majority of land law is unaffected by land registration: the definition of a lease or easement, for example. Land registration has to be seen as fitting within the framework of the old land law we know and, perhaps, love. However, there are two areas in which development of the law can be considered. First, the very structure of land registration, with its threefold structure of registered, overriding and minor interests, demands

---

3   Preface, *A New Landlord and Tenant Law* (2001, Hart).
4   2002 Act, SS. 4, 27.
5   Until 1990 (when conveyances in all parts of England and Wales attracted compulsory registration: SI 1989 No. 1347), a major determinant of whether a title was registered was its geographical location.
6   Lord Chancellor's Department *Consultation Paper on E-conveyancing* (March 2001, hereafter 'LCD E-conveyancing'), Part 1, para. 5. The paper can be accessed at http://www.open.gov. uk/lcd/consult/general/e-conv.htm
7   *Land Registration for the Twenty-First Century: A Consultative Document*, Law Com No. 254, para. 1.5.

that the results of priority disputes must be different on occasion. Whether or not we approve of the outcome in any specific land registration case, the entire system would collapse in ruins if we were not prepared to accept *some* change: guaranteeing the proprietor's title is a sine qua non for the acceptance of conveyancing based upon the register rather than title deeds. The second area for development is that land registration may facilitate change. Radical proposals emanating from the Law Commission and academic writing will be considered later in this chapter, but it may be observed that rules which make sense within an unregistered land system may no longer do so within the registered land system. This is particularly the case for rules based on the need to ensure that a purchaser can rely on obtaining a clear title. In registered land the purchaser will obtain a good title unless there is an entry on the register, in which case the right is brought to his or her attention, or there is an overriding interest. Although overriding interests are quite commonly encountered, in many cases the registered transferee can safely rely on obtaining an unassailable title.

It is against this background that I will investigate three ways of looking at the modern role of land registration. The first is as a system for making the transfer (and other transactions) of land more efficient: what may be described as the conveyancing dimension. Next, land registration may be seen as crucially affecting priority rules. This may be seen as its crucial role as regards substantive law (as opposed to the procedural aspects of buying and selling land) and may be linked with the guarantee accorded to the registered proprietor. Thirdly, it may be seen as a catalyst for a radical overhaul of property principles, extending well beyond priority issues. These three ways of looking at registration are not, of course, mutually exclusive, though they do reflect increasingly more flexible approaches to land law. In particular, the extent to which the third approach is embraced will do much to determine the future direction of land law.

The conveyancing dimension

This is, perhaps, the most obvious role of land registration: the principal reasons underpinning its introduction and extension have been to make conveyancing simpler, quicker and cheaper. We are not here concerned with issues of security of title or protection of interest holders, but rather the nuts and bolts of buying and selling land. Three sub-issues emerge: the ease of conveying registered land, its cost and the potential for future improvements.

Ease and cost

These issues will be dealt with together, as they are so closely linked in practice. I considered them some 15 years ago[8] and concluded that registration offered relatively minor benefits. The core point was that registration is all about the quality of the seller's title. In favour of registration, it is plainly easier to see all the relevant information from a copy of the register than to investigate complex deeds stretching over many years (and to make the necessary land charges searches). Yet two factors have combined to diminish the significance of this. First, unregistered conveyancing is much more straightforward than it used to be. Title has to be searched for a minimum period of 15 years[9] and this relatively short period ensures that few conveyances are likely to be involved. Indeed, the title may well consist of a single conveyance. Not only this, but the style of modern conveyances is simpler than in the past: reading the operative parts of a small number of modern conveyances is scarcely taxing. Whereas complex trusts would complicate many nine-teenth-century titles, this is highly unlikely for the great majority of homes today. There may be complex covenants to interpret, but registration does not solve that difficulty.[10] There may well be advantages in some cases flowing from the better mapping that registration entails, though this will be relevant for a relatively small number of transactions. Perhaps the best conclusion is that for the average transaction the benefits of registration are decidedly minor, though on occasion they may be very significant, especially where the title is unusually complex or the boundaries unusually uncertain. The second factor that has to be considered in assessing the benefits of registration is that title questions form a relatively small part of the work of a lawyer acting for the seller or purchaser of land. Questions relating to local authority searches, inquiries before contract (dealing with many non-title related issues), mortgage finance and the tying together of sales in a chain all take significant amounts of time. When one recalls that lawyers charge around 0.5% of the land value for average house values,[11] it easy to see that title issues account for (let us say) 0.1% of the land value. Even significant benefits in the title

---

8 'Land registration: white elephant or way forward?' [1986] CLP 111.
9 More accurately, to the first conveyance 15 or more years old: Law of Property Act 1969, s. 23 (reducing the period in Law of Property Act 1925 (hereafter LPA), s. 44, from 30 years).
10 Similarly, the complexity of leasehold conveyancing is largely unaffected by registration: the assignee of a lease still has to read the lease and assess the significance of the covenants in it: Ruoff and Roper, *Registered Conveyancing*, para. 21–16; Barnsley, *Conveyancing Law and Practice* (4th ed), p. 341.
11 *Woolwich Cost of Moving Survey* 2000 (http://www.woolwich.co.uk). Costs are (as a percentage of land value) significantly higher for cheaper properties and significantly lower for more expensive properties. The scale is much flatter than that for registration fees: Land Registration Fees Order 2001 (SI 2001 No. 1179).

area (and one may doubt whether these are achieved in practice) are going to have little impact in terms of pounds and pence. Registration has the potential for greater speed, but it is unclear that title questions contribute to the two or three months' delay often experienced between acceptance of an offer and completion. Online access to the land register may save a couple of days in obtaining vital information. This would be terribly important if other factors in the conveyancing process enabled it to be completed virtually instantaneously. As is known only too well, this is not the case. Perhaps the most obvious reasons for the present delays lie in the need to organise the chain of conveyances (as well as mortgage finance) and the obtaining of information from sources such as local authorities.[12]

There are current initiatives to remedy some of these problems, though their details lie outside the scope of this chapter. The Homes Bill[13] (lost on the dissolution of Parliament in May 2001) would have introduced the seller's pack – containing much of the information required by purchasers. The National Land Information Service, when operating, will provide electronic access to the information purchasers need. These are useful developments, but in the medium term it seems highly improbable that investigation of title will provide such a bottle neck in the process as to extend the overall time taken.[14] A decade or so ago, registration was having the opposite effect of delaying transactions, as the Land Registry was unable to cope with the flood of work from the very buoyant housing market of the 1980s. It was taking very long periods (months) to enter certain transactions on to the register, especially first registration. Fortunately, the cooling of the housing market in the 1990s,[15] coupled with greater efficiency and use of computer systems on the part of the Land Registry, has caused these unacceptable delays to evaporate.[16] One significant point is that, under the 2002 Act, chains of transactions will become more transparent and may be managed by the Land Registry, thus avoiding some of the worst problems of the present system.[17]

---

[12] See the response of the Law Society to *The Key to Easier House Buying and Selling*, available at http://www.lawsociety.co.uk

[13] Based on a 1998 government consultation paper, *The Key to Easier House Buying and Selling*. The value of the scheme (especially as regards surveys commissioned by the seller) is controversial and it has not immediately been introduced in the new Parliament.

[14] Note the doubts of Richards (2001) 145 Sol J 401 as to whether electronic conveyancing will by itself significantly speed the process. *LCD E-Conveyancing* predicts a possible time saving of five days: Appendix III, para. 15.

[15] Though the recent upsurge in the property market has led to a quarter of registrations taking more than five weeks: Land Registry, *Annual Report and Accounts*, 1999–2000, pp. 8, 15.

[16] One significant factor is that first registrations have always been labour intensive. As registration has developed, the proportion of business represented by first registrations has declined markedly (12% of the number of transfers in 1998–1999, compared with over a third a decade earlier). This trend will continue over the coming years.

[17] 2002 Act, Sch. 5, paras. 2, 5, 9; Law Com No. 271, paras. 2.52, 13.63–65.

What about the cost of registration? In the mid-1980s, I concluded that registered conveyancing is more expensive because fees have to be paid to the Land Registry, whilst legal costs are virtually identical for registered and unregistered land.[18] At that time, the Land Registry fee might be close to half the fees charged by the purchaser's legal advisers, so the extra amount was by no means trivial. Have things changed since then? The Land Registry has stressed reductions in fee levels, often quoting impressive figures.[19] Yet the reality is a little different. Sharp increases in housing costs bring additional revenue to the Land Registry, as the fees increase according to the value of the land. The average house today is worth a little over £100,000.[20] The cost of registering a transfer of that house will be £100 or £200 according to whether or not the value is above £100,000.[21] That typical house would have cost £42,730 in 1985[22] and its transfer would have incurred a Land Registry fee of £100. So the typical house in fact costs at least as much in terms of registration fees today and perhaps significantly more. On the other hand, one would expect Land Registry costs to increase as a result of inflation: holding the price in cash terms for 15 years would be a tribute to the success of the Land Registry in introducing computerisation and streamlining its procedures.[23]

Accordingly, we can say that the 1980s conclusion still stands: registration of title cannot be defended as a system that is more efficient, fast and inexpensive. That does not mean it does not possess advantages, but rather that the inherent bureaucracy is bought at a not insignificant expense.

The potential for improvement

Computerisation provides continuing opportunities for the improvement of the present system (cutting down on delays and reducing costs) and offers the prospect of radical changes in the methods of dealing with land. Indeed, the Law Commission viewed these possible changes as 'the most

---

[18] [1986] CLP 111 at 112.
[19] See, for example, Land Registry, *Annual Report and Accounts*, 1996–1997 and 1997–1998.
[20] Land Registry, *Residential Property Price Report*, April–June 2000.
[21] Land Registration Fees Order 2001 (SI 2001 No. 1179).
[22] Using the Nationwide Building Society index of all house prices to deflate the current value (the figures are available from http://www.nationwide.co.uk and the *Estates Gazette*). All figures are based on material available in summer 2000. (March 2002 figures show an average house value of a little under £120,000. Save for a reduction in the £40,000–£70,000 band, registration fees have not changed.)
[23] First registration was also more expensive than transfers in 1985. The extra cost has disappeared; indeed, there is a 25% reduction for *voluntary* first registration. Very telling are the figures for unit costs: reduced in cash terms by 13% over the past six years.

revolutionary reform to the conveyancing system in England and Wales that has yet taken place'.[24]

So far, the principal changes have been mostly internal to the Land Registry. Over 95% of titles are now computerised,[25] and this enables searches, transfers and other dealings with registered titles to be undertaken far more simply. More recently, direct access to registers of title has been introduced, enabling lawyers to access titles from their offices and to deliver certain requests electronically.[26] In early 1999[27] there were about 1,350 users of direct access, with about 3,000 daily uses of direct access. The exact figures are not very meaningful, as growth is rapid. It might be said that direct access makes matters marginally simpler and quicker for conveyancers, without making significant changes to conveyancing.

The next stage is to replace conventional documentation with electronic communication to the Land Registry. A first step[28] is to enable electronic applications, though this does not dispense with the normal formalities for dispositions of land. What lies beyond, however, is not merely a glorified system of e-mail. We are referring to the replacement of transfers, leases and virtually all documentation relating to interests in land. This is the starting point for the future conveyancing system envisaged by the Law Commission. As they observe,[29] this would enable the three stages of 1) execution of a transfer (or other dealing); 2) application for registration; and 3) entry on the register to be collapsed into a single step. There already exists a very limited scheme for electronic notification of the discharge of registered charges, viable because of the market domination of a relatively small number of mortgage lenders.[30]

The Electronic Communications Act 2000[31] provides partial statutory authority for a move to this next stage. It authorises the introduction of a system of voluntary electronic conveyancing, though the full exploitation of electronic conveyancing awaits the coming into effect of the 2002 Act

---

[24] Law Com No. 254 (future references to the Law Commission are to this report), para. 1.2. Similar views are expressed in Law Com No. 271, para. 1.1.

[25] Land Registry, *Annual Report and Accounts*, 2000–2001, pp. 8, 20, p. 19. All suitable title plans have now been scanned. Work is progressing in scanning filed documents (consultation of which is often necessary to supplement limited information held on the register, especially in relation to complex covenants and leases), but this is a three-year project.

[26] See the description of the service at http://www.landregistrydirect.gov.uk; it is currently available via an intranet to Land Registry account holders.

[27] Land Registry, *Annual Report and Accounts*, 1998–1999, p. 19.

[28] Authorised by Land Registration Rules 2001 (SI 2001 No. 619), subject to there being a Land Registry notice. Cf. also discharge of mortgages, considered below.

[29] Paragraphs 2.45–48; also Part XI.

[30] Land Registration Rules 2000 (SI 2000 No. 249); the system is controlled by the Chief Land Registrar (see also Land Registry, *Annual Report and Accounts* 1999–2000, p. 19).

[31] Section 8; [2000] Conv. 185.

and the implementation by rules of sections 91 and 93.[32] At present, formality rules require a deed or writing for most transactions involving the creation or transfer of interests in land. A fully electronic system takes the place of such documentation. It would not be surprising if the parties felt the need to have a paper copy of the transaction, but this would be optional. What the future holds is not merely an electronic request to register a conventional transfer, but a transfer that will be immediately effective as a result of electronic communication to the Land Registry.

The 2000 Act does no more than provide outline legislative authority for the disapplication of requirements which would inhibit electronic communication in a wide range of circumstances: subordinate legislation is essential for their relaxation in any given area. That subordinate legislation is proposed by the Lord Chancellor's Department *Consultation Paper on E-conveyancing*.[33] The draft order would have the principal effects of allowing contracts (whether for the disposition of registered or unregistered land) and transfers of registered land to be undertaken electronically. The requirements would be that: a) the time and date the instrument is to be effective are stated; b) there is electronic signature of each person by whom it is authenticated and that signature is certified;[34] c) (for contracts) all expressly agreed terms are included; and d) (for transfers) other prescribed conditions are satisfied.[35]

Electronic conveyancing (even in its initial voluntary and minor role) will involve substantial changes and may prove controversial. One aspect of the changes concerns the security and practical operation of electronic conveyancing. The problems here are highly technical, though many are shared with other areas of electronic commerce. They cannot be readily dismissed,[36] but involve issues that extend beyond legal analysis. Assuming that secure and efficient procedures can be developed, what effect would this have on conveyancing? One obvious point is that it may render conveyancing simpler: the number of steps that need to be taken is reduced. Whether this will make a significant difference may be doubted: the legal advisers will still need to check that they have authority to proceed with the electronic entry (though this might be simpler than obtaining a signature to a transfer) and making the electronic entry may

---

[32] *LCD E-conveyancing*, Part I, para. 2, Part 2, paras. 4, 10.

[33] See fn. 6 above, summarised by Capps (2001) 151 NLJ 862.

[34] For this, see *LCD E-conveyancing*, Part 2, paras. 26–28.

[35] It will be appreciated that, for example, the form of the electronic transfer must be compatible with Land Registry systems.

[36] See the concerns expressed by the Law Society in its response (available at http://www.lawsociety.co.uk); Sagoo [2001] 16 EG 140; Perry (2001) 151 NLJ 1100. A rather different point is that provision must be made for stamp duty to be payable and actually paid: it is currently imposed only on documents.

not be enormously simpler than the present posting of the application for registration.[37] The consultation paper estimates that there will be a net cost saving of £16 per transaction.[38] It may be noted that nearly all the cost savings lie in clerical costs and these may be difficult to realise in smaller firms. External costs of £5 per transaction will be incurred as well as software costs. A more important point is likely to be that (for transfers), the electronic entry will take place at completion.[39] This avoids the problems that result from late applications to register: usually described as the 'registration gap'. These may include being bound by minor interests entered on the register after the date of searching[40] or overriding interests created between the date of completion and registration.[41] It is pleasing to welcome ways to eliminate such traps within the registration system.[42] One must, of course, hope that electronic communications operate as intended. One could see disaster looming if the purchaser were to 'complete' but the electronic entry was delayed for some time. This might, for example, occur if there are problems that have not already been sorted out with the Land Registry. There would be a danger of the purchasers having no rights at all at that stage (other than from any preceding contract) and certainly no elimination of the registration gap.

Looking further ahead, the Law Commission sees electronic entries as *replacing* the current methods of dealing with land. Under the Electronic Communications Act 2000[43] and the proposals in the consultation paper, there can be no compulsion to use electronic documents. This means it will continue to be possible to create interests by the normal formalities (though legal status already frequently requires registration). Thus contracts for the sale of land will remain capable of being made in writing and transfers capable of being made by deed. However, s. 93 of the 2002 Act provides authority for rules to require use of electronic documents, electronically communicated to the Land Registry.[44]

---

37 Note the scepticism of the Law Society, in its response to Law Com No. 254, about the advantages as regards leases (available at http://www.lawsociety.co.uk).

38 For time savings, see fn. 14 above.

39 This will require that all problems are sorted out prior to completion: cf. Land Registry, *Annual Report and Accounts*, 1999–2000, p. 20; Law Com No. 271, paras. 2.49–58, 13.42. It is revealing that at present half of all applications to register entail correspondence: see the Land Registry website (http://www.landreg.gov.uk).

40 The Land Registration (Official Searches) Rules 1993 (SI 1993 No. 3276) provide protection where registration is sought within 30 working days of the search; 2002 Act, s. 72.

41 The purchaser is protected by *Abbey National BS* v. *Cann* [1991] 1 AC 56 as regards the rights of those in actual occupation, but not otherwise: *Barclays Bank plc* v. *Zaroovabli* [1997] Ch 321 at 328 (2002 Act, Sch. 3, para. 2: 'at the time of the disposition' requirement for actual occupation).

42 See Rodrigues [2001] 06 EG 156, concentrating on the present problems for subsequent dealings with land pending registration.

43 Section 8 (6).

44 For individuals doing their own conveyancing, see p. 39 below.

Although it is not contemplated that this will be implemented for several years,[45] network access agreements between conveyancers and the Land Registry are likely to require the use of simultaneous electronic entries much sooner.[46]

It is important to note that (subject to some exceptions) this compulsion will apply to the creation and transfer of all interests in land. It will therefore apply not only to transfers of registered titles, but also, for example, to contracts to sell land and the creation of restrictive covenants. A very important, but fairly obvious, point is that registration will be essential for proprietary status.[47] Of course, many interests already require entry on the register before they can bind registered transferees (or lessees or chargees). However, their proprietary status protects them against others interested in the land, such as holders of subsequent minor interests[48] or a trustee in bankruptcy. More surprisingly, the Law Commission contemplates that even contractual status will be denied without registration.[49] This represents a very significant change, particularly as regards contracts for the sale of land, where present practice is for entry on the register to be the exception rather than the rule. In this last area, however, entry of the contract is likely to be necessary in order that immediate electronic registration of the transfer can be effected without any hitches.

How are we to assess these changes? Four areas suggest themselves for discussion. The first concerns the role of registration. Though registration is already often highly desirable in order to provide protection against purchasers, in the future it will be an integral part of the creation of any property interest. Without registration, nothing will exist. A contract for the sale of land will, for example, not exist without registration. Accordingly, it would not even be possible to sue the other contracting party (presumably this might be cured by a later registration; *quaere* whether that registration would be possible after one party has repudiated the transaction[50]). This represents far more than a mere move to electronic entries: there will be a significantly greater penalty for failure to register. In practice, this means that lawyers must learn to live with the new system or very quickly find themselves liable for breach of duty to their clients. The risks to those not employing lawyers will, in practical

---

[45] Law Com No. 254, paras. 2.47, 11.18; Law Com No. 271, paras. 2.59–61, 13.74, 13.80.

[46] Law Com No. 271, paras. 2.60, 13.49, 13.79; 2002 Act, Sch. 5, para. 2 (2) (a).

[47] This was originally thought to be the position in Torrens systems of registration, but no longer represents the law: Whalan, *The Torrens System in Australia*, (1982, Law Book Co.), 281–284.

[48] See fn. 67 below.

[49] Paragraph 11.10; under the 2002 Act, s. 93 (2), a disposition or contract 'only has effect' if electronically made and communicated to the Land Registry.

[50] If registration remains possible, it is largely meaningless to say there is no contract.

terms, be much greater because they are unlikely to be aware of the need to register (at least for transactions other than transfers of title). The Law Commission envisages that the Land Registry will conduct a public awareness campaign, but one may doubt how effective this is likely to be.

The second area concerns formalities. At least at first sight, we will be able to forget completely about formality requirements for land transactions: the details as to when writing or a deed is required will be rendered obsolete. Thus formalities will neither be effective to create a property interest (registration will be essential) nor be necessary (electronic entry will suffice).[51] One likely consequence is that the mountain of litigation regarding writing requirements for land contracts under the Law of Property (Miscellaneous Provisions) Act 1989 will diminish when electronic entry on the register is effective. Even so, not all the problems are likely to go away. Although the contract itself might be entered into electronically,[52] there may still be problems if some of the relevant terms are not held in electronic form.[53] Similarly, if the contract is entered into by a conventional exchange of documents (as might be anticipated in the early days of electronic conveyancing) and then electronically entered on the register, what is the position if terms are omitted from the writing?

In any event, the old formality rules will continue to have a role, albeit much less significant than at present. First, it was earlier thought that it would be possible to make non-electronic applications to the Registrar.[54] This is particularly important for the 'do-it-yourself' conveyancer, as electronic entries are likely to be limited to authorised persons (anticipated to be solicitors, licensed conveyancers and certain financial institutions).[55] It was not clear whether this would have required satisfaction of the old formality rules. However, this no longer appears to be the way in which transactions by a non-professional person will be dealt with. The second, and clearer, role of formalities will be for transactions exempted from the registration requirement. These will be

---

[51] 2002 Act, sections 93, 91, respectively (more technically, an electronic document is to be regarded as signed writing and a deed).

[52] See *LCD E-conveyancing*, Appendix 1, Draft Law of Property (Electronic Communications) Order 2001, inserting a new s. 2A into Law of Property (Miscellaneous Provisions) Act 1989.

[53] As required by the draft s. 2A (2) (a). Cf. *Record* v. *Bell* [1991] 1 WLR 853. Presumably equity would rectify the electronic agreement if a written agreement could have been rectified.

[54] Law Com No. 254, para. 11.11; Contrast the approach adopted by the 2002 Act. Sch. 5, para. 7; Law Com No. 271, paras. 2.68, 13.72–73. There is likely to be a system whereby the Registrar carries out the electronic transaction on the instructions of the individual. There would be no contract or interest in land prior to the entry and the registration gap might remain in such cases.

[55] See Sch. 5 of the 2002 Act for access to the Land Registry network.

considered below, but would include short leases. These leases would still require a deed, subject to the present exception for leases not exceeding three years.[56]

A third area emerges from the recent Lord Chancellor's Department consultation paper. The nature and current development of electronic signatures are such that it is anticipated that agents (solicitors or licensed conveyancers) will sign on their clients' behalf. This raises the question as to the effect of an agent's electronic signature, most especially when it is on behalf of the seller. If the agent is properly authorised, then no problems arise, but what if this is not the case? It appears from the consultation paper that the agent is intended to have deemed authority to sign transfers on the principal's behalf.[57] It appears that this leaves the owner open to fraud by the solicitor. This deemed authority might apply even if the solicitor or conveyancer was never the agent of the owner. The position is further complicated because the implementation of this proposal[58] shows how it is limited to relieving against statutory requirements[59] – all that is possible under the Electronic Communications Act 2000.[60] In so far as the problem is that the agent lacks authority, it follows there is nothing to validate the electronic document. In practice, this may not be as significant as it at first appears, as registration of the document carries a statutory guarantee of title in favour of the purchaser.[61] Under the 2002 Act,[62] it is clear the owner is affected despite the agent's lack of authority. This is to ensure that the conveyancing process is not held up by any need for paper confirmation of the agent's authority.[63]

The fourth and final area concerning the changes consequent upon fully electronic conveyancing lies in its potential to minimise current areas of difficulty. We have already seen this in the context of the registration gap between completion of transfers and registration (under the *LCD E-Conveyancing* proposals). It will be especially important once (under s. 93 of the 2002 Act) interests cannot be created without electronic registration. This is most relevant, of course, to transfers and other registered dispositions (leases, charges).[64] Further points come into play as regards

---

[56] LPA, ss. 52, 54; *Long* v. *Tower Hamlets LBC* [1998] Ch 197.

[57] See Part 2, para. 33 and, especially, the drafting of Question 8 at the end of that paragraph. Cf. Sagoo [2001] 16 EG 140.

[58] Appendix I, LRA, draft s. 144A (6): 'to be regarded for the purposes of any enactment as authenticated by him under the written authority of his principal.'

[59] See LPA, s. 53 (1) (a).

[60] Section 8 (6).

[61] Subject always to a claim for rectification.

[62] Schedule 5, para. 8.

[63] Law Com No. 271, paras. 13.61–62.

[64] The 2002 Act, ss. 91 (2)(b), 93(1) (6) extends electronic entries to dispositions of interests protected by notice (Law Com No. 271, paras. 13.22–23, 13.81).

minor interests. At present, problems arise as regards unprotected minor interests. Three examples may be given. Are they binding on a registered transferee who is aware of them?[65] This would become irrelevant if they could not exist without entry on the register. Next, they may take effect as overriding interests if coupled with actual occupation.[66] The actual occupation overriding interest is commonly seen as one of the most important blots on the title of a registered proprietor; it is certainly the most litigated. Again, if interests require an electronic entry on the register, there would be no interest capable of protection by actual occupation. Thirdly, there may be difficulty regarding the priority between minor interests.[67] Yet again, there would usually be no minor interest without an entry on the register: the first to be protected will also be the first in time.

Sadly, none of these advances is as comprehensive as the above comments would imply. As has already been observed, there will be exceptions to the requirement of electronic entry and, where these apply, the old problems will continue. It follows that the old problems will be diminished rather than eliminated. At this stage we need to consider the scope of the exceptions.

The Law Commission places these exceptions in four categories:[68] 1) rights arising without any express grant or reservation; 2) dispositions taking effect by operation of law; 3) interests under trusts; and 4) leases that are overriding interests. The first and third categories merit further discussion. The first includes rights by proprietary estoppel,[69] adverse possession, implied and prescriptive easements and mere equities (such as the right to set aside a transfer for fraud). It is plain that none of these rights is likely to be protected by entry on the register, whatever the law were to require. It may also be observed that, although many examples will fall within Sch. 3, para 2, of the 2002 Act (actual occupation),[70] not all will do so: some will be other overriding interests and others minor interests. It is

---

65 *Peffer* v. *Rigg* [1977] 1 WLR 285 holds that purchasers are bound if not in good faith, though the Law Commission would exclude both knowledge and notice as vitiating factors: para. 3.46. Section 29 of the 2002 Act provides no obvious scope for arguing that good faith is required and there is no equivalent to LRA, s. 59 (6), relied upon in *Peffer* (Law Com No. 271, para. 5.16).

66 *Webb* v. *Pollmount Ltd* [1966] Ch 584; *Williams & Glyn's Bank Ltd* v. *Boland* [1981] AC 487; 2002 Act, Sch. 3, para. 2 (Sch. 1 operates on first registration).

67 The current position is that the first in time generally has priority, even if the other is protected by way of caution or notice: *Barclays Bank Ltd* v. *Taylor* [1974] Ch 137 and *Mortgage Corporation Ltd* v. *Nationwide Credit Corporation Ltd* [1994] Ch 49. Section 28 of the 2002 Act hardens the first in time rule into an 'absolute' one: Law Com No. 271, para. 5.5.

68 Paragraph 11.12; they do not appear in the 2002 Act, as they will feature in rules implementing s. 93.

69 Confirmed as proprietary interests by 2002 Act, s. 116.

70 Previously LRA, s. 70(1)(g).

foreseeable that a strict rule about a requirement to register will result in many rights being unenforceable. This is likely to lead to a greater use of proprietary estoppel where one party has acted to their detriment. It may be controversial as to how far the courts would permit this.[71] Turning to interests under trusts, these are important if only because so many actual occupation cases involve trusts. It follows that the practical effect of Sch. 3, para, 2 will remain similar to that of LRA, s. 70(1)(g). As with the first category, entry on the register cannot be expected for constructive and resulting trusts. It would be truly surprising if statute were to deny effect to these trusts as imposed by the courts. It is less clear that express trusts deserve such protection,[72] though these have caused relatively little difficulty in practice.

It may be concluded that these exemptions very significantly limit the benefits that appear to flow from requiring registration. That is not to deny that, in broad terms, the exemptions are justified; quite the opposite, failure to recognise them would cause considerable injustice. Rather, the benefits flowing from requiring registration will be less than one might initially expect. True, there will be cases where purchasers will be better protected,[73] but it cannot be said that purchasers can safely make fewer inquiries than at present. From a schematic perspective, none of the present complications is removed entirely. The problems will still have to studied by students, present opportunities to examiners and have to be borne in mind by practitioners.

Priority rules and the guarantee of title

Guaranteeing the title of the proprietor is an essential aspect of title registration. It is what enables those dealing with the land to rely on the register. One may contrast deeds and charges registration systems, where it is necessary to consider the history of the title. In Torrens title

---

[71] Estoppel cannot be used where there is simple failure to register: *Lloyds Bank plc* v. *Carrick* [1996] 4 All ER 630. However, there was still a contractual right in that case. In the new world envisaged by the Law Commission, there would not even be a contract. The situation may be thought analogous to the use of estoppel where the writing requirements of the Law of Property (Miscellaneous Provisions) Act 1989, s. 2, have not been satisfied: *Yaxley* v. *Gotts* [2000] Ch 162; Smith (2000) 116 LQR 11.

[72] The Law Commission defends their position by invoking the principle that references to trusts should be excluded from the register (cf. LRA, s. 74; 2002 Act, s. 78), yet any sensible beneficiary will seek an entry on the register and frequently a restriction is obligatory (LRA, s. 58 (3); 2002 Act, s. 44).

[73] A good example would be the facts of *Webb* v. *Pollmount Ltd* [1966] Ch 584, in which an estate contract (an option to purchase) was protected as an actual occupation overriding interest.

registration systems,[74] there is much stress on the indefeasibility of registered titles and Whalan[75] describes this as 'the point at which the doctrines of the general law and the Torrens statutes meet most forcefully; from the earliest times it has proved be a flash-point'. The same comment is true of English title registration.

What are the component parts of guaranteeing title? Three may be identified. The first concerns the freedom of a registered title from any adverse claims not entered on the register. The second concerns the freedom from rectification of title. The third is the right to financial indemnity if there is shown to be a flaw in a title.

Freedom from adverse claims

Here we are concerned with priority rules: determining which earlier interests bind a registered proprietor. The registered proprietor will have a legal title. If we look back at unregistered land, we see that a holder of a legal estate is bound by existing legal estates and interests and by equitable interests of which there is notice. One result is that if the seller is not, in law, the true owner then the purchaser will not get a good title. How does the position differ in registered land? For a start, the registered proprietor always has the legal estate, regardless of the earlier state of the title to the land.[76] More importantly, the proprietor is subject only to interests protected on the register or overriding interest: other interests are defeated.[77] It will be seen that the language of legal and equitable interests and notice is replaced by these new registered land categories. Admittedly, the contrast with unregistered land is limited by the development there of registration of land charges, whereby certain interests (mainly equitable interests such as charges, estate contracts and restrictive covenants) have to be registered in order to bind a purchaser. Furthermore, in registered land a number of legal interests are overriding interests, so that many legal interests in fact continue to bind the purchaser, even if title is registered. Examples are provided by easements

---

[74] Found in most Commonwealth countries. These systems developed and spread earlier than title registration in England and Wales and generally give greater protection to the registered proprietor.

[75] *Op. cit.* above fn. 47, p. 297. Whalan is critical of the language of indefeasibility as being misleading and prefers the term 'State-guaranteed'.

[76] LRA, s. 69; 2002 Act, s. 58 (subject to satisfaction of registration requirements). See also ss. 5 (first registration) and 20 (transfers) where title is absolute (almost invariably the case); equivalent provisions apply to the registration of leases. The 2002 Act contains equivalent provisions on first registration (s. 11 (3)), but the effect of a registered disposition is expressed (s. 29) in terms of priorities rather than conferring a legal estate.

[77] LRA, ss. 5, 20; on first registration, trustees are subject to the beneficial interests (s. 5 (c)). 2002 Act, ss. 11 (4) (5), 29 (the drafting no longer employs the phrase 'free from all other estates…').

acquired by implication or prescription, adverse possession (sometimes) and leases not exceeding 21 years.[78]

Accordingly, the contrast with unregistered land is not as great as might be thought. But how far are the courts inclined to accept that differences do exist? Four difficult areas may be identified. The first concerns purchasers with actual notice of unprotected minor interests, where the 1925 legislation on its face appeared to protect the purchaser.[79] Identical policy problems arise in unregistered land as regards the land charges scheme: in each case the question arises as to how far we should protect the purchaser. To put it another way, do we see the role of registration of minor interests and land charges to be to avoid issues of constructive notice or to be the sole and final determinant of what binds a purchaser? The contrast here is not so much between registered and unregistered land, as between the traditional concepts of when purchasers are bound and the registration schemes found in the 1925 legislation (and, today, the Land Charges Act 1972 and the 2002 Act). The question has received, at least in registered land, little judicial attention and no clear outcome emerged before the 2002 Act.[80] There are difficult policy issues here I have considered elsewhere,[81] but the Law Commission[82] has taken the 'registration minded' approach of recommending that knowledge and notice on the part of the purchaser should be irrelevant and this appears to be the effect of the 2002 Act.[83]

Overriding interests – our second difficult area – form a notoriously controversial and heavily litigated aspect of land registration. These interests bind purchasers despite not being entered on the register and they afford greater recognition to unprotected interests than one finds in Torrens registration systems in other Commonwealth countries. It has already been observed that many legal interests are overriding interests. Indeed the only significant exceptions are easements expressly created by a registered proprietor,[84] leases exceeding seven years and legal charges.

---

[78] LRA, s. 70 (1) (a), (f), (k); 2002 Act, Sch. 3, paras. 3 (easements) and 1 (leases not exceeding *seven* years). Adverse possession is protected under the 2002 Act if there is actual occupation (para. 2; see Law Com No. 271, paras. 14.64, 14.70) or (first registration only) there is notice of it (s. 11 (4) (c)). Under the 2002 Act, it will be relatively unusual for an adverse possessor to have a right to the land.

[79] Sections 20, 59 (6); see fn. 65 above.

[80] Contrast *Peffer* v. *Rigg* [1977] 1 WLR 285 (registered land, good faith required on the part of the purchaser) and *Midland Bank Trust Co Ltd* v. *Green* [1981] AC 513 (unregistered land, good faith not required). Though the problem is identical, differences in the legislation may technically justify different solutions.

[81] In Jackson and Wilde, *The Reform of Property Law*, at pp. 135–7.

[82] Paragraph 3.46; but see p. 48 below.

[83] See fn. 65 above.

[84] Even these use to be overriding interests as equitable easements: *Celsteel Ltd* v. *Alton House Holdings Ltd* [1985] 1 WLR 204, relying on Land Registration Rules 1925 (hereafter LRR), r. 257, and *Thatcher* v. *Douglas* (1996) 146 NLJ 282. This has been reversed by Sch. 3, para. 3, of the 2002 Act.

On the other hand, the 2002 Act sets out to diminish the scope of overriding interests[85] and the link between legal interests and overriding interests will in future be significantly less significant. However, by far the most intriguing overriding interest is para. 2 of Sch. 3. of the 2002 Act: An interest belonging...to a person in actual occupation... '. This provides an invaluable safety valve for meritorious claims, protecting 'a person in actual occupation of land from having his rights lost in the welter of registration'.[86] The understandable justification is that it is preferable to require purchasers to make inquiries of occupiers than to defeat the interests of occupiers, which would frequently involve turning them out of their homes.[87] The question I wish to address, however, is how far para. 2) is a simple reflection of the rule that occupation provides constructive notice of an occupier's rights. There is much to be said for the view that land registration is intended to get away from the old concepts of notice which could provide so much uncertainty for purchasers.[88] This appears to have been accepted by the House of Lords in *Williams & Glyn's Bank Ltd v. Boland,* especially when Lord Wilberforce stated 'If there is actual occupation, and the occupier has rights, the purchaser takes subject to them. If not, he does not. No further element is material.'[89] In the place of the old concepts we find the possibilities of entry on the register and actual occupation: both of which involve many more black-and-white issues than does notice. That is not to say there cannot be difficult cases as to whether there is actual occupation,[90] but rather that these cases are likely to possess relatively unusual facts and not to require sophisticated legal analysis.

However, what we in fact observe in more recent cases (before the 2002 Act) is an attempt to introduce the doctrine of notice.[91] This can be seen in the Court of Appeal decisions in *Lloyds Bank plc v. Rosset*[92] and *Abbey National BS v. Cann.*[93] I am not concerned with the question whether the

---

[85] Thus Sch. 3, para. 1 limits overriding interest leases to 7 years (and previously 21 years) and para. 3 both limits easements and profits to legal interests and restricts the circumstances when they can be overriding if not reasonably discoverable. Attempts are also made to get overriding interests entered on the register: Law Com No. 271, paras 8.90–95.

[86] *Strand Securities Ltd v. Caswell* [1965] Ch 958 at 979 (Lord Denning MR).

[87] Paragraph 5.61. The issue was more fully discussed in Law Com No. 158, especially paras 2.60–68.

[88] See, for example, Jackson 'Security of title in registered land' (1978) 94 LQR 239.

[89] [1981] AC 487 at 504, rejecting an argument that 'we should have regard to and limit the application of the paragraph in the light of the doctrine of notice'.

[90] One excellent example is *Lloyds Bank plc v. Rosset* [1989] Ch 350 (reversed on another ground: [1991] 1 AC 107), which involved the superintending of the restoration of a derelict house.

[91] I have described this development in *Property Law* (3rd ed, 2000, Pearson Education Inc.), pp. 266–68; cf. Law Com No. 254, paras. 5.57-58.

[92] [1989] Ch 350.

[93] [1989] 2 FLR 265.

resultant position is defensible in terms of what is most reasonably to be expected of purchasers.[94] What is more interesting is the reluctance of the courts to move away from older concepts within unregistered conveyancing. The actual outcome (protecting a purchaser who cannot readily discover the actual occupation) may be applauded and yet the means by which it is achieved criticised. There was nothing in s. 70 (1) (g) justifying the introduction of notice and it would be most inappropriate for unregistered land principles to be imported in other contexts. The danger is that the courts see the old rules as representing some form of ideal justice and are inclined to invoke them whenever possible. It is not difficult to agree that the old rules do frequently lead to a just result as between the two parties before the court. However, this is apt to overlook the point that the legislation is designed to produce a smooth running system of conveyancing. At least to a limited extent, this may have to take priority over the relative merits of two parties looked at in isolation from the larger picture.

A third difficult area concerns timing issues. In unregistered land, the time of completion is crucial. Prima facie, this is not the case for registered land: the time of registration[95] is what counts. This looks as though it might be problematic, as registration is usually some time after completion. Two factors combine to limit the problem. First, a purchaser who seeks registration within 30 days of an official search (itself usually a few days before completion) is protected against intervening entries.[96] A purchaser risks danger by delaying registration longer than this and the courts have shown little concern for such purchasers.[97] Secondly, the courts have held that actual occupation overriding interests must exist at time of completion.[98] Though this required some inventive construction of the earlier legislation, the result does make practical sense: it avoids the 'registration gap' that even diligent purchasers are unable to prevent.

---

[94] The 2002 Act, Sch. 3, para. 2 (c) (i) requires the occupation to be 'obvious on a reasonably careful inspection of the land'. The Law Commission placed no stress on the doctrine of notice in recommending this, preferring to stress its connection with the seller's duty to disclose latent defects (No. 271, paras. 5.21, 8.62). Note that the occupation must be obvious, not the occupier's interest.

[95] More correctly the time of application, as the entry is backdated to that time (LRR, r. 83 (2); 2002 Act, s. 74).

[96] Land Registration (Official Searches) Rules 1993 (SI 1993 No. 3276), rr. 2, 6; 2002 Act, s. 73 (rules will make provision for the length of the priority period).

[97] See, for example, *Elias* v. *Mitchell* [1972] Ch 652. In Torrens systems lacking this statutory protection for purchasers, the courts have been more inclined to find ways to defeat an equitable interest unprotected on the register at the time of completion: Smith (1977) 93 LQR 541 at 553–55.

[98] *Abbey National BS* v. *Cann* [1991] 1 AC 56, confirmed by the drafting of Sched. 3, para. 2 of the 2002 Act.

Nevertheless, there is an argument that the purchaser has usually brought the problem on him- or herself by delaying registration.[99] It may be hoped that these issues, for both minor and overriding interests, will disappear as we move to a system of electronic registration contemporaneous with completion. The absence of a registration gap will simplify the law considerably.[100]

The fourth and final difficult area involves personal liability: an area of law that has been little developed in England.[101] We normally think of purchasers being bound because there is a property interest binding them on the normal principles applicable to unregistered or registered land as the case may be. However, it is possible for a purchaser to be directly liable to a third party. This may be described as personal, or *in personam*, liability.

The most obvious source of personal obligations lies in contracts. Consider this simple example. Suppose a purchaser of land contracts to resell it to Q. Completion of the transfer to the purchaser then takes place and she is registered as proprietor. It would be outrageous if she could deny liability to Q on the basis that Q had not protected the estate contract on the register.[102] Although there is some authority against the enforcement of personal rights generally,[103] the better view (as adopted by the Law Commission)[104] is that failure to register defeats only proprietary rights.

Personal obligations may, of course, arise from sources other than contract. Although the area has not been much developed, it seems

---

99 Ferris 'Structural differences between registered land and unregistered land law' in Jackson and Wilde, *Contemporary Property Law* especially pp. 145–147. The underlying argument of Ferris is that the courts have paid too much attention to the date of completion, as opposed to the date of registration. This is an example of the courts' reluctance to move way from unregistered land thinking, though arguably the author exaggerates the courts' stress on the date of completion.

100 If there is a delay we need to remember that, when electronic registration systems are fully in force and s. 93 has been applied to the type of disposition involved, no right will be attained until registration: see p. 38 above.

101 Perhaps because of the greater protection of registered proprietors in Torrens registration systems, personal liability has long been recognised. For a modern analysis, see Skapinker, 'Equitable interests, more equities and "personal equities" – distinctions with a difference' (1994) 68 ALJ 593.

102 The priority system introduced by the 2002 Act (s. 29) ensures that only rights binding the disponer defeated: Law Com No. 271, para. 5.10.

103 *Orakpo* v. *Manson Investments Ltd* [1977] 1 WLR 347 at 360 (affirmed on other grounds: [1978] AC 95). In unregistered land, *Phillips* v. *Mobil Oil Co Ltd* [1989] 1 WLR 888 denies the use of privity of estate for unregistered land charges, but that depended on legislation declaring unregistered interests 'void as against a purchaser' (Land Charges Act 1972, s. 4 (5), (6)).

104 Paragraphs 3.48–3.49. There is no explicit provision in the 2002 Act, though personal liability is tangentially recognised in Law Com No. 271, paras. 4.11 (knowing receipt), 7.7 (interference with contract) and supported by s. 29. See also the recent Privy Council support for personal claims in Torrens systems in *Gardener* v. *Lewis* [1998] 1 WLR 1535.

possible for the economic torts to apply to a purchaser. It is no defence to say that an interest has not been registered: the purchaser is being attacked on a tort rather than property basis and registration applies only to the latter.[105] Next, suppose the purchaser tells the holder of an unprotected interest that there is no need to protect it, as he or she will respect it after the purchase. In that case, it may well be that subsequent denial of liability would be such fraud as defeats the statutory protection of registered transferees,[106] but there also appears to be a strong argument that estoppel could be relied upon as a form of personal liability.[107]

Most interesting are personal claims based upon trusts and other equitable claims. These are interesting because the dividing line between personal and proprietary claims is difficult to draw. As a result, there is a danger of enforcing rights on a personal basis when in substance a proprietary right is being enforced. Some trusts clearly justify treatment as personal claims. Easy examples are where a resulting or constructive trust is imposed on a purchaser on the basis of another person's contribution to the purchase price or of a common intention. It is plainly inconceivable that the purchaser could argue that the trust is ineffective because it was not entered on the register.[108] Far more difficult is the argument that 'knowing receipt' can be made the basis of personal liability.[109] It is here that proprietary and personal liability tend to shade into each other. The history of the liability of purchasers towards holders of equitable interests lies in the conscionability of the purchaser's claim not to be bound. Though in modern law we think in terms of equitable proprietary interests, this does some violence to the historical development of liability.[110]

The real danger in areas such as knowing receipt lies in their potential to circumvent the statutory protection for purchasers. The Law Commission expresses itself content that 'there should be no place for concepts of knowledge or notice in registered land',[111] while welcoming personal

---

[105] *Esso Petroleum Co Ltd* v. *Kingswood Motors (Addlestone) Ltd* [1974] QB 142; cf. Smith [1977] Conv. 318.

[106] Cf. *Lyus* v. *Prowsa Developments Ltd* [1982] 1 WLR 1044, where the representation was to the seller.

[107] *First National Bank plc* v. *Thompson* [1996] Ch 231. For an estoppel arising after purchase, see *Taylors Fashions Ltd* v. *Liverpool Victoria Trustees Co Ltd* [1982] QB 133.

[108] Though the beneficiary under the trust might claim an overriding interest by virtue of actual occupation, this would be difficult to prove at the time of completion (as required by *Abbey National BS* v. *Cann* [1991] 1 AC 56).

[109] It is interesting that this basis of liability has not been developed in Australia. However, the quite wide basis for personal rights espoused by Skapinker (1994) 68 ALJ 593 would fairly clearly include such situations.

[110] Maitland, *Equity* (2nd ed.), pp. 112–115. This may be accepted even though doubting his analysis that equitable interests operate *in personam* rather than *in rem*, as legal rights do. Cf. *Underhill's Law of Trusts and Trustees* (15th ed.), p. 369.

[111] Paragraph 3.46; for the 2002 Act, see fn. 65 above.

liability. In so far as personal liability is based on an undertaking by the purchaser, this is eminently justified whether the legal basis is contract or trust: cases such as *Lyus* v. *Prowsa Developments Ltd*,[112] in which the purchaser made a promise to the seller to respect an unprotected interest, exemplify liability which makes good practical sense and can be theoretically justified. Louise Tee argues[113] that it is preferable to deal with the enforceability of interests within the terms of the registration statute. That may well be so, but total rejection of personal liability would be a dramatic over-reaction. However, once one moves from purchasers' undertakings to the imposition of liability then matters do become more difficult.[114] The area of tort liability (briefly considered above) may be moderately well settled, though not free from criticism.[115] Resulting and constructive trusts (at least those based on common intention) may also be justified. What seems more difficult to accept is that a constructive trust can be imposed on a person essentially because he or she is purchaser, in circumstances where the law says that property rights do not bind the purchaser. Thus trusts imposed by virtue of a common intention or a trustee profiting from the position as trustee do not set out to deny the statutory protection of a purchaser: they have a very different root, which need not involve a purchaser. Another sort of case is where the conduct of a purchaser or the circumstances of the purchase give rise to an equitable remedy: rescission for misrepresentation or undue influence[116] and rectification for mistake.[117] These cases may be thought to be closer to knowing receipt in that they do involve purchasers. However, they require more than simple awareness of the equitable interest: specific conduct or circumstances are required for liability to be imposed. One apparently paradoxical point is worth noting in this setting. We often

---

[112] [1982] 1 WLR 1044.

[113] 'Rights of persons in actual occupation' [1998] CLJ 328 at 332–333; cf. Wilde [1999] Conv. 382.

[114] Exemplified by the suggestion of Lord Denning in *Binions* v. *Evans* [1972] Ch 359 at 369 that a trust will be imposed whenever a claimant is in actual occupation (subsequently discredited, at least since *Ashburn Anstalt* v. *Arnold* [1989] Ch 1). These facts would, of course, enable an actual occupation overriding interest to be relied upon: registration was not in issue in *Binions*.

[115] See my views in [1977] Conv. 318.

[116] Most cases involve those dealing with the 'guilty' purchaser: it is assumed that the first purchaser is subject to a remedy: *Re Leighton's Conveyance* [1936] 1 All ER 667; *Norwich & Peterborough BS* v. *Steed* [1993] Ch 116. Note also the *Barclays Bank plc* v. *O'Brien* [1994] 1 AC 180 line of cases, though these are more complex because the purchaser (mortgagee) is not directly responsible for the conduct complained of: the mortgagee can be attacked because it has notice (though not notice in the conventional sense of notice of an equitable interest: *Barclays Bank plc* v. *Boulter* [1999] 1 WLR 1919 at 1924–1925).

[117] Again, the main questions have concerned successors in title: *Blacklocks* v. *JB Developments (Godalming) Ltd* [1982] Ch 183 (see 191 for the original purchaser); *DB Ramsden & Co Ltd* v. *Nurdin & Peacock plc* [1998] *The Times*, September 14; Pascoe [1999] Conv. 421. In Australia, cf. *Tutt* v. *Doyle* (1997) 42 NSWLR 10 (unilateral mistake).

think of equitable remedies against purchasers as being weaker than being able to prove that the conveyance is void.[118] Yet the fact that a transfer is void does not mean the transferor necessarily has a remedy against a bona fide transferee. Forgery by a third party is a good example: there is no personal remedy against an innocent registered transferee. The reason is that there is nothing in the transferee's conduct that justifies a remedy. Once it has been registered, the only effect of the transfer's being void is that it might be relevant in rectification proceedings.[119]

Three further points may be made about the knowing receipt basis of liability. The first is that the precise basis of liability (whether or not registered land is involved) is not yet settled. As the Law Commission recognises, liability might result from there being *notice* rather than *knowledge* of the breach of trust. Alarm bells really should be ringing if we have reached a position whereby notice may be the basis of liability of a registered proprietor. The most recent ruling is that 'The recipient's state of knowledge must be such as to make it unconscionable for him to retain the benefit of the receipt'.[120] This appears to tilt the balance towards knowledge, though the flexibility of the test requires further litigation before we can be certain how it would apply to purchasers of registered land. It is paradoxical that much of the debate has taken place against the background that proprietary liability is easier to prove than personal liability,[121] whereas in our present setting personal liability is being mooted where the purchaser, still holding the property, is free from proprietary liability.

The second point – one which favours a wide personal liability – is that the controversial decision in *Peffer* v. *Rigg*[122] can be justified on the basis of knowing receipt.[123] This will please the many lawyers who share the instinctive reaction that a purchaser who is well aware of a breach of trust does not deserve to succeed. It also fits into the Torrens analysis that a purchaser with actual notice of a breach of trust is fraudulent[124] and as such cannot rely on indefeasibility. It may, however, be observed that personal liability is not actually the basis for *Peffer* v. *Rigg* or the Torrens cases.[125] The third point is somewhat related. Even if knowledge of a

---

[118] In the personal property setting, see the well-known mistaken identity cases exemplified by *Lewis* v. *Averay* [1972] 1 QB 198.

[119] See fn. 132 below.

[120] *Bank of Credit and Commerce International (Overseas) Ltd* v. *Akindele* [2001] Ch 437 at 455 (Nourse LJ); cf. Thomas (2001) 21 OxJLS 239.

[121] See especially Megarry VC in *Re Montagu's Settlement Trusts* [1987] Ch 264 at 272–273, 278.

[122] [1977] 1 WLR 285.

[123] See Bright [2000] Conv. 398 at 412–413.

[124] On the basis of knowledge of the fraud of the trustee: *Assets Co Ltd* v. *Mere Roihi* [1905] AC 176 at 210 (PC).

[125] Though a constructive trust is made an alternative ground for the decision in *Peffer*, the basis for its imposition is not stated.

breach of trust gives rise to personal liability, this does not apply to knowledge of other unprotected equitable rights. The liability is based on receipt of trust property, not property subject to an equitable obligation (proprietary or otherwise).[126] Thus the House of Lords has held that a purchaser of unregistered land is not bound despite clear notice of an unregistered option: *Midland Bank Trust Co Ltd* v. *Green*.[127] One may question whether principles of personal liability should apply to trusts but not other equitable claims. Is it really the case that a breach of trust is necessarily so much more terrible than deliberately selling property to defeat an equitable interest such as an option?[128] Indeed, is this not a case in which interference with contract could be argued?

Rectification

Freedom from statutory rectification of title is the second component part of guaranteeing title. How far are the courts influenced by unregistered land outcomes in considering whether to rectify? The danger is that a purchaser may possess an unencumbered title (because a rival claim is neither entered on the register nor an overriding interest) and yet find that rectification destroys that title.[129] Professor D.C. Jackson has been particularly critical of the use of unregistered land principles as a basis for rectification, writing[130] that 'If we have managed to retain the unregistered land framework we have not only failed to make anything of land registration as a means of ridding ourselves of the defects of unregistered land, we have failed to simplify the rules'.

The Court of Appeal relatively recently provided us with a full discussion of the grounds for rectifying the register under the 1925 legislation: *Norwich & Peterborough BS* v. *Steed*.[131] Although the court denied any general discretion to rectify (which is to be welcomed), there

---

[126] It is similar when applying the fraud test in Australia: *Friedman* v. *Barrett* [1962] Qd R 498; Whalan (1975) 6 NZULR 207, *The Torrens System in Australia* (*op. cit.* above fn. 47), pp. 309–317.

[127] [1981] AC 513. The knowing receipt analysis should apply whether title is registered or not.

[128] A plan between seller and buyer to sell in order to defeat an interest may more readily be taken as fraud: cf. *Waimiha Sawmilling Co* v. *Waione Timber Co* [1926] AC 101 at 106.

[129] See LRA, s. 82 (1; 2002 Act, Sch. 4, para. 2). Until amendments in 1977, there would almost invariably be rectification against a first registered proprietor if there was a flaw in the title: *Re 139 Deptford High Street* [1951] Ch 884 and *Re Sea View Gardens, Claridge* v. *Tingey* [1967] 1 WLR 134.

[130] (1978) 94 LQR 239 at 243, considering *Orakpo* v. *Manson Investments Ltd* [1977] 1 WLR 347.

[131] [1993] Ch 116.

is uncertainty as to how far it invokes unregistered principles.[132] The Law Commission, it is pleasing to note, would exclude unregistered land criteria: 'The principles governing unregistered land should come into play only if there is some issue which arises from the time prior to first registration.'[133] Schedule 4, paras. 2, 5 of the 2002 Act uses the term 'mistake' and it remains to see what this encompasses: it is not defined in the 2002 Act. There is some indication that the Law Commission does not intend to apply unregistered land principles even on first registration,[134] but this would seem to restrict rectification too much.

Even if there is jurisdiction to rectify, it should be remembered that para 3. of Sch. 4 of the 2002 Act affords useful protection to the proprietor in possession. Rectification will normally be awarded only if the proprietor is guilty of fraud or lack of proper care or it would be, in the language of the 2002 Act,[135] 'unjust for the alteration not to be made'. There is no evidence in the cases that the courts will readily apply these exceptions.[136]

Indemnity

The third and final aspect of guaranteeing titles concerns the financial guarantee if loss is caused to the registered proprietor.[137] However well structured the system, it is inevitable that rectification will sometimes deny or damage a registered title. A simple (if rare) example is where there are two inconsistent titles:[138] it is impossible for both rival claimants to get the land! There is no financial guarantee of titles in unregistered land,[139] so indemnity is potentially a very significant benefit for purchasers of registered land. When I reviewed the position in the mid-

---

[132] Contrast my argument that it does do so ((1993) 109 LQR 187, *Property Law* (*op. cit.* above fn. 91), pp. 236–238) with the argument of the Law Commission to the contrary (para. 8.11). See also *Horrill* v. *Cooper* (2000) 80 P & CR D16 (rectification where land charge omitted on first registration, *affg* (1999) 78 P & CR 336 on different grounds); *Kingsalton Ltd* v. *Thames Water Developments Ltd* [2001] EWCA Civ 20, [2002] IP & CR 184 (use of LRA, s. 82 (1)(a) when the wrong person is registered as proprietor).

[133] Paragraph 8.40. The 2002 Act distinguishes between rectification on account of a 'mistake' where the proprietor is prejudicially affected (Sch. 4, para. 1) and the more general category of 'alteration' of the register.

[134] Law Com No. 271, para. 3.47.

[135] Schedule 4, paras. 3 (2), 6 (2). The 'order of the court' exception to the protection of the proprietor in possession is dropped: Law Com No. 271, para. 10.16.

[136] Indeed, the cases show a reluctance to do so: *Hounslow LB* v. *Hare* (1990) 24 HLR 9.

[137] LRA, s. 83; 2002 Act, Sch. 8. Indemnity may also be paid to others who lose out from a mistake (Sch. 8, para. 1 (1) (6), but this is not part of guaranteeing titles.

[138] Explicitly provided for by LRA, s. 82 (1) (e); this has no direct counterpart in the 2002 Act, though doubtless it is covered by Sch. 4, para. 2 (1).

[139] Leaving aside actions against a claimant's solicitor, for which negligence must be proved. The practical limitations on such claims have recently been investigated by Morgan in Jackson and Wilde, *Contemporary Property Law*, pp. 173–174.

1980s, I concluded[140] that just 0.18% of fee income went on indemnity claims, though I thought that a truer figure to take account of inflation and growth in the system would be 0.44%. How do those figures look 15 years on, when inflation is low and the system closer to a steady-state position?

Taking the last five years, the figure has increased to 0.61% of fee income.[141] Given that fee income has been held down,[142] this indicates the level of payments has remained quite steady in real terms. One factor that should have a downwards impact on payments is that errors are most likely to arise on first registration; the numbers and more especially the proportion of first registrations have dropped since the 1980s. However the precise figures are viewed, it is clear that a minute part of the resources of registration is devoted to indemnity: its value to the average purchaser is, in financial terms, minimal. This may demonstrate that the Land Registry makes commendably few errors, but it also defeats any idea that indemnity can be seen as insurance for defects in title. A brave attempt was made by the Law Commission in the 1980s to extend indemnity to purchasers bound by overriding interests.[143] Because of the impossibility of quantifying likely claims, that approach is now regarded as foolhardy and has been dropped by the Law Commission.[144] It may well be that this was essential in order to advance more general reforms of land registration, but it severely limits the extent to which imaginative use is made of registration to guarantee a proprietor's title.

When considering the idea of insuring against defects in title, it is worth comparing commercial title insurance. This has never fully developed in this country, despite the fact that it is the basis of conveyancing in the USA.[145] This may be because the risks have never been perceived as being great in England (especially where title is registered), with the consequence that insurance has usually been sought for questionable titles. Any insurance scheme is unlikely to be financially viable if only high risk business is involved (unless the premiums are prohibitively expensive). However, insurance can offer benefits that go beyond the scope of the

---

[140] [1986] CLP 111 at 116–117. Inflation and growth need to be considered because payments are generally made several years after registration.

[141] See the Land Registry annual report and accounts for the years in question. Occasionally, there are very large claims which skew the figures for a particular year. This was the case in 1992–1993, when payments represented 2.5% of fee income.

[142] See p. 34 above. The total fee income has grown by 177% over 15 years to 1999, in comparison with a 127% increase in house prices. However, the number of registered titles has nearly doubled.

[143] Law Com No. 158, paras 2.9–2.14. Lack of proper care would have denied payment, so the practical impact would have been limited: few overriding interests cannot be discovered by making reasonable inquiries.

[144] Paragraph 4.19.

[145] It is described by Payne in 'American title insurance in an English context' [1976] Conv. 11.

indemnity scheme in land registration.[146] The cost is likely to be about 0.25% of the land value, with a minimum of £262.50.[147] This may be compared with Land Registry charges of less than half that amount and solicitors' charges (which will not be replaced by title insurance in England[148]) of roughly double that amount. Easily the most significant use of title insurance in the USA is to protect lenders: virtually all lenders insist upon it. In England, it would be surprising[149] if the losses of an average lender on account of bad titles were anything like 0.25%: it is not clear what benefit a lender would obtain from insuring against losses at a higher cost than averaging losses across a portfolio of mortgages.[150] This is not to argue that insurance has no place in the conveyancing context. For example, it is quite common to take out insurance in respect of a known (but unlikely to materialise) risk in a particular title.

Developing property principles

Under this heading, we will consider developments that may be encouraged or facilitated by registration of title. Although a few specific possibilities will be discussed, this is an open-ended category and many further future developments can be expected. The challenge for those of us brought up on traditional courses based on unregistered land and concepts of legal and equitable interests, coupled with the doctrine of notice, is to work out how many of our existing rules are based on out-of-date criteria. If they are, then now is the time to consider whether they should be changed.

We will start with two recommendations of the Law Commission: one radical and the other, perhaps, timid. The first, radical, proposal relates to adverse possession. It was proposed to limit very severely both the scope and attraction of adverse possession rules[151] and this is implemented by the 2002 Act.[152] There are two main reasons why such a departure from

---

[146] Morgan (*op. cit.* above fn. 139), noting in particular the benefits to mortgagees. For an earlier assessment, see Adams [1979] Conv. 323.

[147] Stewart Title Insurance Company (UK) Limited: http://www.stewartuk.com

[148] The system in the USA is significantly different in that title insurance companies there vet the title and largely cut out the role of the purchaser's lawyer.

[149] The Nationwide Building Society (with a market share close to 8%) wrote off an amount for bad and doubtful debts of 0.6% of current market lending in 1999: *Annual Report and Accounts*, 1999. Although details are not given, one might surmise that a tiny proportion of this is attributable to defects in title, as opposed to inadequacy of the security.

[150] The cost could be passed on to the borrower, but this would render the lender uncompetitive.

[151] Part X. Reform of prescription, considered in the same part, provides another example, though it is not implemented by the 2002 Act.

[152] Sch. 6, section 96–98.

old principles is desirable and feasible for registered land. The first is that, because titles are guaranteed by the state, adverse possession has little significant function in settling otherwise doubtful titles. The second is that the Registrar[153] can play a role in serving notices and deciding when adverse possession should be allowed. It is significant to note that the role of the Registrar is to be central, not just in giving and receiving notices, but in the much more discretionary areas of deciding (for example) whether the squatter had entered under a reasonable belief as to his or her rights.[154] It would be more difficult to duplicate this role within the unregistered system. The 2002 Act enacting this much watered-down version of adverse possession is undoubtedly one of the most fundamental changes to property law in the past century.

The second recommendation reveals more caution. It concerns the priority of interests other than the registered fee simple (or lease or mortgage). Though the quality of the title enjoyed by a registered proprietor goes to the very heart of land registration (and so was considered above), there is nothing inherent in the scheme which demands that the priorities of other interests should change. Take, for example, two equitable charges over land. It is no part of the registration of title scheme to enable dealings with such interests or to guarantee their position relative to each other. Such interests will benefit considerably from registration of title, as there will be less doubt concerning the title being charged and indemnity will be payable if that title is rectified to their disadvantage.[155] Yet those interests are not guaranteed: thus a forged equitable charge will have no effect, regardless of whether it is protected on the register.

However, it might be thought that title registration provides an opportunity for the old priority rules to be reconsidered. The essence of those rules is that the first of two equitable interests has priority: the second, however much in good faith and without notice, has very little hope of reversing this[156] save for the unusual case in which it can be shown that the equities favour the second interest. The obvious question today is whether we should give priority to the first interest to be protected on the register: this would enable the second interest to rely on the state of the register. Although this increases the risks of failure to protect an interest,[157]

---

153 Disputes will be considered (as with other contested applications) by the adjudicator, though there are some significant changes a new and independent position created by the 2002 Act.

154 Paragraphs 10.51–52. There could, as normal, be an appeal to the High Court. 2002 Act, Sch. 6, 2, 5.

155 LRA, ss. 82 (2), 83 (1): *Freer* v. *Unwins Ltd* [1976] Ch 288 at 295; 2002 Act, Sch. 4, para. 8, Sch. 8, para. 1.

156 *Phillips* v. *Phillips* (1861) 4 De GF & J 208 (45 ER 1164).

157 Most especially where the first interest holder possesses the land certificate, so that under the LRA 1925 that person knows that no registration can take place.

it adds considerable certainty for those dealing with land. A highly material point is that acquisition of an equitable interest may well involve a large financial outlay[158] and arguably the law is defective if it fails to provide certainty as to priority. Such certainty is unobtainable apart from registration, but we now have the basic tools to do more.

When we look at unregistered land, we see that an equitable charge (without deposit of title deeds) may lose priority to a later equitable interest, unless registered under the Land Charges Act 1972.[159] It is, then, surprising to find that there is no equivalent provision in LRA 1925. In the words of Robert Walker LJ:[160]

> Although the purpose of the Land Registration Acts is to achieve greater simplicity and certainty in title to land by a system of central registration of property, ownership and charges, that purpose has not been fully attained and the existence of an entry of some sort on the register is not in every case either a necessary or a sufficient condition for protection...

Perhaps inevitably, the courts concluded that we are thrown back on to the old first in time rule: simple failure to protect the first interest will not postpone priority.[161] There may be exceptions where the first interest holder bears responsibility for arming the proprietor 'with the appearance of absolute and unincumbered ownership',[162] but these will be rare.

In the 1980s, the Law Commission recommended that priority should be accorded to the first person to place an entry on the register,[163] the same rule as benefits registered interests such as the fee simple, lease or mortgage. In Law Com No. 254, however, this recommendation was dropped[164] and the 2002 Act confirms and strengthens the first in time rule.[165] Given that the Law Commission was prepared to be bold in other areas, that it regarded the issues as important and the present law to be uncertain, lacking in security for holders of minor interests and capable of leading to anomalies,[166] why does the Law Commission cling to the old law? Two principal answers appear. The first is that the legislation earlier proposed was thought to be defective, with highly complex provisions

---

[158] Apart from charges, options provide another good example.

[159] Section 4 (5); Harpum, *Megarry & Wade: The Law of Real Property* (6th ed, 2000, Sweet & Maxwell), paras. 19–221, 19–225–6. This does not apply to other land charges, such as estate contracts or restrictive covenants.

[160] *Freeguard* v. *The Royal Bank of Scotland plc* (1998) 79 P & CR 81 at 86.

[161] *Barclays Bank Ltd* v. *Taylor* [1974] Ch 137 (later interest protected by caution); *Mortgage Corporation Ltd* v. *Nationwide Credit Corporation Ltd* [1994] Ch 49 (notice).

[162] *Freeguard* v. *The Royal Bank of Scotland plc* (1998) 79 P & CR 81 (artificial transaction involving a sale (funded by the seller) with an option to get the property back).

[163] Law Com No. 158, paras. 4.94 *et seq*.

[164] Part VII.

[165] Section 28; Law Com No. 271, para. 5.5 (an 'absolute' rule).

[166] Paragraph 7.27.

required (especially for transitional provisions).[167] It is, perhaps, unfortunate that there is no explanation of the nature of these problems, though it is always easier to propose changes than to draft a satisfactory method of introducing them. Stronger reasons are found in the point that, before too long, electronic conveyancing will mean that minor interests will not exist unless entered on the register.[168] In other words, a first to protect rule will in fact be introduced: the first to protect will also be the first to exist.

If we stopped there, the case in favour of the Law Commission's amended position would be overwhelming. However, two considerations must be added. The first is that there will be quite some time before interests require entry in order to be effective. While electronic entries will be upon us quite soon, all recognise that the requirement of electronic protection lies much further down the road. For that extended period, the problems faced by holders of minor interests will continue. While it is true that there has been little litigation in the area, this proves neither that problems do not arise nor that the law is satisfactory. The second consideration is that not all interests will require entry on the register. As we have seen, a significant number of exceptions are planned.[169] It follows that a person taking (for example) an equitable charge or option will have no way in which to discover whether there are rights that will take priority. Some of the exceptions will, of course, be overriding interests and these would have priority anyway by virtue of that status. But minor interests such as a resulting trust in favour of a person not occupying the premises would illustrate the problem. The Law Commission regards any loss of time order priority as being unfair to the sorts of informal rights that will be valid without registration.[170] There is something in this, but they are already at risk as regards subsequent registered interests: there is no loss of nerve in that setting.

At least when electronic conveyancing is fully introduced, it will be true that the problems will be less than at present. Even so, one may express disappointment that the Law Commission succumbed so readily to the drafting difficulties.

So far, we have considered two areas dealt with by the Law Commission. However, other potential developments exist beyond those considered by the Law Commission. One example was investigated recently by Louise Tee.[171] She argued that, as a matter of policy, overriding interests within s. 70 (1) (g), now Sch. 3, para 2, (actual

---

[167] Paragraphs 7.26, 7.30 (2).
[168] See p. 38 above.
[169] See p. 41 above.
[170] Paragraph 7.30 (1).
[171] [1998] CLJ 328.

occupation) should encompass all claims to land and not be restricted to rights conventionally regarded as proprietary. This is, of course, the argument propounded by Donovan LJ in *National Provincial Bank Ltd* v. *Ainsworth*, but roundly rejected by the House of Lords.[172] The argument is important and controversial, as it goes to the heart of our sense of proprietary interests. There is no space in this chapter to do more than comment on some of the issues.

One argument may be readily accepted. Now that we have replaced the complex and uncertain doctrine of notice with the more easily determined issues of entry on the register and actual occupation, some of the reasons for limiting proprietary interests lose their force. In particular, the discoverability of the interest is much less of a problem for purchasers today, even if the case law on actual occupation is less clear than one might have hoped. If one is asking which rights should be admitted to proprietary status, then the registration system might justify a wider range of rights than would have seemed appropriate to judges a century ago. One might, for example, feel more comfortable today about accepting a right to rectify a document, when the person seeking rectification must either have placed an entry on the register or be in actual occupation of the disputed land.[173]

Students new to land law commonly ask why we should have a list of proprietary interests: would it not be simpler to recognise all rights? Though there are fairly standard answers that can be given, there is commonly a lingering doubt whether the justification is more one of historical development rather than modern utility. The issues raised by Louise Tee force us to face these questions in the registration setting. Her argument is presented in the context of overriding interests, yet an initial reaction is that it is difficult to comprehend why actual occupation should empower rights which cannot be protected upon the register. I do not seek to raise an argument on the wording of the legislation;[174] rather I argue that it would be irrational to limit the sorts of interests that can be minor interests (provided they are capable of binding purchasers of registered land). From the point of view of the purchaser, matters are

---

[172] [1964] Ch 665 at 692–693; [1965] AC 1175 especially at 1261 (Lord Wilberforce).

[173] *Blacklocks* v. *JB Developments (Godalming) Ltd* [1982] Ch 183, though one may feel less happy where the actual occupation is consistent with the document as in *DB Ramsden & Co Ltd* v. *Nurdin & Peacock plc* [1998] *The Times*, 14 September. Section 116 of the 2002 Act provides that a 'mere equity' is capable of binding successors in title in registered land, settling doubts expressed in *Collings* v. *Lee* [2001] 2 All ER 332 at 338 (CA) in the context of a transfer procured by fraudulent misrepresentation. See Law Com No. 271, paras. 5.32–5.36.

[174] Under the legisaltion when she wrote , the provisions for notices (s. 49 (1) (f) 'right, interest, or claim') and cautions (s. 54 (1) 'Any person interested . . . in any land') appeared every bit as malleable as s. 70 (1) (g). The 2002 Act refers to 'interest' for both notices (s. 32) and actual occupation overriding interests (Sch. 3. para, 2).

much more certain if a right is protected on the register than if claims of actual occupiers have to be investigated. From the point of view of the incumbrancer, there seems little justification to *prevent* entry on the register. It is not as if actual occupation protects rights entitling occupation: it is well known that all the interests of the occupier are protected.[175] It appears to follow that the dividing line between personal and proprietary rights would entirely disappear in registered land. That is not to argue that the results would be at all bad: many would be happy to see positive covenants bind purchasers[176] and easements lose the requirement of a dominant tenement, to provide just two examples. Yet what these examples do demonstrate is how radical this change would be: many of our rules and preconceptions would disappear.

How far would this change simplify the law? Louise Tee argues strongly that the present law is uncertain as to what interests bind purchasers and that this can cause problems for purchasers. One might add that an occupier who is not legally advised will not differentiate between proprietary and other rights when replying to an inquiry by a purchaser, so that a purchaser may be faced with a mixture of proprietary and personal claims even if the law were to make a clear distinction. It cannot be doubted that some uncertainty exists. Nor can it be doubted that having rules as to which interests bind purchasers complicates the law and renders its study considerably more challenging. Yet one may doubt whether these problems have much significance in practice. In the huge majority of cases, it will be obvious to even a harried and non-specialist legal adviser as to what will bind the purchaser. Louise Tee suggests that cases since *Ainsworth* have widened the scope of actual occupation overriding interests and shown inconsistency. Yet the examples provided are unconvincing. The right to rectify was recognised as proprietary well before *Ainsworth*[177] and Neuberger J has recently regarded it as 'self-evidently' within the paragraph.[178] She also cites cases on the unpaid vendor's lien and statutory rights to buy, but the judges clearly did not see themselves as developing proprietary categories, whatever the rights and wrongs of these cases.

One area has given rise to considerable debate, both academic and to a much lesser extent judicial: the effect of estoppels. This is a controversial area and one that cannot yet be regarded as settled, though the 2002 Act establishes estoppels as proprietary in registered land.[179] Indeed, if we are

---

[175] Exemplified by *Webb* v. *Pollmount Ltd* [1966] Ch 584, in which occupation as tenant protected an option to purchase the freehold.

[176] Though their binding tenants is less obviously justifiable in all cases: cf. Law Com No. 127, para. 11.11.

[177] Cf. *Smith* v. *Jones* [1954] 1 WLR 1089.

[178] *DB Ramsden & Co Ltd* v. *Nurdin & Peacock plc* [1998] *The Times*, 14 September, confirmed by the 2002 Act, s. 116.

[179] Section 116; Law Com No. 271, paras. 5.29–5.31.

to have a distinction between proprietary and personal rights, it is inevitable that such controversies will arise: it would be wrong to straitjacket the law so that no development is allowed.[180] This flexibility necessarily involves a cost in terms of uncertainty. Accordingly, one has to agree that the present legal structures involve some uncertainty for purchasers. But would a revised property structure offer greater certainty? One may express doubts at two levels. The first is that it is recognised that some limits will be necessary: personal obligations and those not relating to the land would not affect purchasers.[181] However these limits may be articulated, it seems probable that considerable difficulty would lie in their application (whether or not the claimant is in actual occupation). Suppose money is lent for work to be done on land: can the creditor claim payment from a purchaser? Or to take a similar example based on the artificer's lien encountered in the USA, can a person who undertakes work on land claim against a purchaser? More generally, there is a real question whether the range of obligations that may affect a proprietor (especially where they are statutory) can readily be identified so as to provide clarity as to what will affect a purchaser. How relevant would it be if equitable relief is not available against the seller,[182] so that it appears as if we have a simple conflict with traditional rules as to contractual liability? There may be a real danger that the incidence of uncertainty would be greater than under the present law.

A further problem for the purchaser lies in knowing the details and incidents of the right claimed. Within a system of well-known proprietary interests, clarified over many years, a purchaser knows what is involved with rights such as leases, mortgages and easements. If we allow any claim to bind a purchaser, much greater uncertainty is inevitable. A written agreement may solve many of the problems, but there will remain issues of interpretation and implication. If we look to the reasoning employed in the House of Lords in *Ainsworth*, we see that much of the stress lies in the difficulty for the purchaser in discovering exactly what rights are likely to be binding. In a much maligned passage,[183] Lord Wilberforce refers to the rights having permanence and stability.[184] This is not a circular reference to the effect of the right; rather it is a description of the nature of the particular right: one that is not limited to a specific house and which depends upon the conduct of the spouses. To quote from a

---

[180] Well shown by reluctance to rely on the proviso to LPA, s. 4 (1) to restrict the development of new interests.

[181] Tee [1998] CLJ 328 at 337–338.

[182] A thought prompted by the stricter application of such remedies in Australia: *Cowell* v. *Rosehill Racecourse Co Ltd* (1937) 56 CLR 605.

[183] Gray and Gray, 'The idea of property in land' in Bright and Dewar, *Land Law: Themes and Perspectives* (1998, Oxford University Press), p. 36.

[184] [1965] AC 1175 at 1248.

few lines earlier in his speech, 'these rights are at no time definitive, they are provisional and subject to review at any time...'. The underlying point is that they are rights which it is extremely difficult for a purchaser to investigate. The same comments can, of course, be made about estoppel claims. Although the authorities predominantly favour purchasers being bound, the present trend is to doubt whether estoppels should continue to bind purchasers. In so far as there is a tension between the law on contractual licences and that on estoppel licences,[185] the trend prior to the 2002 Act was towards unifying it along the lines of contractual licences with neither binding purchasers.[186] Against this background, is it not odd to suggest an approach that would have the opposite effect?

Also relevant in the licence context is the constructive trust. It has already been seen that there are dangers in the widespread use of constructive trusts to defeat the statutory protection of registered proprietors. However, even if purchasers are bound by all rights, the problem of when to impose a constructive trust will not go away in all licences cases. Some cases involve a constructive trust being imposed on a purchaser where the seller was not bound: in this type of case it would continue to be necessary to decide whether to impose a constructive trust.[187] There are similar problems if the claimant of an unprotected right is not in actual occupation: it would still be necessary to consider whether a constructive trust should be imposed to avoid the effects of failure to protect it on the register.

Two further points come to mind regarding the desirability of having a restricted category of proprietary rights. The first is that one traditional reason for restricting rights is that otherwise titles to land might be so burdened as to be detrimental to efficient land use. One suspects that this argument is rather like that of 'floodgates' in torts: frequently invoked, but more rarely justified. Yet it is a factor that has to be borne in mind. For example, with restrictive covenants we have a partial safety valve of discharge or modification under LPA, s. 84. If we were to recognise many more rights as binding purchasers, then thought would need to be given to extending the scope of s. 84. The second thought concerns the approach of the Law Commission to electronic conveyancing.[188] How would this fit within an abandonment of proprietary categories? If Louise Tee's proposal were in fact limited to actual occupation overriding

---

[185] That there is much of a tension may be doubted, especially because estoppel cases generally involve expectations of regular proprietary interests: Moriarty (1984) 100 LQR 376.

[186] Briefly discussed in Smith (*op. cit.* above fn. 132), pp. 441–442 (cf. also p. 172).

[187] *Lyus* v. *Prowsa Developments Ltd* [1982] 1 WLR 1044. The same would have been true in *Binions* v. *Evans* [1972] Ch 359 if the licence had been a bare licence.

[188] Not available to Louise Tee at the time she was writing.

interests, the effect might not be great,[189] but we have seen that it would be difficult to justify this limitation. For other interests, it seems at first sight as if the proposals mesh well together: purchasers would be bound only if there is an entry on the register and it would not matter what the nature of the protected right is. Unfortunately, intractable problems exist. We have seen[190] that the Law Commission intends that in due course an unregistered interest will be wholly void: it will not even have contractual effect as between the parties. If we were to say that contractual rights could bind purchasers but that they have to be entered on the register before being valid, this would bring registration into a wide range of contracts that the parties would not consider as being affected by registration: even a window-cleaning contract might require registration! This could have a disastrous effect upon a wide range of contracts relating to land and is clearly unacceptable.

The second point is as to what lessons can be learnt from leasehold conveyancing. Here, virtually all non-personal covenants are enforceable against purchasers (whether of the lease or of the reversion) since the Landlord and Tenant (Covenants) Act 1995. This illustrates the greater enforceability of covenants in leasehold conveyancing, though even then it certainly does not mean that all obligations affecting the parties will bind successors: the rules apply only to covenants in leases and not to obligations to third parties. Even as regards covenants, it has been warned that it would be unsafe to apply the rules to freehold land without some control over what should be enforced.[191] The lesson from the leasehold context may be that the skies will not fall in if a wider range of obligations were to affect purchasers, but that some problems will arise: simplicity of structure would be bought at a cost.

For these reasons, it is suggested that to abandon the distinction between personal and proprietary rights would cause difficulties and disadvantages outweighing the undoubted advantages that it would bring. However, what is important for the purpose of this chapter is that it is one question which should be asked within the modern registration system: Louise Tee has performed an invaluable task in bringing it to our attention. Registration facilitates and, indeed, requires a wide range of preconceptions to be challenged.

---

[189] Though it is inconsistent with the Law Commission's analysis of what will remain as an actual occupation overriding interest: para. 5.62.

[190] See p. 37 above.

[191] Lord Templeman in *Rhone* v. *Stephens* [1994] 2 AC 310 at 321 refers to 'difficulties, anomalies and uncertainties' and 'social injustice' if the courts were to recognise the running of positive freehold covenants.

Conclusion

It is easy for students to view registration as a mass of incomprehensible rules, with the odd interesting question mainly in the actual occupation overriding interest setting. However, it can be seen that it raises issues of fundamental importance for land law generally and not merely for those engaged in the day-to-day conveyancing process. Of course, success as a conveyancing tool is what land registration is all about and it is vital that registration succeeds at this level: something that has not always been obvious. Yet it can be seen as possessing a significance that transcends practicalities. Many of the issues to be debated in this context, whether in the past or the coming years, are necessarily controversial and split commentators and judges. Yet it is only by engaging with them that the true potential of registration can be realised.

Further reading

Ferris 'Structural differences between registered land and unregistered land law', in Jackson and Wilde, *Contemporary Property Law*.

Jackson, 'Security of title in registered land' (1978) 94 LQR 239.

Law Commission, *Land Registration for the Twenty-First Century, A Consultative Document* (Law Com No. 254).

Law Commission, *Land Registration for the Twenty-First Century, A Conveyancing Revolution* (Law Com No. 271).

Payne, 'American title insurance in an English context' [1976] Conv. 11.

Pottage, 'The originality of registration' [1995] OxJLS 371.

Skapinker, 'Equitable interests, mere equities, "personal" equities and "personal equities" – distinctions with a difference' (1994) 68 ALJ 593.

Smith, 'Land registration: white elephant or way forward?' [1986] CLP 111.

Sparkes, 'The discoverability of occupiers of registered land' [1989] Conv. 342.

Tee, 'Rights of persons in actual occupation' [1998] CLJ 328.

Thompson, 'Registration fraud and notice' [1985] CLJ 280.

Whalan, *The Torrens System in Australia* (1992, Law Book Company).

3

Easements

Anna Lawson

Introduction

The easement does not generally enjoy a good reputation amongst law students. It is often regarded as a symbol of 'the mindless formalism of traditional Property Law'.[1] To some extent this reputation is deserved. The Law Commission, which is currently reviewing the topic,[2] has observed that it can be criticised for being 'illogical, uncertain, incomplete and inflexible'.[3]

Despite its complexity, the easement constitutes a worthy (and often unavoidable) object of study. It is, in many ways, fundamental to the smooth running of our daily lives. For many of us, it is an easement which gives us access to our homes. It is also often an easement which brings us such essentials as water, drainage facilities, electricity and gas. It may also be an easement which gives us the use of a garden or a washing line, or a place to park our car and store our goods. In view of the facilitative role played by such rights, it is not surprising they were christened 'easements'. Non-legal definitions of that term include:[4]

> The process or means of giving or obtaining ease or relief from pain, discomfort, or anything annoying or burdensome; relief, alleviation; redress of grievances.

And:

> Advantage, convenience, comfort; furtherance, assistance,...enjoyment...

---

[1] Rose 'Servitudes, security and assent: some comments on Professors French and Reichman' (1982) 55 S Cal LR 1403 at 1403.

[2] *Seventh Programme of Law Reform* (1999) Law Com. No. 259, item 5 (b).

[3] *Rights Appurtenant to Land* (1971) Law Com. WP 36, para. 31.

[4] *Oxford English Dictionary* (1989, Clarendon Press), vol. 5.

As to the legal meaning of an easement, a refreshingly jargon-free definition is as follows:[5]

> Easements are rights possessed by the owner of one piece of land (the 'dominant' land) whereby the owner of other ('servient') land is obliged either to suffer something to be done on his land, or to refrain from doing something on his own land, for the benefit of the dominant land.

Easements (such as rights of way) that permit the owner of the dominant land to do something on the servient land are often referred to as 'positive'. Conversely, the term 'negative' is often used to describe easements that allow the owner of the dominant land to prevent the owner of the servient land doing something on that land (e.g. a right to light, which prevents the owner of the servient land obstructing the flow of light to the relevant part of the dominant land).[6]

In this chapter an attempt will be made to identify the considerations which frequently influence the judges in easement cases. An appreciation of these underlying themes helps to understand the intricacies of the present law. Two specific issues – the need for dominant land benefited by the easement and the implication of easements – will then be considered in some depth.

Underlying themes

General

It is possible to identify three basic considerations to which courts frequently have regard in this area of the law. Though there is some overlap between them there is also frequently tension, particularly between the second and third. They will now be considered in turn.

Intention of the parties

If an easement has been created expressly, the intention of the parties, as revealed in the document creating the easement, will obviously play a crucial role. It will generally determine the precise nature and extent of the right created. Nevertheless, the courts will not always give effect to the expressed intention of the parties. An intention that a right will bind future owners of the servient land as an easement will not be effective unless the right satisfies the conditions which have been developed to determine whether a right is capable of acquiring easement status.

---

5   Law Com. (1971) WP 36, para. 15.
6   *Ibid.*, para. 16.

The intention of the parties also plays an important role in the creation of implied easements. Here the intention to create an easement is presumed from the existence of particular circumstances. In all cases, with the possible exception of the easement of necessity,[7] the parties can prevent an easement being implied by simply expressing a contrary intention.

The need to ensure that land is fully utilised

As there is only a finite amount of land, there is an important public interest in ensuring that such land as there is should be used as effectively as possible. In support of this objective, judges have insisted that the list of rights which are capable of existing as easements is not closed. As societal conditions change and new facilities become available, new rights may be recognised as easements. The category of easements must, in the words of Lord St Leonard,[8] 'alter and expand with the changes that take place in the circumstances of mankind'. It seems, however, that this expansion is likely only in relation to positive easements. The category of negative easements is not likely to expand as the restrictive covenant now provides an alternative and preferable means of creating the rights in question.[9]

This policy also seems to have been influential in the development of the law on the creation of implied easements. The situations in which the courts have been prepared to presume that the parties intended an easement are ones in which that easement would, at the very least, be necessary for the reasonable use of the land.[10] The implication of easements in such circumstances thus ensures that owners of the dominant land are given the means to use their land fully and effectively. It should be remembered, however, that if this policy were the only relevant consideration, an easement would be implied whenever that was necessary for the effective use of the land concerned. This is plainly not the case.

Protectiveness towards the servient land

An easement imposes a burden, not only on the owner of the servient land who creates the easement, but also on all subsequent owners of that land. This has led Professor Rose to remark that:[11]

---

7   See below.
8   *Dyce* v. *Hay (Lady)* (1852) 1 Macq. 305 at 312.
9   *Phipps* v. *Pears* [1965] 1 QB 76. Law Com WP 36, para. 17.
10 See, however, the discussion of *In Re Webb's Lease* [1951] Ch 808 below fns. 140–154 and accompanying text.
11 (1982) 55 S Cal LR 1403 at 1403.

'[W]hen we consider what easements...*do* – bind land owners to some previous owner's agreements, in which the current owners have had no say – the puzzle is that a free and rational nation permits these arrangements at all.'

As Rose readily acknowledges, however, there are many reasons why such arrangements should be tolerated.[12] Nevertheless, the desire to keep the burden imposed on the servient land to a minimum is evident in many of the rules governing the creation and operation of easements.

The desire to minimise the burden imposed on the servient land explains the general rule that easements will not impose any positive obligation on the servient land.[13] It explains, at least in part, the rule that an easement cannot confer the right to exclusive use of the servient land.[14] Similarly, it helps to explain the rule that a right will not be capable of existing as an easement if it imposes an obligation over a 'very large and indefinite area'.[15] It may also help to explain the need for a dominant tenement and the reluctance of the courts to recognise as easements rights not closely analogous with those already capable of existing as easements.[16]

The judicial protectiveness towards the servient land seems consistent with the view that, '[T]he law of property is driven by an analysis which takes the perspective of exclusion rather than one which elaborates a right to use'.[17] Emphasis is given to the right of an estate holder to exclude (within certain limits) others from the land. As easements represent a constraint on this right to exclude, their extent is subjected to careful control.

The Law Commission has observed that much of the law relating to easements was developed 'at a time when rights of private ownership were held sacrosanct to a degree not now regarded as consistent with the interests of the community as a whole'.[18] It suggested that, in order to take account of those interests, the law needed to be made more flexible.[19] The types of tension which can arise are well illustrated by two Scottish cases in which the plaintiffs (pursuers) experienced difficulty in exercising their rights under an easement due to physical impairments.

Middletweed v. *Murray*[20] concerned the extent of a right of way over a

---

[12] She writes, for instance, that 'We tolerate these "dead hand" arrangements because they provide long lasting security for land arrangement and encourage property owners to invest in the long term improvements that are essential to the productive use of real estate' (*ibid.* at 1403).

[13] The easement of fencing represents an exception *Crow* v. *Wood* [1971] 1 QB 77.

[14] *Copeland* v. *Greenhalf* [1952] 1 Ch 488.

[15] *Pwllbach colliery* v. *Woodman* [1915] AC 634 at 649 *per* Lord Sumner.

[16] *Ackroyd* v. *Smith* (138) ER 68; *Keppell* v. *Bailey* 39 ER 1042.

[17] Penner *The Idea of Property in Law* (2000, Oxford University Press), p. 71. See also Gray, 'Property in thin air' [1991] CLJ 252 particularly at 294.

[18] Law Com WP 36, para. 1. See also para. 37.

[19] *Ibid.*

[20] [1989] SLT 11.

farm track to reach the part of the River Tweed where Middletweed owned salmon-fishing rights. Middletweed had granted time shares in the fishing rights to 32 people, three of whom were disabled and, without vehicular access, would have found it either impossible or 'an ordeal'[21] to reach the relevant bank. Middletweed argued that its right of access along the track (which was suitable for use by vehicles) included vehicular access because this was necessary in order for it to have full beneficial use of the fishings.[22] While the court accepted that this was the governing principle, it did not accept that the disability of the users of the right of way would have any bearing on it whatsoever. All that was required was that the right of way should be sufficiently extensive to allow full beneficial use of the fishings to a person 'of average strength and mobility'.[23] Pedestrian access would suffice for such a person and, consequently, there could be no right to drive vehicles along the track.

Drury v. *McGarvie*[24] concerned the issue of whether or not a right of way along a track, over which there was vehicular access to the pursuers' cottage, had been obstructed by the defender's erection of gates across it. The defender (who owned the servient farmland) had erected the gates in order to prevent his stock straying. The pursuers were both elderly and disabled and found the gates, which were 'heavy, improperly hinged and so placed as to be difficult to reach',[25] almost impossible to open. Consequently, they had become 'virtually house-bound'.[26] Lord Hope, upholding the first instance ruling, held that the gates did not constitute an obstruction as it had not been proved that they would cause 'material inconvenience' to a 'person of average strength and agility or...the ordinary, able-bodied adult'.[27] The fact that they had caused material inconvenience to the pursuers was not relevant.[28]

In both *Middletweed* and *Drury* disabilities of the owners of the dominant land forced the courts to choose between minimising the burden on the servient owner and making a right of way usable by a dominant owner possessing less than average strength and agility. In both cases, they chose to ensure that the burden an easement imposed on the servient owner should be as small as possible.

---

[21] *Ibid*. at 13 *per* Lord Davidson.
[22] Following *Miller* v. *Blair* (1825) 4 S 214.
[23] [1989] SLT 11 at 14 *per* Lord Davidson.
[24] [1993] SLT 987.
[25] *Ibid*. at 988.
[26] *Ibid*.
[27] *Ibid*. at 991.
[28] They were entitled to fall back on the right of the owner of the dominant land to repair the gates at their own expense. They may well also have had a claim against the defender under s. 1 of the Occupiers Liability Act 1984 if, in trying to open the gates, they had been injured in some way. See the discussion of such liability in Gaunt and Morgan, *Gale on Easements* (1997, Sweet & Maxwell), p. 56.

The dominant land requirement

General

As is well known, the characteristics of easements were scrutinised by the Court of Appeal in *Re Ellenborough Park*[29]. Lord Evershed MR, in '[formulating] what can now be taken to be the essential qualities of those rights',[30] adopted the four-fold categorisation set out in a leading textbook.[31] This, now famous, categorisation runs as follows:[32]

> (1) [T]here must be a dominant and a servient tenement: (2) an easement must 'accommodate' the dominant tenement: (3) dominant and servient owners must be different persons, and (4) a right over land cannot amount to an easement, unless it is capable of forming the subject-matter of a grant.

It is immediately striking that the first three of these *Ellenborough* conditions relate, in some way, to the dominant tenement. It is, therefore, important to have a clear understanding of the role played by this concept in the current law of easements.

The need for a dominant tenement

In order for an easement to exist, there must obviously be land over which it is exercised – the servient tenement. Under English law,[33] as the first three *Ellenborough* conditions demonstrate, there must also be land which it benefits – the dominant tenement. Once an easement has been established, it will generally pass with the dominant land to subsequent owners and, subject to registration requirements, be exercisable against subsequent owners of the servient land. The owner of the dominant land, however, will not be able to use the easement for the benefit of land other than the dominant tenement[34] or to transfer the easement to a third party independently of that land. Nor will the owner of the servient land be able to grant an easement to a person who does not own land benefited by the privilege in question. In short, an easement cannot exist in gross but only as an attachment or appurtenance to the dominant tenement.

The rule that an easement cannot exist unless land[35] benefiting from it

---

[29] [1956] Ch 131.

[30] *Ibid.* at 161.

[31] Cheshire, *Modern Real Property* (7th ed., Butterworths) p. 456.

[32] [1956] Ch 131 at 163. Note that a right will not exist as an easement, even if these four conditions are satisfied, if it confers a right to exclusive use over the serviant land – *Copeland* v. *Greenhalf* [1952] 1 Ch 488 at 498 *per* Upjohn J.

[33] This is not the position in the USA. See McLean, 'The nature of an easement' [1966] West LR 32 at 40–42 for a discussion of the operation of easements in gross under US Law.

[34] *Peacock* v. *Custins* [2000] EGCS 132.

can be identified has not escaped criticism.[36] Why should a right to park a car, to land a helicopter or to cross a field to reach a beach be condemned to the precarious status of contractual licence just because the person to whom they are granted has no land benefited by them? It has been argued that there is no good reason for this result and that the rule requiring a dominant tenement is 'without authority or justification'.[37]

Despite the fact that the rule is 'almost universally assumed to have existed for centuries',[38] it seems that it did not fully crystallise until the middle of the nineteenth century.[39] In the case, regarded by Holdsworth as the turning point of the law on this issue,[40] Lord Cairns declared that:[41] '[T]here can be no such thing according to our law ..., as an easement in gross. An easement must be connected with a dominant tenement.' Sturley observes that this assertion was 'a mere dicta, unsupported by authority'.[42] He expresses incredulity that a rule, based on such a flimsy foundation, should become so firmly established 'without even an analysis of the issue in any of the leading cases'.[43] Since his article was written, however, the matter has received some attention from the Court of Appeal in *London & Blenheim Estates Ltd* v. *Ladbroke Retail Parks Ltd*.[44]

In *London & Blenheim Estates* the dominant tenement requirement was upheld and described as 'trite law'.[45] Peter Gibson LJ suggested that one reason for this rule lies 'in the policy against encumbering land with burdens of uncertain extent'.[46] Unfortunately, his analysis is brief and contains no clear explanation of what difficulties, in his view, are embraced by the phrase 'burdens of uncertain extent'. Nevertheless, it is clear that the argument draws heavily on the desire to protect the servient land[47] and it appears to be similar to what Sturley termed the 'surcharge argument'.[48]

Sturley offered the surcharge argument as one of the two commonly

---

[35] Exceptionally, the dominant tenement may consist of an incorporeal hereditament rather than corporeal land (e.g. a right of fishing *Hanbury* v. *Jenkins* [1901] 2 Ch 401). For discussion, see Gaunt and Morgan (*op. cit.* above fn. 28), pp. 15–17.

[36] See, in particular, Sturley, 'Easements in gross' (1980) 96 LQR 557 and McLean [1996] West LR 32 at 36–42.

[37] (1980) 96 LQR 557 at 568. See also McLean [1996] West LR 32 at 42.

[38] Smith, *Property Law* (3rd ed., 2000, Pearson Education Inc.) p. 458.

[39] *Ackroyd* v. *Smith* (138) ER 68; *Rangeley* v. *Midland Ry. Co.* [1868] 3 Ch App 306; and *Hawkins* v. *Rutter* (1892) 1 QB 668.

[40] Holdsworth, *A History of English Law. vol. 7* (1925, Methuen) p. 326.

[41] *Rangeley* v. *Midland Ry Co.* [1868] 3 Ch App 306 at 310–311.

[42] (1980) 96 LQR 557 at 562. See also [1966] West LR 32 at 38.

[43] *Ibid.*

[44] [1994] 1 WLR 31.

[45] *Ibid.* at 36 *per* Peter Gibson LJ.

[46] *Ibid.* at 37.

[47] See above.

[48] (1980) 96 LQR 557 at 562–564.

advanced rationales for the dominant tenement requirement.[49] It is based on the concern that without the constraints imposed by the needs of a dominant tenement, an easement might impose too heavy a burden on the servient land. This concern relates both to the nature of the potential right and to the potential transferees of that right (it might, for instance, be transferred from one person who used the right sparingly to a group of heavy users). Sturley acknowledges the genuineness of these concerns but argues that they would not be difficult to meet.[50] The parties to the original grant of an easement in gross would be free to specify limits both on the extent of the right and the range of possible transferees. In the event of difficulty, the courts would not find the issues too different from ones which currently arise in connection with profits in gross or easements appertaining to dominant land. Should there be the need for further regulation, he suggests that the jurisdiction of the Lands Tribunal could be extended to cover easements.[51]

Though Sturley's responses to the surcharge argument go some way to addressing concerns about uncertainty, they do not address them all. The removal of the dominant tenement requirement would also remove, at least for easements which had no dominant tenement, the requirement that the right should accommodate the dominant land. Uncertainty as to whether alternative limits should be developed and, if so, what they should be, would result – unless possibly the change was effected by a carefully drafted statute. Further, such a change would undoubtedly risk the imposition of heavy, additional burdens on servient land and so, undoubtedly, attract strong judicial suspicion.[52]

It is clear that, at present, an easement cannot exist in the absence of a dominant tenement. This rule is not likely to be relaxed by the judges.[53] It is to be hoped that the continued existence of this rule will be among the questions examined by the Law Commission in its current review of easements. If it is of the view that the rule has 'no conclusive reason'[54] the painstaking task of drafting appropriate legislation could begin.

---

[49] The other being the 'clogs and fetters argument', based on the idea that easements in gross might be difficult for purchasers of the servient land to discover – see *ibid.* at 563–567.

[50] *Ibid.* at 563–564.

[51] The Law Commission recommended such an extension (though it was not concerned with easements in gross) in WP 36, para. 121.

[52] See above fn. 16.

[53] Despite some dicta of Upjohn LJ in *Johnstone* v. *Holdway* [1963] 1 QB 601 at 610, in which he appeared to be prepared to contemplate the possibility that an easement in gross might exist in equity.

[54] Smith (*op. cit.* above fn. 38), p. 459.

Accommodating the dominant tenement

The second *Re Ellenborough* condition requires that a right must accommodate the dominant tenement or, in other words, that 'it must be the land that benefits rather than the individual owner of the land'.[55] Unlike human beings, however, land is not able to enjoy rights in any meaningful sense. The reference to rights being enjoyed by land here is simply a convenient short-hand. What is required in reality is that the right will be of benefit to any owner of that land, present or future, as opposed to being of benefit only to the current owner.

In order to determine whether this second condition is satisfied, Evershed MR in *Re Ellenborough*[56] adopted a test based on the 'normal enjoyment' of the land in question. He said:[57]

> It is not sufficient to show that the right increased the value of the property conveyed unless it is also shown that it was connected with the normal enjoyment of that property. It appears to us that the question whether or not this connection exists is primarily one of fact and depends largely on the nature of the alleged dominant tenement and the nature of the right granted.

The usefulness and appropriateness of the 'normal enjoyment' test has been questioned. McLean,[58] for instance, argues that the law of easements has not traditionally relied on the concept of normal or abnormal user of land. In his view:[59] '[I]t is wrong to say that an easement may attach only to the normal use of land. The law ought to be that an easement may accommodate any lawful use of land.' This rejection of the 'normal enjoyment' test is based on the belief that it carries with it the idea that there are, in absolute terms, 'normal' and 'abnormal' uses of land. The test, however, as Lord Evershed explained,[60] *is* 'primarily one of fact' which 'depends largely on the nature of the alleged dominant tenement and the nature of the right granted'. Thus, what may be connected with the normal enjoyment of property used as a factory may not be connected with the normal enjoyment of property used for agricultural or residential purposes. The test does not require, as McLean seems to fear, that judges should determine whether uses of land are, in absolute terms, normal or abnormal.[61]

---

55 *Ibid.*
56 [1956] Ch 131.
57 *Ibid.* at 170.
58 [1966] West LR 32.
59 *Ibid.* at 43–44. He proposes an alternative approach to the question of whether or not the dominant land is accommodated by a particular right. This would require a judge to ask whether that right was, in the abstract, a reasonably necessary element in the use of land. For example, is a right of way (not the particular one in question) a reasonably necessary element in the use of property of the type concerned (e.g. commercial or residential)?
60 See above fn. 57 and accompanying text.
61 Consequently, the 'normal enjoyment' test and McLean's 'reasonable necessity' test appear, in essence, to be one and the same.

In determining whether a right is connected with the normal enjoyment of the dominant tenement, judges should have regard to 'current social conditions, … prevailing patterns and trends of conduct',[62] and allow a right to pass the test if it is 'currently a not uncommon and not socially undesirable aspect of the type of use to which property is being put'.[63]

In *Re Ellenborough*,[64] where the properties in question were houses, it was held that the right to use a garden would accommodate them. It was sufficiently connected with the normal enjoyment of 'a house as a house, namely, as a place in which the householder and his family live and make their home'.[65] A right to use the Zoological Gardens or to attend Lords Cricket Ground free of charge, on the other hand, would fail the test.[66] Similarly, it has been suggested that a right to use a swimming pool or a tennis court would fail because houses in England and Wales do not normally possess such facilities.[67]

In order to decide whether or not a particular right is commonly enjoyed, a comparitor group must be established. If, for instance, the issue was whether use of a garden accommodated a tower-block flat in a locality where there were very few gardens, should the comparitor be flats of a similar type, residential properties generally in the locality or residential properties across the country? The more narrowly the group is drawn, the less likely the flat occupant would be to succeed. Conversely, a narrowly drawn comparitor group would advantage a claimant living in an unusually luxurious home in an exclusive locality – maybe someone claiming a right to use a swimming pool where comparable houses in the area all possessed such a facility.

This issue has not been expressly considered in the courts but, to date, judges have shown no inclination to draw the comparitor group narrowly. To do so would, in the residential context, accentuate the gap between the rich and the poor and might therefore seem undesirable. Nevertheless, in a different context, this is the approach that has been adopted to the determination of the standard of repair required under a covenant to keep property in 'tenantable repair' in a lease. Here:[68]

> The character of a house must be taken into account, because the same class of repairs as would be necessary to a palace would be wholly unnecessary to a cottage; and the locality of the house must be taken into account, because the state of repair necessary for a house in Grosvenor Square would be wholly different from the state of repair necessary for a house in Spitalfields.

[62] McLean [1966] West LR 32 at 45.
[63] *Ibid.*
[64] [1956] Ch 131.
[65] *Ibid.* at p. 174 *per* Evershed MR.
[66] *Ibid.*
[67] McLean [1966] West LR 32 at 45. See also Smith (*op. cit.* above fn. 38), p. 460.
[68] *Proudfoot* v. *Hart* (1890) 25 QB 42 at 52 *per* Lord Esher MR.

It is suggested, however, that this approach should not be imported into the law of easements. The standard of repair test is based on notions of reasonableness and expectation which vary according to the nature of the property concerned.[69] The normal enjoyment test is not based on such notions and should be regarded simply as a threshold test – is a particular right capable of benefiting land. To adopt the standard of repair approach in this context would be to introduce unnecessary uncertainty and complexity.

Whatever comparitor group is adopted, it is clear that the test of normal enjoyment has regard to the prevalence of particular facilities or advantages. This gives it the flexibility necessary to produce different results over time. Many rights that might today be considered to be connected with the normal enjoyment of a house (e.g. the right to park a car) would not have been so considered a century ago. It therefore permits the categories of rights capable of existing as easements to expand and alter in line with changing social conditions.[70]

Further, though described as 'factual', the 'normal enjoyment' test allows room for value judgments about the types of rights which should receive the protection of easement status.[71] Thus, in relation to commercial property, a right to advertise one's business on neighbouring land may pass the test[72] whereas a right which would result in the establishment of a commercial monopoly would not.[73] In relation to residential property, a right to indulge in the recreations provided by a garden would pass the test whereas a right to race horses or play games might not.[74]

Implied easements

General

The methods by which an easement may be impliedly created are often divided into four main categories, each of which will be considered

---

[69] The required standard is that which renders the property 'reasonably fit for the occupation of a reasonably minded tenant of the class who would be likely to take it' – *Proudfoot* v. *Hart* (1890) 25 QB 42 at 53 *per* Lord Esher MR and 56 *per* Lopes LJ; *Credit Suisse* v. *Beegas Nominees Ltd* [1994] 4 All ER 803 at 821 *per* Lindsay J.

[70] See the discussion of this issue above.

[71] Gray and Gray, *Land Law* (1999, Butterworths), p. 139.

[72] *Moody* v. *Steggles* (1879) 12 Ch D 261.

[73] *Re Ellenborough Park* [1956] Ch 131 at 175 *per* Evershed MR (discussing *Hill* v. *Tupper* (1863) 159 ER 51).

[74] A view suggested by Evershed MR in *Re Ellenborough Park* [1956] Ch 151 at 179. His lordship was there discussing the fourth *Ellenborough* condition rather than the second, but there seems to be some overlap between these two conditions on the issue of rights to recreation. For discussion of rights to recreation see, for example, McLean [1966] West LR 32 at 56–57.

below. While the first three of these represent exceptions to the formality requirements for the creation of interests in land, the fourth – s. 62 of the Law of Property Act 1925 – does not. Indeed, it is arguable that s. 62 results in the creation of express rather than implied easements[75] as it operates by inserting, or implying, words into a conveyance. Nevertheless, some discussion of it seems appropriate here.

All four categories can be used to grant easements over the grantor's land in favour of the grantee. In addition, the first two can be used to reserve easements over the grantee's land in favour of the grantor. None of them can be used to grant or reserve easements over the land of a stranger. Thus, they all presuppose a scenario in which the grantor will retain some land.

The doctrine of non-derogation from grant plays an important role in this area of the law.[76] Not only does it provide a rationale for at least some of the four specific methods of implication, but it can also result in the creation of easements outside these specific methods.[77] Precisely when judges will be prepared to find that an easement has been created on the basis of non-derogation, though none of the specific methods of implication would have been available, is somewhat unclear.[78]

The rule against derogation from grant is often stated in the following terms:[79]

> [I]f the grant or demise be made for a particular purpose the grantor or lessor comes under an obligation not to use the land retained by him in such a way as to render the land granted or demised unfit or materially less fit for the particular purpose for which the grant or demise was made.

As this quotation indicates, the rule is designed to protect grantees by preventing a grantor giving a thing with one hand and taking away the means of enjoying it with the other.[80] Generally, an easement will not be impliedly reserved in favour of a grantor.[81] The doctrine of non-derogation will operate to imply rights only if they were in the contemplation of the parties at the time of the grant.[82] Not all

---

[75] See, generally, Hopkins *The Informal Acquisition of Rights in Land* (2000, Sweet & Maxwell), p. 214.

[76] See, generally, *ibid.*, pp. 185–215 and Elliot 'non-derogation from grant' (1964) 80 LQR 244.

[77] See, for example, *Ward* v. *Kirkland* [1967] 1 Ch 194 though Ungoed-Thomas J preferred to ground his decision on s. 62 (*ibid.* at 227).

[78] Law Com. WP 36, para. 89 (vi).

[79] *Browne* v. *Flower* [1911] 1 Ch 219 at 226 *per* Parker J.

[80] *Birmingham Dudley & District Banking Co* v. *Ross* (1888) 38 Ch D 295 at 313 *per* Bowen LJ.

[81] *Wheeldon* v. *Burrows* (1879) 12 Ch D 31 at 49–50 *per* Thesiger LJ; *In Re Webb's Lease* [1951] Ch 808 at 816 *per* Evershed M.R.

[82] *Johnston* v. *Holland* [1988] 1 EGLR 264; *Harmer* v. *Jumbil (Nigeria) Tin Areas Ltd* [1921] 1 Ch 200.

contemplated rights will be implied, however. Rights will be implied only if, in addition, the property would be 'unfit or materially less fit'[83] for its purposes were the rights denied. They will not be implied if, without them, the grantee would simply suffer some discomfort.[84]

Easements of necessity[85]

Contrary to the general rule that easements will not be impliedly reserved in favour of a grantor,[86] an easement of necessity may be impliedly reserved as well as impliedly granted. The conditions to be satisfied in order for one to arise were set out by Lord Oliver in *Manjang* v. *Drammeh*[87] as follows:

> There has to be found first a common owner of a legal estate in two plots of land. It has secondly to be established that access between one of those plots and the public highway can be obtained only over the other plot. Thirdly, there has to be found a disposition of one of the plots without any specific grant or reservation of a right of access.

Easements of necessity require a high degree of necessity. The guiding principle, laid down by Stirling LJ in *Union Lighterage Co.* v. *London Graving Dock*,[88] has been that such an easement will arise only if, without it, the land could not be used at all. The fact that it may be necessary to permit the land to be used in a reasonable, convenient or effective manner will not suffice. For this reason it is unlikely that an easement of necessity will arise in connection with any right other than a right of way.[89] The fact that a property may lack facilities such as telephone lines, electricity or water does not mean it cannot be used at all. Further, no right of way will be implied by reason of necessity if there is some means of access to the property, however inconvenient or restricted it might be. Thus, the existence of access by a footpath[90] or by water[91] would mean that no

---

83 *Browne* v. *Flower* [1911] 1 Ch 219 at 226 *per* Parker J. See also *Ward* v. *Kirkland* [1967] Ch. 194 at 226–7 *per* Ungoed Thomas J – '...derogation from the grant seems to indicate doing something which defeats in substantial measure the purpose of the grant'.

84 See Hopkins (*op. cit.* above fn. 75), p. 194.

85 The term easements of necessity will be used here to refer only to easements without which the dominant land would be unusable for general purposes.

86 *Wheeldon* v. *Burrows* (1879) 12 Ch D 31 at 49–50.

87 (1991) 61 P & CR 194 at 197.

88 [1902] 2 Ch 557 at 573.

89 See, for example, *Barry* v. *Hasseldine* [1952] Ch 835 and *Union Lighterage Co.* v. *London Graving Dock Co.* [1902] 2 Ch 557. For a general discussion of this issue, see Jackson, 'Easements of necessity' (1981) 34 CLP 133 at 148–150 and Garner 'Ways of necessity' [1960] Conv. 205 at 209–210.

90 *M.R.A. Engineering* v. *Trimster Co. Ltd.* (1988) 56 P & CR 1; Martin [1989] Conv. 355.

91 *Manjang* v. *Drammeh* (1991) 61 P & CR 194.

easement of necessity conferring vehicular access could be created. It was, no doubt, considerations such as these which led Dillon LJ to observe that:[92] 'The law as to ways of necessity is in some respects archaic and it may be that it is time that it was given closer consideration as against modern circumstances.' At present, however, the only situation in which it is clear that an easement of necessity will arise is one in which the land granted or reserved would otherwise be totally inaccessible or landlocked.

Turning now to the basis of the easement of necessity, early cases establishing the doctrine contain many references to the public good of having land that is accessible and therefore available for cultivation and use. Glyn CJ's observation that it is ' ... to the prejudice of the public weal that land should lie fresh and unoccupied',[93] provides a good example. In the nineteenth century, however, judges began to attribute the easement of necessity to the intention of the parties (in line with a general tendency to assume that legal rights and doctrines stemmed from contract and the free will of the parties).[94] The case in which the question of the basis of the easement of necessity has received most attention in recent times is *Nickerson* v. *Barraclough*.[95] It should be stressed, however, that in that case the easement of necessity was not directly in point (it not being argued that at the time of the relevant conveyance the land was inaccessible)[96] and that their Lordships' observations on the subject are therefore *obiter*. There is also a view that those *obiter* observations have no relevance at all to true easements of necessity and apply only to what have been termed here '*Pwllbach* easements'.[97]

In *Nickerson*[98] the Court of Appeal took the view that easements of necessity are implied into relevant transactions because that is what is intended by the parties to those transactions. In the words of Buckley LJ:[99]

> [I]n my judgment, the law relating to ways of necessity rests not upon a basis of public policy but upon the implication to be drawn from the fact that unless some way is implied, a parcel of land will be inaccessible. From that fact the implication arises that the parties must have intended that some way giving access to the land should have been granted.

---

[92] *M.R.A. Engineering* v. *Trimster Co. Ltd.* (1988) 56 P & CR 1 at 5.

[93] *Packer* v. *Welsted* (1658) 82 ER 1244 at 1285. See also *Dutton* v. *Taylor* (1700) 2 Lut 1487 at 1489.

[94] For further discussion of this development, see Simonton, 'Ways by necessity' (1925) 25 Col LR 571 at 576; Bradbrook 'Access to landlocked land: a comparative study of legal solutions' (1982–85) 10 Syd LR 39 at 57.

[95] [1981] Ch 426.

[96] A point noted by Brightman LJ *ibid.* at 437 and 441, and by Buckley LJ at 447.

[97] See, in particular, Crabb, 'Necessity: the mother of intention'[1981] Conv. 442. See also Coldham, 'Easements of necessity' (1982) 132 NLJ 224. '*Pwllbach* easements' will be dealt with in the following section.

[98] [1981] Ch 426.

[99] *Ibid.* at 447. Buckley LJ, like Eveleigh LJ, agreed with the principal judgment which was delivered by Brightman LJ.

The Court of Appeal consequently upheld an express agreement which provided, in effect, that there should be no practicable means of access to a building plot. Both Brightman LJ[100] and Buckley LJ[101] did acknowledge that public policy might, in some circumstances, lead a court to strike down terms in an agreement. They did not indicate, however, whether those circumstances might ever include the need to prevent land becoming inaccessible.[102]

In ruling that easements of necessity are based on the presumed intention of the parties, the Court of Appeal was heavily influenced by the fact that this explanation was consistent with the limits of the doctrine. In particular, easements of necessity will not arise in cases where the land has been acquired by some method not involving an agreement between grantor and grantee – e.g. by escheat[103] or by adverse possession.[104] In the absence of such an agreement it would be inappropriate to presume that there had been a common intention that the land should be accessible. There would be nobody with whom the owner of the inaccessible land could claim to have shared that intention.

The intention-based explanation also seems to be consistent with the rule that a way of necessity will not be created if the necessity arises at some point after the grant of the land.[105] As there was no necessity at the time of the grant, the parties cannot be presumed to have intended that there should be an easement in order to deal with it. It also appears to be consistent with the rule established in *Corporation of London* v. *Riggs*[106] that an easement of necessity may be used only for the purposes for which the parties contemplated that the dominant land would be used at the time of the grant. If they contemplated that the land would be used for agricultural purposes, they cannot be presumed to have intended that there should be a right of way supporting commercial or residential use.

In view of the above, it is easy to understand why Brightman LJ regarded intention as 'such an obvious and convenient candidate for paternity'.[107] Nevertheless, his decision on this point has not escaped criticism. Three main grounds of attack can be identified.

First, it has been argued that the relevant intent is generally fictional – the parties not having considered the issue or not having realised that the

---

[100] *Ibid.* at 441.

[101] *Ibid.* at 447.

[102] By contrast, Megarry V-C, at first instance ([1980] Ch 325), took the view that public policy would invalidate any agreement which deprived land of a suitable means of access without good reason. See also Bodkin, 'Easements of necessity and public policy' (1973) 89 LQR 87 at 90.

[103] *Proctor* v. *Hodgson* 156 ER 674.

[104] *Wilks* v. *Greenway* (1890) 6 TLR 449.

[105] *Midland Ry.* v. *Miles* (1886) 33 Ch D 632; *Chapel* v. *Mason* (1894) 10 TLR 404. For further discussion of this point, see Jackson (1981) 34 CLP 133 at 142–143.

[106] 1879–80) 13 Ch D 798.

[107] *Nickerson* v. *Barraclough* [1981] 1 Ch 426 at 440.

land would be inaccessible without such an easement. If parties intend that an easement should be created, they will usually create it expressly. In the words of one commentator:[108] 'The intent of the parties is immaterial, unless expressed in some way. The so called presumed intent is pure fiction...' What lies beneath that fiction – the factor that motivates the courts to create it – is public policy.[109]

The danger of basing the doctrine on a fictional intent is that concentration on that intent, rather than on the policy underlying it, may cause confusion in the development of the doctrine.[110] It may encourage courts to lay down rules on the basis that they are 'logical deductions from a fictional grant'[111] even when they do not represent 'an effective means of resolving a practical problem'.[112] A frequently used example of such a rule is that laid down in *Corporation of London* v. *Riggs*.[113] This rule flows logically from the intention-based theory but fails to give due weight to the importance of not sterilising land by trapping it into one particular use.[114]

Secondly, though intention seems to provide a good explanation of many aspects of the doctrine of easements of necessity, there are other aspects of the doctrine for which intention does not provide an obvious explanation. It does not, for instance, explain why the degree of necessity required should be so high. Surely the average purchaser would be just as likely to intend to acquire a right of way over the vendor's land when the only alternative access was by water,[115] or by a road running twenty feet below their land,[116] as they would be if there were no alternative access at all?

Finally, the *Nickerson* ruling that easements of necessity are founded on intention has been attacked on the ground that it unduly restricts the operation of the doctrine and, thus, results in plots of land remaining unnecessarily landlocked and sterile. It has been suggested that every jurisdiction should have rules that guarantee that no land will remain landlocked and that, in common law countries, this would best be achieved by recognising that easements of necessity are based on public policy, not intention.[117] Thus, it is assumed that if the doctrine were held to rest on principles of public policy, not intention, it would be able to

---

[108] Simonton (1925) 25 Col LR 571 at 601.
[109] As was explicitly recognised in the early American case of *Buss* v. *Dyer* (1878) 125 Mass 287 at 291.
[110] Simonton (1925) 25 Col LR 571 at 577.
[111] Jackson (1981) 34 CLP 133 at 152.
[112] Bradbrook [1982–85] 10 Syd LR 39 at 46.
[113] See above fn. 106 and accompanying text.
[114] Jackson (1981) 34 CLP 133 at 144-5; J.W. Simonton 'Ways by Necessity' (1925) 25 Col. L.R. 571 at 582–583; Bradbrook (1982–85) 10 Syd LR 39 at 45.
[115] *Manjang* v. *Drammeh* (1991) 61 P & CR 194.
[116] *Titchmarsh* v. *Royston Water Co. Ltd.* (1899) 81 LT 673.
[117] Bradbrook (1982–85) 10 Syd LR 39 at 56.

shake off some of its present restraints and liberate hitherto landlocked land. It would operate regardless of any express contrary intention and would not require the dominant land to be acquired by some transaction into which a term could be implied.[118]

This last criticism is, in essence, an attack on the judiciary for not expanding the scope of the doctrine of easements of necessity. Its assumption that a public policy based doctrine would inevitably result in the expansion of the doctrine is, however, open to challenge.

As Megarry V-C. observed in *Nickerson*:[119] 'If such a head of public policy exists... the question is what its bounds are. I do not think it can be said that, whatever the circumstances, a way of necessity will always be implied whenever a close of land is made landlocked.' Even if courts were to accept public policy as the foundation of the doctrine, they would not be required automatically to recognise an easement of necessity in relation to all landlocked land. They would have to address the question of whether the public policy-driven implication of an easement of necessity should, in some circumstances, give way to other considerations. A not unappealing view of the present law is that the doctrine is based on public policy[120] and that it is confined to cases in which there is a grant of land from a former common owner because, in other situations, the courts have no means of determining on which land the burden of such an easement should fall.[121] In the words of the principal proponent of this view:[122] 'The fact seems to be that the courts use the implied grant or reservation as a means of determining the land on which the burden shall fall. When the servient land cannot be determined in this manner, no easement is allowed.' The problem of identifying a servient tenement in such circumstances is exacerbated by the absence of any judicial power to award compensation to the selected servient owner.[123] On this view it would be for the courts to decide in due course whether the express contrary intention of the parties should be viewed as another factor confining the scope of a public policy-based doctrine of easements of necessity.

In conclusion, intention has undoubtedly played an influential role in the development of the doctrine of easements of necessity. Public policy, however, has also undeniably played an important part. Indeed, it has been persuasively argued that the intention of the parties, in the absence of strong policy arguments (such as the need to prevent land becoming

---

[118] *Ibid.* at 42.

[119] [1980] Ch 325 at 334.

[120] A view propounded by Bodkin (1973) 89 LQR 87.

[121] Simonton (1925) 25 Col LR 571 at 578–579.

[122] *Ibid.* at 579.

[123] See Bradbrook (1982–85) 10 Syd LR 39 for a discussion of a number of statutory schemes permitting such compensation to be ordered.

sterile) or the existence of fault or unfairness, cannot justify the informal creation of rights in land.[124] It is, therefore, tempting to respond to Brightman LJ that if intention has a strong claim to paternity of the doctrine, public policy has an equally strong claim to maternity!

What is important, however, is surely not the parentage of the doctrine but an understanding of its present character. One view of that is that it can be explained simply on the basis of the principle of non-derogation from grant.[125] There are certainly some indications that the courts might be prepared to hold that this principle may operate so as to reserve rights in favour of a grantor[126] as well as to grant them in favour of a grantee. There is as yet, however, no explicit judicial support for the view that this principle provides a complete explanation of the easement of necessity. There are clearly some important differences – the degree of necessity demanded, for instance, is higher for an easement of necessity than that required under the doctrine of non-derogation. Given the infrequency with which the easement of necessity makes an appearance in court,[127] the analysis of its character is likely to keep teams of legal psychoanalysts occupied for many years to come.

Easements necessary to give effect to the common intention of the parties

The starting point for any analysis of easements arising under this heading is the following pronouncement of Lord Parker in *Pwllbach Colliery* v. *Woodman*:[128]

> The law will readily imply the grant or reservation of such easements as may be necessary to give effect to the common intention of the parties to a grant of real property with reference to the manner or purposes in and for which the land granted or some land retained by the grantor is to be used.

It is possible to identify three apparently distinct methods of implying easements based on these words. The first is relatively uncomplicated and will not be considered in any detail here. It operates to confer easement status on a right that is necessary for the enjoyment of some other

---

[124] Davis, 'Informal acquisition and loss of rights in land: what justifies the doctrines?' (2000) 20 LS 198, particularly at 219.

[125] See, for example, Hopkins (*op. cit.* above fn. 75), pp. 207–209.

[126] *Johnston* v. *Holland* [1988] 1 EGLR 264.

[127] Reasons for this include the fact that they could generally be avoided by competent conveyancing; the availability of other methods by which to imply an easement *Wheeldon* v. *Burrows* (1879) Ch D 31, s. 62, etc.; and possibly the fact that there is now very little undeveloped land in England and Wales. See, generally, Jackson (1981) 34 CLP 133 at 133.

[128] [1915] AC 634 at 646–647.

expressly granted right.[129] The second method will be referred to here as the *Pwllbach* easement, as its requirements are drawn directly from *Pwllbach* itself. The third will be referred to as the *Re Webb's Lease* easement as, though broadly based on *Pwllbach*, it is from *Re Webb's Lease*[130] that it derives its specific character. These two methods will be considered in turn, particularly in relation to the type of intention they require. The relationship between these easements and the easement of necessity will then be briefly discussed.

The *Pwllbach* easement, like the easement of necessity, may be impliedly granted or impliedly reserved. It will arise if it is necessary in order for the land to be used in the manner intended by the parties. Necessary, here, is interpreted strictly. According to Lord Atkinson in *Pwllbach*, a right will be implied on this basis only if it is '*necessary* for the use and enjoyment, in the way contemplated by the parties...'[131] It will not suffice that it is 'convenient or...usual or common in the district, or...simply reasonable'.[132]

As to the nature of the required intent, Lord Parker went on to explain that:[133] '[I]t is essential for this purpose that the parties should intend that the subject of the grant or the land retained by the grantor should be used in some definite and particular manner.' Thus, what must be intended is some particular use for the land concerned. Confusingly, given the fact that these easements are commonly referred to as 'intended easements',[134] the easement itself need not be intended. It must simply be necessary to the carrying out of the intended purpose.[135] This distinction is well illustrated by the decision of the Court of Appeal in *Wong* v. *Beaumont Property Trust Ltd*[136] (in which *Pwllbach* was applied though the easement was described as one of necessity[137]). There, parties to a lease intended the premises concerned to be used as a restaurant and provision to this effect was included in the lease. That purpose could not lawfully be carried out unless a ventilation duct was attached to the landlord's adjoining premises. The right to install and use such a duct was therefore

---

[129] See *ibid.* where the example is given of a case in which a right of access to a stream is necessary for the exercise of an expressly granted right to draw water from it.

[130] [1951] Ch 808.

[131] [1915] AC 634 at 643.

[132] *Ibid.* at 643 *per* Lord Atkinson.

[133] *Ibid.* at 647.

[134] See, for example, *Stafford* v. *Lee* (1993) 65 P & CR 172 at 175 per Nourse LJ and Harpum *Megarry & Wade: The Law of Real Property* (2000, Sweet & Maxwell), para. 18.102.

[135] See *Stafford* v. *Lee* (1993) 65 P & CR 172 at 175 where Nourse LJ describes proof of the intended purpose and of the necessity of the easement to that purpose as the 'two hurdles' which a grantee must surmount.

[136] [1965] 1 QB 173.

[137] See Megarry (1964) 80 LQR 322 at 323 for the view that the easement in *Wong* was a true easement of necessity rather than one implied to give effect to the common intention of the parties.

necessary to carry out the intended purpose and it was consequently implied as an easement into the lease. This occurred despite the fact that the parties were unaware of the need for the duct at the time of the lease and the landlord's evident objection to its installation.

In *Wong* there was no doubt that the leased premises were intended to be used as a restaurant as this had been expressly agreed. This was not so in *Stafford* v. *Lee*.[138] There the plaintiff, who owned a piece of woodland, sought to establish that their easement over the defendant's road extended to permit use for the purpose of building, and then inhabiting, a dwelling house. The relevant conveyance to the plaintiff's predecessor in 1955 contained no reference whatsoever to any intended use of the land. Consequently, the plaintiff might have been expected to fail to raise a *Pwllbach* easement, especially given Lord Parker's emphatic warning that:[139] 'It is not enough that the subject of the grant or the land retained should be intended to be used in a manner which may or may not involve this definite and particular use.' The Court of Appeal, however, was prepared to find that at the time of the 1955 grant it had been intended that the woodland should be built upon and used for residential purposes. In reaching this conclusion, Nourse LJ had regard to the fact that the purchaser lived a long way from the woodland and would therefore not be able to use it regularly as a kind of garden; and to the fact that the plan indicated that comparable adjoining plots of land had already been built upon. Thus, the intention to use land in a particular way may be implied as well as expressed.

Re Webb's Lease[140] concerned an alleged implied reservation of a landlord's right to advertise his business on the tenant's walls. *Pwllbach*, narrowly construed, was of no assistance as the claimed right to advertise was not necessary to the contemplated use of the landlord's property. Evershed MR, while recognising that as a general rule a grantor was under a duty to reserve rights expressly, thought it 'implicit in the language of Lord Parker in *Pwllbach*'[141] that an easement could be impliedly reserved if that was necessary to 'make the transaction ... sensible and effective according to its terms'.[142] Jenkins LJ considered the test to be 'whether the circumstances of the case ... are such as to raise the necessary inference that the common intention of the parties was to reserve'[143] the right in question. In order to satisfy this test, it must be proved 'at least that the facts are not reasonably consistent with any other explanation'.[144] Thus, in order to acquire an easement under *Re Webb's*

---

[138] (1993) 65 P & CR 172.
[139] *Pwllbach Colliery Co Ltd* v. *Woodman* [1915] AC 634 at 647.
[140] [1951] Ch 808.
[141] *Ibid.* at 816. See also *ibid.* at 826 *per* Jenkins LJ.
[142] *Ibid.*
[143] *Ibid.* at 828.
[144] *Ibid.* at 829.

Lease, unlike *Pwllbach*, it must be shown that the easement itself was intended by the parties.

In *Re Webb's Lease* itself, the grantor failed to establish the alleged easement. It was on this basis, however, that the Court of Appeal in *Peckham* v. *Ellison*[145] found that the plaintiffs were entitled to an easement across the Defendant's garden which gave the plaintiffs access to the back of their own property. The way in which the requisite intention was found to exist in this case has been criticised on two grounds. First, the Court of Appeal was prepared to find that the parties must have intended the easement as, even though they had not applied their minds to the issue, had they done so they would have agreed that there should be such an easement.[146] The intention was thus imputed to them and in no real sense genuine.[147] Secondly, the court decided that the facts were not reasonably consistent with any explanation other than that the easement had been intended because it was not convinced to the contrary by the defendant.[148] This seems to shift the burden of proof on the issue to the defendant when, as stressed in *Re Webb's Lease*, it should lie firmly on the plaintiff as the person claiming the right.[149]

The Court of Appeal in *Peckham* plainly felt it would have been unjust to deny the claimed right[150] and was prepared to make every effort to find that it had been intended by the parties. Such a finding would have been unnecessary if it had been possible to rely on *Pwllbach*, where the relevant intention relates to the use of the property, not the right itself. This possibility was not expressly considered. The most likely reason for its tacit rejection is that, though there would have been little difficulty in proving that there had been a common intention that the property retained by the council (a predecessor in title of the plaintiff) should have been used as a dwelling house, it could not have been shown that the right to cross the neighbouring garden was necessary to the carrying out of that purpose. Cazalet J did observe that:[151] 'Clearly when dealing with refuse, coal and other like items access to the rear of the house, without going through the house itself, must be, at its lowest, an easement necessary for the reasonable enjoyment of No 16.' Nevertheless, he also acknowledged it had been accepted at first instance that there could be no easement of necessity to reach the rear garden due to the existence of

---

[145] (2000) 79 P & CR 276.

[146] See *ibid*. at 297–298 *per* Cazalet J.

[147] Fox, 'Implied reservation of easements: *Peckham* v. *Ellisson*' [1999] Conv. 353 at 357–358. Compare the similar approach adopted by the Court of Appeal in *Midland Bank plc* v. *Cooke* [1995] 4 All ER 562 in the context of establishing a common intention to acquire an equitable interest in a family home under *Lloyds Bank plc* v. *Rosset* [1991] 1 AC 107.

[148] See (2000) 79 P & CR 276 at 294 *per* Cazalet J.

[149] Fox [2000] Conv. 353 at 359.

[150] See, for example, (2000) 79 P & CR 276 at 283.

[151] *Ibid*. at 295.

internal access to it[152] and that, had the claimed right been denied, the plaintiffs could have secured alternative external access by creating an entrance to a track running along the rear of the properties.[153] The right claimed would thus seem to have fallen short of the required degree of necessity.

The *Re Webb's Lease* easement has been developed as an exception to the general rule that an easement will not be impliedly reserved in favour of a grantor. As yet, there have been no cases in which it has been relied upon by a grantee. This is, no doubt, due to the fact that *Wheeldon* v. *Burrows*[154] and s. 62 of the Law of Property Act 1925 would often be available to a grantee. There may be situations, however, in which neither of these alternatives could be relied upon. In such cases there would seem to be no reason why a grantee should not attempt to argue that an easement should be implied in their favour on the basis of *Re Webb's Lease*.

It is not clear whether *Re Webb's Lease* would put potential grantees in any better position than they would be in were they to rely simply on the doctrine of non-derogation from grant. It is not obvious, for instance, whether the right concerned needs to be necessary to the reasonable enjoyment of the land in order to qualify under *Re Webb's Lease*. It is arguable that it should be viewed simply as an example of the operation of the rule against non-derogation in favour of grantors. This would carry with it the requirement that the right should have a material effect on the enjoyment of the property.

Turning now to the second issue, there is a great deal of uncertainty about the precise relationship between easements of necessity and *Pwllbach* easements. In *Nickerson* v. *Barraclough*[155] Megarry V-C seemed to regard them as 'two distinct but overlapping'[156] ways in which easements might be implied on the basis of necessity. Both require the right to be strictly necessary for the use of the land concerned. The distinction is that for easements of necessity the right must be necessary in order for the land to be used in any manner at all, whereas for intended easements the right must be necessary in order for the land to be used in the particular manner intended by the parties.

The distinction between easements of necessity and the *Pwllbach* intended easement is frequently clouded by a judicial tendency to refer to both as easements of necessity.[157] It may be that, in any event, it is a

---

[152] *Ibid.* at 283.
[153] *Ibid.* at 282.
[154] (1879) 12 Ch D 31.
[155] [1980] Ch 325.
[156] *Ibid.* at 332.
[157] See, for example, *Wong* v. *Beaumont* [1965] 1 QB 173 at 181 *per* Denning MR. See also *Nickerson* v. *Barraclough* [1980] Ch 325 and [1981] Ch 426 (discussed, on this point, in Coldham (1982) 132 NLJ 224).

distinction without a difference.[158] It is arguable that, as the courts are now prepared to imply a common intention to use the land in a specific way, they will be able to find such an intention whenever a landlocked plot is conveyed – thus eclipsing the traditional easement of necessity. The precise limits of the situations in which the courts will be prepared to find that there was an implied intention to use the land in a particular way have not yet been fully explored, however. It has been suggested, for instance, that a court will not be as inclined to find that a use was intended in the case of a reservation as it is in relation to a grant.[159]

The view that the easement of necessity, at least in relation to implied grant, has been subsumed within the *Pwllbach* intended easement is very attractive.[160] Both are driven by the policy that land should not become sterile but be used to its full potential.[161] Though intention is relevant to both, neither requires proof that the parties actually intended the claimed easement. The *Pwllbach* easement could drop the misleading title of 'intended easement' and become a legitimate easement of necessity. The title 'intended easement' could, instead, be reserved for easements implied under *Re Webb's Lease*. These do not require the easement to be necessary for the land to be used and are therefore quite distinct.

On the basis of the authorities at present, however, the easement of necessity and the *Pwllbach* intended easement remain 'distinct but overlapping' concepts. It remains to be seen whether the courts will decide that the overlap has become complete. If they decide it has not, some guidance as to the precise extent of the overlap would certainly be helpful.

The rule in *Wheeldon* v. *Burrows*[162]

The third important method by which an easement may be implied is under the rule in *Wheeldon* v. *Burrows*. This rule derives from the following words of Thesiger LJ:[163]

> [O]n the grant by the owner of a tenement of part of that tenement as it is then used and enjoyed, there will pass to the grantee all those continuous and apparent easements (by which, of course, I mean *quasi* easements) or, in other words, all those easements which are necessary to the reasonable enjoyment of

---

[158] See Wilkinson, 'The basis of the easement of necessity' (1964) 27 MLR 720 at 721.

[159] Harpum (*op. cit.* above fn. note 134), para. 18.102. See also *Aldridge* v. *Wright* [1929] 2 KB 115.

[160] See Crabb [1981] Conv. 442.

[161] Davis [2000] 20 LS 198 at 219. See also *Wong* v. *Beaumont Property Trust Ltd* [1965] 1 QB 173 at 180 where Denning MR described Lord Parker's dictum (quoted above fn. 128 and accompanying text) as being the principle underlying all easements of necessity.

[162] (1879) 12 Ch D 31.

[163] *Ibid.* at 49.

the property granted, and which have been and are at the time of the grant used by the owners of the entirety for the benefit of the part granted.

Unlike the easements already considered here, the *Wheeldon* v. *Burrows* easement can be implied only in favour of the grantee. Thesiger LJ refers to the need for the claimed easement to be 'continuous and apparent' and 'necessary to the reasonable enjoyment of the property'. The meaning of these two requirements, and the relationship between them, will now be considered, followed by a brief discussion of the basis of the rule.

The phrase 'continuous and apparent' was introduced into the common law by Gale (adopting it from the French Code Civile[164]), in the first edition of his textbook in 1839.[165] In the Code Civile 'continuous' meant, broadly, that the land must be arranged in such a way as to permit continuous enjoyment of the right without human intervention (e.g. a watercourse).[166] 'Apparent' meant broadly that the easement must be one which outwardly betrayed its existence by, for instance, a door or window. In other words, it must be one that would be discoverable on a physical inspection of the land.[167]

Gale had argued that English law on the implication of easements was analogous to the French law. This view was rejected by English courts[168] but left as a legacy the requirement that a quasi-easement must be continuous and apparent to pass under *Wheeldon* v. *Burrows*.

English courts have not attempted to interpret the terms 'continuous' and 'apparent' strictly in accordance with their original meanings.[169] Some guidance as to their meaning in current English law is provided by Ungoed-Thomas J in *Ward* v. *Kirkland*.[170] He suggested that:[171] '[T]he words continuous and apparent seem to be directed to there being on the servient tenement a feature which would be seen on inspection and which is neither transitory nor intermittent...' Simpson has argued that this interpretation of the phrase is very similar to the meaning of 'apparent' in the Code Civile and that, consequently, the word 'continuous' might usefully be dropped from statements of the current law.[172] This argument is strengthened by the fact that a right held not to be continuous may nevertheless become an easement under *Wheeldon*.

---

[164] See Simpson, 'The rule in *Wheeldon* v. *Burrows* and the Code Civile' [1967] 83 LQR 240, for a discussion of the relevant French law.

[165] See *ibid.* at 240. See also *Dalton* v. *Angus* (1881) 6 App Cas 7401 *per* Lord Blackburn.

[166] Article 688. See Simpson [1967] 83 LQR 240 at 240.

[167] Article 689. See Simpson [1967] 83 LQR 240 at 241–242.

[168] *Suffield* v. *Brown* (1864) 46 ER 888; *Wheeldon* v. *Burrows* (1879) 12 Ch D 31.

[169] See Harpum, '*Long* v. *Gowlett*: a strong fortress' [1979] Conv. 113 at 116.

[170] [1967] 1 Ch 194.

[171] *Ibid.* at 225.

[172] [1967] 83 LQR 240 at 245. See also Smith (*op. cit.* above fn. 38) at p. 472, describing the judicial tendency to regard the term 'continuous' as 'an inconvenient restriction that can be overlooked'.

Thus, in *Borman* v. *Griffith*[173] Maugham J declared that a right of way along a 'visible and made road' could not be 'continuous'.[174] The reason, though not expressly given, was presumably that the right itself would be exercised only intermittently. The right to use the road, despite not being continuous, became an easement as it was both 'obvious' and necessary for the reasonable enjoyment of the property.[175]

It is not easy to identify rights, traditionally regarded as 'continuous and apparent', which could not be treated as simply 'apparent'. 'Apparent' does not require a physical feature, such as drains,[176] to be immediately visible provided that it would be discoverable on a careful inspection. A right to light would generally be apparent from the existence of physical features such as windows. A right to support would generally be apparent from the physical geography of the property.

Abandoning the word 'continuous' would have the advantage of emphasising the function of this first *Wheeldon* requirement. It was introduced into English law 'as an answer to the dilemma that a man could not be said to have "rights" over his own land, because what he did on that land was referable to his ownership of it'.[177] Its function is not to ensure that grantees acquire only those easements that are continuous. Rather it is to provide a measure of certainty about the rights that will pass to the grantee. This it does by excluding any right that would not be obvious on a careful inspection of the land concerned. Apparency is therefore crucial, but continuousness seems to be little more than a distraction.

The second *Wheeldon* v. *Burrows* requirement – that the right must be necessary for the reasonable enjoyment of the land – derives entirely from English authorities. Simpson suggests that, had Gale not introduced the notion of the 'continuous and apparent' easement, it is likely that English courts would have softened the boundaries of the easement of necessity to allow it to cover easements which were necessary for the reasonable enjoyment of the land.[178] The *Wheeldon* ruling that rights may gain the status of easements if they are necessary to the reasonable enjoyment of the property was a development drawn from the long-established[179] rule that a grantor must not derogate from his grant.[180]

---

173 [1930] 1 Ch 493.
174 *Ibid.* at 499.
175 *Ibid.*
176 *Schwann* v. *Cotton* [1916] 2 Ch 120.
177 Harpum [1979] Conv. 113 at 117.
178 (1967) 83 LQR 240 at 245.
179 See, for example, *Palmer* v. *Fletcher* (1663) 1 Lev 122.
180 See Elliot (1964) 80 LQR 244 at 245; Smith (*op. cit.* above fn. 38), p. 474; Harpum 'Easements and Centrepoint: old problems resolved in a novel setting' [1977] Conv. 415 at 421.

The reasonable necessity requirement in *Wheeldon* seems to be more straightforward than the apparency requirement. Unlike the easement of necessity, it clearly does not require the right to be essential for use of the land in any manner.[181] Nor does it require the right to be essential for use of the land in the specific manner intended by the parties, as would the *Pwllbach* easement. It also seems clear that it requires a right to do more than simply accommodate the dominant tenement. The precise location of the standard within these perimeters, however, is less clear. It has been said that 'it hovers... at some ill defined point between the two'.[182]

Some guidance is provided by the numerous cases in which claims have been made under *Wheeldon v. Burrows*[183] in respect of an alternative means of access. There is no difficulty in establishing that such a right accommodates the dominant tenement. Generally, however, they will not be regarded as necessary for the reasonable enjoyment of the property if they would simply provide a more convenient access than that already existing.[184] They are likely to succeed, however, if the claimed alternative route enables the grantee to avoid genuine dangers connected with use of the original.[185] They are also likely to succeed if, without the claimed access, the grantee would be unable to carry out a business the nature of which had been known to the grantor.[186]

It has been argued, on two grounds, that the requirement that the right must be necessary for the reasonable enjoyment of the property should be abandoned and replaced simply with the requirement that it should accommodate the dominant tenement.[187] First, this would remove the uncertainty connected with the application of the present standard. Secondly, it would make the standard consistent with that operating in s. 62 cases and, since there may be cases in which both *Wheeldon* and s. 62 apply, such consistency is important.

It is highly unlikely that the courts will be prepared to remove the reasonable necessity requirement. To do so would extend the *Wheeldon v. Burrows* easement beyond the scope of the doctrine of non-derogation from grant, which appears to provide its primary rationale. Interestingly, if the reasonable necessity requirement were removed from *Wheeldon*, the effect would be identical to the effect of ruling that s. 62 applied to all

---

[181] See, for example, *Wheeler v. J.J. Saunders Ltd.* [1995] 2 All ER 697 at 702 *per* Staughton LJ and 707–708 *per* Peter Gibson LJ.

[182] Thompson, 'Paths and pigs' [1995] Conv. 239 at 240.

[183] (1879) 12 Ch D 31.

[184] *Wheeler v. J.J. Saunders Ltd.* [1995] 2 All ER 697; *Goldberg v. Edwards* [1950] Ch 247; cf. *Schwann v. Cotton* [1916] 2 Ch 120.

[185] See *Milman v. Ellis* (1996) 71 P & CR 158, particularly at 163 *per* Sir Thomas Bingham MR.

[186] *Borman v. Griffith* [1930] 1 Ch 493.

[187] Thompson [1995] Conv. 239 at 240–242. This is, it seems, the position under the French rules which Gale had thought applicable in England (see above fns. 164–167 and accompanying text); Simpson (1967) 83 LQR 240 at 246.

continuous and apparent easements regardless of diversity of occupation.[188] In either event, continuous and apparent easements would pass to a grantee whether or not they were necessary for the reasonable enjoyment of the property granted.

Since *Wheeldon* v. *Burrows*[189] there has been a great deal of confusion as to the relationship between the continuous and apparent requirement and the reasonable necessity requirement. This is largely due to the fact that, although they would appear to have quite different meanings, Thesiger LJ, after referring to 'continuous and apparent' easements, said that 'in other words' ones which are necessary to the reasonable enjoyment of the property. Thus, generations of lawyers have been asking:[190] 'Are these requirements synonymous, alternative or cumulative?' The question has remained live for so long largely because '[w]henever judges show awareness of there being a problem, they are frequently wise enough to say relatively little...'[191] Nevertheless, despite the continued appearance of decisions in which only one of the conditions is relied upon[192] and judicial observations that the requirements are synonymous,[193] the widely favoured view is that the tests are cumulative[194] – i.e. that each must be satisfied.

The basis of the rule in *Wheeldon* v. *Burrows* was considered by the House of Lords in *Sovmots Investments Ltd.* v. *Secretary of State for the Environment*.[195] Lord Wilberforce described it in the following terms:[196] 'The rule is a rule of intention, based on the proposition that a man may not derogate from his grant.'

Similarly, Lord Edmund-Davies[197] regarded the *Wheeldon* v. *Burrows*[198] line of cases as illustrating the principle of non-derogation from grant and identified as the 'very basis' of the rule the need to imply easements necessary to give effect to the common intention of the parties.

---

[188] See below fn. 211 and accompanying text for discussion of this argument. See also Thompson 'The aquisition of easements' [1997] Conv. 453 at 457 where the argument based on s. 62 seems to be preferred.

[189] (1879) 12 Ch D 31.

[190] Harpum [1977] Conv. 415 at 421.

[191] Smith (*op. cit.* above fn. 38), p. 474.

[192] *Simmonds* v. *Dobson* [1991] 1 WLR 720.

[193] *Wheeler* v. *J.J. Saunders Ltd* [1995] 2 All ER 697 at 707 *per* Peter Gibson LJ. Despite this observation, the case is frequently used to support the view that the requirements are *cumulative see*, for example, Thompson [1995] Conv. 239 at 240, [1997] Conv. 453 at 457; Hopkins (*op. cit.* above fn. 75), pp. 212–213.

[194] See, for example, Harpum [1977] Conv. 415 at 421, Harpum *op. cit.* above fn. 134, para. 18.104; Smith (*op. cit.* above fn. 38), p. 474 (though Smith goes on to suggest an 'answer' to the problem which would seem to reduce the role of the continuous and apparent requirement to virtual non-existence).

[195] [1979] AC 144.

[196] *Ibid.* at 168.

[197] *Ibid.* at 175.

[198] (1879) 12 Ch D 31.

Their Lordships in *Sovmots Investments* treated the rule against derogation as one of intention. It is based on the presumption that parties will intend the granted land to carry with it rights necessary to its reasonable enjoyment in the manner envisaged. The apparency requirement of *Wheeldon*, assuming the requirements to be cumulative, operates so as to restrict this presumption to cases in which quasi-easements should be obvious to a grantee. It can be argued that this is perfectly consistent with the doctrine of non-derogation from grant which requires the parties to have had an expectation or intention that the right should be granted – only if a grantee is aware of a quasi-easement can they genuinely expect to receive it.[199] The traditional view, however, is that the need for a right to be continuous and apparent in order to fall within *Wheeldon v. Burrows* separates the operation of *Wheeldon v. Burrows* from the pure doctrine of non-derogation from grant.[200]

Thus, like the easement of necessity and the intended easement, the *Wheeldon v. Burrows* easement seems to be based on the presumed intention of the parties combined with the policy of maximising the utility of land. It has long been accepted that the rule will not apply if there is evidence of a contrary intent.[201] Nor will it apply in cases of compulsory purchase where there cannot realistically be said to have been any common intention between the parties.[202]

Section 62 of the Law of Property Act 1925

According to s. 62 (1):

> A conveyance of land shall be deemed to include and shall by virtue of this Act operate to convey, with the land, all...ways, waters, watercourses, liberties, privileges, easements, rights, and advantages whatsoever, appertaining or reputed to appertain to the land, or any part thereof, or, at the time of conveyance, demised, occupied, or enjoyed with...the land or any part thereof.

The section originally appeared as s. 6 of the Conveyancing Act 1881 and was introduced in order to simplify conveyances. Before its introduction (and, indeed, afterwards), legal easements existing at the date of the

---

[199] See Davis (2000) 20 LS 198 at 218. For a discussion of the expectation requirement in the rule against derogation from grant, see Elliot (1964) 80 LQR 244 at 255–260.

[200] See Hopkins (*op. cit.* above fn. 75), pp. 212–213.

[201] *Squarey v. Harris Smith* (1981) 42 P & CR 118. *Millman v. Ellis* (1996) 71 P & CR 158 establishes that the existence of a more limited express easement than the one claimed will not be treated as evidence of a contrary intent (as in relation to s. 62 – *Hansford v. Jago* [1921] 1 Ch 322; *Gregg v. Richards* [1926] Ch 521).

[202] *Sovmots Investments Ltd. v. Sec. of State for the Environment* [1979] AC 144; cf. *North Eastern Ry. v. Elliot* (1861) 10 HLC 333 and Elliot (1964) 80 LQR 244 at 250.

conveyance would automatically pass to a purchaser.[203] Easements that were equitable, however, or that had previously existed but been extinguished because the dominant and servient tenements had fallen into common ownership would not.[204] In order to ensure that a purchaser would acquire such rights, conveyancers had to make express provision in the conveyance – often achieved by the insertion of what became known as the 'general words'. Section 62 was enacted simply to imply these general words into all conveyances, unless expressly excluded,[205] and thus save time and paper. For a section with such a simple, unambitious aim, s. 62 has generated a bewildering amount of controversy and confusion. Indeed, even today, there is scarcely any aspect of its operation that is free from uncertainty and debate.

The context in which the section operates is not completely clear. Sargant J held in *Long* v. *Gowlett*[206] that the section would not apply unless, at the time of the conveyance, the two tenements had been owned or occupied by different people. This rule has been approved, *obiter*, by the House of Lords[207] and upheld by the Court of Appeal.[208] Its basis, according to Lord Wilberforce, is that 'when land is under one ownership one cannot speak in any intelligible sense of rights ... being exercised over one part for the benefit of another'.[209] If the section (which does not require the rights to be reasonably necessary to the enjoyment of the land) were allowed to apply in such cases, it would be extremely difficult to identify which of the activities of the common owner should be treated as rights appertaining to the quasi-dominant tenement and so within its scope.[210]

Despite the fact that the *Long* v. *Gowlett* diversity requirement is regarded by some as an 'unjustified limitation on the scope of the statutory general words',[211] it now seems unlikely it will be reconsidered by the courts. Sargant J accepted that an easement of light represents an

---

[203] *Godwin* v. *Schweppes Ltd.* [1902] 1 Ch 926.

[204] See discussion in Tee 'Metamorphoses and Section 62 LPA 1925' [1998] Conv. 115 at 116.

[205] Section 62 (4).

[206] [1923] 2 Ch. 177.

[207] *Sovmots Investments Ltd.* v. *Secretary of State for the Environment* [1979] AC 144 at 169 *per* Lord Wilberforce and at 176 *per* Lord Edmund-Davies.

[208] *Payne* v. *Inwood* (1997) 74 P & CR 42 at 47–49 *per* Roch LJ.

[209] *Sovmots Investments Ltd.* v. *Sec. of State for the Environment* [1979] AC 144 at 169.

[210] See Smith *op. cit.* above fn. 38, p. 476, using the example of the sale of an orchard by somebody who owned an adjoining house – would the use of the toilet in that house pass to the purchaser of the orchard under s. 62? See also Harpum [1977] Conv. 415 at 418–420.

[211] Jackson, 'Easements and general words' [1966] Conv. 340 at 346. Jackson's reasons include lack of authority and the argument that the requirement is based on the factual difficulty of identifying quasi easements which should not prove insuperable, particularly given that courts already have to identify quasi continuous and apparent easements under *Wheeldon* v. *Burrows* (see *ibid.* at 346–349). See also Smith 'Centrepoint: faulty towers with shaky foundations' [1978] Conv. 449 at 450–455.

exception to the general rule and will pass under the section whether or not there is diversity of ownership or occupation.[212] What is less clear is whether this exception extends to embrace all quasi-easements that are continuous and apparent. Harpum[213] has argued vigorously in favour of this view, which derives some support from *Long* v. *Gowlett*[214] itself. Whether it represents present law is unclear, however, as little mention of it has been made in subsequent cases.[215]

Turning now to the nature of the rights to which the section will apply, it is clear there is no need for the right to be necessary for the reasonable enjoyment of the property.[216] What is less clear is whether the section requires rights to be apparent in some way. Sargant J was troubled by the notion that the section might apply to rights which were 'non-apparent'.[217] So too was Ungoed-Thomas J in *Ward* v. *Kirkland*.[218] In that case, however, Ungoed-Thomas J was able to apply the section with a clear conscience as the right concerned would have been 'clear and obvious'[219] to a purchaser on a physical inspection of the land.

It has been argued that, in order to enable purchasers to identify what rights attach to the land they are buying, s. 62 should apply only to rights that are continuous and apparent in the *Wheeldon* v. *Burrows* sense.[220] This argument has been criticised on the grounds that it is not supported by the language of the statute or other authority;[221] that it confuses the operation of s. 62 with the common law rules on the implication of easements; and that it is based on a misplaced analogy with the doctrine of notice.[222] In *Ward* v. *Kirkland*,[223] the notion that s. 62 would apply only to rights that were continuous and apparent was specifically rejected. What is unclear is whether the courts will develop some lesser standard of apparency, perhaps based on Ungoed-Thomas J's term 'clear and obvious'.

---

[212] [1923] 2 Ch 177 at 202–203, relying on *Broomfield* v. *Williams* [1897] 1 Ch 602.

[213] [1977] 41 Conv. 415 at 420–421; [1979] Conv. 113. See also Harpum *op. cit.* above fn. 134, para. 18.114; Thompson [1997] Conv. 453 at 457–458. For criticism, see Smith [1978] Conv. 449, [1979] Conv. 311.

[214] [1923] 2 Ch 177. Sargant J distinguished *Broomfield* v. *Williams* [1879] 1 Ch 602 on the grounds that an easement of light was 'a physical fact, plainly visible to anyone buying a house' and described it as 'extremely similar to a continuous and apparent easement' (*ibid.* at 202).

[215] See, however, *M.R.A. Engineering* v. *Trimster Co Ltd* (1988) 56 P & CR1 at 6–7 where Nourse LJ seems to be of the view that s. 62 is applicable to quasi easements and appears to suggest that it has replaced *Wheeldon* v. *Burrows* (1879) 12 Ch D 31.

[216] *Goldberg* v. *Edwards* [1950] Ch 247.

[217] *Long* v. *Gowlett* [1923] 2 Ch 177 at 203 though it is not entirely clear whether this concern was limited to cases in which there had been no diversity of ownership or occupation.

[218] [1967] 1 Ch 194 at 228.

[219] *Ibid.* at 230.

[220] See, for example, Harpum [1977] Conv. 415 at 420.

[221] Apart from Kekewich J in *Titchmarsh* v. *Royston Water Co. Ltd.* (1899) 81 LT 673 at 674–675.

[222] Jackson [1996] Conv. 430 at 340–345; Smith [1978] Conv. 449 at 450–454 and [1979] Conv. 311.

[223] [1967] 1 Ch 194 at 229.

The effect of s. 62 seems to be clearly established by the authorities but has attracted considerable criticism. It was established in *International Tea Stores Co.* v. *Hobbs*[224] that the section will have the effect of converting what were mere precarious and revokable licences or permissions before the conveyance into legal easements, provided that they are capable of existing as easements and not intended to be temporary[225] or personal[226] only. According to Jenkins LJ,[227] the reason for this is 'clear' and is simply that inclusion in the deed, through s. 62, confers legal status on the former licence. This 'metamorphosis from personal into proprietary right'[228] has been described as 'remarkable',[229] 'surprising',[230] 'startling'[231] and 'magical'.[232] It has been criticised on three main grounds.

First, it has been criticised on the ground that it is founded on 'dubious logic'.[233] The section, it is argued, applies only to rights that appertain (or are reputed to appertain) to the land.[234] Licences therefore should lie outside its ambit. The term right, however, was used loosely by Farwell J to refer to permissions granted by licences. This linguistic inaccuracy led him to the view that such permissions were rights which fell within the scope of the section.[235]

Secondly, the *International Tea Stores* rule seems to punish, and therefore deter, acts of kindness by landlords towards their tenants. Knowledgeable landlords might well avoid granting favours (such as the use of a track or a coal shed) to their tenants for fear that s. 62 may transform them into irrevocable easements on the execution of a conveyance[236] between them. This viewpoint is well illustrated by the following lament of Tucker LJ:[237]

> The result is that the defendant, through his act of kindness in allowing this lady to use the coal shed, is probably now a wiser man and I may perhaps regret that the decision in this case may tend to discourage landlords from acts of kindness to their tenants. But there it is. That is the law.

---

[224] [1903] 2 Ch 165.
[225] *Goldberg* v. *Edwards* [1950] Ch 247; *Birmingham, Dudley & District Banking Company* v. *Ross* (1883) 38 Ch D 295; *Hair* v. *Gillman* (2000) 48 EG 117.
[226] *Goldberg* v. *Edwards* [1950] Ch 247; *Dewsbury* v. *Davis*, LEXIS 21 May 1992. For criticism of these distinctions, see Tee [1998] Conv. 115 at 115–116.
[227] *Wright* v. *Macadam* [1949] 2 KB 744 at 751.
[228] Tee [1998] Conv. 115 at 115.
[229] Smith (*op. cit.* above fn. 38), p. 476; Harpum (*op. cit.* above fn. 134), para. 18.111.
[230] Harpum (*op. cit.* above fn. 134), para. 18.111.
[231] Tee [1998] Conv. 115 at 115.
[232] *Ibid.*
[233] *Ibid.* at 124.
[234] *Ibid.* at 119.
[235] *Ibid.* at 121–122.
[236] Including a written lease *Wright* v. *Macadam* [1949] 2 KB 744.
[237] *Wright* v. *MacAdam* [1949] 2 KB 744 at 755. See also *Green* v. *Ashco Horticulturist Ltd* [1966] 1 WLR 889 at 897 *per* Cross J.

It should be noted, however, that as it is possible expressly to exclude the application of s. 62,[238] such favours may still be safely granted.

Finally, this aspect of the operation of s. 62 has been attacked on the ground that it results in the creation of easements regardless of the parties' intentions. Tee[239] has argued that before 1881 when the section was first introduced, the Court of Exchequer Chamber, though reluctant to hold that the general words would create easements from licences, would be prepared to do so if it was clearly demonstrated that this was the true intention of the parties.[240] Thus, intention played a 'determinative'[241] role in the transformation of licences into easements on conveyance. Though s. 62 and its predecessor were not designed to change the law which had been developed around the general words, under the *International Tea Stores* rule the intention of the parties certainly does not enjoy its former importance. As Tee[242] points out, it will now be relevant only to *prevent* the transformation taking place in cases where it can be shown that the permission was intended to be temporary or personal.

Section 62, then, was introduced simply to save parties the trouble of including the general words expressly in their conveyances. The intention of the parties would, therefore, seem to provide its rationale. It appears legitimate to assume, in the absence of evidence to the contrary, an intention that easements existing (or reputed to exist) before the conveyance should continue to exist.[243] To assume an intention that what were revocable licences before the conveyance should become irrevocable easements, on the other hand, is not legitimate. The easements thus created are not required to be necessary in any way to the enjoyment of the land. It is consequently extremely difficult to find any justification for the creation of new easements under s. 62.[244]

Summary of the discussion of implied easements

In *Wheeler* v. *J.J. Saunders*,[245] Peter Gibson LJ expressed the view that: 'It is

---

[238] Section 62 (4). Such exclusions have long been inserted into conveyances on an extremely widespread *basis see* Law Com. WP 36, para. 87.

[239] [1998] Conv. 115 at 117–118.

[240] See, in particular, *Kay* v. *Oxley* (1875) LR 10 QB 360 and *Bayley* v. *Grt. Western Ry.* (1884) 26 Ch D 434.

[241] [199] Conv. 115 at 121.

[242] *Ibid.* at 122–123.

[243] cf. Davis (2000) 20 LS 198 at 210 where it is suggested that 'the implication of rights here cannot be said to have anything to do with the intention of the parties'. Though this seems to refer to s. 62 as a whole, it may refer only to its creative aspect (its ability to create easements from what were previously merely licences).

[244] See *ibid.*; [1998] Conv. 115.

[245] [1995] 2 All ER 697 at 707.

perhaps surprising that so important a matter as a right of way should be capable of being granted merely by implication in a modern conveyance...'. The Law Commission, in its 1971 working paper,[246] contemplated the 'drastic solution' of a system in which no easements would be implied but a court or tribunal given jurisdiction to award one if it was considered to be reasonably required. This possibility was rejected on the ground that it might cause injustice, particularly in relation to leases created informally and without the benefit of legal advice.[247] In addition, the commission felt that:[248] 'parties to contracts are entitled to expect that the law will give their contracts business efficacy without the expense...of proceedings.' These are convincing reasons for continuing to imply easements.

The present system for the implication of easements is, however, unnecessarily complex and confused. Thirty years ago the Law Commission[249] suggested a statutory formula which might replace the current system of specific but overlapping rules. This would have transferred to the purchaser of part only of a piece of land:

(a) Any facilities which were previously available to the occupier of that part of the land and which, in all the circumstances of the case, it is reasonable to contemplate as continuing and

(b) Any new facilities which are either necessary to the proper enjoyment of that part at the time of the transaction or which in all the circumstances it is reasonable to contemplate as having been intended by the parties to be imposed upon completion of the transaction.

This would have simplified the law and removed the difficulties caused by *International Tea Stores Co.* v. *Hobbs.*[250] It is a great pity the idea was allowed to drop.[251]

Conclusion

Though easements have been part of English and Welsh property law for many centuries, a considerable amount of controversy surrounds many aspects of their existence and operation. Only two of these aspects have been explored in detail here, but there are many other equally contentious areas – e.g. prescription and termination. These controversies and confusions make the subject both frustrating and fascinating. An

---

[246] No. 36, para. 91.
[247] *Ibid.*
[248] *Ibid.*
[249] *Ibid.*, Proposition 9.
[250] [1903] 2 Ch 165.
[251] For further discussion, see Tee [1998] Conv. 115 at 123–124.

appreciation of the underlying themes that have influenced the development of the current rules can help to reduce the bewilderment often felt by those embarking on the study of the easement.

Further reading

Davis, 'Informal acquisition and loss of rights in land: what justifies the doctrines?' (2000) 20 LS 198.

Harpum, 'Easements and Centrepoint: old problems resolved in a novel setting' [1977] Conv. 415.

Harpum '*Long* v. *Gowlett*: a strong fortress' [1979] Conv. 113.

Hopkins, 'The Informal Acquisition of Rights in Land' (2000, Sweet & Maxwell).

Jackson, 'Easements of necessity' (1981) 34 CLP 133 and JF.

Simonton, 'Ways by necessity' (1925) 25 Col LR 571.

Simpson, 'The rule in *Wheeldon* v. *Burrows* and the Code Civile' [1967] 83 LQR 240.

Smith, 'Centrepoint: faulty towers with shaky foundations' [1978] Conv. 449.

Sturley, 'Easements in gross' (1980) 96 LQR 557.

Tee, 'Metamorphoses and Section 62 LPA 1925' [1998] Conv. 115.

4

Leases – contract, property and status

Stuart Bridge

Introduction

The lease straddles the worlds of contract and property. It is an estate the duration of which is determined by the agreement of the landlord and the tenant. It is also highly significant as a status, tenants enjoying rights and incurring obligations that are denied to others. The law of leases is extraordinarily complex, and the search for order out of the inherent chaos can at times seem an almost futile exercise. The student of land law (at whom this book is principally directed) tends to concentrate on the 'general principles' affecting the leasehold relationship, covering important conceptual matters as the defining characteristics of a lease, the nature and extent of certain leasehold obligations, the proprietary impact of leases, the enforceability of leasehold covenants by and against successors to the original parties, and the termination of the lease by notice to quit, forfeiture for tenant default, surrender and so forth. It is inevitable that this emphasis on 'general principles' provides a view of the law of landlord and tenant which is some way removed from the practical realities of the leasehold relationship. One obvious divergence relates to security of tenure. It may be that according to the 'general principles', a lease can be terminated by notice, but there may be statutory restrictions on such termination, nor does it necessarily follow that recovery of possession ensues upon termination of the lease. The landlord and tenant practitioner must be aware that specific types of lease are dealt with by statute in very different ways, and that engrafted on to the 'general part' are principles which may or may not apply according to the specific kind of lease.[1]

---

[1] The traditional demarcation of landlord and tenant law into 'general principles' and specific parts has been recently criticised by Peter Sparkes who advocates wholesale dispensation with the 'general part' and division of the core into a threefold classification of commercial leases, short residential leases and long residential leases: *A New Landlord and Tenant Law* (2001, Hart).

Not only are there are many statutory regimes, it is also the case that the formality of the relationship (and the length of the term) is highly variable. Residential accommodation such as bed-sits are frequently let on 'periodic tenancy', where the tenant pays rent on a periodic basis and the landlord-tenant relationship continues until either party determines it by serving written notice on the other. Commercial property, such as offices, shops and garages, is more likely to be let on a 'fixed-term tenancy' for five, or ten, or fifteen years. The rent may be subject to review pursuant to a preordained procedure at defined intervals during the lease. Then there is the 'long lease', used principally in relation to developments of houses or flats, which involves the grant of a lease for hundreds, sometimes thousands, of years, in consideration of the payment of a capital sum known as a premium and a 'ground-rent'. These leasehold interests are conceptually much closer to freeholds (the so-called 'fee simple absolute in possession') than periodic tenancies, and they are traded on the housing market in much the same way.

This chapter is intended to take the land law student on a brief journey into the territory of the landlord and tenant practitioner, to illustrate the diversity of the landlord-tenant relationship, and the difficulties of policy the law is continuing to address.

The lease as property

The student of land law sees the lease as part and parcel of the law of property.[2] It is an estate, indeed as a 'term of years absolute' it is one of the only two legal estates capable of being created.[3] Although a deed is usually necessary to create a legal estate, there is a major exception in favour of leases taking effect in possession for a term not exceeding three years at the best rent which can be reasonably obtained without taking a fine.[4] Such leases, even if created by parol, may nevertheless comprise legal estates. Thus almost all periodic tenancies and fixed-term tenancies for three years or less will take effect as legal estates. But in the event of a lease not complying with necessary statutory formalities, it will be at best an equitable interest. The classic example of an equitable lease is where, pursuant to the rule in *Walsh* v. *Lonsdale*,[5] a landlord agrees to grant a lease to a tenant (for a term exceeding three years), but no deed is executed. Equity 'looks on as done that which ought to be done', and thus the

---

[2] Historically, leases were 'chattels real' and formed part of the law of personalty: see Harwood, 'Leases: are they still really real?' (2000) LS 503.

[3] Law of Property Act 1925, s. 1 (1).

[4] *Ibid.*, s. 54 (2).

[5] (1882) 21 Ch D 9.

agreement, if specifically enforceable,[6] will take effect as a lease in equity. The equitable lease is an estate contract for the purposes of the Land Charges Act 1972, as it is a contract to create a legal estate, and where title to the land is unregistered the lease should be registered as a Class C (iv) land charge.[7] A failure to register will result in the equitable lease being void against a purchaser for money or money's worth of the landlord's legal estate.[8]

In the more usual situation, where title to the land is registered, a lease can be protected by registration in two ways. First, it is possible to register a leasehold interest in land where the lease is for a term of years absolute of which more than 21 years are unexpired.[9] In this case, the registered title is leasehold. Secondly, it is possible to register notice of a lease, save where the term is an overriding interest.[10] A legal lease will take effect as an overriding interest where it is granted for a term not exceeding 21 years.[11] It is thus possible to register by way of notice a legal lease with over 21 years unexpired pending substantive registration of the leasehold title, and to register by way of notice an equitable lease. An equitable lease may also take effect as an overriding interest where the tenant is in actual occupation of the land or in receipt of the rents and profits thereof, save where inquiry is made of the tenant and the rights are not disclosed.[12] The protection afforded to those holding both legal and equitable leases is excellent. It is perfectly logical to offer those holding a legal lease the security of an overriding interest, as where title is unregistered the legal lease will bind all-comers. Where the lease is equitable, the tenant is nevertheless likely to be protected, as the nature of the lease is such that he or she will usually either be occupying the property or be receiving rent as a result of sub-letting.

The position of those holding leases will be significantly affected when the Land Registration Act 2002 comes in force. In an attempt to encourage the registration of all significant estates, almost all leases for a term exceeding seven years will require substantive registration.[13] Such leases will become registered estates, the leaseholder or tenant registering his or her interest by way of notice against the title of his or her immediate landlord. Overriding status will be accorded to leases granted for a term not exceeding seven years.[14] This expression implies that such leases must

---

[6] This will require the agreement, if made on or after 27 September 1989, to be made in writing, incorporating all the terms in one document (or two, where contracts are exchanged): Law of Property (Miscellaneous Provisions) Act 1989, s. 2.

[7] Land Charges Act 1972, s. 2.

[8] *Ibid.*, s. 4 (6); *Hollington Bros Ltd* v. *Rhodes* [1951] 2 TLR 691, [1951] 2 All ER 578 n.

[9] Land Registration Act 1925, s. 8 (1), as amended.

[10] *Ibid.*, s. 48.

[11] *Ibid.*, s. 70 (1) (k); see *City Permanent Building Society* v. *Miller* [1952] Ch 840, limiting the application of this provision to legal leases.

[12] Land Registration Act 1925, s. 70 (1) (g).

[13] Land Registration Act 2002, s. 4 (1) (c).

[14] Land Registration Act 2002, Sched. 1, para 1, Sched. 3, para 1.

be legal.[15] The equitable tenant who fails to enter a notice will have to establish that he or she was in actual occupation – the receipt of rents and profits will no longer suffice.

It is important to realise, not least because it is rarely the actual issue in the cases, that an occupier of land who wishes to assert occupational rights against purchasers or mortgagees of a superior interest will almost always be seeking to establish the existence of a lease. The distinction between the lease and the licence has been of central importance to land lawyers in drawing the line between an estate in land which is, as we have seen above, potentially binding on purchasers or mortgagees of the reversion (in other words, an interest in property) and a mere agreement between two parties which is mutually enforceable but which lacks the element of 'durability'.[16] It is an over-simplification to suggest that licences have no proprietary consequences whatsoever,[17] but courts have in recent years rejected earlier attempts (of Lord Denning in particular[18]) to promote the contractual licence to the level of a property interest.[19] However that is not to deny all extra-contractual significance to licences: for example, certain kinds of licensee have been accorded the right to protect their possession in the tort of trespass.[20]

When Mr Roger Street, a solicitor of the Supreme Court, agreed on 7 March 1983 to allow Mrs Wendy Mountford to occupy a furnished room he owned in Boscombe for a weekly payment of £37, neither could have imagined that the dispute over the true effect of this contractual arrangement would be ultimately decided by the House of Lords, and would become the leading case in English law on the definitional characteristics of the lease.[21] The argument between the parties was

---

[15] See *City Permanent Building Society* v. *Miller*, [1952] Ch 840.

[16] See Hill, 'The proprietary character of possession' in *Property 2000* (2001, Hart). A tenant is to be regarded as in actual occupation only if he, his agent or employee is physically present there.

[17] See, for instance, Hill (*op. cit.* above fn. 14)- p.22.

[18] *Errington* v. *Errington* [1952] 1 KB 290 at 299 ('Neither the licensor nor anyone who claims through him can disregard the contract except a purchaser for value without notice.') See also *Binions* v. *Evans* [1972] Ch 359; *DHN Food Distributors Ltd* v. *Tower Hamlets LBC* [1976] 1 WLR 852; *Re Sharpe (A Bankrupt)* [1980] 1 WLR 219; *Lyus* v. *Prowsa Developments Ltd* [1982] 1 WLR 1044.

[19] *Ashburn Anstalt* v. *Arnold* [1989] Ch 1 at 13–27, *per* Fox LJ. There remains the possibility, in limited circumstances, of the imposition of a constructive trust to give effect to contractually agreed stipulations. See, for further developments, *Camden LBC* v. *Shortlife Community Housing* (1992) 90 LGR 358 at 373; *Canadian Imperial Bank of Commerce* v. *Bello* (1992) 64 P & CR 48 at 51. There is an extensive academic literature on this subject, concisely summarised in Gravells, *Land Law: Text and Materials* (2nd ed., 1999, Sweet & Maxwell), pp. 520–522 and 532–533.

[20] Hill, (*op. cit.* above fn. 14) at p.31 *et seq.*, criticising the recent decision of the Court of Appeal in *Manchester Airport Plc* v. *Dutton* [2000] QB 133

[21] 'Is there a more important landlord and tenant case?' ask Williams and Luba in their 'A to Z of Landlord and Tenant' (2001) 12 L & T Rev 10.

whether the agreement entered into comprised a lease or a licence, but the wider issue was whether it was possible to contract out of the statutory regime of the Rent Acts which was then widely applicable to private sector residential lettings.[22] By the Rent Act 1977, s. 1: 'Subject to this Part of this Act, a tenancy under which a dwelling-house (which may be a house or part of a house) is let as a separate dwelling is a protected tenancy for the purposes of this Act.' In the event of Mrs Mountford having a protected tenancy, she could seek to have a 'fair rent' registered in respect of the property, as a result of which Mr Street would be unable to enforce the contractually stipulated sum of £37.[23] He would instead be bound by the rent officer's assessment of what rent was reasonable, almost inevitably at a lower sum than that agreed, and he could not react to Mrs Mountford's application by seeking to terminate their agreement and to recover possession as she would be accorded statutory security.

Mr Street's view of the Rent Acts was stridently expressed in the pages of the _Conveyancer_ a short time after his defeat in the House of Lords:

> The Rent Acts are grossly unfair to landlords. A stranger obtains a weekly tenancy of a house: half a century may pass before the owner can have his property again. In the meantime he can only charge a so-called 'fair' rent which in many cases does little more than cover the cost of keeping the property in repair. As a result of all this the capital value of the property drops to between one-third and one-half of its vacant possession value. Little wonder that over the years landlords and their legal advisers have sought various ways of avoiding the potentially horrendous consequences of being caught by the legislation.[24]

Mr Street's argument before the courts was straightforward: the terms of the written agreement which the occupier had signed were quite clear, and effect should be given to them. Mrs Mountford had been given the 'right to occupy' the room for a consideration described as a 'licence fee'. The agreement was terminable by either party giving the other 14 days' written notice, or by the landlord in the event of non-payment of the fee, payable weekly, or breach of any other term. The final clause of the agreement, separately signed by Mrs Mountford, stated that she understood and accepted that a licence in the above form did not and was not intended to give her a tenancy protected under the Rent Acts. This was the simplest possible attempt to avoid the consequences of Rent Act protection, and it convinced the Court of Appeal, no less a judge than Slade LJ asserting the supremacy of contract over status:

[22] See Sparkes (_op. cit._ above fn. 1), p. 150: '_Street_ v. _Mountford_ decided that a tenant could not contract out of the security of the Rent Act 1977.'
[23] Rent Act 1977, s. 44.
[24] [1985] Conv. 328.

Having regard to the form of the document and the declaration at the foot of it, I do not see how the plaintiff could have made much clearer his intention that what was being offered to the defendant was a mere licence to occupy and not an interest in the premises as tenant. And I do not see how the defendant could have made clearer her acceptance of that offer than by her two signatures.[25]

The decision of the House of Lords in *Street* v. *Mountford* can be seen, on one level, as status reasserting itself over contract. The words used, and the terminology chosen, by the contracting parties, are of strictly limited importance. The parties' intention is material, but only in so far as there is an intention to grant exclusive possession. Thus it is irrelevant that they may have indicated an intention to confer a licence rather than to grant a lease. Their Lordships' approach is paternalistic and interventionist, necessarily so they would argue, as the economics of the rental housing market would otherwise operate routinely so as to deny to occupiers the rights that Parliament has expressly conferred. The consequential restriction of contractual autonomy is justified by reference to the imbalance of the parties' negotiating strengths and the desirability of ensuring that rented homes are affordable and are not repossessed by landlords save where absolutely necessary.[26] The House of Lords gives a resoundingly negative answer to the question whether parties are free to contract out of the Rent Acts.

It is important to realise what *Street* v. *Mountford* does not decide. It is not directly concerned with that central question of land law: namely, the extent to which an interest, whether or not derived from a contract, is binding on a purchaser of an estate in the land. Nor did their Lordships have to consider the true meaning of exclusive possession, as Mr Street conceded that his standard-form agreement had conferred exclusive possession on Mrs Mountford. Indeed, the single major attempt of Lord Templeman to explain and analyse exclusive possession in the residential sector foundered badly, when he stated, somewhat dogmatically: 'An occupier of residential accommodation at a rent for a term is either a lodger or a tenant.'[27] This was clearly not the case, as is quite obvious from the context of the speech, several 'exceptional circumstances' being listed where a grant of exclusive possession does not result in the grant of a tenancy, and yet the occupier would not be ordinarily described as a 'lodger'.[28] According to Lord Templeman, an occupier is a lodger 'if the landlord provides attendance or services which require the landlord or his servants to exercise unrestricted access to and use of the premises'. Such a person is a licensee, but it is clearly nonsense to suggest that all licensees are lodgers, and Lord Templeman cannot have intended to do so. Indeed,

---

[25] (1984) 271 EG 1261 at 1264.
[26] See further *AG Securities* v. *Vaughan* [1990] 1 AC 417.
[27] *Ibid.* at 817.
[28] For example, a service occupier: see *per* Lord Templeman, *ibid.* 818.

it is an exaggeration to describe the status of 'lodger' as 'critically important',[29] and subsequent to *Street* v. *Mountford*, the Court of Appeal has sought to play down the significance of the lodger, emphasising that it is whether a person is a licensee or a tenant that is crucial.[30]

The temptation of landlords to attempt to deny exclusive possession where they were negotiating with more than a single occupier has always been strong. In the 1970s the device of the 'non-exclusive occupation agreement' had evolved, whereby the landlord required a couple who intended to cohabit to sign separate documents, usually in identical terms, acknowledging that they agreed to share the property with such other licensees whom the landlord should permit to use it. The high-water mark of these agreements was the decision of the Court of Appeal in *Somma* v. *Hazelhurst*,[31] which was subsequently overruled by the House of Lords in *Street* v. *Mountford* on the grounds that the agreements in question were obviously sham and were not intended to be acted upon by the parties thereto. The usual construction of such agreements following *Street* v. *Mountford* is as a joint grant of exclusive possession to the two occupiers.[32] Thus, in *Antoniades* v. *Villiers*,[33] an unmarried couple who had signed two identical written agreements permitting the landlord to occupy the rooms himself at any time, and permitting other persons to use them with the licensee were held to have been jointly granted exclusive possession of the property. The agreements were clearly interdependent. Had one member of the couple refused to sign their agreement, the other would have been denied the opportunity to do so.

When, as Mr Street himself had anticipated,[34] a later court was called upon to consider in detail the implications of the centrality of the exclusive possession concept where multiple occupiers were concerned, the decision of the House of Lords in *AG Securities* v. *Vaughan, Antoniades* v. *Villiers* comprised both a justification and an exposition of the radically interventionist approach to the construction of agreements providing for the occupation of residential property initially advocated in *Street* v. *Mountford*. In the earlier case, Lord Templeman had articulated the nature of the problem:

> Although the Rent Acts must not be allowed to alter or influence the construction of an agreement, the court should, in my opinion, be astute to detect and frustrate sham devices and artificial transactions whose only object is to disguise the grant of a tenancy and to evade the Rent Acts.

[29] Gray and Gray, p.365.
[30] *Brooker Settled Estates* v. *Ayers* (1987) 54 P & CR 165 at 169–170; *Nicolaou* v. *Pitt* (1989) 21 HLR 487 at 493.
[31] [1978] 1 WLR 1014.
[32] For an exception, see *Mikeover Ltd* v. *Brady* [1989] 3 All ER 618 (no unity of interest as the parties were (genuinely) severally liable for the rent).
[33] [1990] 1 AC 417.
[34] [1985] Conv. 328 at 333.

This approach was justifiable, as was hinted in *Street* v. *Mountford*, by the imbalance in the respective bargaining positions of landlord and occupier who, in a situation where demand for housing exceeds supply, 'may concur in any expression of intention in order to obtain shelter'.[35] Thus, where two persons have signed separate documents providing them with accommodation, the court deciding whether a tenancy or licence has been created 'must consider the surrounding circumstances, including any relationship between the prospective occupiers, the course of negotiations and the nature and extent of the accommodation and the intended and actual mode of occupation of the accommodation'.[36] It is even legitimate to take account of the parties' subsequent conduct, not to construe the terms of their contract but to determine whether the documents were or were not genuine and, if not, which terms of their written agreement were seriously intended to be acted upon.[37]

Although the House of Lords in both *Street* v. *Mountford* and *AG Securities* v. *Vaughan* refused to give their views on the impact of the Rent Acts on the availability of housing,[38] the combined effect of these decisions was to make it well nigh impossible for private sector landlords to avoid the Rent Acts and other protective legislation, at least by the device of denying tenant status to the occupiers of their property. However, a few months after the House of Lords handed down its decision in *AG Securities*, legislation came into force that rendered avoidance of the Rent Acts themselves no longer necessary, and which largely removed the landlords' incentive to prefer licensees to tenants. Although these decisions are still of major significance in expounding the lease/licence distinction, and thereby the definition of the leasehold estate, their implications in terms of status, the reason why the disputes were litigated, have changed significantly.

The lease as status

The status-conferring dimension of the landlord–tenant relationship is given little attention in modern land law courses. Yet, as we hope has been already observed, the leading cases have frequently been motivated by a desire on the part of the landlord to avoid legislative status and, as we shall see in due course, there are many other cases where the courts have been faced with the interaction of the general principles of landlord

---

[35] *Per* Lord Templeman in *AG Securities* v. *Vaughan* at p. 458.
[36] *Ibid.*
[37] *Per* Lord Oliver in *AG Securities* v. *Vaughan* at p. 469.
[38] 'The court lacks the knowledge and the power to form any judgment on these arguments which fall to be considered and determined by Parliament. The duty of the court is to enforce the Acts...' *per* Lord Templeman in *ibid.* at 459.

and tenant law with specific statutory provisions that apply to certain kinds of lease. The landlord–tenant relationship does not exist within a vacuum, it exists within a factual context, and the type of property let (a house, a flat, a farm, an office), for instance, will make considerable differences to the legal regime applicable. There is insufficient space here to do justice to the multifarious forms of statutory intervention in the landlord–tenant relationship. However, it may be useful to mention three particular areas in an attempt to show how the legal background has moved on, even since the days of *Street* v. *Mountford*, to illustrate why it is that private sector residential landlords have changed their practices, and to compare the operation of principle in the residential sector of property with that in the commercial field.

Part I of the Housing Act 1988 came into force on 15 January 1989, less than four years after the decision in *Street* v. *Mountford*. The Conservative government had taken the view that the decline in the private rented sector of residential property was attributable to the impact of rent control, and that any revival would require landlords to obtain a commercial return for their investment.[39] The 1988 Act sought to phase out the Rent Acts by providing that tenancies granted after the legislation came into force would be taken out of the operation of the Acts altogether. Instead, a new regime of letting, known as the 'assured tenancy', would apply to them, pursuant to which landlords could charge whatever rent the tenant agreed to pay.[40] The assured tenant was given statutory security and a limited form of succession on death was also enacted. Eight years later, by the Housing Act 1996, the statutory security of private sector tenants was dealt a further blow. As from 28 February 1997, any new tenancy was to take effect as an 'assured shorthold tenancy', unless the parties expressly agreed otherwise, under which the landlord can recover possession once any fixed term has expired by giving notice of a sufficient length. The legislative matrix is extremely convoluted, but the sum effect is clear. Since the enactment of the Housing Act 1988 there has been a highly significant diminution in the statutory rights of the tenant of residential property in the private sector. The spectre of the Rent Acts, which cast a long shadow over residential lettings, has been vanquished, and market forces are now allowed to prevail. Over the course of the last decade, private sector landlords have ceased to care whether they grant tenancies or licences.

The Rent Acts have not entirely disappeared from the picture. Indeed, their continued existence is in some way a tribute to the potency of the

---

[39] Housing: The Government's Proposals (1987), Cm 214.

[40] Although the Court of Appeal has recently shown a readiness to reject escalating rent provisions where the term is not seriously intended to be acted upon the parties, but has been included to facilitate the recovery of possession by the landlord: *Bankway Properties Ltd* v. *Penfold-Dunsford* [2002] 1 WLR 1369. See Bright [2002] CLJ 146.

statutory rights they conferred. Not only did the Rent Act-regulated tenant obtain the benefits of rent control and excellent statutory security, which made it very difficult for landlords to recover possession, the tenant's immediate family also enjoyed important rights to succeed to the regulated tenancy on death of the incumbent tenant. Thus in 1999, over a decade after the death knell of the Rent Acts was sounded, the House of Lords was faced with a claim to succeed to a Rent Act-regulated tenancy in the celebrated case of *Fitzpatrick* v. *Sterling Housing Association*.[41] However, the impact of rent control is now far less severe on landlords of such property which continues to be regulated under the Rent Acts, the Court of Appeal having held, in two important decisions, that a rent officer or rent assessment committee determining the 'fair rent' of a dwelling should take account not only of rents on properties which were let on regulated tenancies but also of rents on properties let on assured tenancies (in other words, 'open market' rents).[42] The effect of these decisions was that certain tenants, whose rents were previously registered at levels well below the market rent, were faced with sharp and unexpected increases in the rent payable. The government reacted by imposing a maximum limit on rent increases by statutory instrument based on index-linking.[43] Following a successful challenge to the legitimacy of this delegated legislation before the Court of Appeal, the House of Lords held, in December 2000, that it was lawful, and the relevant order is now to be treated as being in force.[44] It remains the case, however, that over the next few years the substantial difference between rents of properties let under the different regimes will be gradually eroded.

The public sector of housing has never been subjected to the regime of the Rent Acts, as it was for many years assumed that local authorities would act in the interests of their rate-paying tenants and not be influenced by unseemly market forces. Council tenants were therefore left to resort to public law remedies in cases where they fell into dispute with their local authority landlords over matters such as the negotiation of council rents.[45] The systematic conferment of security of tenure on public sector tenants was initiated by Margaret Thatcher's first Conservative administration, contemporaneously with its highly publicised promotion

---

[41] [2001] 1 AC 27.

[42] *Spath Holme Ltd* v. *Manchester & Lancashire Rent Assessment Committee* [1995] 2 EGLR 80, *Curtis* v. *London Rent Assessment Committee* [1999] QB 92.

[43] Rent Acts (Maximum Fair Rent) Order 1999 (SI 1999 No. 69).

[44] *R* v. *Secretary of State for the Environment, Transport and the Regions, ex parte Spath Holme Ltd* [2001] AC 349. The order was made pursuant to powers reserved in Landlord and Tenant Act 1985, s. 31.

[45] There has never been any systematic regulation of public sector rents, aggrieved tenants having to rely on the somewhat cumbersome processes of judicial review: *Wandsworth LBC* v. *Winder* [1985] AC 461.

of the tenant's right to buy the reversion of their landlord.[46] Thus there arose, in the public sector, the status of 'secure tenant', conferring security of tenure, rights to exchange tenancies, and succession rights on death.[47]

The numerous systems of security operative in both private and public sectors of housing have been criticised as being unnecessarily complex, and as contributing to cost and delay in the courts. The case for reform and codification has been strong for some years, and Lord Woolf recommended in 1996 that a review of housing law should be carried out by the Law Commission 'with a view to consolidating the various statutory and other provisions in a clear and straightforward form'. The law reform process is now in train.[48] A 'Scoping Paper' was published by the Law Commission in March 2001, heralding a 'comprehensive review' of housing law, leading to the development of law reform proposals for its simplification and modernisation. The first Consultation Paper[49] contains highly significant provisional proposals for the promulgation of a new scheme providing for the security of residential occupiers in the public and private sectors.

Where the commercial sector of lettings is concerned, statutory protection is given to tenants by virtue of Part II of the Landlord and Tenant Act 1954.[50] This legislation was initially enacted to provide business tenants with some security beyond that conferred by the lease, as it was felt to be in the interests of the economy as a whole.[51] It applies to 'any tenancy where the property comprised in the tenancy is or includes premises which are occupied by the tenant and are so occupied for the purposes of a business carried on by him or for those and other purposes'.[52] 'Business' is widely defined to include a trade, profession or employment, and it includes any activity carried on by a body of persons, whether corporate or unincorporate.[53] Part II of the 1954 Act does not interfere with the terms freely negotiated between landlord and tenant – there is no rent control machinery. However, the landlord's right to recover possession is restricted by the statute, which directs that a business tenancy 'shall not come to an end' unless it is terminated in accordance with the provisions of the Act.[54] Thus, a fixed-term tenancy will continue by force of statute on its contractual expiry date provided that the tenant does not cease to occupy the premises for business purposes.

[46] Housing Act 1980.

[47] The provisions are now to be found in the Housing Act 1985, Parts IV and V.

[48] See the Law Commission's 35th *Annual Report*, 2000, para. 1.46 and text below.

[49] Law Commission Consultation Paper No. 162, *Renting Homes 1: Status and Security*.

[50] For the proposed reform of this statute, currently subject to a consultation exercise, see text below.

[51] For an excellent short history of statutory control of business tenancies, see Haley (1999) 19 LS 207.

[52] Landlord and Tenant Act 1954, s. 23 (1).

[53] Ibid., s. 23 (2).

[54] Ibid., s. 24 (1).

It remains possible for the landlord to terminate the lease by forfeiture, and for the tenant to terminate by giving notice or by surrender, but otherwise the special statutory machinery must be used. This requires the landlord to give not less than six nor more than 12 months' notice in the statutorily prescribed form (the 's. 25 notice') to expire not earlier than the date when the tenancy could have been determined by notice to quit, or would have expired.[55] The tenant may respond to such a notice by claiming a new tenancy.[56] On application by the tenant for a new tenancy, the landlord can oppose only on certain statutory grounds.[57] The court has jurisdiction to determine the terms of any new tenancy that is granted, and will exercise that jurisdiction utilising its discretion within certain statutory parameters, which limits the maximum length of the term of the new tenancy to 14 years.[58] Contracting out of the 1954 Act is expressly prohibited.[59] It will be no surprise that landlords of commercial property have from time to time attempted to confer licences rather than leases, on the basis that a licence would not confer the statutory rights enjoyed by business tenants and that recovery of possession would ultimately be rendered considerably simpler. Courts have usually striven to frustrate such attempts, and in doing so have adopted the rigorous approach endorsed by the House of Lords in *Street* v. *Mountford*.[60] Unlike the residential tenancy legislation, however, the 1954 Act does provide a means of contracting out by obtaining the sanction of the court. This somewhat unusual procedure, which applies only where the tenancy to be granted is 'for a term of years certain',[61] requires the parties to make a joint application, and the court to give its blessing, prior to the lease being executed.[62] It has been criticised. The function of the court in hearing applications is unclear, and it is sometimes very difficult for parties to a commercial transaction to fit a court application, with the litigation and other risks involved, into the tight timetable for completion of the lease.

[55] Ibid., s. 25.
[56] This requires the tenant to give written notice to the landlord that he or she is not willing to give up possession of the premises, and to apply to the court for a new tenancy not less than two nor more than four months after receipt of the s. 25 notice: 1954 Act., ss. 25 (5), 29 (2), (3).
[57] *Ibid.*, s. 30.
[58] *Ibid.*, s. 33.
[59] *Ibid.*, s. 38.
[60] *London & Associated Investment Trust Plc* v. *Calow* [1986] 2 EGLR 80; *Vandersteen* v. *Agius* (1993) 65 P & CR 266. *cf. R (National Car Parks Ltd) v Trinity Development Co (Banbury) Ltd*, Court of Appeal, October 18 2001; [2001] 2 EGLR 43, HH Judge Rich QC.
[61] It has been recently decided, resolving an issue of some doubt, that this phrase includes fixed-term tenancies containing a break clause exercisable by either or both parties: *Metropolitan Police District Receiver* v. *Palacegate Properties Ltd* [2001] Ch 131 at 139; [2000] 3 All ER 663 at 669.
[62] Landlord and Tenant Act 1954, s. 38 (4).

Assuming that both parties are entering the agreement with full awareness of its legal consequences (ideally by proof of receipt of independent legal advice), does the excursion to court serve any real purpose? The court is not empowered nor entitled to consider the fairness of the bargain the parties propose to make, nor is the provision intended to give the court the right to dictate to the parties what the terms of the lease should be.[63]

The business tenancy legislation was reviewed by the Law Commission in 1992.[64] The report concluded that the legislation generally worked well, and provided an effective code regulating the security of the tenant with regard to commercial leases. Although certain reforms were then proposed, no action was taken until November 2000, when an announcement was made by the DETR that they intended to consult on the possible implementation of detailed improvements to Part II of the Landlord and Tenant Act 1954. A consultation paper was then published,[65] which made clear that the reforms being contemplated flowed substantially from the 1992 Law Commission report.[66] The reforms are detailed and, if enacted,[67] will radically transform the way in which commercial leases are negotiated and litigated. The most significant proposal involves the facilitation of contracting out of the legislative machinery. The requirement that parties obtain the prior sanction of the court has been much criticised as serving little obvious purpose,[68] and the government now proposes that it would be possible to contract out provided that the lease contained a prominent 'health warning' informing the tenant about the consequences of giving up the statutory rights of renewal and that a written acknowledgement was then signed by the tenant to the effect that he or she had read and understood this statement. While this reform will clearly be welcomed by those negotiating commercial leases, it remains to be seen whether the government's desire that 'most business tenants should continue to enjoy security of tenure' will be frustrated by the ease with which such a procedure can be utilised. If use of the 'health warning' becomes routine as parties (in particular landlords) realise that the statute provides no more than a purely voluntary code, the significance of Part II of the

---

[63] *Metropolitan Police District Receiver* v. *Palacegate Properties Ltd* [2001] Ch 131 at 138; [2000] 3 All ER 663 at 668 *per* Pill LJ.

[64] *Business Tenancies: A Periodic Review of the Landlord and Tenant Act 1954, Part II*, Law Com No. 208.

[65] *Business Tenancies Legislation in England and Wales – Consultation Paper*, available on the Internet at http://www.planning.detr.gov.uk/conindex.htm

[66] Law Com No. 208.

[67] It is currently intended to promulgate the reforms by use of the order-making procedure recently instigated by the Regulatory Reform Act 2001.

[68] See, most recently, the comments of the Court of Appeal in *Metropolitan Police District Receiver* v. *Palacegate Properties Ltd* [2001] Ch 131; [2000] 3 All ER 663.

Landlord and Tenant Act 1954 will be much diminished and the proposals for the streamlining of the statutory machinery extensively set out in the remainder of the consultation paper will have limited impact. Long experience in the area of landlord and tenant law has shown that to allow the ready qualification or restriction of status by contract will result in the exploitation of the commercially weaker party whom Parliament had intended to protect. The amendment currently contemplated, if it takes effect, will give landlords the upper hand, and it is possible that the proportion of commercial leases to which the statute applies may fall. The return to the free market, and the respect thereby accorded to contractual autonomy, will reduce still further the significance of status.

The agricultural lease has the longest history of statutory security. In a recent move that parallels that in the residential sector, there has been an application of market ethos, and the system of security carefully built around the 'agricultural holding' has been dismantled in favour of the 'farm business tenancy'. The Agricultural Holdings Act 1986 broadly applies to tenancies beginning before 1 September 1995, whereas those entered into on or after that date will fall within the jurisdiction of the Agricultural Tenancies Act 1995. The 1986 Act rendered mandatory one year's notice to quit as a precondition to recovering possession of the holding, and prevented the operation of notices to quit save in certain statutorily prescribed cases. This legislation incited landlords to attempt to avoid its impact, and some devices were well recognised and indeed accepted by the courts.[69] However, a simple statement that the tenant was not able to invoke the protective legislation (by serving a counter-notice on the landlord in response to the notice to quit) was held to be ineffective,[70] and the courts were prepared to strike down shams and collusive arrangements with third parties designed to obviate the protection the statute had intended to accord to the tenant.[71] As with residential tenancies, the incentive to avoid the legislative machinery has now disappeared following the relaxation of the consequences for landlords. The landlord who grants a farm business tenancy can recover possession as of right by giving the appropriate degree of notice.[72]

In the leading case of *Johnson* v. *Moreton*,[73] the House of Lords conducted an illuminating analysis of the rationale for intervening with parties' freely negotiated agreements where the consequence of uphold-

---

[69] For instance, a fixed-term tenancy for more than one year but less than two years fell within a legislative lacuna, giving rise to the so-called *Gladstone* v. *Bower* tenancy: *Gladstone* v. *Bower* [1960] 2 QB 384, sanctioned post-*Street* v. *Mountford* in *EWP Ltd* v. *Moore* [1992] QB 460.

[70] *Johnson* v. *Moreton* [1980] AC 37.

[71] See, in particular, *Gisborne* v. *Burton* [1989] QB 390.

[72] Agricultural Tenancies Act 1995, s. 6.

[73] [1980] AC 37.

ing them would be the frustration of the very objectives of the legislature. The tenant, who had entered into a lease of a farm for a term of ten years, had covenanted that he would give possession of the farm immediately upon determination of the term and that he would not serve a counter-notice or take any other steps to claim the benefit of any statutory provision granting security of tenure. Their Lordships held that the tenant could not by the terms of the agreement deprive himself of the opportunity to exercise his statutory rights. There was a public interest which Parliament had clearly identified and which the agricultural holdings legislation was intended to protect 'for the sake of the soil and husbandry of England of which both landlord and tenant are in a moral, though not of course a legal, sense the trustees for posterity'.[74] Nowhere is there a stronger assertion of the pre-eminence of statutory protection over contractual autonomy, the famous speech of Lord Simon of Glaisdale being articulate, perceptive and humane:[75]

> Generally, a man became a tenant rather than an owner-occupier because his circumstances compelled him to live hand-to-mouth; the landlord's purse was generally longer and his command of knowledge and counsel far greater than the tenant's. In short, it was held, the constriction of the market and the inequality of bargaining power enabled the landlord to dictate contractual terms which did not necessarily operate to the general benefit of society. It was to counteract this descried constriction of the market and to redress this descried inequality of bargaining power that the law – specifically in the shape of legislation, came to intervene repeatedly to modify freedom of contract between landlord and tenant. Since Maine, the movement of many 'progressive' societies has been reversed.
>
> The movement from status to contract was largely a creature of the common law. The reverse movement has been largely a creature of legislation. As a result lawyers sometimes tend to regard freedom and sanctity of contract as still of special and supervening juristic value. But freedom of contract and its consequences are quite likely to be 'mischiefs' as that word is used in statutory construction.

Much has changed in the 20 years since *Johnson* v. *Moreton*. It can be seen, with the benefit of hindsight that, in its overt hostility to attempts to contract out of protective legislation, *Street* v. *Mountford* was the high-water mark for status. Since then, with the phasing out of Rent Act protection in the residential sphere, the widespread invocation of essentially 'contrac-tual' assured shorthold tenancies and the commercialisation of agricultural lettings, the movement has been very much back in the direction of contract. The enactment of the proposed reforms to the business tenancy legislation will be a further step along the road to a free market.

[74] *Ibid. per* Lord Hailsham at 59.
[75] *Ibid.* at 66 *et seq.*

The lease as contract

The lease is an estate the duration of which is determined by the agreement of the landlord and the tenant. Thus the lease is both an estate and a contract. The extent to which the contractual aspect of the lease can influence and affect other legal consequences of the leasehold relationship has been placed in sharp focus in recent years. Although the lease has always been viewed as a somewhat amphibious concept, as suggested by its one-time categorisation in the list of 'chattels real', the contractual flavour of the lease was traditionally of less significance than its property dimension. Once the tenant had been granted the legal estate, it was felt that the contract had been completed, and so the estate rather than the contract then governed the ensuing relationship. This was exemplified by certain speeches in *Leighton's Investment Trust Ltd* v. *Cricklewood Property and Investment Trust Ltd*[76] denying the applicability of the contractual doctrine of frustration to leases generally. The effect of the dominance of the estate over the contract was to limit not only doctrines but also remedies. While certain remedies were viewed as distinctive incidents of the landlord–tenant relationship, such as distress for non-payment of rent and forfeiture (with its associated discretion to relieve tenants and others from the consequences of breach of covenant), other more general remedies were not considered to be available. The essential preoccupation of the law of leases was with the 'possession–rent' relationship.[77] The landlord 'granted' exclusive possession of the land to the tenant, and 'reserved' rent to be payable out of the land in return. While the language of the lease might take the form of contract (the tenant covenanting to pay the rent), the essence of the relationship was proprietary, and little concern was expressed for the fulfilment of the parties' contractual expectations.

Yet, as has been seen in the USA, the influx of contractual thinking can have enormous influence on the definition and development of the rights of residential tenants. In *Javins* v. *First National Realty Corp.*,[78] the landlord argued that the common law implied no conditions as to the fitness or repair of demised premises, and that in the absence of express obligations in the lease document itself the landlord was under no liability to maintain the condition of the property: *caveat emptor*. The District of Columbia Court of Appeals held that the common law rule was obsolete in the light of the realities of modern living. A residential lease was not for the use of land as such, but for the occupation of a habitable dwelling with the services one would expect. A lease of a dwelling-house or flat should be equated to a consumer contract, and it was consistent with

[76] [1943] KB 493.
[77] Bright and Gilbert, p.78 et seq.
[78] (1970) 138 App DC 369.

modern attitudes to the protection of consumer expectations that the landlord should warrant the habitability of the premises in question. Moreover, breach of the warranty would give rise to contractual remedies against the landlord:

> Stripped to its essentials, the doctrine rejects the premise that a lease is only a transfer of land to be governed by special principles of real property law. Instead, the implied warranty of habitability theory treats the transfer of the demised premises as analogous to a sale of goods, and protects the expectations of the landlord and the tenant by applying ordinary notions of contract law including mutual dependency of lease covenants.[79]

The application of contractual doctrine to leases by the English courts has been somewhat more hesitant, and certainly less exuberant. In *Liverpool City Council* v. *Irwin*,[80] decided by the House of Lords in 1976, a landlord local authority had no formal document of lease detailing the respective rights and obligations of the parties, but merely sent each of its tenants a list of 'conditions' by which the tenant was to abide. A tenant of a flat complained about the state and condition of the common parts of the block in which they were living, and stopped paying rent in protest. Lord Wilberforce applied orthodox contractual doctrine in determining whether any repairing obligations should be implied into the parties' agreement. The tenant had rights, in the nature of easements, to use the stairs, the lifts and the rubbish chutes, and the landlord was therefore under an obligation to take reasonable care to keep those parts of the premises in a condition of reasonable repair and usability. This conclusion was reached by reading into the contract such obligations as the nature of the contract implicitly requires: 'a test, in other words, of necessity.' The potential for development of the *Irwin* decision was undoubted, but it was not fully realised, the English judges, for the most part less proactive than their American counterparts, being quite understandably reluctant to innovate in areas where Parliament had legislated. Thus in *Quick* v. *Taff Ely BC*,[81] the Court of Appeal emphasised the limitations of the current statute-based liability of landlords to repair residential premises, in particular that there is no generally applicable obligation on a landlord of residential property to ensure that the property is fit for human habitation during the currency of the lease. At the same time, the court indicated, in no uncertain terms, that this was an area ripe for reform. Although the Law Commission made important proposals in 1996 in its *Report on Responsibility for the State and Condition of Property*, invocation of the legislative process has yet to ensue.[82]

---

[79] Schoshinski, *American Law of Landlord and Tenant*, p.123 (3:16).
[80] [1977] AC 239.
[81] [1986] QB 809, construing the Landlord and Tenant Act 1985, ss. 8, 11.
[82] Law Com No. 238, noted by the current author in [1996] Conv. 342.

In 1980, the decision of the House of Lords in *National Carriers* v. *Panalpina*[83] held that the doctrine of frustration applied to leases as to any other contracts. In doing so, a purposive view of the lease was taken, as in *Irwin*, looking at the type of the letting, the surrounding circumstances and the parties' contractual expectations. The contemplated use of the property was again recognised. It was, according to Lord Simon of Glaisdale, not realistic to argue that:

> on execution of the lease the lessee got all that he bargained for. The reality is that this lessee, for example, bargained, not for a term of years, but for the use of a warehouse owned by the lessor, just as a demise charterer bargains for the use of this ship.[84]

Their Lordships also rejected the argument that once the estate was granted, the contract was fully executed and therefore no longer capable of frustration: 'a lease is partly executory: rights and obligations remain outstanding on both sides throughout its currency.' But this was not to say that frustration would be easy to establish. On the contrary, in taking a broad view of the contract, it was necessary for the court to consider the long-term nature of the relationship which the parties may have initially envisaged. On the facts in *Panalpina*, access to the warehouse which was the subject matter of the lease was rendered impossible for a period of just over 18 months as a result of a local authority order closing the street. However, at the time of the closure the lease had nearly five years to run and, out of the ten-year term, less than two years of use would have been lost in total. This did not therefore amount to frustration of the lease.

Irwin and *Panalpina* may not seem ground-breaking decisions. The former was subsequently found to be of strictly limited application, as the courts showed considerable reluctance to trespass upon the statutory realm of repairing liabilities. The latter was important in asserting that frustration could apply, but it was admitted that its operation would be minimal in view of the long-term nature of the leasehold relationships involved. But the mould had been broken, and in the years that followed, arguments based on the contractualisation of leases came thick and fast. The advantages of applying contractual doctrine and remedies were clear in terms of flexibility, allowing the parties the ability to dictate the terms of their relationship, and enforcing those terms in the most effective way.

A third House of Lords decision to give effect to a contract-based approach was *Hammersmith & Fulham LBC* v. *Monk*.[85] The question that arose was whether a notice to quit given by one of two joint tenants was effective to determine the lease. Adopting a property analysis of the lease, it can be strongly argued that the two joint tenants should act jointly in

[83] [1981] AC 675.
[84] *Ibid.*, at 705.
[85] [1992] 1 AC 478.

giving notice to determine their right to exclusive possession of the flat. As joint tenants, they are treated by the outside world as if they were a single owner, and therefore to discontinue the tenancy would require the will of both (or all) the joint tenants. If the lease was viewed as contract, the unilateral decision by one tenant to remove himself from liability for the rent and other covenants should be respected.[86] The House of Lords, in holding that a notice by one joint tenant was indeed sufficient to terminate the lease, adopted a contract-based approach, emphasising that a lease should be treated no differently from any other kind of contract: 'As a matter of principle I see no reason why this question should receive any different answer in the context of the contractual relationship of landlord and tenant than that it would receive in any other contractual context.'[87] One remedy that could be extremely useful, particularly for tenants, was terminating the lease in response to a serious 'repudiatory' breach of covenant by the landlord. It would be most unlikely that the lease, drafted no doubt by the landlord, would contain such a right, although it would of course allow the landlord to forfeit and re-enter in the event of non-payment of rent or breach of covenant by the tenant. In *Hussain* v. *Mehlman*,[88] Stephen Sedley QC, as he then was,[89] held that a tenant could respond to the landlord's failure to comply with, in this case, statutory repairing obligations by terminating the tenancy, giving up vacant possession and returning the keys to the landlord. Such action would thereupon extinguish the tenant's future rental liability. This historic decision, albeit arrived at in the county court, is tightly reasoned and is based on an essentially contractual vision of the residential tenancy. The Court of Appeal has given its express sanction to this radical approach, which has been applied in the context of commercial as well as residential leases.[90]

The process of contractualisation of leases was now growing apace. Frustration, rescission for fraud, termination for breach, implication of terms for business efficacy (contractual doctrines all) have been applied in recent years to leases, unobjectionably in my view, on the ground that a lease is as much a contract as an estate.[91] But the *coup de grace*, or some might say the *reductio ad absurdum*, of the contractualists, was to come in

---

[86] See in particular Lord Browne-Wilkinson at 491–492.

[87] *Ibid. per* Lord Bridge at 483.

[88] [1992] 2 EGLR 87.

[89] The successful counsel for the respondent local authority in *Monk*, Stephen Sedley QC, has since been elevated to the judiciary and is currently a member of the Court of Appeal.

[90] *Re Olympic & York Canary Wharf Ltd* (No 2) [1993] BCC 159 at 166; *Kingston upon Thames RLBC* v. *Marlow* [1996] 1 EGLR 101 at 102; *Chartered Trust plc* v. *Davies* [1997] 2 EGLR 83; *Nynehead Developments Ltd* v. *R.H. Fibreboard Containers Ltd* [1999] 1 EGLR 7.

[91] See also the central role assumed by contract in the future version of the landlord-occupier relationship in Law Commission Consultation Paper No 162, *Renting Home*, 1.32 et seq, Part VI.

the decision of the House of Lords in *Bruton* v. *London & Quadrant Housing Trust*.[92] A lease is a contract, and it may be nothing more than a contract. It need not be an estate at all.

A local authority granted a charitable housing trust a licence to use a block of flats (which had been compulsorily acquired) to provide short-term accommodation for the homeless. No estate or interest in the land was granted to the defendant trust. The defendants then entered into a written agreement with the plaintiff for occupation of a flat in the block. The agreement, which purported to confer a 'weekly licence' on the plaintiff, explained the arrangement with the council and expressed a condition that the plaintiff would vacate upon receiving reasonable notice from the defendants of 'not normally less than four weeks'. The plaintiff also agreed to allow the defendants, their staff and agents access 'at all times during normal working hours... for all purposes connected with the work of the trust'. Seven years after entering into occupation, the plaintiff brought proceedings in the county court claiming damages against the defendant trust for breach of the covenant to repair implied by statute[93] into leases of dwelling-houses for a term of less than seven years. The defendant raised as a preliminary issue that the plaintiff occupied as a licensee and did not have a lease. Successful in this contention before the county court and the Court of Appeal,[94] the defendants lost before the House of Lords.

Lord Hoffman, giving the leading speech, held that the agreement conferred exclusive possession on the occupier. Under normal *Street* v. *Mountford* principles, therefore, this would be a tenancy unless 'special circumstances' could be shown. Lord Hoffman rightly rejected the defendant's argument that the identity of the landlord, or its agreement with the council not to grant tenancies, or the plaintiff's agreement that he was not to be a tenant, comprised 'special circumstances'. But he went on to hold, much more controversially, that the defendant's lack of any property interest in the land was immaterial. Although the defendant trust could not grant a legal estate in the land, the plaintiff had nevertheless obtained a lease in the flat.

Lord Hoffmann advanced two arguments in support of this result. First, the term 'lease' (or 'tenancy') refers to a bilateral relationship between the landlord and the tenant, and nothing more:

> It is not concerned with the question of whether the agreement creates an estate or other proprietary interest which may be binding upon third parties. A lease may, and usually does, create a proprietary interest called a leasehold estate or, technically, a 'term of years absolute'. This will depend upon whether

---

[92] [2000] 1 AC 406. For comment and criticism, see Bright (2000) 116 LQR 7; Dixon [2000] CLJ 25; Rook [1999] Conv. 517.

[93] Landlord and Tenant Act 1985, s. 11.

[94] [1998] QB 834, [1997] 4 All ER 970, Kennedy and Millett LJ, Sir Brian Neill dissenting.

the landlord had an interest out of which he could grant it. Nemo dat quod non habet. But it is the fact that the agreement is a lease which creates the proprietary interest. It is putting the cart before the horse to say that whether the agreement is a lease depends upon whether it creates a proprietary interest.[95]

This has been aptly described as advancing a 'relative' or 'relational' concept of exclusive possession, pursuant to which the court asks simply whether the occupier has exclusive possession as against their immediate landlord.[96] By adopting this focused approach, it is possible to concentrate on the two parties to the contract and to disregard wider issues such as capacity to grant a proprietary interest. But its undoubted effect is to recognise that an agreement which does not confer an estate in the property can nevertheless be a lease. This kind of lease, being non-proprietary, is unique.

Lord Hoffmann held that a tenancy also arose by virtue of estoppel. Here, the articulation of principle ('it is not the estoppel which creates the tenancy, but the tenancy which creates the estoppel') is unexceptionable.[97] But its application to the facts of the case is. While it may be necessary for there to be a tenancy to create the estoppel, there was no tenancy in *Bruton*, for the reasons given above. There are two accepted circumstances in which a tenancy by estoppel may arise. The estoppel may be by deed (the grantor being precluded from disputing the validity of his or her grant[98]), or by representation (the grantor being estopped by an unambiguous and material representation as to his or her title on the strength of which the tenant takes a lease[99]). The facts of *Bruton* cannot be forced into either analysis. The trust took great care to communicate the limited nature of their interest in the flat to the plaintiff, and throughout the agreement referred to him only as a licensee. The trust had never purported to grant the plaintiff a tenancy – on the contrary.[100]

---

[95] [2000] 1 AC 406. at 415.

[96] See Bright (2000) 116 LQR 7.

[97] For subsequent citation by way of approval, see *Wroe (t/a Telepower)* v. *Exmos Cover Ltd* [2000] EGLR 66.

[98] *First National Bank plc* v. *Thompson* [1996] Ch 231 at 237.

[99] See Harpum, *Megarry & Wade: The Law of Real Property*, 6th ed., 2000, Sweet & Maxwell, para. 14.095.

[100] Millett LJ set out the position lucidly in the Court of Appeal: 'In the present case both parties knew that the trust had no title and could not grant a tenancy. That is not sufficient to prevent the creation of a tenancy by estoppel. But the trust did not purport to grant a tenancy. The document was carefully drawn by the trust and accepted by Mr Bruton as a licence. There is no inconsistency between the terms of the document and the trust's assertion that it has not granted a tenancy. There is no ground for holding that the parties must be taken to have adopted an assumed basis for the transaction. They did not agree that the trust should grant a tenancy even though it had no title; they agreed that it should grant a licence because it could not grant a tenancy.'

Lord Jauncey, supporting Lord Hoffmann, felt persuaded by the result of the Court of Appeal decision in *Family Housing Association* v. *Jones*,[101] where on similar facts 'special circumstances' were found not to exist. However, counsel for the landlord in *Jones* did not argue the significance of the landlord having no title: it was decided on the basis that the identity and function of the particular landlord did not prevent the grant of a tenancy on the facts of the particular case – a perfectly satisfactory application of reasoning to the arguments that were advanced.[102] Lord Hoffmann's dismissal of counsel for the defendant's argument in *Bruton* that *Jones* was therefore immaterial is cursory. The failure to advance an argument along the lines of *Bruton* in the earlier case was, according to Lord Hoffman, 'easily explained by the fact that the grantor's title or lack of title was irrelevant to the issue in the case'.[103]

The one speech that takes a slightly different tack is that of Lord Hobhouse. As befits a commercial judge, he adopts what might be described as a 'contractual' approach. The claim was to enforce a contractual course of action. The existence of a contractual relationship of landlord and tenant sufficed to trigger the statutory implication of the repairing covenant. The housing trust had capacity to enter into the contractual agreement. No problem arose from the fact that the trust had no legal estate, as no interest was being asserted by the plantiff against any third party to the agreement. Lord Hobhouse's speech does not satisfactorily answer the objections already outlined, but it may indicate a possible way for future courts to deal with the precedent set by *Bruton*. Indeed, on policy grounds – that a landlord should not be able to escape statutorily repairing obligations by denying that they had capacity to grant a tenancy – the decision is perfectly acceptable. As a precedent it is much more difficult, as it creates a hybrid interest of a seemingly non-proprietary nature, the full implications of which we will only come to understand and appreciate with its further judicial exposition.[104]

Prior to *Bruton*, one would have thought that the conferment of a proprietary interest was absolutely essential to the characterisation of an agreement as a lease. The bare minima of a lease would have seemed to be the grant of exclusive possession for a term, and the capacity to make a grant of exclusive possession in the absolute sense (so that the tenant can defend his or her possession against all-comers) of the very essence. In an earlier House of Lords decision, *Prudential Assurance Co Ltd* v. *London Residuary Body*,[105] an attack was made on the necessity for the 'term' of a lease to fulfil the requirement of certainty. Previous cases had held that it

---

[101] [1990] 1 WLR 779, [1990] 1 All ER 385.

[102] Although compare the subsequent decision of the House of Lords in *Westminster City Council* v. *Clarke* [1992] 2 AC 288, [1992] 1 All ER 695.

[103] At p.414.

[104] See Bright (2000) 116 LQR 7 at 9.

[105] [1992] 2 AC 386.

must be possible to say, at the beginning of a lease, when it would terminate by effluxion of time.[106] However, despite argument that the contractual autonomy of the parties should be respected and their freely negotiated agreement duly enforced, the House of Lords held that the principle must prevail. This assertion of the power of property law to limit the extent to which parties can modify property interests was welcomed in some quarters.[107] Most conveyancers would agree that freedom of contract must occasionally be sacrificed on the altar of property, and Lord Templeman did not seem unduly concerned by the consequences of applying strict property principles to the facts before him. However, Lord Browne-Wilkinson, while accepting that under the current law it was necessary for an effective lease to satisfy tests of certainty, considered that the result in *Prudential Assurance* was unsatisfactory, and proposed that the issue should be referred to the Law Commission so that it could contemplate future reform.[108] The decision in *Bruton* presents a further challenge for those who believe that the division between contract and property should be clear and easily drawn.

Covenant: the lease as contract and property

As we have seen, the lease is a method of disposition of land, and it offers investment opportunities in providing, in exchange for exclusive possession for a defined period of time, a commercial return by way of income (in the form of rent) and possibly also capital (a premium paid at the time of grant). But the popularity of the lease can also be attributed to another factor. If a freehold estate is sold, the purchaser or vendor may make covenants concerning the future use of the land. Those covenants may be enforced by and against the original parties to them pursuant to their contract and, in so far as the covenant touches and concerns the land and is restrictive of the use to which the burdened land is to be put, they may also be enforced, traditionally by way of injunction, against successors in title.[109] Positive covenants do not, however, 'run with the land'.[110] Thus it is extremely difficult to enforce covenants requiring successors in title to maintain the condition of their property, a potentially very serious problem where housing developments or industrial estates are concerned.[111] The lease, on the other hand, makes use of the wider

---

[106] *Lace* v. *Chantler* [1944] KB 368.

[107] Sparkes (1993) 109 LQR 93.

[108] *Prudential Assurance Co Ltd* v. *London Residuary Body* [1992] 2 AC 386 at 396.

[109] *Tulk* v. *Moxhay* (1848) 2 Ph 774.

[110] *Rhone* v. *Stephens* [1994] 2 AC 310.

[111] The current Commonhold and Leasehold Reform Bill, if enacted, will introduce a 'commonhold' system into which parties can contract. This will facilitate the mutual enforcement of covenants between the relevant parties.

doctrine of privity of estate, which enables both restrictive and positive covenants to be enforced by and against those who succeed to the original parties to the landlord–tenant relationship. Thus for centuries covenants have been given a proprietary effect, subject only to the proviso that the covenant in question had a proprietary flavour that, in legal parlance, it 'touched and concerned' the land. This doctrine has led to the widespread use of leases, not only in the disposition of flats and other forms of housing development., but also in the case of commercial property.

The enforceability of leasehold covenants by and against parties to the lease and their successors in title is based upon the twin notions of privity of estate and privity of contract. By the doctrine of privity of contract, the original landlord and the original tenant bind themselves to comply with their mutual obligations for the duration of the contractually agreed term. The contractual nexus may be detectable beyond the original parties who signed the lease, most significantly where landlords require assignees of the lease to covenant directly with them to comply with all the obligations of the lease for the duration of the term. By the doctrine of privity of estate, any successor in title of those original parties is bound to observe the covenants that touch and concern the land for the time during which that successor has that title. Whereas privity of contract is based on the parties' agreement, privity of estate is based on the parties' property relationship.

It has been difficult sometimes to distinguish the influences of contract and estate as litigants seek to use whichever offers the sounder basis for their arguments, and the more effective remedy for their grievance. In the notorious case of *Centrovincial Estates plc* v. *Bulk Storage Ltd*[112] the original parties had agreed a rent of £17,000 p.a. Following assignment of the lease, a subsequent tenant agreed on review that the rent should be increased to £40,000 p.a. When that tenant defaulted, the landlord sought recourse from the original tenant, and he was held liable to pay the rent at the higher rate. Harman J held that:

> each assignee is the owner of the whole estate and can deal with it, so as to alter it or its terms. The estate so altered then binds the original tenant, because the assignee has been put into the shoes of the original tenant and can do all such acts as the original tenant could have done.

In the later case of *Selous Street Properties Ltd* v. *Oronel Fabrics Ltd*,[113] this reasoning based on the vesting of power in the assignee to vary the terms of the estate was applied by Hutchison J to permit the landlord to claim against a former tenant for rent which was increased on review taking

[112] (1983) 46 P & CR 393.
[113] (1984) 270 EG 643, [1984] 1 EGLR 50.

account of alterations made to the premises by the assignee. As the tenant had assigned the lease to the assignee, it had empowered the assignee to negotiate variations to the lease. Only if those variations were so substantial as to amount to a surrender and re-grant (such that the arrangement now took effect as a new lease) would the former tenant's liability be extinguished.

In *Friends Provident Life Office* v. *British Railways Board*,[114] the Court of Appeal identified the fallacy in the reasoning of these decisions. The original tenant was bound by contract to the original landlord, and that contract remained enforceable despite the assignment of the leasehold interest. However, the variation effected by the assignee amounted to a variation of the estate, not the contract. It was the estate, not the contract, which the assignee was now empowered to deal with, and while such action might increase the liability of the assignee, or subsequent holders of the estate thus varied, it could not affect predecessors in title. Central to the analysis in *Friends Provident* is the distinction between contract and estate. As Susan Bright concisely puts it: 'The *Friends'* case at last recognises that the original tenant should be bound only by his own promises, not by later changes to the lease that were not authorised by him. Nor does he authorise later changes simply by selling the lease to the assignee.'[115]

However, the wording of the covenant may allow scope for a subsequent increase in the level of liability. Thus it is usual for a tenant entering into a lease to covenant to pay the rent as agreed and as reviewed from time to time. A landlord may then be able to enforce an increased rent against a tenant although the rent being claimed had been increased on review, or by agreement at the time of review. But where the landlord had agreed with a later tenant to vary covenants in the lease which variation was outside the reasonable contemplation of the original parties to the contract, then the obligation as varied could not be enforced against a predecessor. This was the fallacy of the *Selous Street* decision.

The judgments in *Friends Provident* were given within a week of Royal Assent being granted to the Landlord and Tenant (Covenants) Act 1995.[116] This important and complex statute, which has had huge consequences for the enforceability of leasehold covenants, focused primarily on the vicissitudes of the doctrine of privity of contract and the invidious position of former tenants and their guarantors faced by claims accruing after they had acquitted themselves of such interest as they had in the relevant property. Initially inspired by the recommendations of the

---

114 [1996] 1 All ER 336.
115 'Variation of Leases and Tenant Liability' in 'The Reform of Property Law', at p.82.
116 Note in particular s. 18, which was intended to reverse the effect of the *Selous Street* decision.

Law Commission in its *Report on Privity of Contract and Estate*,[117] the Act in its final form bears the scars of political wheeler-dealing and skullduggery which accompanied its passage through Parliament. The admirably clear notion that tenants should be released from liability once they have assigned their interest under the lease (at least with the landlord's consent) was lost in the translation, and practitioners and law students have had to deal with new concepts and devices including statutory notice procedures, authorised guarantee agreements and overriding leases. The detailed provisions of the Act have been fully explained elsewhere.[118] Its essential effect can be summarised as follows.

In relation to leases whenever granted

1.   Where a landlord wishes to recover payment of rent or any other fixed charge payable under the lease from a former tenant or a guarantor, a notice must be served on that person within six months of such sum becoming due. A failure to serve a statutory notice will be fatal to the landlord's claim, as the former tenant or guarantor will cease to be liable. This provision was intended to prevent the landlord from allowing considerable arrears of rent to accumulate prior to notifying potentially liable parties who would otherwise be wholly unaware of the nature or extent of the liability.

2.   In the event of a notice being served as above, the recipient who pays the required amount is entitled to have an overriding lease of the premises granted by the landlord. This lease will be interposed between the reversion of the landlord and the interest of the current tenant, and will have the effect that the recipient will be empowered, in most cases, to act against the defaulter, perhaps invoking a right of re-entry to recover possession and thereby facilitating dealing with the property to compensate for the losses incurred.

In relation to leases granted on or after 1 January 1996 (the date the Act came into force):

1.   On an assignment of the reversion or the term, the benefit and burden of all landlord and tenant covenants of the tenancy (and the benefit of a landlord's right of re-entry) will pass to the assignee.[119] This will occur whether the assignment is legal or equitable.[120] A

---

[117] Law Com No. 174 (29 November 1988).
[118] [1996] CLJ 313.
[119] Landlord and Tenant (Covenants) Act 1995, s. 3.
[120] s. 28 (1).

covenant that is expressed to be personal to any person cannot be enforced against any other person.[121] A restrictive covenant can be enforced against any person owning or occupying premises to which the covenant relates.[122] Thus the common law requirement that a leasehold covenant would only run if it touched and concerned the land has been abolished with prospective effect.

2.	On an assignment of the term, the tenant is released from the tenant covenants of the tenancy (and at the same time ceases to be entitled to the benefit of the landlord covenants of the tenancy). However, the tenant may be required by the landlord to enter into an 'authorised guarantee agreement' (AGA) under which the tenant will guarantee the performance of the tenant covenants by the immediate assignee. It is necessary, for an AGA to be effective, that the lease contains an absolute or qualified covenant against assignment without the consent of the landlord (or some other person) and that the landlord must impose as a condition of the grant or consent that the tenant enter into the AGA. The condition of entry into an AGA must be 'lawfully imposed' – in other words, the imposition of the condition must be reasonable in circumstances where the Landlord and Tenant Act 1927, s. 19, applies. However, in certain 'qualifying leases' the landlord will be able to insist on the tenant entering into an AGA, as the lease will have contained express provision specifying the entry into an AGA as a condition subject to which consent may be granted. The overall effect of these provisions on commercial leases is that the landlord will usually have the security of the tenant's covenant until their immediate assignee in turn assigns the term to another tenant. At that time, the immediate assignee will be required to guarantee the performance of the covenants by the new tenant pursuant to another AGA.

3.	On assignment of the reversion, there is no automatic statutory release of the landlord from the landlord covenants. However, the assigning landlord can apply to the tenant to be released by serving notice on the tenant before or within four weeks of date of the assignment. If the tenant objects to the landlord's release, it must serve a counter-notice to that effect. The landlord can then apply to the court for a declaration that it is reasonable for the release to take place. If release does occur, the landlord will at the same time cease to be entitled to the benefit of the tenant covenants.

---

[121] s. 3 (6).

[122] s. 3 (5); see *Oceanic Village Ltd* v. *United Attractions Ltd* [2000[Ch 234, noted at [2000] CLJ 450.

The decision of the Court of Appeal in *Chesterfield Properties Ltd* v. *BHP Great Britain Petroleum Ltd*[123] concerned an attempt by a landlord to deny liability for breach of covenant on the ground that a release had been effected by force of statute. BHP was granted a lease for a 20 year fixed term with effect from June 1997. By a collateral agreement, the original landlord (L1) agreed to undertake certain refurbishment works prior to the tenant going into possession and covenanted to remedy any defects arising. This latter covenant was acknowledged by the tenant to be an obligation personal to L1, although it was an obligation which could be enforced by the tenant's successors in title. Subsequently L1 assigned the reversion to L2 (its associated company) and served notice on the tenant requesting release from its obligations under the tenancy and informing the tenant that they must notify them of any objection to the release within four weeks. No such notification was given, and when the tenant brought a claim against L1 for failure to remedy allegedly defective works, L1 argued that they were no longer bound to comply with this obligation.

Both Lightman J, at first instance, and the Court of Appeal took the view that despite service of the release notice by the landlord prior to assignment of the reversion, the landlord remained liable to remedy the defective works. The procedure applied to 'landlord covenants', defined in the Act as covenants 'falling to be complied with by the landlord of premises demised by the tenancy', and 'the landlord' was defined as 'the person for the time being entitled to the reversion expectant on the term'.[124] This provision clearly contemplated release only of liability under those covenants which could be enforced by successive landlords (landlords 'for the time being'). Thus it was not possible for a landlord to invoke the release procedure with regard to personal convenants. The result was clearly just, as there was more than a hint of the landlord, in transferring the reversion to its associated company, seeking to take advantage of the statute to escape its convenanted obligations.

However, *Chesterfield Properties* does raise an issue which has been largely dormant since the enactment of the 1995 Act, namely the distinction between covenants which run with the land and those which do not. The old test, whether the covenant 'touches and concerns' the land (or, in its statutory translation, 'has reference to the subject-matter of the lease'), was abolished in relation to new leases by that Act on the ground that it was arbitrary and illogical. The new test is whether a covenant is '(in whatever terms) expressed to be personal to any person'.[125] Whereas the court has in the past been expected to decide whether a covenant, viewed objectively, 'touches and concerns' the land, the matter is now essentially one for the parties themselves. If they do not

---

[123] [2001] EWCA Civ 1797, 30 November 2001.
[124] S.28(1)
[125] S.3(6).

intend a covenant to be enforceable by or against their successors, that should be stipulated expressly in the lease. It is perfectly possible for a covenant, which is proprietary in nature, to be rendered unenforceable by or against successors, or even (as was the case in *Chesterfield Properties*)[126] enforceable one way only subsequent to assignment. 'A covenant which relates to the land may nevertheless be expressed to be personal to one or other or both of the parties to it. This is a matter for the contracting parties.'[127] Thus, there appears to be nothing to prevent the terms of the lease from stipulating that the covenant to pay rent, or to repair, is a covenant which is purely personal to the original parties and thereby to restrict its application exclusively to those parties.

The 1995 Act has been accurately described as effecting a 'sea-change' in the law affecting the tenant's liability after he assigns the lease.[128] Moreover, it has led many landlords of commercial properties to change their practices as they strive to enforce as best they can the obligations of the lease and to obtain the best possible security for the payment of the rent and the performance of the covenants. We have already seen how the landlord and tenant may specify in advance conditions subject to which licence or consent may be granted and which cannot be subsequently challenged by the tenant on the grounds of unreasonableness.[129] It has become standard for the covenant against alienation to be drafted in such a way that the landlord can require as a condition of granting consent to assignment that the assigning tenant enter into an authorised guarantee agreement. Thus when T1 assigns, with the landlord's consent, the landlord will then have the security of the new assignee (T2) and that of T1 pursuant to the AGA. This practice does not offend any of the provisions of the Act provided that the condition requiring the tenant to enter into an AGA was contained in the lease or in some other agreement made before the tenant makes application for the landlord's consent.[130]

---

[126] It was exressly stated that the landlord's personal covenant to remedy defects could be enforced by successors in title of the tenant.

[127] Per Jonathan Parker LJ, giving the judgment of the court.

[128] Per Neuberger J in *Wallis Fashion Group Ltd* v. *CGU Life Assurance Ltd* [2000] 2 EGLR 49, 52.

[129] It may be that no such conditions have been specified in advance and that the landlord is therefore in a somewhat weaker position when the tenant seeks consent to assign. It is still open to the landlord to argue for the imposition of conditions, but in each case it will be necessary for the landlord to show that the condition is 'reasonable'. If the landlord seeks to impose unreasonable conditions, there is potential liability under the Landlord and Tenant Act 1988 (see in particular section 1 thereof).

[130] Landlord and Tenant Act 1927, s. 19(1A), added by the Landlord and Tenant (Covenants) Act 1995, s. 22. This provision applies to 'qualifying leases', defined as any lease which is a new tenancy (see 1995 Act s.1) other than a residential lease, i.e. a lease by which a building or part of a building is let wholly or mainly as a single private residence.

An important related question arose in *Wallis Fashion Group Ltd* v. *CGU Life Assurance Ltd.*[131] Commercial leases negotiated and granted prior to the 1995 Act would obviously not require the tenant to enter into an AGA on assignment. Yet when a tenant now seeks renewal of such a tenancy pursuant to Part II of the Landlord and Tenant Act 1954, should the court impose a covenant against assignment in the new lease in such terms? In *Wallis Fashion*, the landlord argued that a tenancy being granted by the court pursuant to Part II of the Landlord and Tenant Act 1954 should include provision requiring as a condition of any assignment by the tenant that the tenant enter into an authorised guarantee agreement guaranteeing the liability of the immediate assignee. Neuberger J refused to include such a provision in the tenancy being granted. It was more consistent with the current lease[132] to allow a landlord the security of an AGA only if it was reasonable in the circumstances which applied at the time when consent to assignment was sought, rather than to permit the landlord to require the assignor to enter into an AGA whatever circumstances were then prevailing. Moreover, it was an unattractive contention of the landlord that he should be entitled to the benefit of a covenant in a tenancy which 'entitles him to be unreasonable'. Neuberger J did not say that a landlord will never be able to contend successfully for the new lease to contain provision entitling the landlord to an AGA as of right, as it will depend on the circumstances of each application, but it is clear that a landlord seeking to uphold such a term will have an uphill struggle.

A further problem, much discussed, but yet to be judicially decided, concerns the position of a guarantor of the original tenant. A guarantor, although not in a relationship of privity of estate with the landlord, offers an alternative means of satisfaction where the tenant fails to comply with the obligations under the lease. The 1995 Act aims to release guarantors from liability at the same time and to the same extent as the tenant whose obligations they are guaranteeing is released by the statute.[133] Is it therefore possible for the landlord to require the assigning tenant's guarantor to be a party to an authorised guarantee agreement? Although this would have the obvious advantage to the landlord of an additional defendant in the event of non-payment of rent, or other breaches of covenant by the tenant in possession, the legislation is silent and unsupportive. In particular, section 16 (which defines AGAs) appears to envisage that it is only the assigning tenant which can enter into the AGA

---

131 [2000] 2 ELGR 49.
132 See *O'May* v. *City of London Real Property Co Ltd* [1983] 2 AC 726, imposing the burden on the party seeking a departure from the terms of the current lease to justify the proposed change.
133 S. 24 (2).

with the landlord.[134] In offering landlords an opportunity of pursuing the tenant after assignment, AGAs provide an exception to the basic principle that on assignment of the lease the tenant's future liability is extinguished. Had Parliament intended to allow landlords to demand or request that contractual sureties enter into AGAs, clear wording would have been expected. [135] Looking outside the Act, the recommendations of the Law Commission which provided the catalyst for the legislation appear to limit AGAs to the assigning tenant, and there is no express affirmation that sureties could be parties to an AGA (although it should also be said that there is no express denial either).[136]

The ingenuity of solicitors advising landlords is not, however, rebuffed by simple reference to section 16. It may be that a guarantor cannot be a party to an AGA as such, but there may be other ways in which they can be compelled to provide the desired security. One possibility, discussed at length in the practitioner periodicals, is an agreement of sub-guarantee. The parties to the lease, L, T1 and G1 could stipulate at the outset that G1 would guarantee the liability of T1 both during the time that T1 was tenant under the lease (or until T1 was himself released by virtue of the statute) *and during the currency of any AGA T1 might subsequently enter into.* There are different schools of thought on the effectiveness of such a provision.[137] Less likely to be challenged (and attractive therefore to cautious landlords) is the inclusion of a condition in the lease to the effect that a guarantor of objectively stated financial standing must be provided by the assigning tenant to guarantee the obligations now being under-taken by the assignee. If the guarantor then proposed by the tenant, and accepted by the landlord, were a different person from the guarantor of the assigning tenant, it is difficult to see how any challenge could be made.[138] If the existing surety were taken on by the landlord as the surety for the assignee's liability, then the position may be more doubtful. Certainly, any stipulation in the lease (or other agreement preceding the second guarantee) requiring the original surety to be surety for the assignee would be liable to be struck down, as this would frustrate the operation of the Act – the tenant covenants being guaranteed by the

---

[134] This is the constant theme throughout the provision, but a good example is sub-section (1): 'Where on an assignment a tenant is to any extent released from a tenant covenant of a tenancy by virtue of this Act...nothing in this Act (and in particular section 25) shall preclude *him* from entering into an authorised guarantee agreement with respect to the performance of that covenant by the assignee.'

[135] Compare s. 17(3), which makes provision for the service of a 'problem notice' on a guarantor. It would have been possible for a similar extension to have been made in respect of such persons in section 16.

[136] Law Com No. 174.

[137] See Cullen & Potterton (1996) E. G. 118, Slessenger (1998) E. G. 102.

[138] I cautiously advanced this argument in [1996] CLJ 313 at 351. See also Walker (1998) L & T Review 124.

surety would be the same tenant covenants as before, albeit that the person primarily liable to perform them will have changed. But if the original surety volunteers, without any pre-existing obligation, to guarantee the assignee's liability under those covenants, then the mischief of the anti-avoidance provisions would appear to be averted, and it may be more difficult to say that the operation of the Act is being frustrated.

It was inevitable that the Landlord and Tenant (Covenants) Act 1995 would result in disagreement between protagonists about the meaning of certain provisions and the extent to which parties are free to come to their own agreements. As we have seen, the tension between statute and contract is ever present in landlord and tenant litigation. It has been argued that at a suitable opportunity Parliament should be invited to clarify the uncertainties that are most prevalent (for example, to enable a landlord to join a guarantor of the assigning tenant as a party to an AGA).[139] But it is doubtful that this will happen in the foreseeable future. It is more likely that further exploration of the boundaries of liability will be by means of test litigation.

Into the future: restructure and reform

It should be clear thus far that the law of landlord and tenant encompasses an almost infinite variety of contractual and proprietary relationships which are disparately governed by a profusion of statutory enactments. We have seen how status is of massive significance in all spheres of the law of leases, and how the interrelation of property and contract impacts throughout. As will have been seen in the course of this chapter, which proceeds from an essentially conceptual view of the subject, taking 'contract', 'status' and 'property' as particular aspects of the lease which can illustrate the practical impact of legal principle upon the flexibility and availability of remedies, certain areas are of much greater importance in the context of the commercial rather than the residential sector or vice versa. Take, for instance, the enforceability of covenants by and against those who are not parties to the original lease. This is of greatest application in the context of commercial leases, where fixed-term tenancies are granted subject to the exercise of rights of re-entry in the event of tenant default and where assignment of the reversion and the term is a common occurrence. The rules are far less frequently applied in relation to residential leases, where periodic tenancies are the norm and where assignment of the interest may never come into the head of the tenant. But that is not to say that the rules have no application. Indeed, there are many residential leases that are expressly granted for very long terms indeed.

---

139 Williams (2000) L & T Review 49.

The law of landlord and tenant has seen much change in recent years, much of the legislation, as we have seen, being of a political flavour – notably the phasing out of the Rent Acts and the stealthy deregulation of both residential and agricultural tenancies. As has been remarked recently by Peter Sparkes, we have now reached a stage where the political differences on the future of landlord and tenant between the two largest parties are much fewer than they have been.[140] The Law Commission has, over the years, had a relatively limited impact on the development of landlord and tenant law, for the most part due to its understandable reluctance to become embroiled in an area where the complexion of the government would make a very considerable difference to the chances of any proposals they might make coming to fruition. The difficulty faced by the Commission in proposing politically contentious reforms has been well documented. That said, it is not always easy to predict which proposals will face opposition or disapproval from certain political sectors. The enactment of the Landlord and Tenant (Covenants) Act 1995 was the culmination of a process which the Law Commission had initiated, but as a result of the parliamentary mauling suffered by the Bill, the end-product was far removed from, and many would argue, significantly inferior to, the initial proposals.

At its very inception, the Law Commission had a grand design for a codification of landlord and tenant law,[141] but it was pragmatically realised some years ago that this was too ambitious a programme and it was abandoned.[142] This must have been in some respects due to the recognition of the way in which the law of landlord and tenant was fragmented into different regimes for different kinds of leasehold property, making a rationalisation of the entirety of the law a somewhat unnecessary and arguably ineffectual exercise. Indeed, possibly the only significant piece of legislation that has given full effect to proposals of the Law Commission is the Landlord and Tenant Act 1988, conferring stronger remedies on tenants whose landlords had unreasonably with-held their consent to assignment of the lease.[143] But there are signs that further progress is being made. As we have already mentioned, the proposals for reform of the statutory procedures concerning business tenancies may finally bear fruit. Termination of leases (the law of forfeiture) has been on and off the Commission's agenda for a very long time, but work on a final report and draft Bill is being currently conducted.[144] The problem of disrepair of residential property, high-

---

[140] In *Property 2000*, at p. 219.
[141] See the First Programme of Law Reform, Law Com No 1 (1965).
[142] The Thirteenth Annual Report of the Law Commision 1977–1978, Law Com No 92, para 2.34
[143] The 1988 Act is based on proposals in Law Com No 141 (1985).
[144] Law Com No 142 (1985), Law Com No 221 (1994).

lighted in its 1996 report, remains of vital importance, and is also under active consideration.[145]

As the current Chairman of the Law Commission, Sir Robert Carnwath, has stated: 'It is possible to look forward to a period of reasonable political consensus on the essential elements. Such a consensus provides a promising climate for the Law Commission to carry out its proper role of modernisation and simplification, without becoming involved in matters of political controversy.'[146]

The problem in many areas of landlord and tenant law has been the achievement of consensus, and it is this vital element which has given the Commission the opportunity to carry out its major project on housing law. The Government has stated that it does not intend to alter the basic balance between landlords and tenants in the residential sectors.[147] There is an obvious need to remove the current complexity and to clarify the law as it affects people on an everyday basis in the occupation of their homes. The next few years are likely to see reform of much of the law of landlord and tenant, with an ultimate objective of clarification and simplication of legal principle.

Further reading

Bridge, *Former Tenant, Future Liabilities and the Privity of Contract principle: the Landlord and Tenant (Covenants) Act 1995* [1996] Cambridge Law Journal 313.

Bright, *Uncertainty in Leases: is it a vice?* (1993) Legal Studies 38.

Bright & Gilbert, *Landlord and Tenant Law, the Nature of Tenancies* (1995, Oxford) *passim.*

Glendon, *The Transformation of American Landlord-Tenant Law* (1982) 23 Boston College Law Review 503.

Hill, *The Proprietary Character of Possession* in *Modern Studies in Property Law: Property 2000* (2001, Hart Publishing).

Rabin, *The Revolution in Residential Landlord-Tenant Law* (1984) 69 Cornell Law Review 517.

Sparkes, *A New Landlord and Tenant Law* (2001, Hart Publishing), *passim.*

---

[145] Law Com No 238 (1996).

[146] (2001) 5 L & T Rev 3.

[147] *Quality and Choice: A Decent Home for All*, DETR.

5

Co-ownership and trusts

Louise Tee

The law relating to co-ownership and trusts is paradoxically both one of the oldest established areas of land law and one of its most dynamic areas today, showing quite dramatic developments over the past 30 years. The result is a patchwork of jurisprudence, with ancient concepts, originating in feudal times, standing cheek by jowl with new legislation and the imaginative decisions of some of the braver members of the judiciary. Not surprisingly, such a heady mix is intricate and arcane, with subtleties to tax the unwary practitioner as well as the hapless student. The complexity of source is mirrored by an underlying fragmentation of policy. For the law of co-ownership and trusts deals with people's homes, and this all-too-human dimension naturally brings in its train policy considerations which may conflict with traditional land law objectives. Differing policies vie for prominence and sometimes achieve an uneasy co-existence, which can either be extolled as a creative tension or dismissed as incoherent.

This is therefore an area of the law that has attracted, and continues to attract, much critical comment, and calls for wholesale reform. But of course the issues are not straightforward and, although the calls for reform are widespread, there is little consensus as to how the law should be amended. So the debate continues, with both principles and policy subjected to lively scrutiny.

Co-ownership

Background

When the land law reforms that culminated in the 1925 property legislation were being considered, patterns of landholding were very different from those now prevailing. The vast majority of people lived in privately rented accommodation, with the (male) head of the household as sole tenant. Owner-occupation was very unusual – indeed, the 1910 census did not even mention the possibility – and co-ownership arose in quite a different context, when property was passed down the generations. A testator with investments in land might well leave his land to his children, and they would continue to rent out the land, and receive the rents. Or otherwise, they would sell the land and divide the proceeds of sale. The significant point is that, in either case, the co-ownership was connected with the economic value of land rather than the provision of a home.

The structure of the law at that time may have created some problems for those individuals – and their lawyers – who wished to deal with co-owned land. When tenants in common held the legal estate in a plot of land, their number could multiply over the years to produce a fragmented title that could cause management problems or daunt a conveyancer in search of a secure title. When co-owners were embroiled in intractable dispute, the only solution could be cumbersome and expensive partition. So, there were problems; but, even so, there does not seem to have been any sustained or vocal campaign for reform of the law of co-ownership – nothing anyway to explain the breath-taking radicalism of the 1925 property legislation.[1] So its genesis is still unclear – and possibly the result of the vision of one man, Benjamin Cherry, who was the driving force behind the legislation. But whatever the motivation behind the reform, the result was spectacular. With stunning simplicity, the Law of Property Act simply abolished legal tenancy in common. It provided that henceforth all co-owners would hold a legal estate as joint tenants and the Trustee Act imposed a limit of four on the number of individuals who could hold a legal estate at any one time. The legislation was able to achieve this remarkable reform by using a trust mechanism. Other than when land was held in strict settlement, co-owned land was to be held on trust for sale.[2] When two or more trustees for sale sold land, the beneficial interests under the trust would be overreached and transferred to the proceeds of sale. By means of this unique solution, beneficial tenants in common could continue to multiply, but not so as to affect a purchaser of the legal estate. The investment value of co-owned land was recognised and retained, and conveyancing was simplified. The reform was startling in its ingenuity and clear-sightedness.

But since then, of course, the pattern of landholding in England and Wales has changed out of all recognition. First, there was the rise in owner-occupation. This trend was discernible in the 1930s and it

---

[1] Anderson, *Lawyers and the Making of English Land Law 1832-1940* (1992, Clarendon); Anderson, 'The 1925 property legislation' in Bright and Dewar, *Land Law: Themes and Perspectives* (1998, Oxford University Press), p. 123.

[2] Although this was hidden within the statutory provisions rather than clearly stated – see Anderson (1998), *op. cit.* above fn. 1, p. 122.

accelerated after the Second World War. The proportion of owner-occupiers then rose inexorably, reflecting new economic and social norms and, subsequently, the introduction of the right-to-buy legislation by the Conservatives under Mrs Thatcher.[3] Today, nearly 70% of households are owner-occupied, and the private rental sector only amounts to some 10%.[4] The other material change has been the rise in express co-ownership with, typically, both husband and wife taking legal title to their matrimonial home. But this rise in co-ownership has not been continuous – instead, the numbers peaked in the early 1980s, with a total of 74% of new mortgages being taken out by couples in 1984. Since then, there has been a decline – to just 56% in 1998. Similarly, the proportion of mortgages taken out by one person alone rose from around 25% in 1984 to 39% in 1998, with the proportion to single women doubling over the period.[5] Perhaps the rise in the divorce rate is relevant here, together with the changing aspirations of women and the increasing number of single-person households. It is not yet clear when, if at all, the figures will stabilise. At present, we can merely say that express co-ownership is still the most popular choice for people when buying a home, but that many single people are also entering the market.

Obviously, as co-ownership shifted from the investment market to the purchase of matrimonial homes, the trust for sale mechanism became increasingly inappropriate. The reforms introduced by the Trusts of Land and Appointment of Trustees Act 1996, which converted such trusts for sale into trusts of land, were a timely – indeed laggardly – response to the new circumstances in which co-ownership now arises, but they merely dealt with the detail of the trusts and left intact much of the essential 1925 structure which still governs co-ownership today. The pressing question is whether this structure is still appropriate for the twenty-first century.

A valid declaration of beneficial entitlement

Those couples who purchase homes together are unlikely to understand the intricacies of land law. The best practice is obviously for their legal adviser to explain to them the different options – beneficial joint tenancy or tenancy in common in declared proportions – and for the transfer then to record their chosen beneficial entitlements. This seems quite simple, and so it is extraordinary that many transfers have failed to declare the beneficial interests, and solicitors have been fairly criticised for such sloppy practice.[6] But, until recently, the first of the many pitfalls for the

---

[3] Housing Act 1980 and then Housing Act 1985.

[4] *Social Trends* 30 (2000, The Stationery Office).

[5] *Ibid.*, Chart 10.25.

[6] See *Cowcher* v. *Cowcher* [1972] 1 WLR 425 at 442 *per* Bagnall J and *Bernard* v. *Josephs* [1982] Ch 391 at 403.

unwary solicitor in the area of co-ownership lurked in the mere process of including a declaration. For before new Land Registry forms were issued under the Land Registration Rules 1997, the short form of transfer did not expressly invite a declaration as to beneficial interests.[7] Instead, from 1974, the form merely included a statement as to whether the survivor of joint tenants could give a valid receipt for capital money arising on sale. In the usual course of events, a survivor would only be able to give such a receipt if she and her co-owner had held as beneficial joint tenants, and so the practice developed of using such a statement as a substitute for an express declaration of beneficial interests.[8]

This would not have mattered too much had it not been for a decision of the Court of Appeal that invalidated the practice and so, presumably, destroyed the desired effect of many existing transfers. The case was *Huntingford* v. *Hobbs*,[9] and it concerned the extent of the respective beneficial interests of an estranged couple in their jointly owned home. The transfer had contained the common declaration that the survivor of the couple could give a valid receipt for capital money arising on a disposition of the land. Dillon LJ understood this to mean that the transferees were taking the house as beneficial joint tenants, but Slade and Steyn LLJ refused to interpret the statement as such, on the ground that the declaration about receipts did not *necessarily* indicate beneficial joint tenancy. They pointed out that if the couple had purchased their house as mere nominees for a third party, then the survivor, as a bare trustee of the legal estate, would also have been able to give a valid receipt. In refusing to imply into the transfer a declaration of trust, the court followed an earlier case where in fact a shadowy third party had been glimpsed in the wings,[10] but there was no such ghostly presence in the *Hobbs* scenario. The result was that the court could ignore the intention that informed the Hobbs transfer. This then allowed the court to use a resulting trust analysis instead – and reach an apportionment that the majority obviously preferred. The caselaw is now clear,[11] so solicitors should know what to do. But this will not save all those transfers made

---

[7] Now, as from 1 April 1998, applications for first registration of title in joint proprietors and for any subsequent transfer to joint proprietors must specify the nature and extent of the intended beneficial entitlements (Land Registration Rules 1925, Sch. 1, inserted by Land Registration Rules 1997, r. 2(2)).

[8] Farrand, *Emmet on Title* (19th ed.) para. 10.137 states that it was 'not the usual practice to include the "usual joint tenancy clauses" of unregistered conveyancing in transfers of registered land to beneficial joint tenants. Instead the names of the transferees are simply inserted as such in the appropriate form of transfer with, *at most*, the following habendum added "to hold unto themselves as joint tenants beneficially"' (emphasis added).

[9] [1993] 1 FLR 736.

[10] *Harwood* v. *Harwood* [1991] 2 FLR 274.

[11] See now *The Mortgage Corporation* v. *Shaire* [2000] 1 FLR 973. Thompson, 'Secured creditors and sales' [2000] Conv. 329, is critical.

before 1993. The number of transfers with such a formula must be very large, and many co-owners who believe they own as express beneficial joint tenants – and so intended – must be mistaken. This is – at the least – an unfortunate outcome.

Express beneficial joint tenancy

This difficulty aside, if the transfer expressly declares the beneficial entitlement, then in the absence of fraud or rectification, this will generally determine how the couple own their home.[12] And it seems, from such evidence as there is, that most couples choose to hold as beneficial joint tenants. It is unclear why this is. One suspects that solicitors ask the hopeful couple if they would like their new home to pass automatically to the survivor in case of death. A question so framed, in the context of the excitement of buying a new (possibly first) home, when presumably the couple feel well disposed towards each other, is in reality unlikely to elicit any other response.[13] The main advantage of beneficial joint tenancy is that upon the first death, the survivor will automatically enjoy the full legal and beneficial ownership of the home, without the need for any action on her part. If the deceased's estate was very small, this may mean that probate can be avoided altogether. And the attraction of this to happy couples, who can fully imagine the trauma of bereavement and who want to minimise the necessary post-death formalities for their loved ones, is very understandable. A more dubious benefit – morally speaking – concerns creditors. When a beneficial joint tenant dies, her interest in what was the jointly owned property is immediately extinguished. This means that any unsecured creditors of the deceased will not be able to claim against the property for the settlement of their debts – the property being no longer part of the deceased's estate. One can only hope that this 'advantage' does not weigh with too many couples at the time of purchase.

So these are the benefits of beneficial joint tenancy but, of course, that is not the end of the story. There are also serious disadvantages which may make the choice of joint tenancy disastrous for some luckless purchasers.

---

[12] The only difficulty may be if one or other of the couple then claims an increased share on the basis of a constructive trust or, indeed, a share under s. 37 of the Matrimonial Proceedings and Property Act 1969. For a consideration of this possibility, see p. 162.

[13] *Harwood* v. *Harwood* ([1991] 2 FLR 274) shows an example of the advice proffered by a solicitor to a purchasing couple – in effect, he advises them to hold as beneficial joint tenants.

Disadvantages of beneficial joint tenancy

Unwanted property devolution

The first problem is that survivorship operates automatically, without any contemporaneous input from the couple themselves. And so, it is not always certain that, at the time of death, survivorship is what the deceased actually wanted. Indeed, from the caselaw, it is clearly often the opposite of what was wanted, or intended. When a couple buy a house, and agree they want to hold as beneficial joint tenants, the solicitor will no doubt explain survivorship to them, and severance, and how severance operates. In particular, the solicitor will (one hopes) stress that property held under joint tenancy cannot be left by will. But it is unlikely that, in the excitement of buying a house, many people will remember this particular esoteric point. Indeed, it seems to be a common, and perfectly understandable, misconception that one can leave one's 'half' of the house by will. If a solicitor is employed to draw up the will, and fails to sever a joint tenancy so as to enable the testator's wishes to be fulfilled, then at least the disappointed beneficiary can sue the solicitor in negligence.[14] But, increasingly, people eschew legal advice – or at least legal fees. Instead, they buy do-it-yourself will-forms from stationers, or download them from the Internet. Then the hapless testator may well make a will that tries to leave jointly owned property to a third party. Let us hope that at least the testator dies happy – because alas the third party is going to be bitterly disappointed.

This issue seems particularly worrying now, in view of the rise in the divorce rate and the increase in serial cohabitation. Although most marriages still survive (just), a sizeable proportion do not, and it is likely that the failure rate of cohabitation is similarly high. In the context of such familial instability, it seems increasingly inappropriate that property should automatically pass[15] in accordance with a half understood agreement, possibly made many years previously, rather than as the deceased subsequently intended. Indeed, this is a clear example of a law that fails to accord with people's reasonable expectations. And whenever that happens, one needs to question the law most carefully to see if it is in fact justifiable.

'Equal share' trap

A further objection to beneficial joint tenancy is perhaps less weighty, but can still cause distress. This is that upon severance, the couple will automatically hold equal shares, whatever their original contributions. No

---

[14] As in *Kecskemti* v. *Rubens Rabin & Company*, The Times, 31 December 1992, and *Carr-Glynn* v. *Frearsons* [1998] 4 All ER 225.

[15] 'Pass' is used here in a practical, rather than technical sense.

doubt this is also explained to couples at the start, but again – no doubt-many couples will not fully understand the implications. It has been suggested that this trap could be circumvented by creating an express trust to provide that, in the case of severance, the respective shares should be other than equal.[16] Whether this would be acceptable to a court without legislation is unclear – the possibility seems to undermine the theoretical basis of joint tenancy as two (or more) identical interests. But in the meantime, and pending any decision, caselaw provides examples of the annoyance felt when this particular trap is sprung on the unwary major contributor to the purchase.[17]

Uncertainty as to whether severance has taken place

The third and possibly most serious problem is that it is not always clear whether a testator has previously severed her interest. The question can be crucially important to both loved and estranged survivors. For if the deceased made a valid will, leaving her 'share' of the former joint home elsewhere, then a previous severance would allow the will to take effect as drawn; but obviously an ineffective severance would not. In the latter case, survivorship would operate. It is difficult to overemphasise the emotional and financial distress that survivors must suffer in the face of such uncertainty, especially when the only solution is an application to the court. Legal advisers also must find it hard – imagine having to explain to the bereaved loved one that the will may – or may not – take effect as drawn, and that the court will have to decide.

And this continues to happen. For there are several reasons why it may be unclear whether severance has occurred. The substantive law itself generates continuing debate, and then there are also the familiar difficulties in applying legal principles to the infinite number of untidy and ambiguous arrangements which people so inconveniently enter into.

Severance: issues of principle

At first sight the law concerning severance seems relatively straightforward, with the three methods described by Page-Wood V-C in *Williams* v. *Hensman*,[18] and then s. 36 (2) of the Law of Property Act 1925. But of course appearances are deceptive, and important issues of principle still

---

[16] *Goodman* v. *Gallant* [1986] Fam 106 at 119.

[17] As in *Goodman* v. *Gallant* itself.

[18] (1861) 1 J & H 546 at 557: 'A joint-tenancy may be severed in three ways: in the first place, an act of any one of the persons interested operating upon his own share may create a severance as to that share…Secondly, a joint-tenancy may be severed by mutual agreement. And, in the third place, there may be a severance by any course of dealing sufficient to intimate that the interests of all were mutually treated as constituting a tenancy in common.'

remain undecided. In particular, the scope of the first heading under *Williams* v. *Hensman*, acting upon one's own share, remains unclear. Despite the logical anomaly of a joint tenant, who owns 'all, yet nothing',[19] being able to transfer a share without first severing, it is well-established that a total alienation by a joint tenant both severs and then transfers her share in one magical sleight of hand. However, there is much less certainty about a partial alienation, for example a lease or a mortgage.

A partial alienation

Obviously, if all the joint tenants grant a lease, then there is no problem, but what if just one joint tenant purports to let the property? One can imagine a situation where, for example, a joint tenant has moved out of the house upon a relationship break-up, and the remaining occupant decides to let some or all the house for income. It seems that in principle this is possible, and a valid lease can be created,[20] but there is little consensus as to the legal effect.[21] Some sixteenth-century cases provide authority that, in these circumstances, a sub-lease severs, and in principle there seems no reason why a sub-lease should have any different effect from a lease. But the cases are very old[22] and the reports brief, and they do not seem a very solid foundation upon which to reach a firm conclusion. In more modern times, the Irish case of *Re Armstrong*[23] held that a lease severed but, as Crown has pointed out,[24] the ratio is rather circular and unsatisfactory. The case was distinguished by the Canadian courts in *Sorensen* v. *Sorensen*,[25] where a lease for life was held not to sever. In Australia, it has been suggested that a lease could effect *temporary* severance, just for the duration of the lease.[26] Gray and Gray[27] tend to favour this idea of temporary severance, while Harpum prefers permanent severance.[28] The jury is still out.

Similar doubts could be harboured about the effect of a mortgage, now that it is generally created by charge rather than outright conveyance. It is arguable that, as the right of survivorship is not destroyed by the grant of

---

[19] 'Totum tenet et nihil tenet', Bracton, fo. 430 (Woodbine's edn), Vol. 4, p. 336.

[20] *Tilling* v. *Whiteman* [1980] AC 1 at 24. Though note that the lessor would only be able to grant exclusive possession of her interest. The other joint tenants would still be entitled to assert their rights of possession, unless they were estopped in any way. Disputes would be governed by the Trusts of Land and Appointment of Trustees Act 1996.

[21] Fox, 'Unilateral demise by a joint tenant: does it effect a severance?' [2000] Conv. 208.

[22] *Pleadal's Case* (1579) 2 Leon 159; *Sym's Case* (1584) Cro. Eliz. 33.

[23] [1920] 1 IR 239.

[24] 'Severance of joint tenancy of land by partial alienation' (2001) 117 LQR 477.

[25] [1977] 2WWR 438.

[26] *Wright* v. *Gibbons* (1949) 78 CLR 313 (*obiter*).

[27] In Gray and Gray, *Elements of Land Law* (3rd ed., 2000, Butterworths), p. 861.

[28] *Megarry & Wade: The Law of Real Property*, (6th ed., 2000, Sweet & Maxwell), para. 9.040.

a mere encumbrance, such as an easement,[29] it should also survive the grant of a charge. And, indeed, this argument has been accepted in the Supreme Court of Victoria, which held, in *Lyons v. Lyons*,[30] that because a mortgage was now simply a charge and not a conveyance, there was no destruction of the unities and no severance. This seems logical and in accord with principle, but in England mortgages have so far been held to sever.[31] The caselaw is not overwhelming, however; in *First National Securities Ltd v. Hegerty*, Bingham J merely stated, without reasons, that the grant of an equitable charge severed,[32] and the other authority that is usually cited, *Re Sharer*, was only at first instance and contained no discussion as to the actual form that the mortgage had taken. So it is still possible that a more careful judicial consideration could reach a different conclusion.

A unilateral declaration of intent to sever

Another unresolved issue concerns the effect of a unilateral declaration of intention to sever, and whether or not this comes within Page-Wood V-C's first heading. Before 1925 it seems quite clear from the caselaw[33] – and indeed from the elaborate procedures that conveyancers used to effect severance – that it did not. And this seems correct in principle. When talking about acting upon one's share, Page-Wood V-C was referring to transactions which necessarily severed a joint tenancy so as to have any effect – in other words, alienations. An effective transfer of a joint tenant's interest to another would automatically destroy the unities of title and time that underlie joint tenancy. So when Havers J, in *Hawkesley v. May*,[34] casually remarked that a unilateral declaration came within the first heading of severable actions, he was obviously wrong. Likewise, when the heresy was repeated by Plowman J in *Re Draper's Conveyance*,[35] it could be ignored, and his alternative, and rather more orthodox ratio based on s. 36 (2) of the Law of Property Act 1925, could be accepted as correct.[36] Walton J, in *Nielson-Jones v. Fedden*,[37] criticised the dicta in these two cases to devastating effect, and the matter seemed closed. But, alas, a fateful

---

[29] *Hedley v. Roberts* [1977] VR 282.

[30] [1967] VR 169.

[31] *Re Sharer* (1912) 57 SJ 60; *First National Securities Ltd v. Hegerty* [1985] QB 850.

[32] He took comfort from the criticism in *Williams & Glyn's Bank Ltd v. Boland* [1981] AC 487 of *Cedar Holdings Ltd v. Green* [1981] Ch 129; but the criticism was directed at the artificiality of the doctrine of conversion.

[33] *Re Wilks, Child v. Bulmer* [1891] 3 Ch 59. Though see Luther, 'Williams v. Hensman and the uses of history' (1995) 15 LS 219.

[34] [1956] 1 QB 304 at 313.

[35] [1969] 1 Ch 486.

[36] In *Harris v. Goddard* [1983] 1 WLR 1203 (CA) Dillon LJ specifically limited his approval of Re Draper to the ratio based on s. 36.

[37] [1975] 1 Ch 222.

scripture rally held in Trafalgar Square, and a rose wrapped in newspaper, were, in time, to have unforeseen repercussions upon the law of severance. For in the tragicomic case of *Burgess* v. *Rawnsley*,[38] Lord Denning MR endorsed the idea that, prior to 1925, a mere declaration of intent would sever in equity. His reasoning was based on the poorly drafted s. 36 (2) of the Law of Property Act 1925 and a very clumsy 'other' inserted into the proviso.[39] On the strength of this hapless adjective, a whole new interpretation of the law of severance was constructed. And although this was all *obiter*, it still stands within a judgment in the Court of Appeal and has merely been gently queried in England.[40] The High Court of Australia, on the other hand, has robustly signified its disapproval of the heresy.[41]

Paradoxically, although it seems clear that Lord Denning MR was wrong, his argument could be useful in the future. Because his (mistaken) conclusion could be used to remedy yet another drafting defect in the notorious s. 36 (2). A strict reading of the subsection suggests that severance by written notice is only available to beneficial joint tenants who also hold the legal estate. This would exclude the position where A and B hold the legal estate on trust for X and Y as beneficial joint tenants. No one has been able to identify any reason at all for such a limitation, and one can only hope that, if the matter ever came before a court, the judge would adopt a purposive construction and allow the statutory procedure. But judges come in all shapes and sizes, and a literal interpretation could throw X back on equity if her written notice to sever were held not to come within the statutory powers. If this were the case, then Lord Denning MR's suggestion in *Burgess* could be a life-line, albeit illegitimate, and X could argue that her written notice had severed anyway under the first heading of *Williams* v. *Hensman*. The result, of course, would be a rather pleasing example of a situation where two wrongs do indeed make a right.

Severance: issues of application

Even when the principles are clear, the way in which the courts apply them to cases can seem unpredictable. It is difficult to trace any consistent policy in applying the law, other than a marked reluctance on the part of the courts to find that there has ever been a mutual course of dealing

---

[38] [1975] Ch 429.

[39] 'Provided that, where a legal estate (not being settled land) is vested in joint tenants beneficially, and any tenant desires to sever the joint tenancy in equity, he shall give to the other joint tenants a notice in writing of such desire or do such *other* acts or things as would, in the case of personal estate, have been effectual to sever the tenancy in equity...'(emphasis added).

[40] *Hunter* v. *Babbage* [1994] 2 FLR 806 at 814–815.

[41] *Corin* v. *Patton* (1989–1990) 169 CLR 540 at 584.

sufficient to sever. So even when brothers divided a house into two separate maisonettes, or a deserted wife had lived in one of the jointly owned houses while the errant husband had lived with his mistress in the other, no sufficient mutual course of dealing was found.[42] Indeed, the last reported case in England where severance upon this ground was successfully urged is over 50 years old and concerned the division of receipts from a fund.[43] This is not especially helpful for cases concerning homes. All in all, it must be very difficult for the high-street solicitor to advise with confidence as to whether or not an informal severance has occurred.

Reform of severance

In view of all these uncertainties, it is not surprising that various commentators have thought about reform and have come up with ideas as to how severance could be simplified, modernised, restricted or, indeed, expanded. It is worth looking briefly at the ideas, and the most significant are listed below. Note that these suggestions do not undermine beneficial joint tenancy as such, but merely tinker at the edges, so as to aid its smooth functioning.[44] Some of the ideas seem very sensible, as will be seen, but none of the suggestions offers an unmitigated and cost-free benefit. So it becomes a matter of judgment as to whether any reform would provide an overall improvement on the present position.

Necessity for consent or knowledge of other joint tenants

One idea is that severance should not be possible without the consent or knowledge of the other joint tenants. McLean, in a seminal article in 1979,[45] makes the point that both parties to a joint tenancy probably expect that their consent is needed to a severance, which after all changes the nature of their interest; he thinks this should be acknowledged. In Saskatchewan, such consent is necessary:[46] no instrument purporting to transfer the share of a joint tenant can be registered unless accompanied by the written consent of the other joint tenant(s). But such an idea is unlikely to attract any support in England and Wales. Lord Denning's doomed attempt in *Bedson* v. *Bedson*[47] to reintroduce some need for consent was strongly criticised. It was argued that a requirement for

---

[42] *Greenfield* v. *Greenfield* (1979) 38 P & CR 570; *Gore and Snell* v. *Carpenter* (1990) 60 P & CR 456. See also *Nielson-Jones* v. *Fedden* [1975] Ch 222; *McDowell* v. *Hirschfield Lipson & Rumney and Smith* [1992] 2 FLR 126.

[43] *Re Denny* (1947) 116 LJR 1029.

[44] See Law Com WP No. 94, paras 16.11 – 16.14; Tee, 'Severance revisited' [1995] Conv. 105.

[45] 'Severance of joint tenancies' (1979) 57 Can Bar Rev 1.

[46] Land Titles Act, RSS 1978, c.L-5, s 240.

[47] [1965] 2 QB 666.

consent would unreasonably restrict individual freedom of action, and could lock people into unhappy situations.[48]

But although it would be undesirable to require consent, it seems reasonable to provide that severance should not take effect without the other joint tenants having been given notice. At present, it is still possible to sever secretly, behind the backs of the others, and this can cause great injustice. If a joint tenant in England secretly mortgages her equitable interest, her co-tenant will be blissfully unaware of the severance. If the mortgagor then dies, the co-tenant may be horrified to discover that survivorship will not operate. And it is possible to imagine even more unsavoury scenarios. Imagine that our enthusiastic mortgagor then repays the loan, while still keeping the co-tenant and others in ignorance. Our mortgagor can then cleverly hedge her bets, and either take under survivorship if she outlasts her partner, or allow her papers to reveal the severance to her executors if she is unlucky enough to die first. A severance would, of course, permit an effective testamentary disposition to a third party. If that were to happen, the surviving joint tenant would understandably feel betrayed as well as disappointed.

A requirement of notice would prevent such unscrupulous secrecy and, *prima facie*, it seems a useful and sensible reform of the law. But there is a problem with the idea – for it would put at risk any third party who took a contract, mortgage or lease from a single beneficial joint tenant. Unless the other beneficial tenants had been given notice, the third party could find that her interest suddenly evaporated in the magic of survivorship. This has weighed with commentators, but the difficulty can be exaggerated. After all, is it really unreasonable to suggest that a third party should investigate the grantor's title before entering into a transaction? Beneficial joint tenancy – or at least a trust and co-ownership – will invariably be apparent from the most cursory inspection of a register or title deeds. The third party could then decide whether to insist upon severance first, or whether to bear the risk that the grantor might predecease her partner.

Abolition of informal methods of severance

A more drastic reform would be to abolish all the informal methods of severance, so that only written statutory notice (and homicide) severed.[49] This would reduce much of the uncertainty that has bedevilled this area, and so also seems attractive as an idea. But of course there would again be losers, and they would be those people who perhaps need the law's

---

[48] The requirement for consent would reintroduce a type of co-ownership similar to the now obsolete tenancy by entireties, whereby a joint tenancy held by a husband and wife was in effect unseverable without the agreement of both.

[49] Involuntary alienation – through bankruptcy – is a further complicating factor, though that could always be considered a special case and treated exceptionally.

protection. For the losers would be those beneficial joint tenants who do not understand the law – and that is probably most of them. The reform would mean that even joint tenants who had agreed with each other to separate out their shares could find themselves then subject to unwanted survivorship. This would be imposing an outcome that most clearly was against the wishes of the people involved. All the difficulties that surround beneficial joint tenancy would be visited on unwilling people unless they took legal advice at the right moment. So, yes, the certainty would perhaps reduce some of the stress caused by not knowing how property should devolve, but the cost of achieving this would be high, and at the expense of lay people. The need to balance the conflicting interests is clear – but how to achieve that balance is less obvious. Here indeed is displayed one of the perpetual tensions in land law – between the need for clarity and certainty, on the one hand, and the need to promote fairness and discretionary justice on the other.

Severance by will

Another, ingenious, reform would be to introduce severance by will.[50] The great advantage of this would be that it would avoid unwanted property devolution. If the errant husband made a will leaving his 'share' in the matrimonial home to his new love, and then died before lawyers became involved to effect severance, his share would at least go as he had wished. It would also be a reform that would align the law with people's reasonable expectations, and that is always a desirable outcome. The main issue is whether or not such a reform would fatally undermine the theoretical underpinning of survivorship and leave the law in an unprincipled mess. That perhaps is a matter of judgment – and the reform would involve judgments elsewhere as well. For it could result in difficult questions of construction as to whether the testator meant to include the jointly held property in the will or not. 'All to Sue' could show an intention to leave Sue the house share, or it could mean everything other than jointly-held property. The other main problem is that such a reform seems to extend the opportunities for secret severance and, as has been discussed above, this allows for unhappy and rather unsavoury betrayal.

Severance by separation and divorce

Finally, a simple but very attractive reform has been suggested by Ziff[51] – and this is that separation should suspend, and divorce terminate, the right of survivorship automatically. This would be useful when the joint tenants are married, and it is a pity it has not yet attracted widespread

---

50 Prichard, 'Beneficial joint tenancies: a riposte' [1978] Conv. 273.
51 Ziff, *Principles of Property Law* (2nd ed, 1996, Carswell) p. 303.

support. Of course, it could lead to uncertainty as to what constituted a separation, but that does not seem insuperable. The main drawback with the idea is that its scope would be limited because it would not be much help to the many unmarried couples who hold as beneficial joint tenants.

A more radical solution – abolition of beneficial joint tenancy

Because of all these problems, a few bold commentators[52] have suggested that the best way to cut the Gordian knot is to abolish beneficial joint tenancy entirely, so that co-owners always hold the legal estate as joint tenants and the beneficial interest as tenants in common. At a stroke, this would destroy all the problems of uncertainty surrounding informal severance, and property would devolve by will in accordance with the testator's wishes – and, indeed, in accordance with the reasonable expectations of lay people. Thompson also notes that such a solution would avoid potential problems under the Forfeiture Act 1982, in the rare, but still real, cases where one beneficial joint tenant kills the other. He also suggests, though this is perhaps more speculative, that if couples could only hold as beneficial tenants in common, it would encourage them to agree at the outset the proportions in which they should own the property.[53]

The main advantages of such an abolition are clear. No longer would property automatically pass in a way which the people involved might not expect and, instead, from the beginning, each individual would have a 'share' in the house, which he or she could then deal with, and leave in a will, as desired. This legal structure would really accord with the general assumptions of the population, and it would avoid the necessity to try to explain to hopeful purchasers the arcane concepts governing beneficial joint tenancy. Under such a reform, the daring sweep of the reformers in the 1920s would be mirrored – to provide yet more simplicity and certainty.

So is it appropriate to introduce such a reform when, as mentioned above, beneficial joint tenancy seems to be the more popular arrangement with couples? It becomes an issue of freedom of choice. Should one make life (and death) more complicated for happily married or cohabiting couples just because of the difficulties caused by dysfunctional and unhappy couples? Most marriages still survive and so it can be argued that such a reform would be a case of the tail wagging the dog – and a rather unruly and undeserving tail at that. The questions are important, because any law that restricts people's freedom to arrange their affairs as they think fit must be carefully scrutinised. One needs to be satisfied that any legislative intervention into people's private property arrangements

---

[52] Bandali, 'Injustice and problems of beneficial joint tenancy' (1977) 41 Conv. (N. S.) 243; Thompson, 'Beneficial joint tenancies: a case for abolition?' [1987] Conv. 29.

[53] It seems probable that a couple buying a house together would find it difficult, between themselves, to agree to shares other than fifty/fifty.

is indeed justified. Here, one can make a case. The solution for happy couples is simple – they merely need to make a will leaving their property to each other. This hardly seems disadvantageous – instead, it seems a wise precaution and, with all the competing providers, it no longer need be an expensive exercise. The necessity for probate, where otherwise it might have been avoided, also seems less problematic these days. With increasing owner-occupation, visiting a solicitor has become more common and therefore less intimidating for large groups of the population, and the real costs of probate have declined over the years. A simple estate is now relatively cheap to wind up. Also, it is worth noting that in an increasing number of households, other assets vie for value with the house – in these households, probate will in any event probably be necessary. All these trends mean that the advantages of beneficial joint tenancy – the avoidance of probate and the need to make a will – have steadily diminished in value and significance over the years.

So there are strong arguments in favour of abolishing beneficial joint tenancy and restricting co-ownership to beneficial tenancy in common. And indeed the arguments seem to grow stronger every year, as relationships waver and probate becomes cheaper and easier. But so far there is no general call for this reform. It is noticeable that the most recent legislative foray into this general area – the Trusts of Land and Appointment of Trustees Act 1996 – resolutely failed to trespass upon anything to do with beneficial joint tenancy or tenancy in common – even though some issues, such as the poor drafting of the Law of Property Act 1925, ss. 34–36, are crying out for action. Unfortunately, until now the political will has been absent, but one must hope this is a matter that is revisited in the near future.

Co-ownership and housing

Of course, it is not just owner-occupiers who have so willingly embraced co-ownership – joint tenancy is now common in rented accommodation as well. And this has led to a complex interaction between ancient principle, on the one hand, and, on the other, the pragmatic requirements of a local authority to manage its housing stock as efficiently (and cheaply) as possible. Local authorities have found support for their practical ambitions in the House of Lords who, within a single decade, have been prepared to adopt first a strictly theoretical argument and then an aggressively pragmatic ratio in order to prevent tenants out-manoeuvring local authority landlords.

Hammersmith & Fulham L.B.C. v. *Monk*[54] allowed a single joint tenant (a woman who wanted rehousing away from her estranged partner) to give

---

[54] [1992] 1 AC 478. Noted Tee [1992] CLJ 218.

an effective notice to quit to the council landlord. Thus she terminated the joint tenancy of the council flat against the wishes of her male partner, who was still living there. At first sight, the result seems perverse. It is, after all, axiomatic that joint tenants have to act unanimously in their dealings with their jointly-held estate, and indeed such a requirement accords with both common sense and reasonable assumption. However, the House of Lords reached their decision by means of a particular interpretation of the mechanism underlying a periodic tenancy. By emphasising Blackstone's point that a periodic tenancy lasted only 'so long as both parties please', their Lordships were able to argue that yes, indeed, joint tenants had to act unanimously, but the unanimity required was in permitting the tenancy to continue from period to period (in this case, from week to week) rather than in serving a notice to quit. Thus, theoretically, a notice to quit should be viewed, not as an effective terminating mechanism, but merely as an indication that the necessary intention to continue a tenancy was absent. An apparently positive act – the serving of a notice to quit – was translated in the judgments into an essentially passive, 'negative' action. Black was white. The judgment has been praised by those land lawyers who enjoy the conceptual and historical basis of the present law. However, it was by no means an inevitable result. It would have been quite possible to conclude that periodic tenancies had developed in character quite considerably since Blackstone's day, and that the increasing strictness in the cases concerning the validity of a notice to quit showed that the nature of such a notice, even if it had been originally merely declaratory, had now changed to become positive and proactive. The case has spawned a succession of further ones, but the courts have had their hands tied by the House of Lords, and the orthodoxy has persisted. The practical result of *Monk* was that the local council was able to evict the man without needing to rehouse him, and thus they could provide a separate home for the woman at no additional cost to their housing stock. The result is politically and economically convenient, but the route is questionable, and the judgment can be criticised for divorcing law from the practical realities of everyday life. It also, as an additional point, now undermines the statutory intention of the Trusts of Land and Appointment of Trustees Act 1996 which encourages consultation with beneficiaries.[55]

However, the House of Lords differed utterly in their approach in *Burton* v. *Camden London Borough Council*,[56] where they were willing to eschew artificial reasoning to radical effect. Here, the majority held that a deed of release executed by one departing joint tenant in favour of the other amounted to an assignment of her interest. This was the finding desired by Camden, which wanted to move the remaining tenant into

[55] Section 11.
[56] [2000] 2 WLR 427. Noted Bridge [2000] Conv. 474.

smaller accommodation and so did not want her to become the sole tenant of the flat. Section 91 of the Housing Act 1985 prohibits the *assignment* of a secure tenancy, and so by categorising the deed of release as an assignment which came within the statute, the House of Lords effectively avoided the deed. The cavalier disregard of centuries of learning about joint tenancy is quite impressive. Lord Nicholls labelled as an 'esoteric concept'[57] the fundamental characteristic of joint tenancy – that each joint tenant owns the whole. He was indeed right when he called this 'remote from the realities of life' but that he was prepared to reinterpret the common law as a result is quite astounding.

And so we have two cases, both with convenient conclusions (for local authorities) but with quite different approaches to legal reasoning and old-established principle. It is indeed good to recognise that ancient legal principle can be remote from the realities of life – and there is much to be said for trying to ensure that law and reality march side by side. The difficulty is when one is unable to predict which principles will be swept aside with a flourish and paean to modern life, and which will be lovingly preserved in the aspic of Blackstonian reasoning. Such unpredictability provides further support for the suggestion that this area is ripe for reform.

Trusts of Land and Appointment of Trustees Act 1996 (TOLATA)

But so far, statutory reform has been restricted to TOLATA. The thinking behind this Act was that the trust for sale was an anachronistic vehicle for co-ownership.[58] And this was right. The trust for sale – 'the rentier's settlement par excellence'[59] – bore little relationship to the purchase by a hopeful couple of their future home. TOLATA retained the trust device, but substituted for the statutory trust for sale, a trust of land, without any duty to sell.[60] The Act also confirmed that a beneficiary under a trust of land is entitled to occupy that land, and thus reinforced the statutory recognition of present-day realities. Indeed, the Act went even further in recognising the contemporary family context by enabling a court to take into account, when making an order concerning the trust under s. 14, the welfare of any child living in the home. This acknowledgment that a non-property consideration is relevant is a departure from conventional

---

[57] [2000] 2 WLR 427 at 431.

[58] *Transfer of Land: Trusts of Land*, Law Com No. 181 (1989), paras. 3.2, 3.5, 3.6.

[59] Murphy and Roberts, *Understanding Property Law* (3rd ed., 1998, Sweet & Maxwell), p. 224.

[60] It is still possible to create an express trust for sale – though such a trust has been emasculated by s. 4 of TOLATA, which provides that a power to postpone sale indefinitely is implied into every trust, even where the trust provides to the contrary. Pettit, 'Demise of trusts for sale and the doctrine of conversion' (1997) 113 LQR 207.

orthodoxy; but its impact should not be exaggerated – in practice judges had previously managed to take such matters into account by looking at the underlying purpose of the trust.

TOLATA and overreaching

Indeed, TOLATA was not as radical as it might have been for, although it recognised that trusts for sale were anachronistic, it did not pursue the logic to the ultimate conclusion that overreaching also needed reform. Basically, overreaching ensures that if a purchaser of land subject to a trust pays the purchase monies to two trustees, then she will take the land free of any beneficial interests under that trust. The interests will be transferred from the land to the purchase monies. This is only fair to the beneficiaries if one accepts the premise that a claim against the purchase monies is equivalent to, and as good as, an interest in the land itself. While this premise might well have been true in 1925, when co-owned land was held for investment purposes, it is patently not true today. Mr and Mrs Flegg would confirm this.

Overreaching, of course, is one of the cornerstones of the 1925 property reforms, and a crucial element in the scheme of protection offered to purchasers of both registered and unregistered land. This is why, when the scope of overreaching was attacked in *City of London Building Society* v. *Flegg*,[61] the issues at stake were considered so important that the case went to the House of Lords. *Flegg* highlighted an unresolved conflict in the 1925 legislation between the principle of overreaching and the extent of overriding interests in registered land. For the trusting Mr and Mrs Flegg were in actual occupation of Bleak House at the time that their trustees, the Maxwell-Browns, secretly granted the mortgage to the building society. The Fleggs had a beneficial interest in the house and so were apparently able to call upon the protection offered to them by s. 70 (1) (g) of the Land Registration Act 1925. But the House of Lords safeguarded the position of a purchaser – here the mortgagee – in registered land, by holding that, in effect, the overreaching card trumped overriding interests. This was, of course, very convenient for mortgagees, who thereafter could deal with trustees with minimal risk. Indeed, the position of mortgagees was even further assured when *State Bank of India* v. *Sood*[62] confirmed the overreaching effect of a disposition by two trustees, even though no capital monies were transferred at the time. In the aftermath of *Flegg*, the Law Commission recommended that the consent of full-age beneficiaries in occupation of trust property should be a necessary precondition for overreaching to take effect,[63] but this

---

[61] [1988] AC 73.
[62] [1997] Ch 276.
[63] *Transfer of Land: Overreaching: Beneficiaries in Occupation*, Law Com No. 188 (1989), para 4.3.

apparently sensible suggestion was quietly dropped and the Law Commission clearly did not intend TOLATA to affect overreaching.

Since then, there has been some lively debate as to the effect of TOLATA, for Ferris and Battersby[64] have argued that TOLATA has accidentally overturned the effect of *Flegg* and reduced the protection offered to purchasers of registered land. Their reasoning is that although subs. 6 (1) of TOLATA gives trustees all the powers of an absolute owner, subss. 6 (5), (6), and (8) then restrict the powers of trustees with new and extensive limitations.[65] Trustees who dispose of land in contravention of the limitations will be acting in breach of trust. Such a breach of trust will, in the absence of a statutory provision to the contrary, prevent overreaching from occurring. Ferris and Battersby have pointed to particular provisions in TOLATA which protect purchasers from specific instances of a breach of trust by vendors,[66] and deduced from this that purchasers are not protected from other breaches of trust – for example, those coming within the scope of s. 6. There is also a general statutory protection[67] offered to purchasers in good faith – but this only extends to unregistered land and does not protect a bona fide purchaser of registered land. She could find herself vulnerable to overriding interests under a trust, even though she had paid her money to two trustees.

Dixon has disagreed. He has argued[68] that even if the powers of trustees are more restricted by TOLATA, it does not necessarily mean that a disposition in contravention would be ultra vires so that overreaching could not occur. A disposition might be in breach of trust, but have no effect upon the actual validity of the transaction.

It is likely that the courts will strive to follow Dixon and construe TOLATA in such a way as to preserve the impact of *Flegg*, even if the construction has to be rather strained as a result. Some flavour of this can be discerned in *Birmingham Midshires Mortgage Services Ltd* v. *Sabherwal*.[69]

---

[64] 'The impact of the Trusts of Land and Appointment of Trustees Act 1996 on purchasers of registered land' [1998] Conv. 168; 'Overreaching and the Trusts of Land and the Appointment of Trustees Act 1996 – a reply to Mr Dixon' [2001] Conv. 221. See also Hopkins, 'Overreaching and the Trusts of Land and Appointment of Trustees Act 1996' [1997] Conv. 81.

[65] TOLATA: 'In exercising the powers conferred by this section trustees shall have regard to the rights of the beneficiaries' s. 6 (5); 'The powers conferred by this section shall not be exercised in contravention of, or of any order made in pursuance of, any other enactment or any rule of law or equity' s. 6 (6); 'Where any enactment other than this section confers on trustees authority to act subject to any restriction, limitation or condition, trustees of land may not exercise the powers conferred by this section to do any act which they are prevented from doing under the other enactment by reason of the restriction, limitation or condition' s. 6 (8).

[66] *Ibid.*, ss. 9 (2), 10 (1).

[67] *Ibid.*, s. 16.

[68] 'Overreaching and the Trusts of Land and Appointment of Trustees Act 1996' [2000] Conv. 267.

[69] (2000) 80 P & CR 256 (CA).

At first instance, counsel for Mrs Sabherwal had argued that the decision in *Flegg* had been affected by the 1996 Act and that overreaching had not occurred, even though the purchase monies had been paid to two trustees. The judge gave ten separate reasons for refuting this argument, and the case went to the Court of Appeal on different grounds. Even so, Robert Walker LJ adverted to the point, and mentioned the three reasons he considered the most cogent. That the overreaching effect of the relevant legal charges would have occurred six years before TOLATA took effect was, naturally enough, quite convincing. The second reason that Robert Walker LJ favoured is more relevant to the future. He noted that s. 2 of the Law of Property Act 1925, which contains the essential overreaching provision, had been amended to meet the new terminology of TOLATA – this, he thought, showed in effect statutory confirmation of overreaching inherent within TOLATA.

The debate will become largely academic with the new Land Registration Act 2002, because s. 26 offers general protection to purchasers of registered land. A limitation on the power of a vendor will not affect a purchaser unless the limitation is reflected on the register. So over-reaching will be secured again. However, the impact of TOLATA on transactions conducted before s. 26 takes effect will remain a contentious issue. And indeed, so may overreaching itself. The injustice that can be caused to beneficiaries in occupation whose interests are overreached is grave and, as a result, it is likely this issue will return to the courts in the future, perhaps supported by arguments from the Human Rights Act.

Section 15 of TOLATA

A second current debate concerns the effect of s. 15 of TOLATA. Under s. 30 of the Law of Property Act 1925, the court had the power to order a sale of trust property and an extensive body of caselaw developed around the question of when a sale would, or would not, be ordered. The Law Commission stated that it intended to 'consolidate and rationalise'[70] the approach that the courts had adopted under s. 30, and TOLATA repealed s. 30 and instead granted the courts enhanced powers of adjudication in s. 14. Section 15 lists the criteria to be considered, without prioritising, and the inevitable question has been asked – is the s. 30 caselaw still relevant to applications under s. 14? In *TSB plc* v. *Marshall*,[71] Judge Wroath, sitting in the County Court, thought that the purposes of s. 30 and s. 14 were the same – to do what was equitable, just and fair – and he endorsed the old s. 30 approach – that where there was a conflict between an innocent

[70] *Transfer of Land: Trusts of Land*, Law Com No. 181 1989 para. 12.5.
[71] (1998) 3 EGLR 100.

spouse and a chargee, the interests of the chargee should prevail, unless there were exceptional circumstances, and that the court should not defeat a collateral purpose of the trust if it were still subsisting. However, Neuberger J has now disapproved *Marshall* in *The Mortgage Corporation* v. *Shaire*.[72] He construed the new Act and concluded that the interests of creditors were now just one interest among others to be considered when deciding whether to order a sale.[73]

This has attracted fierce criticism from Pascoe.[74] She argues that s. 15 was not meant to change the law and that Neuberger J is wrong. She underpins her argument with reference to the Law Commission report, and to Lord Mackay, then Lord Advocate, who introduced the Bill on its second reading in the House of Lords,[75] and indicated that the old caselaw would still apply. However, these arguments have to contend against the strong evidence of the statute itself[76] for, as has been said, s. 15 does not prioritise any of the criteria. Pascoe also disapproves of the effect upon creditors. Under s. 30, a secured creditor could feel fairly confident that the court would order a sale in order to satisfy the charge – under the new, *Shaire* approach, such confidence may be misplaced. But this is not to say that TOLATA has dramatically altered the balance of advantage. For even if a creditor is refused a sale, all is not lost. It may decide to institute bankruptcy proceedings against the debtor and, if successful, it can then take advantage of s. 335 (3) of the Insolvency Act 1986, which in effect allows a sale a year after a bankruptcy order is made.

TOLATA – practical effect

Ultimately, TOLATA is a disappointment. Yes, it has tidied up the law by turning trusts for sale into trusts of land, but its practical effect is limited. It has ostensibly protected beneficiaries against their trustees but, unless Ferris and Battersby are proved right, it has failed to offer any practical benefit against that most deadly weapon in a trustee's armoury – overreaching. Since the high-water mark of protection offered to beneficiaries in *Williams & Glyn's Bank Ltd* v. *Boland*,[77] there has been a steady retreat, and TOLATA has made little attempt to redress any balance.[78] Section 15 only minimally enhances the protection of

---

[72] [2000] 1 FLR 973.

[73] Neuberger J refused to order a sale on condition that the mortgagee had its equity converted into a loan and that Mrs Shaire pay interest on the loan.

[74] 'Section 15 of the Trusts of Land and Appointment of Trustees Act 1996 – a change in the law?' [2000] Conv. 315.

[75] HL Debs. Vol. 569, col. 1719.

[76] Thompson, 'Secured Creditors and Sales' [2000] Conv. 329.

[77] [1981] AC 487.

[78] Contrast this with the judicial activism which has culminated in *Royal Bank of Scotland plc* v. *Etridge* (No. 2) [2001] 3 WLR 1021.

beneficiaries against third parties. As has already been mentioned, the statute also resolutely failed to attempt any reform of beneficial joint tenancy or tenancy in common. An opportunity to introduce a considered and wholesale reform was missed.

Implied trusts

Formality requirements and implied trusts

By s. 53 (1) (b) of the Law of Property Act 1925, some formality is required for the successful declaration of a trust in land – it must be evidenced in writing. This requirement, which dates back to the Statute of Frauds,[79] does not seem especially onerous, and it can be justified as a means of preventing fraud, ensuring certainty in dealings with land and perhaps protecting settlors from casual or over-impulsive generosity. But, inevitably, any formality requirement provides an opportunity for the unscrupulous to take advantage of their more naive neighbours, and circumstances may arise when an insistence upon formality may seem in itself to support fraud. So equity developed a jurisdiction whereby even trusts that did not comply with the requisite formalities would be recognised, if it would be fair and appropriate to do so (or, at least, unconscionable *not* to do so). Such 'implied' trusts are specifically exempt from the formality requirements of s. 53 (1).[80] It is these implied trusts that have generated a lively academic discussion and much controversy.

In land law, an implied trust is typically claimed where a couple share a house that is in the name of only one of them. If the couple are unmarried, and the relationship breaks down, the court will have only very limited powers to reallocate property,[81] and the non-title holder will have to claim an interest under an implied trust, or proprietary estoppel, if she is to succeed in salvaging any part of the house's equity for her own future use. If the couple are married, the court will have very wide discretionary powers under the Matrimonial Causes Act 1973 to redistribute the property to produce a fair and just result, so a breakdown in the relationship does not call for a claim under an implied trust. However, during the continuation of the marriage, a third-party creditor may claim against the apparent property of one spouse, and the other

---

[79] Statute of Frauds 1677, s. 7.

[80] By Law of Property Act 1925, s. 53(2). See Statute of Frauds 1677, s. 8.

[81] If the couple have a child, the court has the power to order a property adjustment order for the child's benefit under Sch. 1 to the Children Act 1989. If the couple are heterosexual and the family home is rented, then under Part II of Sch. 7 to the Family Law Act 1996, the court may transfer the tenancy from one to the other. So far, courts have been reluctant to use their powers under Sch. 1 in a way that results in a 'windfall' for the resident parent. See *A* v. *A (Financial Provision)* [1994] 1 FLR 657.

spouse may then assert some beneficial interest, to the disadvantage of the creditor but to the advantage of the family unit.[82]

There is general unhappiness with the present law and, indeed, in acknowledgment of this, the Law Commission has, for several years now, been considering the problem of homesharers.[83] The criticisms take various forms. The basis of the law itself is questioned, as is its doctrinal coherence. Its practical effect has also been subjected to much consideration and comment.

The theoretical basis of resulting trusts

An implied trust may be either constructive or resulting. Resulting trusts are the older – the jurisprudence was already well established by the time of the seminal eighteenth-century case, *Dyer* v. *Dyer*.[84] This case confirmed that if A contributed to the purchase of land then, in the absence of evidence to the contrary (and in the absence of a stronger equitable presumption), equity would presume that A should acquire a commensurate beneficial interest in the land. A would hold this interest under a resulting trust.

Recently, the whole theoretical basis of resulting trusts has become a subject of debate. Birks[85] has argued that they should be seen as essentially restitutionary in character, and that they are best analysed as a response to unjust enrichment.[86] A self-contained law of restitution is comparatively new in English taxonomy, and its boundaries, especially with the law of property, are still being delimited. So it is understandable that those lawyers who are trying to establish the bounds of restitution should be receptive to new analyses that incorporate within its sphere established areas of jurisprudence, and a battle-ground at present is the resulting trust. A clear exposition of the restitutionary case is found in Chambers's book on resulting trusts.[87] He has developed Birks's ideas and has produced a careful exploration of the underpinning of the presumption. His argument is that a resulting trust is presumed when (a) A has contributed to the purchase of property and (b) A *did not intend* to give the benefit of that property to the recipient. This means that the *only* evidence that will rebut the presumption of resulting trust is positive evidence of an intention to give. An alternative, and perhaps more

[82] See, for example, *Williams & Glyn's Bank Ltd* v. *Boland* [1981] AC 487.
[83] *29th Annual Report*, (1994) Law Com No. 232 (1999), para. 2.78. The publication of the Law Commission's report is expected shortly.
[84] (1788) 2 Cox Eq Cas 92.
[85] 'Restitution and resulting trusts' in Goldstein, *Equity and Contemporary Legal Developments* (1992, Oxford).
[86] Also see Hopkins, *The Informal Acquisition of Rights in Land* (2000, Sweet & Maxwell) for further support of the restitutionary nature of resulting trusts.
[87] *Resulting Trusts* (1997, Clarendon Press).

traditional or orthodox analysis, is that the presumption applies when (a) A has contributed to the purchase of property and (b) A *intended* to create a trust for herself.

It matters which of these alternative analyses is correct, because that then affects the relevance of any evidence that may be adduced in rebuttal or support of a resulting trust. If Birks and Chambers are right, and the only evidence that will rebut the trust is evidence of the contributor's intention to benefit the recipient, then a resulting trust can (and will) be presumed even when the claimant quite clearly had no intention to establish a trust in her own favour. And it is indisputable that there are some cases in the law reports where resulting trusts have been found even though the claimant lacked any intent to create a trust. Thus, Chambers is able to point to the 'ignorance' cases, where a claimant had not realised that he had contributed to the purchase of property in the name of another, and yet still successfully established a resulting trust.[88] Also, Chambers uses the 'incapacity' cases, where a resulting trust has been presumed even though the contributor lacked the legal or mental capacity to consent to a transfer. As an example of the latter, he cites *Goodfellow* v. *Robertson*,[89] where Spragge C considered that evidence of incapacity (unsoundness of mind) did not rebut the presumption of resulting trust in the invalid's favour.

The argument is persuasive in theory, although it is unfortunate that Chambers is unable to point to additional, and more recent, cases in support of his thesis. He only refers to a handful of cases, several of which date back to the eighteenth or nineteenth centuries.[90] This seems an insecure foundation upon which to build a whole new theoretical structure and so, despite increasing support for the restitutionary analysis,[91] it is still vulnerable to criticism.

And criticism such analysis has received. Swadling[92] has argued strongly against a restitutionary role for resulting trusts and points to caselaw in support of his contention that a resulting trust arises on the presumption that the contributor *intended* to create a trust. Swadling's argument has been expressly endorsed at the highest level by the House

---

[88] See, for example, *Williams* v. *Williams* (1863) 32 Beav 370, where a father purchased land but, through an honest mistake, and unknown to the father, the land was put into the son's name. After the son died, a resulting trust was found in the father's favour. If a resulting trust were based upon a presumption that the contributor intended to establish a trust, then the evidence of the father's ignorance should have rebutted the presumption.

[89] (1871) 18 Gr 572.

[90] See Chambers (*op. cit.* above fn. 87), pp. 19–27.

[91] Millett L.J. (writing extra-judicially) 'Restitution and constructive trusts' (1998) 114 LQR 399; see also Lord Millett in *Air Jamaica Ltd* v. *Charlton* [1999] 1 WLR 1399, noted (2000) 116 LQR 15.

[92] 'A new role for resulting trusts?' (1996) LS 110.

of Lords in *Westdeutsche* v. *Islington LBC*.[93] Lord Browne-Wilkinson rejected the notion of a restitutionary resulting trust and stated that 'a resulting trust is not imposed by law against the intentions of the trustee ... but gives effect to his presumed intention.' If Swadling's thesis is correct, then *any* evidence that is inconsistent with the contributor's intention that the recipient is to be a trustee will rebut the presumption of resulting trust. This obviously makes a resulting trust easier to rebut; much more evidence will be relevant. Those, like Swadling, who are worried about 'proprietary overkill' – that is, the expansion of proprietary claims into those areas where previously only personal claims existed – prefer these more limited circumstances in which a resulting trust can be implied.

Possibly, there is a certain amount of empire-building in progress. This, at any rate, is a perception among some property lawyers. As Lord Browne-Wilkinson rather caustically remarked, 'the search for a perceived need to strengthen the remedies of a plaintiff claiming in restitution involves, to my mind, a distortion of trust principles'.[94]

As if this very fundamental uncertainty were not enough, the matter has been further obfuscated by recent judicial suggestions that the intentions of *both* contributor and recipient are relevant for the presumption of resulting trust. Mee[95] blames Lord Diplock for this development, and his famous dictum in *Gissing*[96] that conflated resulting and constructive trusts and premised them both upon the inequitable conduct of the recipient/trustee. This departure from orthodoxy has been reinforced by Lord Browne-Wilkinson in *Westdeutsche*, who talked of resulting trusts giving effect to the common intention of the parties.[97] Likewise, in *Tinsley* v. *Milligan*,[98] although Lord Browne-Wilkinson considered that the presumption of resulting trust was crucial to the case, he seems to have conflated resulting and constructive trusts and talked of common intention in relation to resulting trusts.

---

[93] *Westdeutsche Landesbank Girozentrale* v. *Islington London Borough Council* [1996] AC 669, at 689, 709. Lord Goff, referring to Birks's paper (at fn. 85 above), said 'his thesis ... is written to test the temperature of the water ... The temperature of the water must be regarded as decidedly cold'.

[94] [1996] AC 669 at 709.

[95] *The Property Rights of Cohabitees* (1999, Hart), p. 39.

[96] *Gissing* v. *Gissing* [1971] AC 886 at 905: 'A resulting, implied or constructive trust – and it is unnecessary for present purposes to distinguish between these three classes of trust is created by a transaction between the trustee and the cestui que trust in connection with the acquisition by the trustee of a legal estate in land, whenever the trustee has so conducted himself that it would be inequitable to deny to the cestui que trust a beneficial interest in the land acquired. And he will be held to have so conducted himself if by his words or conduct he had induced the cestui que trust to act to his detriment in the reasonable belief that by so acting he was acquiring a beneficial interest in the land.'

[97] [1996] AC 669 at 708.

[98] [1994] 1 AC 340.

The general confusion engendered by all this can be seen only too clearly in that sad case of middle-aged love, *Springette* v. *Defoe*.[99] The parties both contributed towards the purchase of a house in their joint names, but in the proportions of three quarters to one quarter. Although the transfer did not contain a declaration of their beneficial interests (and so there was no express trust), the evidence showed that both parties had thought they would share the house equally. However, they had never discussed this with each other – it was just what they both assumed. Now in effect this meant that Springette intended to give Defoe a quarter share of the house – and this should have been enough to rebut the presumption of resulting trust, whatever the theoretical underpinning of the presumption, and whether or not one adopts a restitutionary analysis. If the presumption of resulting trust had been rebutted, then that would have allowed equity to follow the law so that the parties would have held as beneficial joint tenants. Such a result would most nearly have been in accord with their intentions. But, instead, the Court of Appeal held that the presumption of resulting trust could only be rebutted by evidence of a common intention between the parties, which they then failed to find because the parties had not discussed their property shares. The bizarre result of the case was that a trust was found which bore no relationship to the intention of either party. Although the case has been strongly criticised,[100] it continues to attract judicial approval.[101]

And so uncertainty reigns, and it is probable that this contributes to the confusion between resulting and constructive trusts that now bedevils this area, as is discussed below.

The theoretical basis of constructive trusts

The jurisprudence underpinning constructive trusts has developed very rapidly over the last 30 years or so, and it is an impressive example of how caselaw can develop to deal with the changing requirements of an evolving society. For the rigidity of family life, which typified the first half of the twentieth century, then evaporated in the aftermath of the Second World War and was replaced by something much more fluid and volatile. In this new heady society, typified by 'women's lib' and the 'swinging sixties', relationships foundered, cohabitation became more common and women became more active in the market place. This sounds as though it was fun and liberating, and to a certain extent it was. But this new family instability could also leave women very vulnerable financially. Women who had shared homes and lives with partners over many years found

[99] [1992] 2 FLR 388.
[100] Mee (*op. cit.* above fn. 95), 40–41.
[101] See *Allen* v. *Rochdale BC* [2000] Ch 221 at 232.

they were potentially destitute and homeless if their name was absent from the title deeds and their shared life came to an end. The reader will not be surprised to learn that Lord Denning MR recognised and responded to these new trends, and tried to provide a judicial solution by developing the idea of 'family assets'. This was given short shrift by a conservative House of Lords, but it was the same House of Lords, and particularly Lord Diplock in *Gissing* v. *Gissing*,[102] who provided the essential mechanism to help these women (and, of course, the occasional man) by recognising informal co-ownership. The idea that a trust would be imposed where there had been an offer or agreement as to beneficial entitlement, and then detrimental reliance thereupon, was a convenient way to tackle the perceived problem and to remedy the more extreme cases of unfairness. That a Court of Appeal under the stewardship of Lord Denning MR was only too ready to embrace (and try to extend) the jurisprudence and the judicial success of constructive trusts is not surprising. But perhaps inevitably, Lord Denning MR's infectious enthusiasm, berated by Battersby as 'inconsistent with precedent, not based upon identifiable principles and detrimental to third parties',[103] led to a backlash, and in *Lloyds Bank plc* v. *Rosset*,[104] Lord Bridge attempted both to circumscribe the ambit of constructive trusts – to bring more certainty and principle into the area – and also to analyse their essential character.

Lord Bridge's premise, that constructive trusts are based upon the agreement of the parties, has been criticised as incorrect in principle. Glover and Todd[105] argue that it is the settlor's intention that is necessary, not a common intention. In practice, this does not seem to make much difference, because the claimant also has to show detrimental reliance and so logically needs to be aware of the settlor's apparent intention that she should enjoy a beneficial share in the property; it is difficult to see how she could rely on this without agreeing to it. But anyway the constructive trust in connection with the family home seems to have developed its own special jurisprudence, which is now quite distinct from the law of trusts in other areas. This is a reflection of the centrality that issues concerning ownership of family homes have achieved over the last half century.

The distinction between resulting and constructive trusts

A main difficulty is how, within the area of family homes, constructive and resulting trusts relate to each other. In *Rosset*, Lord Bridge divided

---

[102] [1971] AC 888 at 906.
[103] 'How not to judge the quantum (and priority) of a share in the family home, *Midland Bank plc* v. *Cooke*' (1996) 8 CFLQ 261.
[104] [1991] 1 AC 107.
[105] 'The myth of common intention' (1996) 16 LS 325.

constructive trusts into two categories: (a) when there was an express agreement between the parties that the claimant should share in the beneficial entitlement to the property; and (b) when there was not. In the latter case, Lord Bridge considered that a direct contribution to the purchase price of property would allow the court to infer a common agreement to share, and could therefore form the basis of a constructive trust. The contribution would serve the dual role of allowing the inference of agreement, and fulfilling the necessity for detrimental reliance thereon. Such an 'implied agreement' constructive trust looks very like the traditional type of resulting trust. In both cases, and in the absence of evidence as to intention, a direct contribution to the purchase of land generates a beneficial share in that land. But if that is the case – then how does one know when to use a resulting trust analysis, and when a constructive trust?

The question matters because, conventionally, a resulting trust has produced a share commensurate to the contribution while, under constructive trust jurisprudence, the court tries to give effect to the agreement between the parties, whatever that might have been. This can therefore result in quite different shares being awarded, depending upon which type of trust one finds – as the different judgments of *Drake* v. *Whipp*[106] show. But since the judgments in *Midland Bank plc* v. *Cooke*,[107] it is unclear whether this distinction as to quantification still holds good. In *Cooke*, the Court of Appeal was faced with a wife who had contributed a small sum directly to the purchase of the matrimonial home. There was evidence that, at the time of purchase, neither she nor her husband had thought about the ownership of the house, which had been put into his name alone. When a third party – the bank – subsequently claimed against the husband's share, it became vital for Mrs Cooke's financial well-being to claim as large a proportion of the house as possible. And the Court of Appeal strove to help her. They managed to reject the strictly proportionate (6%) allocation of the judge, and to award her a half share in the house. How the court succeeded in doing this is a little unclear. Either they imposed a resulting trust, but with a novel, expansive approach to quantification of share or, alternatively, they imposed an implied constructive trust as explained by Lord Bridge in *Rosset*. The problem about the latter analysis is that, in principle, constructive trusts are imposed to prevent unconscionability – and it is difficult to see any unconscionable behaviour on the part of Mr Cook when neither he nor his wife discussed or even thought about ownership of the home. The motives of the court, to salvage some remnants of equity in the family home for a deserving hard-working wife, are no doubt understandable, but the juridical basis is very difficult to reconcile with any traditional

[106] [1996] 1 FLR 826.
[107] [1995] 4 All ER 562.

principle, and the implications of the case are still unclear.[108] Possibly, resulting trusts now allow for an enlarged quantification. Or possibly, the courts can now impute an intention in order to justify a constructive trust in the family home whenever there has been a direct contribution by the claimant. Whichever is correct, one expects that the development will be confined to trusts of a family home.

The distinction between constructive trusts and proprietary estoppel

Another area of interest concerns the distinction between common intention constructive trusts and proprietary estoppel. The law concerning estoppels has developed separately from the constructive trust jurisprudence but, in recent years, the two have grown ever more similar in character. An estoppel may arise when a claimant has relied upon a representation to her detriment; and it is easy to see that the same facts may appear to allow both a claim for a constructive trust and a claim in proprietary estoppel. This has led to spirited debate as to whether or not the two principles are now essentially indistinguishable, and both commentators and judges have contributed their thoughts. Lord Bridge in *Rosset*,[109] for example, stated that reliance upon an express agreement could engender a constructive trust or a proprietary estoppel, and the tenor of his judgment seemed to suggest that it did not matter which was claimed.

With regard to overreaching, it is now clear that indeed this is the case, and that it does not matter whether one frames one's claim in terms of estoppel or a constructive trust. For the ingenious argument of Mrs Sabherwal, that her interest in the family home was estoppel-based and therefore not subject to overreaching, was firmly rejected by the Court of Appeal in *Birmingham Midshires Mortgage Services Ltd* v. *Sabherwal*.[110] The court refused to allow the claimant to manipulate the identification of her interest to her advantage in this way. As Robert Walker LJ feelingly said, 'To do so would cause vast confusion in an area which is already quite difficult enough', to which one can only say, hear, hear.

But it has been possible to identify some distinctions between a constructive trust and an estoppel – one is that the courts have been prepared to use a wide range of remedies to satisfy an estoppel, whereas the remedy for a constructive trust is merely the awarding of an appropriate beneficial share. In this respect, an estoppel claim can be seen

---

[108] For further discussion, see Tee, 'Division of property upon relationship breakdown' in Herring, *Family Law: Issues, Debates, Policy* (2001, Willan).

[109] [1991] 1 AC 107 at 132. See also Browne-Wilkinson V-C in *Grant* v. *Edwards* [1986] Ch 638 at 656. But see *Stokes* v. *Anderson* [1991] 1 FLR 391.

[110] (2000) 80 P & CR 256.

as permitting the courts a welcome flexibility – which is perhaps why most claims in this area have been framed in terms of constructive trust.

Another possible distinction concerns the enforceability of the trust or estoppel against a third party. It seems clear that when the court finds a constructive trust, the proprietary nature of the beneficial interest dates back to the time of the relevant detrimental reliance. Hayton[111] has criticised this aspect of the jurisprudence and has argued that there should be no retrospective recognition of a common intention constructive trust. He thinks that constructive trusts should not be enforceable against a third party until they have been adjudicated.

In contrast, the question whether an inchoate estoppel – that is an estoppel that has not yet been adjudicated – was enforceable against a third party was a live issue until very recently.[112] A persuasive argument ran that, as the court could satisfy the estoppel by means of a licence or other non-proprietary remedy – or even by saying that no equitable intervention was required – it was illogical and inappropriate to accord the inchoate creature a proprietary status. The argument was not only persuasive, it was also supportable. For the caselaw yielded no ready answer one way or the other, and so there was room for argument from principle. There were indeed many cases that suggested that inchoate estoppels were enforceable against third parties, but the third parties involved generally turned out to be intimately connected with the representor rather than genuinely independent, and the cases were often susceptible to alternative analysis.[113] So the jury was still out.

The Law Commission, however, has now taken a robust view of the matter. In its commentary on the Land Registration Bill, it stated that the weight of authority was in favour of recognising an inchoate estoppel as proprietary.[114] Accordingly, s. 116 of the Act provides that 'for the avoidance of doubt' (always a give-away) and 'in relation to registered land' an inchoate estoppel can bind successors. In the future therefore there will be little to distinguish a claim for proprietary estoppel from a claim for an interest under a constructive trust, provided the land is registered. Both will allow retrospective recognition of an interest, and both will therefore be equally threatening to third parties. Perhaps only a judicial attitude that a wider discretion is permissible for estoppel claims

---

[111] 'Equitable rights of cohabitees' [1990] Conv. 370, and 'Constructive trusts of homes – a bold approach' (1993) 109 LQR 485. See, *contra*, Ferguson, 'Constructive trusts – a note of caution' (1993) 109 LQR 114.

[112] See Smith, 'How proprietary is proprietary estoppel?' in Rose, *Consensus ad Idem* (1996, Sweet & Maxwell).

[113] See Tee, 'The rights of every person in actual occupation' [1998] CLJ 328 at fn. 36.

[114] The Law Commission, in a novel argument, dismissed the opposition to this principle on the basis that it came from academics 'defending their published views' (Law Com No. 271, 2001, para 5.30).

will remain as a difference, and that is fairly shadowy and insubstantial. The new Act could theoretically result in the intriguing prospect of estoppels being treated differently in unregistered and registered land, because the matter is not as clear cut as the Law Commission claims, but the inexorable march of registered land will soon diminish that possibility. For within a generation only land owned by a corporation will remain unregistered.

The relationship between express and implied trusts

An unresolved issue is whether or not the beneficial proportions under an express trust can be increased by the identification of an implied trust on top of the expressly agreed share. The available caselaw is not especially helpful. In *Pettitt* v. *Pettitt*, [115] Lord Upjohn declared that an express declaration of trust, when duly evidenced by signed writing, 'necessarily concludes the question of title ... for all time'. Similar statements can be found elsewhere.[116] However, it seems unclear why a claimant should only be able to argue that she had acquired a share of property under a constructive trust if the property was originally in the sole name of her partner. In principle, a promise of a share – or an increased share – in property, followed by sufficient and relevant detrimental reliance upon that promise, would seem to require equity's intervention however the property was originally held. One can imagine, for example, a scenario where a house was purchased in joint names, legally and beneficially, and upon the relationship breakdown, the departing cohabitant saying, 'you take over the mortgage and all the outgoings, and you can have the whole house'. That could possibly engender a proprietary estoppel, but could it not also found a constructive trust to build upon the express trust? The most recent judicial pronouncement is found in *Re Schuppan (a Bankrupt) (No 2)*,[117] in which Maddocks J declared that 'it is not easy to find room for a second trust where one has been expressly declared'. One can, of course, interpret this in one of two ways – either that it is in effect impossible, or that the court just has to be a little more careful before finding the second trust. Related to this conundrum is the effect of s. 37 of the Matrimonial Proceedings and Property Act 1970, which quite clearly seems to provide that a spouse can enlarge her beneficial share in the matrimonial home by paying for substantial improvements to the property.[118]

---

[115] [1970] AC 777 at 813.

[116] For example, *Gissing* v. *Gissing* [1971] AC 886 at 905 *per* Lord Diplock; *Goodman* v. *Gallant* [1986] Fam 106.

[117] [1997] 1 BCLC 256 at 269.

[118] Harpum (in *Megarry & Wade: The Law of Real Property, op. cit.* above fn. 28, at para. 9.041) points out that this could result in unexpected severance of a beneficial joint tenancy.

Just as it seems unclear whether one can claim a constructive trust to add to a share under an express trust, so it is unclear whether the share under an implied trust can then be informally altered. In so far as the share can be created informally, it would seem logical to conclude that it can also be altered informally, but there is no clarity in the caselaw. In *Cowcher* v. *Cowcher*,[119] Bagnall J rejected an argument that a wife could increase her share informally, but in *Re Densham (A Bankrupt)*[120] Goff J disagreed with Bagnall J and considered that a constructive trust could give effect to a subsequent agreement. Likewise, *Re Schuppan*[121] seems to suggest that a share can be altered by subsequent informal agreement, but the judge's thinking on this point is not clearly expressed.

Implied trusts – issues of policy

So, the substantive law generates some discussion and disagreement. But this is nothing to the thousands of words that have been written about the effect of the present law and the issues of policy that inform or should inform implied trusts.

Criticisms range over the unreality of the search for common intention and detrimental reliance, the unpredictability of outcome, the devaluation of non-financial contributions, the capricious results and the underlying gender-bias endemic in the whole process of searching for an implied trust. These criticisms are trenchant and important.

The role of intention

A problem in premising an implied trust upon the intentions of the parties is that, generally speaking, happy couples do not think in proprietary terms. People tend to be motivated by love or affection (or of course the opposite) in their dealings with their spouses or cohabitants, rather than by mercenary calculation. Couples tend to share their homes and arrange their finances as is convenient for the present, and with no thought of, or indeed knowledge of, the legal implications for beneficial ownership in the future. Thus it is unrealistic to look for an agreement as to how the home is owned.

As a result, some commentators have suggested that the courts should abandon the search for elusive intention and, instead, premise beneficial ownership upon other criteria. The seminal article was written by Gardner in 1993.[122] He argued that where the law identifies a relationship of trust and collaboration (by taking an objective approach rather than

---

[119] [1972] 1 WLR 425.
[120] [1975] 1 WLR 1519.
[121] *Re Schuppan (a Bankrupt) (No 2)* [1997] 1 BCLC 256.
[122] 'Rethinking family property' (1993) 109 LQR 263.

heart-searching) a community of property regime should be imposed to give effect to the requisite values of the relationship. The article has provoked much discussion, both supportive and critical.

The difficulty is that any attempt to abandon the intention of the parties as the crucial trust-generating factor in effect results in the imposition, by the courts, of possible alien or unwelcome value judgments as to how couples should own property, and results in effective redistribution of private property without legal redress. At present, such interference in property rights, and an effective judicial power to redistribute property, is confined to statutory powers awarded to courts, in connection with divorce (or some children-related) proceedings. The confining of such powers to divorce proceedings means that the individuals involved chose, by marrying, to acquire a specific legal status with implications for future freedom of action and property rights. Such cannot be said of the cohabiting couple, who may have deliberately chosen not to marry and may resent any outside interference as to how they order their property as between themselves.

A possible development, which would still place intention firmly in the centre of the jurisprudence but which would also take account of the unreality of couples thinking in proprietorial terms, would be to recognise an imputed intention. That would allow the court to impute to the parties the intentions that they would have had, had they thought about property rights. By retaining a close connection to the intention of the parties, respect for individual autonomy could still be retained. People would still be encouraged to take personal responsibility for their own lives, but a note of reality would creep into the judicial inquiry. Bottomley argues for this.[123] She thinks that intention should be the starting point of a consideration of ownership – but she recognises the reality of sexual-domestic relationships – and favours a readiness to find an objective test for intention. This could take into account the relationship and interrelations between the couple. The difficulty is that the House of Lords has rejected this idea. In *Pettitt* v. *Pettitt*[124] both Lord Reid and Lord Diplock argued against a subjective test for intention They were in the minority. In *Gissing* v. *Gissing*,[125] Lord Reid again argued his case, but Lord Diplock rather reluctantly abandoned his previous arguments ('I must now accept the majority decision...')[126] and instead proposed his classic formulation for implied trusts.

---

[123] 'Women and trust(s): portraying the family in the gallery of law' in Bright and Dewar, *Land Law: Themes and Perspectives* (1998, Oxford University Press).
[124] [1970] AC 777 at 795.
[125] [1971] AC 886 at 897.
[126] *Ibid.* at 904.

The unreality of detrimental reliance

The idea of 'detrimental reliance' is also problematic. Superficially, the requirement seems reasonable and necessary. It provides the equivalent of consideration for the promise of a share in the house – without such a requirement, a claimant could argue that she was entitled to a beneficial interest just on the strength of an oral agreement that would not even have contractual force. The detrimental reliance also provides that element of unconscionability upon which a constructive trust is founded – for once the claimant has relied upon the agreement to her detriment, it becomes unconscionable for the paper owner to deny her a share in the property.

So it is very understandable that the courts have insisted upon this criterion. The difficulty is that, like common intention, the requirement shows a fundamental disregard for human nature.[127] On the whole, people who live together and share their lives contribute willingly and generously to the common good of their family unit without thought of reward or proprietary interest. The mythical individual who embarks upon a course of conduct only because she thinks she has an ownership share in the house is – thankfully – an unlikely construct. As O'Donovan has noted,[128] this subject, a rational, capable individual in charge of his own destiny, is a particular kind of person with a set of characteristics associated with masculinity rather than femininity. She argues that this reflects a masculine bias within the law. The feminine qualities of co-operation and sharing and context are not reflected in the legal subject, nor the legal requirements, and therefore disadvantage women.

Considerations of gender-bias

The gender-bias underlying the present jurisprudence has attracted much comment.[129] In form, constructive (and resulting) trusts are gender-neutral. Indeed, they are also neutral as to sexual orientation, race, religion and any other potentially discriminatory factor that a prejudiced society may conjure out of its wounded psyche. But it has long been recognised that this neutral form masks a discriminatory substance.

The reality operates against women on various levels. As noted above, the mythical legal subject who in theory enters into an agreement as to property rights with a loved one seems characteristically more masculine than feminine. On a less abstract level, the contributions a woman often makes to family life, the nurturing and emotional support, the home-

---

127 Lawson, 'The things we do for love: detrimental reliance in the family home' (1996) 16 LS 218.
128 'With sense, consent or just a con? Legal subjects in the discourse of autonomy' in Naffine and Owens, *Sexing the Subject of Law* (1997, Sweet & Maxwell).
129 The literature is extensive. A good starting point is Bailey-Harris, 'Law and the unmarried couple – oppression or liberation' (1996) 8 CFLQ 137.

making generally, are discounted by a judiciary unable to view such contributions as either 'detrimental' or 'in reliance'. Even a woman who assists in renovation may find her work dismissed as 'natural' and therefore as not qualifying.[130] The search for 'detrimental reliance' to found a constructive trust devalues non-monetary contributions and, even more, contributions that are not susceptible to an easy evaluation in monetary terms.

The way forward: statutory reform

The idea that seems to be gaining in popularity is that there should be some limited form of statutory intervention, so that couples who have lived together for a qualifying period may then apply to the courts for discretionary property transfer orders or other orders along the lines of those available to divorcing couples. Barlow and Lind[131] have elaborated upon the idea of statutory intervention to develop a proposed system of modified community of property. They suggest a sliding scale of allocation of property rights, whereby the non-owner partner gradually acquires a larger share in the family home. They also suggest that contracting out should be permitted, and that the courts should have a discretion to adjust the proportions to prevent 'manifest disadvantage'.

A statutory scheme is attractive on various levels. One of the problems with this area is that reform suggestions often involve intervention into people's private lives and, in effect, if a beneficial interest in the home is recognised against the wishes or intention of the titleholder, confiscation of private property. This can be criticised as inappropriate and undesirable behaviour on the part of the state and an erosion of the principle that the law should respect private property. However, a statutory rather than a common law development would at least be democratically legitimised, and this should help counter some of the more extreme constitutional arguments. A statutory provision that allowed homesharers to claim some proportion of the beneficial interest in their home would be supported by those who consider that the role of the law is not merely to protect established property owners but extends to protecting the vulnerable and disadvantaged. It would also reduce the present stark distinction between the statutory protection offered to spouses and that offered to mere 'common law' wives or husbands. With increasing rates of cohabitation, and less social or, indeed, economic difference between the married and the unmarried, such a reduction seems resonant with the times.

---

[130] Note Lord Bridge's dismissive description of Mrs Rosset's work in *Lloyd's Bank plc* v. *Rosset* [1991] 1 AC 107.
[131] 'A matter of trust: the allocation of rights in the family home' (1999) 19 LS 468.

No doubt there would need to be an opt-out provision, for even though that is vulnerable to manipulation by the emotionally less dependent partner, it is still an important safeguard to preserve individual choice. But the details can be worked out without too much difficulty once the principle is established. A statutory reform, which enabled a cohabitant to claim a share of her home, would be a welcome initiative. It also seems likely. We await the publication of the Law Commission's report on homesharing with anticipation.

Final thoughts

In this chapter we have ranged over a wide area of jurisprudence and debate. The discourse can be presented in various ways. Thus implied trusts are relevant to the debate between liberalism – with its emphasis on individuality and rights – and communitarianism – with its emphasis on status and social relationships. In addition, the discussion involves the public/private debate – the extent to which the state – via the law – should interfere in private, i.e. domestic sexual, relationships. The continuing tension in land law between the need for certainty and the desire for flexibility to ensure fair results in particular cases is only too clearly evident in this whole area. The subject has also attracted feminist attention because, while the present law of implied trusts is formally gender-neutral, it arguably exhibits gender bias. All these view points and interpretations inform the law of co-ownership and trusts, even though the subject-matter is the relatively common one of a couple setting up home together, and then either living together in harmony until death, or moving on to other relationships. But of course, though the scenario is common, even typical, individuals and their relationships are unique. The trick is to provide a law that facilitates and supports, but does not unduly constrain or unfairly restrict people in their domestic arrangements. Put like that, it is clear why the law engenders such debate and controversy. In the circumstances, although the present law could certainly be improved in many particulars, one can also conclude that it could be a whole lot worse.

Further reading

Barlow and Lind, 'A matter of trust: the allocation of rights in the family home' (1999) 19 LS 468.
Bottomley, 'Women and trust(s): portraying the family in the gallery of law, in Bright and Dewar, *Land Law: Themes and Perspectives* (1998, Oxford University Press).
Chambers, *Resulting Trusts* (1997, Clarendon Press).

Dixon, 'Overreaching and the Trusts of Land and Appointment of Trustees Act 1996' [2000] Conv. 267.

Ferris and Battersby, 'The impact of the Trusts of Land and Appointment of Trustees Act 1996 on purchasers of registered land' [1998] Conv. 168, 'Overreaching and the Trusts of Land and the Appointment of Trustees Act 1996 – a reply to Mr Dixon' [2001] Conv. 221.

Gardner, 'Rethinking family property' (1993) 109 LQR 263.

Hopkins, *The Informal Acquisition of Rights in Land* (2000, Sweet & Maxwell).

Lawson, 'The things we do for love: detrimental reliance in the family home' (1996) 16 LS 218.

Mee, *The Property Rights of Cohabitees* (1999, Hart).

6

Mortgages

Mika Oldham

It is tempting to conceptualise the residential mortgage as a sort of David and Goliath transaction, in which some poor, powerless and guileless individual is crushed by the might of the huge and emotionless financial institution. But of course it is not that simple. Mortgages confer significant benefits on both parties to the bargain, and they also have wider political, economic and social importance.

The mortgage market and the wider economy

It is difficult to overemphasise the economic importance of the mortgage. In terms of scale, mortgages constitute the most important source of consumer credit in the UK and consequently represent huge business for the financial sector[1]. At the end of 1997 total sterling loans to the private sector totalled £836.2 billion, of which mortgages accounted for £403.2 billion. Mortgage lending was more than double all lending to industrial and commercial companies.[2]

But market size is not the sole reason for the economic importance of the mortgage. In terms of function, mortgages constitute a key economic institution – the means by which assets are mobilised, capital generated and productivity and the wider economy boosted. The mortgage is a mechanism that transforms 'passive' land value into 'active' value in that it allows the value of land to be released for other purposes while the

---

[1] In 1999, banks' assets totalled some £1,321,485 million, of which £337,899 million was invested in mortgages. For building societies, total sterling assets amounted to £155,380.4 million, of which mortgages accounted for £123,183.4 million (*Annual Abstract of Statistics*, No. 137, 2001, pp. 389, 400).

[2] Robertson (Lombard Street Research), *Strategic Analysis of the UK Mortgage Business* (1998, The Financial Times).

freeholder or leaseholder is still able to enjoy the benefits of physical occupation or possession. It has even been argued that the ability to mortgage land is the key to the fundamental distinction between rich and poor countries. In poor countries, asset mobilisation is not possible because the capital invested in housing is incapable of being released because of inadequate underlying structures of property ownership and of social, political and legal control.[3] From such a perspective, the stability of the entire economy of a country is dependent on a proper functioning of the law of mortgages.

The state and the mortgage market

This pivotal importance of the mortgage within the economy provides the first of three broad reasons for the state's interest in the mortgage market generally, and in the law of mortgages in particular. The state plays a critical role in the process of asset mobilisation, in that the state must establish and safeguard the underlying legal structures that create the conditions necessary for the maintenance of a healthy flow of capital within the private economy.

A second, albeit rather different, explanation for the state interest in the mortgage is the fact that successive governments have used the mortgage – or, more specifically, promoted or facilitated the use by others of mortgages – as a means through which to reduce public expenditure on both housing and health care. As regards housing, state encouragement of home ownership has impacted on both public and private sectors of the housing and property market. Within the public sector, sales by successive governments of public housing stocks under 'right to buy' schemes have been effected through parallel rights of access to mortgage financing.[4] At the same time, measures were introduced that prevented local authorities from using the proceeds of those sales to build new public housing. Within the private sector, government rhetoric extolling the virtues of home ownership has been accompanied by more material encouragement in the form of economic and budgetary incentives, such

---

[3] De Soto, *The Mystery of Capital* (2000, Bantam).
[4] The key legislation was the Housing Act 1980, which gave most council tenants and some housing association tenants the right to buy their homes at discounted prices, with a statutory right to a local authority mortgage. A revised scheme now operates under the Housing Act 1985, as amended. For details, see Arden and Partington, *Housing Law* (2nd ed., 1994, Sweet and Maxwell), Chap. 18.

as mortgage interest tax relief.[5] In the result, owner-occupation levels have risen from around 10% at the start of the twentieth century to 69% by 1999.[6] As regards health care, public expenditure is saved because, having encouraged people to buy their homes, the state may then force them to sell them should they eventually require long-term residential care that would otherwise fall to be publicly funded.[7]

The third broad reason for the state interest in the mortgage market is related to the second but is wider than the purely economic. In political terms, home ownership has long been recognised as conducive to social stability. The homeowner takes on a personal stake in the success, security and prosperity of a particular neighbourhood, but he also buys a stake in the wider capitalist economy upon which the value of his property depends. Thus, home ownership is recognised as politically significant in that it encourages responsible sentiments of law-abiding and productive citizenship. Property ownership invites commitment.

But present levels of home ownership are not without negative implications. Over the last 15 years the traditional link between housing tenure and social class or economic status has become less pronounced than it previously was,[8] and there is some concern that levels of home ownership have reached unsustainable levels. What one study describes as 'disjunctions between housing policy, labour market policy and systems of social security'[9] have resulted in new record levels of repossessions. The number of warrants issued for repossession of properties peaked at 134,000 in 1991, then fluctuated but overall declined to 111,000 in 1996. By 1999, however, the number of warrants issued reached a new high of 137,000. A similar pattern emerges in respect of the number of warrants executed. The number remained fairly steady at around 50,000 between 1993 and 1997; but by 1999 it rose by 40% to 71,000,[10] thus exceeding even the peak of the immediate boom-and-bust

---

[5] Mortgage interest tax relief (MITR) was phased out, disappearing totally in 2000. MITR was considered inefficient in terms of state intervention in the housing market because it represented a general subsidy that gave greater benefits to those with larger mortgages and higher levels of taxable income. The government was also concerned to control house prices and to curb consumer spending, fuelled in part by equity release. The abolition of MITR was intended to have a powerful deflationary effect, and was offset in the short term by interest rate and tax rate reductions (which of course again benefited most the better off). See, further, Pearce and Wilcox, *Home-ownership, taxation and the economy: the economic and social effects of the abolition of mortgage interest tax relief* (1991, Joseph Rowntree Foundation).

[6] *Social Trends* 31 (2001), p. 178.

[7] For details, see the report of the Royal Commission on Long Term Care, *With Respect to Old Age: Long Term Care – Rights and Responsibilities* (1999, HMSO), Chap. 4.

[8] *Social Trends* 31 (2001), p. 181.

[9] Nettleton, Burrows, England and Seavers, *Losing the Family Home* (1999, Joseph Rowntree Foundation), p. v.

[10] *Social Trends* 31 (2001), pp. 190–191.

period. One study reports that between 1990 and 1998, some 454,280 households (an estimated 1.32 million adults and children) experienced repossession. And, of course, the social consequences for the families involved are significant.[11]

Benefits to the mortgagor

For mortgagors, the mortgage serves two main functions: it provides a means of funding for house purchases, and it acts as an 'equity release' vehicle that allows money to be borrowed at relatively low cost.

Housing is a need rather than a luxury, and choice is increasingly restricted. Both public and private rental markets offer only limited and relatively unattractive alternatives to house purchase. Reduced stocks of public housing mean long waiting lists for prospective tenants, and public housing is generally of a low standard and often in poor repair. The private rental sector is depressed, until relatively recently because of legislation that granted tenants security of tenure and controlled the levels of rent payable, thereby rendering the sector unattractive to private investors.[12]

For the borrower, the mortgage provides by far the cheapest source of loan and, indeed, the only way the majority of mortgagors could raise the sort of sum needed to finance a house purchase. Around three quarters of house purchases are effected with the aid of mortgage finance.[13] For the typical homeowner, the mortgage is also a vehicle of wealth creation and a fruitful form of investment. Because the borrower retains the fee simple or leasehold interest in the land that is the subject of the mortgage, the whole of any increase in the value of that land belongs to the borrower. So the mortgage loan of £100,000, that seems at its time of execution in 1992 an enormous burden, takes on a different perspective when the house is sold in 2002 for £500,000. Like any investment, property ownership is a form of speculation,[14] but one that provides an excellent hedge against rapid inflation.

The mortgagor also enjoys certain social benefits, since property ownership effects a form of social inclusion or community bonding. The purchase of a house affiliates the mortgagor to a particular locality and to a particular societal group. The purchaser acquires a sense of belonging

---

[11] See Nettleton *et al*, (*op. cit.* above fn. 10).

[12] There is some evidence of the beginning of a shift towards a more buoyant private sector, although in 2000 it was still the case that over 50% of all rented homes in Great Britain were rented from a local authority: *Social Trends* 31 (2001), p. 179. By contrast, at the beginning of the twentieth century some 89% of homes were privately rented: *ibid.*, p. 178.

[13] *Ibid.*, p. 189. This figure includes, of course, those buyers who could purchase outright but who decide to mortgage their properties as a cheap form of loan.

[14] And of course in a falling market may result in some mortgagors facing a 'negative equity'.

not only to the neighbourhood in which the house is located, but also to a larger group, that of homeowners generally. Home ownership signals respectability, responsibility and, usually, also upward mobility. The peculiarly English ideology surrounding home ownership has had the result that non-homeowners have become almost second-class citizens. Home ownership brings with it additional knock-on benefits that affect the purchaser's future economic dealings, since his or her credit ratings automatically improve. The simple fact that it is less easy for a homeowner than for a tenant to abscond means that even unsecured loans are more readily available, often on better terms, than to a non-homeowner.

Benefits to the mortgagee

The essence of the mortgage transaction is the charging of property as security for the performance of an obligation: usually, but not necessarily,[15] the discharge of a debt. Inevitably the primary anticipated benefit to the mortgagee is the profit that will be earned through the interest payable on the loan. But because the debt is secured, the lender in the mortgage transaction acquires not only the undertaking of the borrower to repay, but also an interest in the mortgaged land. The mortgagor cannot deal freely with the land that is the subject of the mortgage, although he may exercise his right to redeem by discharging his obligation to the mortgagee. The mortgagee, as a secured creditor, enjoys certain additional means of enforcing the performance of the obligation, or extracting the money equivalent. In the case of non-payment, the mortgagee may exercise his rights and remedies so as eventually to destroy the borrower's equity of redemption.[16] In the case of the insolvency of the debtor the mortgagee has a prior call over general creditors on the property that is the subject of the mortgage.[17] Residential mortgages constitute a particularly safe investment for the mortgagee, since people will generally go very far to avoid the loss of a home.

The law's intervention in the mortgage transaction

The intervention of equity into mortgage transactions had, and continues to have, a profound impact on the law of mortgages. But there has been a marked shift in the focus of that intervention, from an early concern to

---

[15] See, for example, *Santley* v. *Wilde* [1899] 2 Ch 474, where the mortgage was both security for a loan and security for a one-third share of future profits.
[16] By sale or foreclosure.
[17] *White* v. *Simmons* (1871) LR 6 Ch App. 555.

protect the mortgagor to a recognition today of a need to achieve a balance between the interests of both mortgagor and mortgagee.

Early developments had as their aim the protection of the impecunious landowner who was at the mercy of unscrupulous moneylenders. The attitude of the courts is exemplified by the frequently cited words of Lord Henley LC: 'Necessitous men are not, truly speaking, free men, but, to answer a present exigency, will submit to any terms that the crafty may impose upon them.'[18] Equitable intervention in mortgage transactions was viewed as one aspect of a general policy of providing relief against penalties and forfeitures and protecting persons from the unconscionable enforcement of legal rights. This policy was given effect in various ways. By the end of the seventeenth century the concept of the debtor's power to redeem had developed into that of the mortgagor's 'equity of redemption'. The doctrine against clogs and fetters on the equity of redemption developed in order to ensure that redemption was not hindered by provisions in the mortgage or by the activity of the mortgagee. From the seventeenth century onwards, the general theory accepted in Chancery was that a mortgage, whatever its outward form, was no more than a security for a debt, and that the mortgagee's rights must be so limited as to ensure that he obtained a security and no more. This theory justified equity's intervention into mortgage transactions – in no area of law was sanctity of contract less regarded.[19]

By the twentieth century, the attitude of the courts had shifted. Changing patterns of property ownership, the emergence and growth of commercial mortgages as forms of investment, and market competition created new imperatives. Legal recognition of the changing functions of the mortgage impacted on equitable intervention with the result that the courts were more prepared to uphold contractually agreed terms. Today, the typical mortgage is a transaction between parties who bear no resemblance to the usurer and the desperate and impoverished land-owner of earlier times. In consequence, the doctrine of clogs on the equity of redemption has declined in importance, but it is not yet defunct. In 2001 in *Jones* v. *Morgan and another* the Master of the Rolls expressed the view that 'the doctrine of a clog on the equity of redemption is, so it seems to me, an appendix to our law which no longer serves a useful purpose and would be better excised'.[20] Nevertheless the Court of Appeal in that case held that a clog on the equity of redemption was created by a clause in a document which was executed some three years after the mortgage.[21]

---

18 *Vernon* v. *Bethell* (1762) 2 Eden 100 at 113, 28 ER 838 at 839.

19 Simpson, *A History of the Land Law* (2nd ed. 1986, Clarendon Press), pp. 240–246.

20 *Jones* v. *Morgan* [2001] EWCA Civ. 995 at para. 86 *per* Lord Phillips MR. See also Law Com. No. 204, *Transfer of Land: Land Mortgages* (1991).

21 The later agreement varied the original mortgage to allow part of the land to be sold and included a clause by which the mortgagor agreed to transfer to the mortgagee a 50% interest in the retained land.

The law is still concerned to guard against differing forms of unconscionable dealing in relation to mortgages, although the focus of protective concern is largely the residential homeowner. The remainder of this chapter is concerned with two areas where the law continues to develop in order to protect vulnerable parties to mortgage transactions. The first of these areas is that of undue influence – more specifically, the extent to which a debtor's undue influence over a surety or chargee will affect the validity of the resulting contract between the surety and a mortgagee. The second area concerns statutory rather than equitable intervention – the creation of a regulatory scheme aimed at improving consumer protection in the mortgage market. Both these areas can be explained in terms of the need to achieve and maintain a proper balance between competing interests. The exercise involves not only consideration of the interests of the parties directly concerned, but also an assessment of the wider significance and the potential effect of the law upon these broader issues.

Undue influence and the law of mortgages

For some time now the issues of undue influence and misrepresentation have provided an important area of interest in the law of mortgages. In 1993 the House of Lords in *Barclays Bank plc* v. *O'Brien*[22] and *CIBC Mortgages* v. *Pitt*[23] qualified in important respects the more restrictive approach it had adopted in 1985 in *National Westminster Bank plc* v. *Morgan*.[24] The decisions seemed to suggest the reappearance of an approach more sympathetic to the victim of undue influence or misrepresentation and consequently triggered a volley of litigants, who tested the limits of *O'Brien* in their attempts to shoot down possession proceedings brought by mortgagees. Some of these later cases settled points that had been left undecided by the House of Lords; others injected new uncertainties and inconsistencies, or 'watered down'[25] the requirements set out by Lord Browne-Wilkinson in *O'Brien*. Alongside the litigants came a parallel flood of articles and commentaries as practitioners and academics grappled with the developing case law.[26] In 2001, in *Royal Bank of Scotland plc* v. *Etridge (No. 2)*,[27] the House of Lords revisited the

---

[22] [1994] 1 AC 180.

[23] [1994] 1 AC 200.

[24] [1985] AC 686.

[25] A phrase used in *Royal Bank of Scotland plc* v. *Etridge (No. 2)* [2001] 3 WLR 1021 by Lord Hobhouse of Woodborough at 100.

[26] See, *inter alia*, Battersby (1995) 15 LS 35; Hooley [1995] LMCLQ 346; Oldham [1995] 7 CFLQ 104; Lawson [1995] CLJ 280; Haley [1998] JBL 335.

[27] [2001] 3 WLR 1021.

topic of undue influence in the law of mortgages. The decision refines and reformulates the principles laid down in *O'Brien* and sets out new minimum requirements for mortgagees who take third party security from wives or partners and for solicitors whose task it is in such cases to advise the surety.

Etridge involved eight conjoined appeals. In each case the wife charged her interest in the home in favour of a bank as security for her husband's indebtedness or the indebtedness of a company through which he carried on business.[28] In seven of the eight cases the wife later sought to resist possession on the grounds that she signed the charge under the undue influence of her husband and the bank was fixed with notice of the undue influence. The eighth case involved a wife who claimed damages from a solicitor who advised her before she entered into a contract of guarantee with the bank. Although some differences of approach are disclosed in the opinions of their Lordships, the speech of Lord Nicholls of Birkenhead received the approval of each of the other Law Lords and should as such be read as the leading opinion.

Undue influence between debtor and surety

Etridge clarifies and reformulates various aspects of the law of undue influence as applied to transactions between debtors and sureties. The importance of the case is enhanced by the fact that the House of Lords took the opportunity 'to go back to first principles'.[29]

Meaning of undue influence

Undue influence is not concerned with understanding or intention,[30] but with improper pressure or taking of advantage, or 'how the intention was produced'.[31] In line with earlier authorities,[32] the House of Lords declined to define in any precise manner the degree of pressure required to establish undue influence. Where commercial interests are involved, as in the surety cases, the absence of more specific guidelines might be considered unfortunate because it derogates from the certainty that

---

[28] The facts of each case are set out in the opinion of Lord Scott of Foscote.

[29] *Per* Lord Nicholls of Birkenhead, at 6.

[30] *Allcard* v. *Skinner* (1887) 35 Ch. D 145, at 182–183 *per* Lindley LJ: 'Courts of Equity have never set aside gifts on the ground of the folly, imprudence, or want of foresight on the part of donors'; *National Westminster Bank plc* v. *Morgan* [1985] AC 686 at 705 *per* Lord Scarman; *Banco Exterior Internacional* v. *Mann* [1995] 1 All ER 936, at 946 *per* Hobhouse LJ.

[31] *Huguenin* v. *Baseley* (1807) 14 Ves. Jun. 273 at 300 *per* Lord Eldon LC, cited by Lord Nicholls at [2001] 3 WLR 1021, at 7. See, generally Gordley, *The Philosophical Origins of Modern Contract Doctrine* (1991, Clarendon Press), pp. 180–185.

[32] See, for example, *Poosathurai* v. *Kannappa Chettiar* (1919) LR 47 Ind. App. 1 at 4 *per* Lord Shaw of Dumferline; *National Westminster Bank plc* v. *Morgan* [1985] AC 686 at 709 *per* Lord Scarman.

facilitates commercial transactions. Nevertheless the view taken in *Etridge* is perhaps the only appropriate approach. Undue influence is of its very nature an invidious form of pressure, usually exercised over some period of time, which operates within the infinitely varied sphere of close human relationships and frequently plays upon the particular weaknesses of the victim: 'The circumstances in which one person acquires influence over another, and the manner in which influence may be exercised, vary too widely to permit of any more specific criterion.'[33]

Revising the analysis of undue influence – burden of proof and presumptions

Their Lordships in *Etridge* questioned the usefulness of the traditional analysis of undue influence. In *O'Brien* the House of Lords had adopted the analysis of the Court of Appeal in *Bank of Credit and Commerce International S.A.* v. *Aboody*.[34] Under that analysis, Class 1 or 'actual' undue influence was distinguished from Class 2 or 'presumed' undue influence. Class 2 was subdivided into two types, Class 2 (A) and Class 2 (B). Class 2 (A) related to certain specific relationships (for example, solicitor/client, medical adviser/patient) which as a matter of law raise an irrebuttable presumption that one party has influence over the other. Class 2(B) comprised situations where the relationship fell outside the Class (2A) categories of 'special' relationship[35] but where the complainant proved the 'de facto existence of a relationship under which the complainant generally reposed trust and confidence in the wrongdoer'.[36] Their Lordships in *Etridge* criticised this analysis as confusing and objected in particular to the use of the term 'presumed undue influence' when applied to cases falling outside the categories of 'special' relationship.[37] For the future, the term 'Class 2 (B)' should be abandoned as a tool of analysis.[38] Whether a transaction was brought about by undue influence is a question of fact. The word 'presumption' is used to describe a shift in the evidential burden of proof on this question of fact; a 'forensic tool'[39] that should not be allowed to obscure the overall position.

---

[33] [2001] 3 WLR 1021 at 7 *per* Lord Nicholls; see also 92 *per* Lord Clyde.

[34] [1990] 1 QB 923 at 953 *per* Slade LJ.

[35] The relationships of banker/client (*National Westminster Bank Plc* v. *Morgan* [1985] AC 686); husband/wife (*Howes* v. *Bishop* [1909] 2 KB 390); fiancé/fiancée (*Zamet* v. *Hyman* [1961] 1 WLR 1442); and unmarried cohabitants (*Rhoden* v. *Joseph* (1990) Lexis transcript) have all been held not to fall within the special categories of relationship that raise the presumption of undue influence.

[36] *O'Brien* [1994] 1 AC 180 at 189 *per* Lord Browne-Wilkinson.

[37] *Per* Lord Nicholls at 17–18; *per* Lord Clyde at 92; *per* Lord Hobhouse of Woodborough at 98, 105; *per* Lord Scott at 161.

[38] *Per* Lord Nicholls at 16–17; *per* Lord Clyde at 92; *per* Lord Hobhouse at 107; *per* Lord Scott of Foscote at 161.

[39] *Per* Lord Nicholls at 16, 17; *per* Lord Hobhouse at 107.

As revised, the position becomes as follows. Whether a transaction was brought about by the exercise of undue influence is a question of fact. The burden of proof rests on the person who claims to have been wronged.[40] The evidence required to discharge that burden depends on the nature of the alleged undue influence, the personality of the parties, their relationship, the extent to which the transaction cannot readily be accounted for by the ordinary motives of ordinary persons in that relationship and all the circumstances of the case.[41] Proof that a complainant reposed trust and confidence in the other party in the management of her financial affairs, coupled with a transaction which calls for explanation, will normally be enough to discharge that burden of proof. In the absence of evidence to the contrary, the court will infer that the transaction was brought about by undue influence. The evidential burden on a question of fact then shifts to the defendant, and the term 'presumption' is merely descriptive of this evidential shift, a 'forensic tool' that is the equitable counterpart of the principle of *res ipsa loquitur*.[42]

Independent advice

In line with earlier authorities,[43] the House of Lords in *Etridge* held that as against the alleged wrongdoer, proof that a complainant received independent advice is a factor to be taken into account by the court, but does not necessarily negate a finding of undue influence. It is possible for a person fully to understand the implications of a proposed transaction but still be acting under undue influence. There is also authority, not adverted to in *Etridge*, that in some cases such advice may not be necessary in order to negate a finding of undue influence.[44]

Manifest disadvantage

The House of Lords in *CIBC Mortgages* v. *Pitt*[45] had held that where there has been actual undue influence, the claimant need not prove that the transaction in question was to his or her 'manifest disadvantage'. In cases based on the presumption of undue influence, however, proof of 'manifest disadvantage' continued to be an essential part of the claim. In *Pitt* itself,[46] and in later cases,[47] there are suggestions of a possible need

---

40 *Per* Lord Nicholls at 13; *per* Lord Hobhouse at 103; *per* Lord Scott at 154.

41 *Per* Lord Nicholls at 13; *per* Lord Scott at 153 *et seq*.

42 *Per* Lord Nicholls at 16; *per* Lord Hobhouse at 107; *per* Lord Scott at 161.

43 See, for example, *Inche Noriah* v. *Shaik Allie Bin Omar* [1929] AC 127, at 135–136 *per* Lord Hailsham LC *Tate* v. *Williamson* (1866) LR 2 Ch App. 55 at 65 *per* Lord Chelmsford LC.

44 *Re Brocklehurst's Estate* [1978] Ch 14, at 36–37 *per* Lawton L.J; *Inche Noriah* v. *Shaik Allie Bin Omar* [1929] AC 127, 135 *per* Lord Hailsham LC (advice from a non-lawyer may be sufficient depending on the circumstances).

45 [1994] 1 AC. 200 at 209 *per* Lord Browne-Wilkinson.

46 *Ibid*.

47 See, for example, *Barclays Bank plc* v. *Coleman* [2001] QB 20 at 30-32 *per* Nourse LJ. See also Lehane (1994) 110 LQR 167; Oldham [1995] 7 CFLQ 104.

to reconsider the requirement of 'manifest disadvantage' in establishing undue influence. The difficulty adverted to in *Pitt* was that the requirement of manifest disadvantage is at variance with the long-established principle applied in abuse of confidence cases. Under that principle, if a fiduciary enters into a transaction with a person to whom he or she owes fiduciary duties, the fiduciary is placed under a duty to establish affirmatively that the transaction was fair.[48] The requirement of manifest disadvantage also ran counter to Court of Appeal authority that adequacy of consideration and/or size of gift are factors to be taken into account, but are not necessarily determinative of whether undue influence has been exerted.[49]

In *Etridge*, their Lordships took the view that the term 'manifest disadvantage' should be abandoned as it causes difficulties and ambiguity. Nevertheless, for the shift in the burden of proof to occur there should be both a relationship of trust and confidence and also a 'transaction that is not readily explicable by the relationship'.[50] The second prerequisite is a 'necessary limitation' upon the width of the first.[51] In place of 'manifest disadvantage', there should be a return to the test outlined by Lindley LJ in *Allcard* v. *Skinner*[52] and adopted in *National Westminster Bank plc* v. *Morgan*.[53] The second prerequisite is 'an advantage taken of the person subjected to the influence which, failing proof to the contrary, was explicable only on the basis that undue influence had been exercised to procure it.'[54]

This aspect of *Etridge* is perhaps its most potentially problematic. Nevertheless, the reformulation of the second prerequisite may resolve at least one difficulty created by the requirement of 'manifest disadvantage'. The need to establish manifest disadvantage as a component element of undue influence effectively meant that a claim could not succeed where the claimant had been paid the market rate. The requirement of 'manifest disadvantage' ran counter to Court of Appeal authority that adequacy of consideration and/or size of gift are factors to be taken into account, but are not necessarily determinative of whether undue influence has been exerted. In *Tate* v. *Williamson*[55] a presumption of undue influence had been raised by proof of a relationship of de facto trust and confidence between a young and extravagant Oxford student who was heavily in debt and an older man to whom he had turned for financial help and

[48] *Demerara Bauxite Co Ltd.* v. *Hubbard* [1923] A.C. 673; *Moody* v. *Cox and Hatt* [1917] 2 Ch 71.
[49] See, for example, *Tate* v. *Williamson* (1866) L.R. 2 Ch App. 55.
[50] *Per* Lord Nicholls at 21–31.
[51] *Ibid.*
[52] (1887) 36 Ch D 145.
[53] [1985] AC 686.
[54] [2001] 3 WLR 1021, at 25 *per* Lord Nicholls, citing *National Westminster Bank plc* v. *Morgan* [1985] AC 686, at 704 *per* Lord Scarman.
[55] (1866) LR 2 Ch. App. 55.

advice. In setting aside the sale by the younger man to the older of a moiety of a freehold estate, Lord Chelmsford LC stated that '[e]ven if the Defendant could have shewn that the price which he gave was a fair one, this would not alter the case against him'.[56] This earlier approach has much to commend it. As pointed out by Slade LJ in the Court of Appeal in *Morgan*, '[I]t is still possible that the relationship and influence therefrom has been abused, even though the transaction is, on the face of it, one which, in commercial terms, provides reasonably equal benefits for both parties'.[57] Dunn LJ in the same case argued that there might be all sorts of reasons why a person might not wish to sell a certain article, even though he is offered a fair price.[58] It seems likely that the *Etridge* reformulation of the second prerequisite from 'manifest disadvantage' to 'a transaction not readily explicable by the relationship' will return the law to this earlier position.

More potentially difficult is Lord Nicholls' discussion of wives who guarantee payment of their husband's business debts. The view adopted in *O'Brien* was that 'manifest disadvantage' was not precluded by the mere fact that a wife is financially dependent on her husband or her husband's business for support. Earlier and, indeed, some later cases had taken the view that a wife who is primarily dependent upon her husband's business for her support and who agrees to stand surety for his debts thereby acquires the speculative benefit 'that her husband's business might have recovered'.[59] On the basis of this analysis, only those wives who were financially independent of their husbands would be able to prove 'manifest disadvantage', with the unfortunate result that the weaker financially the claimant, the less likely she was to succeed in having the impugned transaction set aside. *Etridge* threatens a return to such an approach. Lord Nicholls expressed the view that 'in the ordinary course' a wife's guarantee of her husband's business debts is not to be regarded as a transaction which, failing proof to the contrary, is explicable only on the basis that it has been procured by the exercise of undue influence by the husband.[60] His Lordship emphasised the phrase 'in the ordinary course' and added that there will be cases where a wife's signature of a guarantee or a charge of her share in the matrimonial home does call for explanation. He also noted that courts will take account, as a matter of fact, of 'the opportunities for abuse which flow from a wife's confidence in her husband'. Where there is evidence that a husband has

---

[56] *Ibid.*

[57] [1983] 3 All ER 85, at 92. Lord Scarman in the House of Lords in *National Westminster Bank plc* v. *Morgan* [1985] AC 686 at 704 disagreed with the view of Slade LJ.

[58] [1983] 3 All ER 85 at 90.

[59] *National Westminster Bank plc* v. *Morgan* [1985] AC 686, at 702, 703, 709 *per* Lord Scarman.

[60] [2001] 3 WLR 1021 at 30–31.

taken unfair advantage of his influence over his wife, or her confidence in him, 'it is not difficult for the wife to establish her title to relief'.[61] It is to be hoped that future courts will take note of both these statements so the result will not be a wholesale return to the restrictive approach adopted in the pre-*O'Brien* case law.

Lord Nicholls of Birkenhead added what he termed a 'cautionary note' to the effect that because undue influence has connotations of impropriety, courts should not too readily treat a husband's 'reasonable conduct' as amounting to undue influence.[62] He drew a distinction between natural hyperbole and exaggeration when forecasting the future of a business (which are acceptable), and 'inaccurate explanations' of a proposed venture (which are not). The distinction may well provide a focus for future litigants.

The more restrictive aspects of *Etridge* may be explained in terms of a wish on the part of the House of Lords to reduce the large number of undue influence cases that have been brought in recent years. That desire is understandable, particularly where the claimant seeks to escape liability from a guarantee or charge she has concluded with a third party. In such situations there is a risk that spouses, facing the possible loss of their family home, will be tempted to invent or at least to exaggerate the circumstances by which the wife was persuaded to agree to the security. But it should be remembered that the restrictions will apply equally to situations that do not involve any third party and may result in grave injustice. The need for such restrictions may be open to question, since the Lords' reformulation of the principles to be applied in suretyship cases, discussed below, creates a practical and straightforward means for mortgagees to protect themselves even where there has been undue influence between the debtor and the surety.

Suretyship transactions

The goal in suretyship cases is balance.[63] The law should protect the victim of undue influence, but should also protect the interests of the bank and the wider economic community. If lending institutions cannot with confidence create binding charges, they will stop lending on the security of concurrently owned homes. In *O'Brien* the House set this balance by recourse to a new and unconventional use of the doctrine of constructive notice.[64] *Etridge* builds upon this development to create a

---

[61] *Ibid.* at 19, citing *In re Lloyds Bank Ltd; Bomze and Lederman* v. *Bomze* [1931] 1 Ch 289, 302 *per* Maugham J.

[62] [2001] 3 WLR 1021 at 32–3.

[63] *Barclays Bank plc* v. *O'Brien* [1994] 1 AC 180, at 188–189 *per* Lord Browne-Wilkinson; *Royal Bank of Scotland plc* v. *Etridge (No. 2)* [2001] 3 WLR 1021 at 37 *per* Lord Nicholls

[64] [2001] 3 WLR 1021, at 38–42 *per* Lord Nicholls, at 147 *per* Lord Scott of Foscote.

revised set of minimum requirements to be met by mortgagees and solicitors. In rejecting the approach adopted by the Court of Appeal, their Lordships were sensitive to the need to create a test that was 'simple, clear, and easy to apply in a wide range of circumstances'.[65] At the same time, the *Etridge* reformulation enhances in important respects the protection afforded to wives.

(1) The bank

A bank is put on inquiry[66] whenever, in a non-commercial situation, one person offers to stand surety for the debts of another, or for the debts of a company through which the other carries on business. It is irrelevant that the surety may be a shareholder and/or director of the company in question. The principle extends to spouses, to unmarried couples (whether heterosexual or homosexual) and to non-sexual relationships such as that in *Credit Lyonnais Bank Nederland NV* v. *Burch*,[67] where an employee charged her home as security for the debts of her employee. In cases of joint loan, by contrast, the bank is put on inquiry only if it is aware that the loan is for the husband's purposes as distinct from the parties' joint purposes.[68]

Once put on inquiry, the bank may escape liability by taking 'reasonable steps to satisfy itself that the wife has had brought home to her, in a meaningful way, the practical implications of the proposed transaction'.[69] In *O'Brien* Lord Browne-Wilkinson had prescribed for this purpose the holding by the bank of a private meeting with the wife, at which she is told the extent of her liability, warned of the risks and urged to take independent legal advice. Their Lordships in *Etridge* acknowledged that banks have good reasons for resisting such meetings and formulated an additional and alternative route by which banks may discharge their obligation.

The bank must communicate directly with the wife and obtain from her the name of the solicitor she wishes to act for her. She must be told 1) that the bank will require, for its own protection, written confirmation from a solicitor that he has fully explained to her the nature of the documents and the practical implications they will have for her; 2) that the purpose of this requirement is that thereafter she should not be able to dispute that she is legally bound; and 3) that she may be advised by the same solicitor as her husband, but she may nominate a different solicitor if

---

65 *Ibid.* 46 *per* Lord Nicholls.
66 The House noted that the term 'put on inquiry' is strictly a misnomer in this context, since there is no requirement that the bank make any inquiries: *Ibid. per* Lord Nicholls at 44; *per* Lord Scott at 147.
67 [1997] 1 All ER 144.
68 *Ibid.* at 48.
69 [2001] 3 WLR 1021 at 54.

she chooses. The bank must not proceed with the transaction until it has received an appropriate response from the wife.

The bank must provide the solicitor with the financial information needed to advise the wife, including details of the debtor's current indebtedness, current overdraft facility and the amount and terms of any proposed new facility. If the husband refuses to consent to such disclosure, the bank should not proceed.

If the bank believes or suspects that the wife is being misled by her husband or is not entering the transaction of her own free will, it should insist that she receive separate legal advice and inform her solicitor of the relevant facts. In every case the bank should obtain written confirmation from the solicitor, and is entitled to rely on that confirmation. The House of Lords rejected an argument that a solicitor who advises a wife does so not for her benefit, but for the benefit and protection of the bank, and is therefore acting as the bank's agent. The bank has no control over the advice given to the wife and the solicitor is not accountable to the bank for the advice he gives. In advising the wife, the solicitor acts for the wife alone and does not act as the bank's agent.[70]

As regards past transactions, the bank will ordinarily have discharged its obligations if a solicitor acting for the wife gave the bank confirmation to the effect that he had brought home to her the risks she was running by standing as surety.

2) The solicitor

Practitioners will be pleased to learn that the House felt that the duties imposed in the Court of Appeal placed too heavy a burden on solicitors. In particular, unless it was 'glaringly obvious' that a wife was being grievously wronged, it was not for solicitors to veto transactions by declining to provide the confirmation sought by the bank. The decision whether to proceed is for the wife, not the solicitor. Nevertheless, the role of the solicitor is important and not a mere formality. Because many of the disputed cases involved allegations of extremely poor legal advice, the House provided detailed guidance on what was required.

A solicitor acting for both husband and wife, who at any stage becomes concerned that other interests or duties may inhibit his advice to the wife, should cease to act for her. The meeting with the wife must be in person, in the absence of the husband, and couched in suitably non-technical language. The solicitor must first explain that his involvement is to allow the bank to counter any later suggestion of undue influence or misrepresentation. If the wife confirms that she wishes him to act for her, he should then, as a 'core minimum':

---

[70] *Ibid.* at 75–78.

- Explain the nature of the documents and the practical consequences for the wife if she signs them – that she could lose her home, or be made bankrupt, if her husband's business does not prosper.

- Point out the seriousness of the risks involved, giving details of the purpose and terms of the proposed facility and the amount of her liability. She should be warned that without reference to her the bank might increase the amount, change its terms or grant a new facility. They should discuss her resources and her understanding of the value of the property being charged.

- The solicitor should state clearly that she has a choice and that the decision is hers alone.

- He should ask whether she wishes to proceed; if so, whether she wishes him to confirm to the bank that he has explained the nature of documents and their practical implications, or whether she would like him to negotiate the terms on her behalf. Such negotiation could include, e.g., the sequence in which securities are called in, or the limit of her liabilities. The solicitor should not give any confirmation to the bank without the wife's authority.

Etridge constitutes a very welcome further development of the principles expounded in *O'Brien*. The reformulated principles do not have the effect that wives will never enter into such transactions under the undue influence of their husbands – as Lord Nicholls pointed out,[71] it is possible for a person fully to understand a transaction and still be acting under undue influence. But the decision provides a workable compromise that goes further than *O'Brien* in reducing the risk of undue influence. *Etridge* benefits potential victims in setting a very low threshold to determine when banks are put on inquiry; moreover it involves the surety at an early stage and ensures that the full implications of the proposed transaction are clearly explained. Lending institutions benefit in that even though the threshold is low, the steps required to avoid liability are clear, simple and sufficiently formulaic to keep compliance costs within manageable bounds.

And the wider public interest is not compromised – as their Lordships pointed out, if lending institutions cannot be confident of the validity of charges, there is a risk they will refuse to lend on the security of co-owned houses.[72] Since the rate of default necessarily impacts on interest charges generally, the interests of mortgagors as a whole require that mortgage

---

[71] *Ibid.* at 20.
[72] *Ibid.* at 35.

default should be kept to a minimum. Mortgagors generally will do everything they can to avoid defaulting on their mortgages, precisely because they anticipate that default will result in repossession and the loss of their home. If this perception is removed, the rate of default will inevitably rise.

Mortgage regulation

A new regulatory regime is to be introduced for mortgages. The regime, intended to increase consumer protection in the mortgage market, was prompted by a number of factors. Perhaps predictably, the discussion about mortgage regulation has taken the form of rather polarised views. And as with undue influence, the appropriate solution must be one of achieving balance. But the balance to be struck here is one that allows the benefits of consumer protection but does so without raising prices unacceptably, stifling market competition or blunting incentives to innovate.

The changing business climate

There is a perception, shared by both sides of the debate, that the deregulation of building societies has resulted in 'a growing industrialisation of banking'[73] in which the mortgage market has become less consumer-driven and more concerned with the maximisation of profits. In the words of the Banking Ombudsman, '... competition for market share has seen a move away from a banking culture to a sales culture'.[74] Deregulation has resulted in increased competition, which in turn has prompted the introduction of an ever-widening range of mortgage products.[75] This proliferation of mortgage products is seen both as good, in that it increases consumer choice, and as bad, in that it leads to consumers who are confused by the range and complexity of mortgages now available. Both views, of course, are right.

---

[73] Banking Ombudsman, *Annual Report of the Banking Ombudsman 1998–1999*, p. 29.

[74] *Ibid.* The 1999–2000 report confirmed that the Ombudsman receives more complaints about mortgages than about any other topic: *Annual Report of the Banking Ombudsman 1999–2000*, p. 16.

[75] Research suggests that some 4,000 mortgage products are available: *Annual Report of the Building Societies Ombudsman 1999–2000*, p. 16. The Cruickshank review (*Competition in UK Banking: A Report to the Chacellor of the Exchequer*, March 2000, para 4.37) put the figure at 'over 1,000'.

Arguments in favour of regulation

Those in favour of regulatory control argue that consumer confusion is caused and exacerbated by mortgage industry practices. Consumers cannot make meaningful comparisons between products because different providers are inconsistent in their use of terminology and methods of calculation. Problems of poor, misleading or incomplete information add to a general lack of transparency and lead to poor consumer choices and consumer detriment. Some advertising of mortgage products is confusing and so contributes to the lack of consumer awareness and the absence of effective competition.[76] Consumers have inadequate representation and inadequate avenues of redress. New record levels of repossessions[77] have fuelled anxieties about the plight of those who experience the trauma of losing their home and about the treatment of mortgagors in arrears.[78] Finally, there are growing criticisms of certain administrative practices. Poor systems and controls can facilitate the commission of financial crime.[79] Other practices, such as the imposition of charges (for example, on arrears or for early redemption), which do not reflect the true cost to the lender, are deprecated as unfairly detrimental to the consumer.

Arguments against regulation

Those who would resist the introduction of mortgage regulation point to the significant increase in mortgage-related consumer benefits since the deregulation of banks. Increased competition has resulted in extremely cheap interest rates;[80] in a wide choice of type of lender and distribution channel; and in a wide choice of mortgage products with ever more flexible features. Types of mortgage now available range from very straightforward mortgages that meet the Treasury CAT standard,[81] to specialised 'niche' products for particular borrowers such as the self-

---

[76] See generally, HM Treasury, *Evidence of Consumer Damage reported during Treasury Consultation* (2000, HMT); Financial Services Authority, *Mortgage Regulation: The FSA's High Level Approach* (CP70, 2000, FSA) para. 3.4.

[77] See above.

[78] See, for example, Nettleton *et al*, (*op. cit.* above fn. 10).

[79] CP70, para 3.5.

[80] The Council of Mortgage Lenders (*Response by the Council of Mortgage Lenders to the Financial Services Authority Consultation Paper 98*, 27 September 2001) claims that interest rates are 'historically low', which is true, but so are base rates, therefore no credit can be claimed on behalf of the mortgage market. The indicator of whether mortgages are cheap is the difference *between* the base rate and the interest rates.

[81] CAT standards (Charges, Access and Terms) for mortgages were introduced in April 2000 by the Treasury. Use of the standards is voluntary and intended to indicate to consumers that a mortgage product offers a reasonable deal.

employed, those with poor credit ratings, or older borrowers who wish to arrange an equity release mortgage. Other new products include mortgages that treat the loan as a current account and those that offset loans and savings products.[82] The adverse effects of regulation include an inevitable impact on price, and consequently higher interest rates for borrowers; the hampering of product innovation; and the restriction of consumer choice. There is evidence to suggest that the provision of additional information is unlikely to affect consumer behaviour[83] – if true, the regulatory exercise may well be nothing more than a costly and time-consuming exercise.

The arguments from both sides of the debate have merit. There are undoubted problems in the mortgage market. The majority of consumers do not understand the range of products available nor, in many cases, the products they hold,[84] and the mortgage industry does little to improve consumer awareness.[85] But it is also true that the mortgage market is, by and large, a success story. Competition for market share since the deregulation of building societies has brought many benefits to consumers, including cheap and readily available mortgages, and increased choice. Pressures to regulate have made regulation inevitable, but it is important to safeguard these consumer benefits. Public regulation in a market economy is most effective where it enhances competition. Economies of scale in meeting the compliance costs of regulation give a marked advantage to larger organisations: additional costs that seem negligible to a huge institution can, for a small firm, make continued operation impossible. To maintain and encourage competition, regulation should not make new entry into the mortgage market difficult, should not blunt incentives to introduce new products and should not disadvantage the small firm.

The new regime

The new regulatory regime will bring most mortgage business within the scope of the Financial Services and Markets Act 2000 (FSMA) and under the regulatory authority of the Financial Services Authority (FSA).[86] The regime will require most mortgage lenders and mortgage administrators

---

[82] The Cruickshank review, (*op. cit.* above fn. 77).

[83] The Cruickshank review (*ibid.*, para. 4.46) reported that 65% of consumers did not compare the products of more than one provider before selecting their mortgages.

[84] *Ibid.*, para. 4.67.

[85] *Ibid.*, para 4.85: 'Firms have an interest in exaggerating the difficulties involved in changing suppliers and making sure that consumers are not in a position to make informed choices.'

[86] The constitution, duties and objectives of the FSA are governed by the FSMA 2000, Part 1 and Sch.1.

to be authorised by the FSA and to comply with rules and guidance issued by that body. The regime also incorporates provisions to regulate the form, content and communication of 'qualifying credit promotions'.[87]

'High level standards' and mortgage-specific rules and guidance

The FSA Handbook comprises all the rules and guidance relating to authorised persons, and will apply in varying degrees to mortgage lenders, mortgage administrators and firms that communicate or approve qualifying credit promotions. The present discussion will focus on those parts of the scheme of most relevance to students of land law.

'High level standards'

'High level standards' are standards that all authorised firms must meet and are in the main concerned with issues such as principles for businesses, systems and controls. With a few exceptions, these standards will not be of great interest to students of land law.

Mortgage-specific rules and guidance

The rules and guidance relating specifically to mortgage business will be contained in the Mortgage Sourcebook, a separate volume within the FSA Handbook. A draft Mortgage Sourcebook (hereafter MORT) is included in the FSA's Consultation Paper, *The Draft Mortgage Sourcebook, including Policy Statement on CP70.*[88]

'The general prohibition', regulated activity and authorisation

Three key concepts in the new regulatory scheme for mortgages are 'the general prohibition', regulated activity and authorisation.

'The general prohibition'

Central to the new regulatory regime is 'the general prohibition', contained in s. 19 of the FSMA. Section 19 provides that no person may carry on, or purport to carry on, a regulated activity unless he is an authorised person or an exempt person. Breach of the general prohibition gives rise to criminal liability[89] and also has consequences on the enforceability of resulting controlled agreements.

---

[87] The financial promotions provisions will not be considered here.

[88] CP98, June 2001. The Draft Mortgage Sourcebook is at Annex B. Both CP98 and the FSA's earlier consultative document, *Mortgage Regulation: the FSA's High Level Approach* (CP70), may be accessed through www.fsa.gov.uk

[89] FSMA, s. 23 (punishable by fine and/or imprisonment for up to two years). Section 24 creates an offence of falsely describing oneself as authorised or exempt.

An authorised person cannot be guilty of an authorisation offence, even if he or she undertakes regulated activity for which he or she has not obtained permission from the FSA.[90] In such cases the authorised person has 'contravened a requirement imposed on him by the Authority'[91] and will be subject to disciplinary action by the FSA. Such contravention has no effect on the validity or enforceability of any transaction,[92] although a person who has suffered loss as a result of the contravention may have an action for breach of statutory duty.[93]

Enforceability of agreements

An agreement made by a person in the course of carrying on a regulated activity in contravention of the 'general prohibition' is unenforceable against the other party and voidable at his instance.[94] Equally unenforceable is an agreement made through an unauthorised person – that is, where the contract is concluded by an authorised person but in consequence of something said or done by a third party who acts in contravention of the general prohibition.[95] In either case the avoiding party is entitled to recover any money or property transferred under the agreement, and compensation for any loss incurred as a result.[96] The amount of compensation recoverable is by agreement between the parties, or as determined by the court on application by either.[97] The court has discretion, if satisfied that it is 'just and equitable' in the circumstances, to allow the contract to be enforced, or to allow money or property transferred under the agreement to be retained.[98]

In exercising its discretion, the court is directed to have regard to whether the person carrying on the regulated activity reasonably believed that he was not contravening the general prohibition;[99] or whether (in the case of agreements made through unauthorised persons) the provider knew that the third party was contravening the general prohibition.[100]

[90] *Ibid.*, s. 20 (2).
[91] *Ibid.*, s. 20 (1).
[92] *Ibid.*, s. 20 (2) (b).
[93] *Ibid.*, s. 20 (3). See the FSMA 2000 (Rights of Action) Regulations 2001, reg. 4, discussed below, p. 205.
[94] FSMA., s. 26 (1).
[95] *Ibid.*, s. 27.
[96] *Ibid.*, ss. 26 (2), 27 (2). The avoiding party must also repay any money and return any other property received by him under the agreement: s. 28 (7).
[97] *Ibid.*, s. 28 (2).
[98] *Ibid.*, s. 28 (3).
[99] *Ibid.*, s. 28 (4), (5).
[100] *Ibid.*, s. 28 (4), (6).

'Regulated activity'

A 'regulated activity' is an activity of a specified kind, carried on by way of business[101] in relation to an investment of a specified kind.[102] As regards mortgages, there are two separate regulated activities – entering into a regulated mortgage contract as lender,[103] and administering a regulated mortgage contract.[104]

'Regulated mortgage contract'

A contract is a 'regulated mortgage contract' if, at the time it is entered into, the following conditions are met:

(i) the contract is one under which a person ('the lender') provides credit[105] to an individual or to trustees ('the borrower');

(ii) the contract provides for the obligation of the borrower to repay to be secured by a first legal mortgage on land (other than timeshare accommodation) in the United Kingdom;

(iii) at least 40% of that land is used, or is intended to be used, as or in connection with a dwelling by the borrower or (in the case of credit provided to trustees) by an individual who is a beneficiary of the trust, or by a related person.[106]

The scheme is thus broad enough to include most first mortgages of land, including equity release mortgages. The definition does not require a regulated mortgage contract to be for a particular purpose, such as house purchase, but includes loans for other purposes where the loan is secured by a first charge. It was initially intended to include a condition that the original maturity of a regulated mortgage contract be at least five years, but this restriction was abandoned during the consultation process.[107] In consequence, a broad range of loans secured by a first charge will fall within the scheme, including loans for purposes as varied as home improvements, debt consolidation, business financing, and banking products such as secured overdrafts, secured credit cards, bridging loans and loans secured by 'all monies' charges.

---

[101] The FSMA 2000 (Carrying on Regulated Activities by Way of Business) Order 2001 makes provision as to the circumstances in which a person is, or is not, to be regarded as carrying on a regulated activity by way of business.

[102] FSMA, s. 22 (1).

[103] The FSMA 2000 (Regulated Activities) Order 2001, art. 61 (1).

[104] *Ibid.*, art. 61 (2).

[105] 'Credit' is defined to include a cash loan and any form of financial accommodation: *ibid.*, art. 61 (3) (c).

[106] *Ibid.*, art. 61(3)(a), as substituted by the FSMA 2000 (Regulated Activities) (Amendment) Order 2001, art. 8.

[107] For details, see CP98, para 1.3.

The new regime does not cover mortgages where the mortgagor is a business, or mortgages of dwellings where less than 40% will be used as or in connection with a dwelling by the mortgagor, a beneficiary under a trust held by mortgagor-trustee(s) or a related person. These exclusions are understandable since the expressed intention of the new scheme is to provide increased protection to consumers in the case of mortgages of dwellings.[108]

Given that intention, however, it is surprising that all second or subsequent mortgages, and all equitable mortgages, are also excluded.[109] Many owner-occupiers in financial difficulties will consider a second mortgage as a possible means of alleviating their problems and as such must comprise a peculiarly vulnerable class that would certainly benefit from the stricter disclosure rules contained in the Mortgage Sourcebook. It is similarly difficult to see the justification for excluding equitable mortgages. Equitable mortgages include not only mortgages of equitable interests, but also mortgages of a legal estate (1) where the mortgage is informal or imperfect; (2) where an enforceable agreement to mortgage is not completed by the execution of a deed of charge; or (3) where the mortgagee fails to complete by registration at the Land Registry.[110] It seems illogical to create a regulatory regime that denies its protection to a mortgagor if, as occurred in *Barclays Bank plc* v. *Zaroovabli*,[111] the mortgagee fails to register the charge. On the facts of that case the mortgagors, in breach of the terms of the mortgage, granted a tenancy in the property to a third party. Had the regime been in place the mortgage would no longer have ranked as a regulated mortgage contract because the house was no longer at least 40% occupied by the borrower as a dwelling. But even if the Zaroovablis *had* remained in occupation, the incompetence of the mortgagee would have denied them the benefit of the regime intended to protect them from such incompetence.

A policy decision was taken not to adopt a purpose-based definition on the grounds that it would be difficult to police and 'would carry the risk that unscrupulous lenders could artificially arrange that some borrowers did not in practice get the protection of the regulatory regime.'[112] Even if one accepts these Treasury sentiments – which perhaps suggest an inappropriate lack of confidence in the effectiveness of its own regulatory

---

[108] HM Treasury, *Regulating Mortgages* (October 2000, HMT), p. 11: 'the policy intention [is] to give regulatory protection to people borrowing money secured on a mortgage on the family home.'

[109] Nor will the regime apply to mortgages which, although second charges at the time of execution, later become regulated mortgage contracts by reason of the discharge of the prior mortgage: MORT, para 6.1.3.

[110] See Gray and Gray, *Elements of Land Law* (3rd ed., 2001, Butterworths), para. 6.18.

[111] [1997] 2 All ER 19 (charge executed in 1988 but not registered by Barclays until 1994).

[112] HM Treasury, *Regulating Mortgages* (October 2000, HMT), p. 12.

regime[113] – it would have been possible to include equitable mortgages and second mortgages of homes by the simple omission of two words from the definition. Some second mortgages, though by no means all of them, will continue to be governed by the provisions contained in the Consumer Credit Act 1974.[114]

Administering a regulated mortgage contract

'Administering a regulated mortgage contract' is defined in art. 61 (3) (b) of the FSMA 2000 (Regulated Activities) Order 2001 as either or both of:

  (a) notifying the borrower of changes in interest rates or payments due under the contract, or of other matters of which the contract requires him to be notified; and
  (b) taking any necessary steps for the purposes of recovering or collecting payments due under the contract from the borrower.[115]

Outsourcing of mortgage administration, which is common practice in the banking world, will continue to be possible, even where the person to whom the administration is delegated is not an authorised person within the regulatory regime.[116] In such cases, however, the authorised mortgage administrator will continue to be held responsible for the way in which the administration is conducted.[117]

Authorisation

Once the scheme is in force, only 'authorised persons' within s. 31 of the FSMA and exempt persons will be able lawfully to engage in mortgage-related regulated activities. The most common route to becoming an authorised person will be through an application made under Part IV of that Act.[118] For those without any existing authorisation, application is made to the FSA under s. 40 for permission to carry on one or more specified regulated activities.[119] Firms such as banks and building societies, which are already authorised by the FSA in respect of some

---

[113] And some inconsistency of approach, since the application of the 'cooling off' rules is determined by means of a purposive distinction between mortgages for property purchase and mortgages for other purposes: CP98, para. 14.1, and see below.

[114] See below.

[115] Administration does not include merely having or exercising a right to take action to enforce the regulated mortgage contract, or to require that action is or is not taken: art. 61 (3) (b).

[116] *Ibid.*, art. 63.

[117] MORT para. 1.2.4; Systems and Controls module, para. 3.2.4.

[118] Different considerations apply to EEA credit institutions and other EEA firms and Treaty firms: for details, see Threshold Conditions Manual, para. 1.1.1.

[119] FSMA, s. 40.

other regulated activity, will need to apply under s. 44 to have their authorisation varied. Schedule 6 of the FSMA contains certain 'threshold conditions'[120] that must be satisfied in order to obtain permission.

Exempt persons

The Act provides for the making of exemption orders to apply to specified persons or classes of person.[121] In relation to regulated mortgage activity, certain bodies, including local authorities,[122] registered social landlords[123] and the Housing Corporation,[124] are exempt[125] from the requirement of authorisation. The exemptions apply only to the bodies themselves and do not extend to subsidiaries of those bodies, which will therefore require FSA authorisation to undertake mortgage-related regulated activity.[126]

FSA supervision

Authorised persons are subject to the regulatory and supervisory controls of the FSA.[127] The Authority has a wide range of disciplinary powers, which it may exercise in case of any breach by an authorised person of any relevant principle or rule.[128]

The mortgage-specific rules and guidance

The mortgage-specific rules and guidance are contained in the Mortgage Sourcebook. As noted earlier, and as acknowledged by both consumer groups and the mortgage industry, one of the key problems in the current market is lack of consumer awareness. Lack of consumer awareness not only results in consumer detriment, but also impedes effective competition: 'Knowledgeable consumers provide the best incentive to effective competition. With the right information, consumers can take responsibility for their own financial well being, shop around and exert the

---

[120] As amended by FSMA 2000 (Variation of Threshold Conditions) Order 2001. The conditions relate to issues such as legal status, resources, systems controls, etc. The FSA has power to impose conditions and to vary or cancel the authorisation of its own initiative: FSMA, ss. 43, 45.

[121] FSMA. s. 38; FSMA 2000 (Exemption) Order 2001, as amended by FSMA 2000 (Exemption) (Amendment) Order 2001.

[122] The FSMA 2000 (Exemption) Order 2001, art 5 (2), Schedule, para. 47.

[123] Within the meaning of Part I of the Housing Act 1996: FSMA 2000 (Exemption) Order 2001, art. 5 (2), Schedule, para. 48 (a).

[124] FSMA 2000 (Exemption) Order 2001, art. 5 (2), Schedule, para. 48 (c).

[125] FSMA s. 38; FSMA 2000 (Exemption) Order 2001.

[126] CP98, para. 3.8.

[127] Broad policy as regards supervision of regulated mortgage lenders is discussed at CP70, para. 7. For further details, see the FSA Supervision Manual.

[128] CP70, para. 8; FSA Enforcement Manual.

pressures on suppliers which drive a competitive and innovative market.'[129]

One of the main objectives, therefore, of the mortgage-specific rules and guidance is to address this problem through the provision of what the FSA describes as an 'information package' for consumers.[130] The regime imposes specific disclosure requirements on mortgagees at different stages of a mortgage transaction, with additional obligations that arise where a mortgagor falls into arrears or where a mortgagee in possession sells the mortgaged property. Other new controls, again addressing problems described by the Treasury as 'preventable',[131] regulate business conduct generally, the quality of communications, methods of calculation, the practice of 'responsible lending', charges imposed in specific circumstances, and other aspects of arrears and repossessions.

General requirements relating to standards of business conduct

When a mortgage lender or mortgage administrator communicates information to a customer, it must take reasonable steps to communicate in a way which is clear, fair and not misleading.[132] Other general requirements relate to the prohibition of inducements where these are likely to conflict to a material extent with any duty owed by the mortgage lender to its customers,[133] the extent to which a mortgage lender or administrator may rely on others for information,[134] and exclusion clauses.[135] Electronic communications may be used to satisfy the requirements for communications 'in writing' unless a particular rule states otherwise.[136]

Disclosure requirements

The scheme imposes specific disclosure requirements at different stages of the mortgage transaction. The precise requirements depend on the stage

---

[129] Cruickshank review (op. cit. above fn. 77), para. 1.104.

[130] CP70, para. 5.45 *et seq.*; CP98, paras. 1.10–1.11.

[131] See HM Treasury, *Evidence of Consumer Damage reported during Treasury Consultation* (2000, HMT).

[132] MORT, para. 2.1.

[133] See CP98, para. 5.11–12; MORT para. 2.2.

[134] See CP98, para. 5.13; MORT para. 2.3.

[135] MORT, paras. 2.4.4, 2.4.5. It will not be possible to exclude or restrict any duty owed under the FSMA or the FSA rules, and any other exclusion or restriction of liability must be 'reasonable'. The FSA is of the view that the provisions are broadly similar in impact to the Unfair Terms in Consumer Contracts Regulations 1999.

[136] CP98, paras. 5.16, 6.21; MORT para. 2.5.2. Appropriate security systems must be in place: MORT, para. 2.5.3.

of the transaction and the type of loan involved. In all instances, in order to facilitate meaningful comparisons between mortgage products by prospective or actual mortgagors, the use of the annual percentage rate (APR) is compulsory and there is strict control of the method by which both the APR and the total charge for credit are calculated.[137] The rules govern pre-application disclosure, disclosure at offer stage and at start of contract, and after sale disclosure. Somewhat different requirements are imposed in respect of 'lifetime mortgage contracts', which are equity release mortgages aimed specifically at older mortgagors.[138]

Responsible lending

The principle of 'responsible lending', which comprises principle 6 of the FSA's Principles for Businesses, has been incorporated into a separate rule within the Mortgage Sourcebook. The aim of this rule, according to the FSA, is to ensure that mortgage lenders and administrators pay due regard to the interests of their customers and treat them fairly: 'The FSA regards it as important that customers should not be exploited by lending in circumstances where they are self-evidently unable to repay through income and yet have no alternative repayment plans.'[139] The Authority's view is that the practice of lending on the basis of security value alone should be curtailed, in part in order to protect consumers and in part because of the risks to the mortgagee of imprudent lending practice.[140]

The draft rule requires mortgage lenders to be able to show that before deciding to enter into a regulated mortgage contract, or making a further advance on such a contract, account was taken of the customer's ability to repay.[141] Examples of relevant factors to be considered include, where the repayments are initially discounted, the mortgagor's ability to repay at the end of the discounted period and any proposals of the mortgagor to repay from resources other than income.[142] The mortgagee is instructed, in the absence of evidence to the contrary, that any regular payments are to be met from the mortgagor's income.[143]

---

[137] MORT, para. 8 contains details of how the APR is to be calculated.

[138] For details, see CP98, para. 10; MORT, para. 7.

[139] MORT, para. 9.2.1.

[140] CP70, paras. 5.23–5.26.

[141] MORT, para. 9.3.1.

[142] *Ibid.*, para. 9.3.2. The rule is not intended to prevent legitimate self-certified lending, or lending where the customer has indicated a source of repayment other than income: CP98, para. 1.19; MORT, para. 9.3.4.

[143] MORT, para. 9.3.2.

Charges

The disclosure requirements of the new regime include transparency in relation to charges at all stages of the mortgage transaction.[144] Although the level of charges within regulated mortgage contracts are not generally subject to regulation, the proposed regime will control the setting of charges in three specific situations. The new provisions are intended to address certain mortgage industry practices that can result in the imposition of unfair or unexpected charges in these situations.

(1) Early redemption charges

The first such practice identified by the Authority is where a mortgagor seeks early redemption and the charges imposed do not represent the cost of termination to the lender. Early redemption charges often attach to fixed rate mortgages[145] or capped rate mortgages.[146] The redemption charge is payable if, during the fixed or capped rate period (and sometimes beyond that period), the borrower decides to redeem the mortgage, perhaps to change to another type of mortgage or to another lender. The charges are often substantial and expressed in different terms. The Cruickshank review reported that the majority of consumers were confused about early redemption charges, largely because such charges are not typically expressed in cash values.[147]

Under the proposed new rules, any early redemption charge imposed by the mortgagee must be able to be expressed as a cash value and must be a reasonable pre-estimate of the costs to be incurred by the mortgagee as a result of the early repayment.[148]

(2) Charges applicable on arrears

The second practice to be addressed by the new rules occurs where the charges imposed by a lender on a mortgagor in repayment difficulties do not represent the costs incurred by the lender. The new rules require a charge for arrears to represent a reasonable estimate of the costs, in additional administration, that result from the mortgagor being in arrears.[149] The effects of this change will be first, to prevent the imposition of penalties that exceed the administrative costs to mortgagees

---

[144] *Ibid.*, paras. 4.5.48, 5.4.2, 7.4.42, 7.5.4 (4).

[145] Under which the interest rate is fixed for a specified period – typically five years or less – after which it reverts to a variable rate.

[146] The interest rate is variable, but capped at a maximum rate – again for a specified period.

[147] Cruickshank review, above fn. at 77, para. 4.73.

[148] MORT, para. 10.3.1. Details of the charges must be included as part of disclosure at pre-application, offer and post-completion stages, in post-sale annual statements and in lifetime mortgage disclosure: *ibid.*, para. 10.3.3.

[149] *Ibid.*, para. 10.4.1.

and second, to prevent the practice of 'dual interest rates' under which the higher rate, payable when in arrears, imposes charges that are unrelated to the costs incurred.[150]

(3) Exorbitant credit charges

The third new rule is intended to prevent the situation where the charges (including interest) imposed on a customer are exorbitant and contrary to his or her interests. This rule is likely to be of considerable future importance, since for regulated mortgage contracts it will replace the provisions in ss. 137–140 of the Consumer Credit Act 1974 relating to extortionate credit bargains.[151] Extortionate credit is outside the scope of the Unfair Terms in Consumer Contracts Regulations 1999, which do not affect core terms such as price.[152] The proposed wording of rule 10.5.1 is that:

> 'A mortgage lender must ensure that any regulated mortgage contract that it enters into does not impose, and cannot be used to impose, exorbitant charges upon a customer.'[153]

The guidance accompanying the rule states that in determining whether a charge is exorbitant, a lender should consider the amount of charges for similar products or services on the market, and the nature and extent of the disclosure of the charges to the customer.[154]

Comparison with present provisions

The FSA rule is not an exact counterpart to the Consumer Credit Act provisions. The Authority, having considered the available research on extortionate credit, took the view that the relevant issues are covered either by r. 10.5.1 or by other rules and guidance in the Mortgage Sourcebook.[155] Under the Consumer Credit Act, if the court finds a credit bargain (of whatever amount[156]) extortionate, it may reopen the

---

[150] *Ibid.*, para. 10.4.2.

[151] On the new regime and the Consumer Credit Act generally, see further below.

[152] Regulation 6 (2). A term is a core term, however, only if it is 'in plain intelligible language'. The House of Lords has recently held, in the context of an unsecured loan, that a contractual term regulating the rate of interest payable on default and until discharge of any judgment is not a 'core term': *DGFT* v. *First National Bank* [2001] 3 WLR 1297. (Albeit on the facts the term, which imposed the same interest rate as was agreed in respect of the loan, was not unfair.)

[153] MORT, para. 10.5.1.

[154] *Ibid.*, para. 10.5.2.

[155] See CP98, para. 13.14.

[156] The usual financial ceiling of the Consumer Credit Act (see further, below) does not apply to the provisions on extortionate credit bargains.

agreement so as to do justice between the parties.[157] An 'extortionate' bargain is defined to include an agreement that (a) requires payments (whether unconditionally or on certain contingencies) which are grossly exorbitant, or (b) otherwise grossly contravenes ordinary principles of fair dealing.[158] In determining whether a credit bargain is extortionate, the court is directed to take into account a list of factors.[159] In making its assessment the court considers not only prevailing rates, but also the nature of the agreement and the risks involved.[160]

By contrast with the very specific definition of 'extortionate credit bargain', neither the new rule itself, nor the Definitions section of the Sourcebook contain any amplification on the meaning of 'exorbitant'. Section 139 of the Consumer Credit Act allows an application to be brought by a debtor or a surety,[161] but it is far from clear, from the wording of the rule and the definition of 'customer', that a surety would be covered by the new rule. If sureties are excluded, then since the 1974 Act will no longer apply to regulated mortgage contracts,[162] a regulatory gap has been created. The new regime gives the FSA no power, equivalent to that of the court, to rewrite the terms of an exorbitant bargain, although the FSA would be able to take disciplinary action against non-compliant firms. In particular, the FSA has power to vary or even cancel a Part IV permission on its own initiative and, in appropriate circumstances, could use that power to require a firm to take urgent remedial action.[163] Breach of the new rule against exorbitant charges would not entitle the borrower to treat the contract as void or unenforceable,[164] although he or she would have right of access to the dispute resolution processes of the Financial Ombudsman Service[165] and could bring a civil court action in appropriate circumstances.[166]

---

[157] Section 137.

[158] *Ibid.*, s. 138 (1).

[159] *Ibid.*, s. 138 (2)–(5). The determination is to be made as at the date of the agreement: *Harris v. Classon* (1910) 27 TLR 30.

[160] In the colourful words of Darling J in *Jackson v. Price* (1909) 26 TLR 106, at 107: 'If you had to lend a mutton chop to a ravenous dog, on what terms would you lend it?'

[161] And *First National Bank plc v. Syed* [1991] 2 All ER 250 seems to leave open the possibility that a court could raise the issue of its own motion.

[162] FSMA 2000 (Regulated Activities) Order 2001, arts. 90, 91.

[163] See FSA Enforcement Manual, paras 1.2.1, 3, 5.

[164] FSMA, s.151 (breach of an Authority rule does not constitute a criminal offence, nor does it render any transaction void or unenforceable).

[165] See further, below.

[166] See further, below.

'Cooling off' periods

In some cases a 'cooling off' period of seven days will be introduced to give mortgagors time to reconsider.[167] No cooling off period is required where the purpose of the mortgage is the purchase of land, or where a new regulated mortgage contract is concluded with the mortgagor's existing mortgage lender, or in the case of bridging loans.[168] If there is an existing regulated mortgage contract, no cooling off period is imposed where a further advance or variation is made. Where a cooling off period applies, the content of the offer document must be adapted so as to provide clear information to the borrower of his or her right to reconsider.[169]

Arrears[170] and repossessions

The FSA aims were to introduce measures to reduce the incidence of arrears (and subsequent repossessions) and to ease the position of mortgagors once they have fallen into arrears.[171] To this end, disclosure requirements both before and after entry into the mortgage contract are intended to help consumers to assess whether they can afford a mortgage product and to understand the risks associated with it and where to go for advice if arrears seem likely. Controls on the provision of information once a mortgagor is in arrears are intended to provide certain minimum standards rather than to intervene substantially in lenders' management of such situations.[172]

Mortgage lenders and administrators are required under the new regime to put in place a written policy and procedures for dealing fairly with any customer who is in arrears under a regulated mortgage contract.[173] The policy and procedures should include:[174]

(a) using reasonable efforts to reach an agreement with the mortgagor on the method of repayment, having regard to the desirability of agreeing with the customer an alternative to taking possession of the land;

---

[167] CP98, paras. 1.17, 14; MORT, para. 11. No cooling off period is required where a further advance is made on, or there is some other variation to, an existing regulated mortgage contract.

[168] MORT, para. 11.3.2.

[169] *Ibid.*, para. 5.4.10; see above.

[170] 'Arrears' is defined in the definitions section of MORT as 'the shortfall (equivalent to two or more monthly payments) in the accumulated total payments actually made by the customer measured against the accumulated total amount of payments due to be received from the customer'.

[171] CP70, paras. 5.91–5.93.

[172] CP98, para. 15.2.

[173] MORT, para. 12.3.1.

[174] *Ibid.*, para. 13.3.2.

(b) liaising with a third party source of advice[175] regarding the arrears if the customer so requests;

(c) adopting a reasonable approach to the time over which arrears should be repaid, having particular regard to the need to establish a plan that is practical in terms of the customer's circumstances;

(d) unless it has good reason not to do so, granting a customer's request for a change to the date on which or the method by which payment is due, and giving a written explanation of reasons in case of a refusal;

(e) repossessing the land only where all other reasonable attempts to resolve the position have failed.

In relation to (c) above, the FSA draft Mortgage Sourcebook specifically states that lenders will be expected to have regard to the decision of the Court of Appeal in *Cheltenham and Gloucester Building Society* v. *Norgan*,[176] where it was held that for the purposes of s. 36 of the Administration of Justice Act 1970 and s. 8 of the Administration of Justice Act 1973, a 'reasonable period' should be assessed taking into account the remaining term of the original mortgage.

Outsourcing of arrears handling

The common practice of outsourcing aspects of arrears handling, as with other outsourcing, will continue to be possible under the regulatory regime, although the authorised principal will remain responsible for the way in which the work is carried on.[177]

Information to be provided to mortgagors in arrears

Mortgage administrators must as soon as possible, and in any event within five working days of becoming aware that a mortgagor is in arrears, provide the mortgagor with the following: a list of the due payments that have been missed; the total sum of the arrears outstanding; the arrears charges incurred; charges likely to be incurred as a result of remaining in arrears; information as to the consequences, including repossession, of remaining in arrears; a statement that the mortgage administrator is willing to discuss any proposal for clearing the arrears which reflects the interests of both parties; and details of organisations that provide free advice to those in arrears.[178]

While a mortgagor is in arrears, the mortgage administrator must send him or her a monthly statement of the payments due, the actual arrears,

---

[175] The source of the third party advice must be free of charge to the mortgagor, such as a Citizens' Advice Bureau or the Consumer Credit Counselling Service.

[176] [1996] 1 All ER 449.

[177] MORT, para. 12.3.6; see further, above.

[178] MORT, para. 12.4.1.

the charges incurred and the debt.[179] Mortgage administrators must respond promptly to communications from mortgagors who are in arrears[180] and must not put undue pressure on them through excessive telephone calls or correspondence, or contact 'at an unsocial hour'.[181]

Repossessions

Before the mortgagee commences repossession action, it must 1) provide the mortgagor with a written update of the information provided when the mortgagor first went into arrears; 2) ensure the mortgagor is informed of the need to register with the local authority to be eligible for local authority housing; and 3) clearly state the action the mortgagee intends to take regarding repossession.[182]

Duties imposed on selling mortgagees

The duties imposed on selling mortgagees under the new regime do not correspond exactly with the equivalent duties developed in the courts. By rule 12.6.1 of the Mortgage Sourcebook:

> A mortgage administrator must ensure that where a mortgage lender or a holder of a legal mortgage repossesses a property ... it must endeavour:
>
> (1) to market the property for sale as soon as possible; and
> (2) to obtain the best price that might reasonably be paid, taking account of
>   (a) market conditions; and
>   (b) the continuing increase in the amount owed by the customer under the regulated mortgage contract.

As regards timing, it is not clear that the new rule will always operate in the best interests of the mortgagor. For regulated mortgage contracts, the new rule will effectively replace the general common law principle that a selling mortgagee is prima facie entitled to sell at any time he chooses.[183] Presumably the intention was to avoid both any unnecessary prolongation of the distress inevitably occasioned by a forced sale of the family home, and situations such as that in *Palk* v. *Mortgage Services Funding*

---

[179] *Ibid.*, para. 12.5.1. No statement needs to be sent where there is an agreed repayment plan and payments are being made in accordance with that plan.

[180] *Ibid.*, para. 12.5.2.

[181] *Ibid.*, para. 12.5.3. An unsocial hour includes generally Sundays, or before 9.00 a.m. or after 9.00 p.m. on any other day. It may also include other days or times the mortgage administrator knows a particular customer would not wish to be called, (e.g., for reasons of religious faith or shift working): *ibid.*, para. 12.5.4. For further information on 'putting pressure on a customer', see *ibid.*, para. 12.5.5.

[182] *Ibid.*, para. 12.4.3.

[183] *Cuckmere Brick Co Ltd.* v. *Mutual Finance Ltd.* [1971] Ch. 949; *China and South Sea Bank Ltd.* v. *Tan Soon Gin* [1990] 1 AC 536.

Plc.[184] In *Palk,* the mortgagee's wish to postpone sale was very much against the financial interests of the mortgagors, and the court exercised its discretion under s. 91 (2) of the Law of Property Act 1925 to order immediate sale.

But there may be circumstances – for example, in a rapidly rising property market – where it is in the interests of the mortgagor to postpone sale, and where both mortgagor and mortgagee agree that sale should be delayed. Even in the absence of such agreement, there may be circumstances where the law will imply a duty to delay sale for a short period. In *Meftah* v. *Lloyds TSB Bank plc (No. 2)*[185] it was held that although in principle mortgagees are entitled to sell when they wish, they cannot ignore the fact that a short delay may lead to a higher price being obtained. Accordingly, the bank or its agents must fairly and properly expose the property in the market to avoid possible liability.

The wording of the FSA rule, which could be construed to impose a duty to sell as soon as possible at current market price,[186] should be amended. The revised wording should make clear (i) the circumstances in which immediate sale of the mortgaged property is not required; and (ii) the circumstances in which a reasonable postponement of sale is prescribed.

As regards duty in respect of price, the common law duty is to 'take reasonable care to obtain the true market value of the mortgaged property'.[187] For regulated mortgage contracts, the new rule reintroduces the former statutory duty imposed on building societies to take reasonable care to ensure that the price obtained on a sale of a mortgaged property was the best price that could reasonably be obtained.[188]

Shortfall recovery

The FSA rules provide that where the proceeds of sale are less than the amount owing by the mortgagor, the mortgage administrator must take reasonable steps, as soon as possible after the sale, to inform the customer in writing of the mortgage shortfall debt.[189] As regards shortfall recovery, the position under general law is that recovery of arrears of interest is

---

[184] [1993] Ch. 330.

[185] [2001] EGCS. 44. This duty extends to security held in a foreign country.

[186] It might be argued that a selling mortgagee would comply with the rule if he put the property on the market as soon as possible but postponed sale by refusing any offer to purchase. That construction must be treated with caution, however, since it would effectively mean that the rule imposes *no* duty as to timing of sale, which is unlikely to have been the drafters' intention.

[187] *Cuckmere Brick Co. Ltd.* v. *Mutual Finance Ltd.* [1971] Ch. 949.

[188] Building Societies Act 1986, s.13 (7), Sch. 4, para. 1. The duty was repealed by the Building Societies Act 1997, s.12 (1), (2) with effect from 1 December 1997.

[189] MORT, para. 12.6.2.

statute-barred six years after becoming due,[190] and recovery of principal is statute-barred twelve years from the date when the right to receive that money accrued.[191] Departing from these provisions and drawing on good practice standards such as those contained in the *Mortgage Code*,[192] the new regulatory regime limits the commencement of any action for recovery of the shortfall to six years from the date on which the proceeds of sale were received.[193]

Exclusion clauses

It will not be possible under the new regime for the parties to a regulated mortgage contract to agree to exclude or restrict any duty owed under the FSMA or the FSA rules. Any other exclusion or restriction of liability must be 'reasonable'.[194] The position is the same for the majority of residential mortgages that do not qualify as regulated mortgage contracts,[195] since they will fall within the purview of the Unfair Terms in Consumer Contracts Regulations 1999.[196] Beyond these instances – for example where the mortgagee is not acting in a business capacity – an exclusion clause restricting the duties imposed on the selling mortgagee may be effective. The courts have held that the equitable duties imposed on a selling mortgagee may be excluded, where the exempting words are clear and susceptible of one meaning only.[197]

FSA enforcement and remedies available to the mortgagor

FSA enforcement
The FSMA confers on the FSA a wide range of enforcement and disciplinary powers to use in the pursuit of its statutory objectives. Those powers likely to be relevant in the context of mortgage regulation include: the power to investigate and gather information;[198] to fine;[199] to vary[200] or

---

[190] Limitation Act 1980, s. 20 (5). For exceptions, see Gray and Gray (*op. cit.* above fn. 112), p. 1412, n. 16.

[191] Limitation Act 1980, s. 20 (1).

[192] See below.

[193] MORT, para. 12.6.4.

[194] *Ibid.*, paras. 2.4.4, 2.4.5.

[195] For the requirements for a regulated mortgage contract, see below.

[196] Regulation 5 (unfair terms).

[197] *Bishop* v. *Bonham* [1988] 1 WLR 742 at 752 *per* Slade LJ; *Raja* v. *Lloyds TSB plc* [2001] EWCA 210 (CA), at 20.

[198] FSMA ss.165–169, 284. On the powers of investigators see further, Enforcement Manual, para 2.4.

[199] FSMA, ss. 66, 206. A warning notice and decision notice must be given: ss. 207, 208. See further, Enforcement Manual, para. 13.

[200] FSMA, s. 45. See, further, Enforcement Manual, para. 3.

cancel[201] a Part IV permission on the Authority's own initiative; to make prohibition orders;[202] to apply to the High Court for injunctions;[203] to obtain restitution (through the courts[204] or the FSA's statutory power[205]); to prosecute certain criminal offences;[206] to issue a private warning[207] or a formal caution;[208] to issue public censures and public statements.[209]

The Authority's powers to impose disciplinary sanctions are subject to referral to the Financial Services and Markets Tribunal.[210] Complaints against the FSA are handled through a complaints scheme established under Sch. 1 of the FSMA.[211]

Remedies available to the mortgagor

The 2000 Act gives the FSA the power to make rules relating to the internal handling of complaints by authorised persons and provides[212] for the establishment of an independent dispute resolution scheme – the Financial Ombudsman Service – to resolve complaints about financial services providers.

In-house complaints procedures: The FSA has exercised its powers[213] to make rules for the establishment and operation by authorised persons of internal complaint-handling procedures. The rules cover matters such as procedure, time limits for dealing with complaints, record-keeping and reporting requirements, and compensation.[214] These in-house procedures are the required first port of call for a dissatisfied mortgagor. The final response of the authorised person must inform the complainant of his

---

[201] FSMA, s. 45. Certain procedural requirements are imposed: s. 54. See further, Enforcement Manual, para. 5.

[202] FSMA, s. 56. A prohibition order prohibits an individual (whether or not he is approved under the FSMA) from carrying out functions in relation to regulated activities. See further, Enforcement Manual, para. 8.

[203] FSMA, s. 380. See Enforcement Manual, para. 6.

[204] FSMA, s. 382.

[205] *Ibid.*, s. 384 (1). See, further, Enforcement Manual, para. 9.

[206] FSMA, ss. 401, 402. See Enforcement Manual, para. 15. A list of the relevant offences is included in *ibid.*, para. 15.2.1.

[207] See Enforcement Manual, para. 11.3.

[208] See *ibid.*, para. 15.6.

[209] FSMA, ss. 66, 205. See Enforcement Manual, para. 12. Public warnings and public censure are subject to procedural requirements contained in FSMA, ss. 67, 92, 126 and 207.

[210] Set up under the FSMA, Sch. 13.

[211] Paragraphs 7, 8. The scheme includes the appointment of an independent Complaints Commissioner. For further details, see FSA Handbook module, Complaints Against the FSA.

[212] FSMA, Part XVI, Sch. 17.

[213] *Ibid.*, s. 138 (as amended by FSMA 2000 (Consequential and Transitional Provisions) Order 2001), Sch. 17, para. 13.

[214] For details, see FSA Dispute Resolution Manual: Complaints, para. 1.

right to refer the matter to the Financial Ombudsman Service within six months if he is dissatisfied with the firm's response.[215]

The Financial Ombudsman Service: If a mortgagor is dissatisfied with the response of the authorised mortgage lender or administrator, or he or she fails to receive a response within eight weeks of the complaint, he or she may refer the matter to the Financial Ombudsman Service (FOS). When the new regime is in force, complaints against authorised persons about mortgage lending will be dealt with under the compulsory jurisdiction of the FOS.[216]

The Ombudsman may dismiss a complaint without considering its merits if he is satisfied that a complainant has not suffered, or is unlikely to suffer, financial loss, material distress, or material inconvenience.[217] He may attempt to negotiate a settlement between the parties,[218] conduct an investigation,[219] and determine[220] the dispute either with or (after consideration of representations by either party) without a hearing.[221]

If a complaint is determined in favour of the complainant, the determination may include a direction that the authorised person take such steps towards the complainant as the Ombudsman considers just and appropriate.[222] In addition to (or instead of) financial compensation for financial loss, the determination may include compensation for pain and suffering; for damage to reputation; and/or for distress or inconvenience.[223] The maximum award the Ombudsman can make is £100,000.[224]

Civil court proceedings

The regulatory regime will create certain new and potentially useful rights of action for mortgagors.

Breach of 'the general prohibition' or the restrictions on financial promotion: As already noted,[225] breach of the general prohibition in s. 19 will render a

---

[215] *Ibid.*, para. 1.4.12.
[216] CP98, para. 19.24. With a few exceptions, which are dealt with under the compulsory jurisdiction, complaints about unauthorised persons are dealt with under the voluntary jurisdiction. For full details of the jurisdictions of the FOS, see Dispute Resolution Manual, para. 2.
[217] Dispute Resolution Manual, para. 3.3.1. The rule lists some 17 grounds for such dismissal.
[218] *Ibid.*, para. 3.2.9.
[219] *Ibid.*, para. 3.2.11.
[220] *Ibid.*, para. 3.8.
[221] *Ibid.*, 3.2.12–3.2.13.
[222] FSMA, s. 229 (2) (b).
[223] *Ibid.*, s. 229 (2) (a), (3); Dispute Resolution Manual, para. 3.9.3. Financial loss includes 'consequential or prospective loss'.
[224] FSMA, s. 229 (4); Dispute Resolution Manual, para. 3.9.5.
[225] See above. Similar provisions apply in relation to the restrictions on financial promotions.

contract unenforceable and voidable at the instance of the mortgagor. In each case, a 'due diligence' defence is available, and the court has a discretion to allow enforcement and/or retention of money or property transferred.

Authorised person acting otherwise than in accordance with permission: Breach of s. 20 (1) occurs where an authorised person acts otherwise than in accordance with permission granted under Part IV or resulting from any other provision of the Act. The contravention has no effect on the validity or enforceability of any transaction, but may give rise to an action for breach of statutory duty. By the FSMA 2000 (Rights of Action) Regulations 2001, contravention of a requirement imposed by the Authority (other than a Part IV financial resources requirement)[226] is actionable by a private person who has suffered loss as a result.[227]

'Private person' is defined to include (1) any individual (or, in some circumstances, his fiduciary[228]), unless he suffers the loss in question in the course of carrying on any regulated activity; and (2) any person who is not an individual, unless he suffers the loss in question in the course of carrying on business of any kind.[229]

Contravention by an authorised person of FSA rules: Contravention by an authorised person of Authority rules does not incur any criminal liability,[230] nor does it render any transaction void or unenforceable.[231] It may, however, give rise to an action for damages. By s. 150 (1) of the 2000 Act, contravention by an authorised person of a rule made by the Authority is actionable at the suit of any private person who has suffered loss as a result.[232] The action is subject to the defences and other incidents applying to actions for breach of statutory duty, and subject to any rule specifying that contravention of a specified provision gives no such right of action.[233]

---

[226] Regulation 4 (2) (b).

[227] *Ibid.*, reg. 4.

[228] A fiduciary or representative may act on behalf of a private person where the remedy would be exclusively for the benefit of that person and the remedy could not be effected through action brought otherwise than at the suit of the fiduciary or representative: *ibid.* reg. 4 (2) (a) (ii).

[229] *Ibid.*, reg. 3.

[230] FSMA, s. 151 (1).

[231] *Ibid.*, s. 151 (2).

[232] *Ibid.*, s. 150 (1); FSMA 2000 (Rights of Action) Regulations 2001, reg. 6.

[233] FSMA, s. 150(2).

The FSMA and the Consumer Credit Act

The biggest flaw of the new regulatory system is its failure to bring all consumer mortgage lending, or even all consumer lending, within a single, coherent and modernised regime. Instead, the new regime will operate within a wider, fragmented and complex framework of other regulatory regimes. The complexity of the Consumer Credit Act in its application to mortgages has long been criticised,[234] not least because it is difficult to ascertain whether or not a particular mortgage falls within its purview. The further fragmentation effected by the FSMA is unfortunate, since it can only compound this difficulty. The result will be consumer confusion and unnecessary additional compliance costs for the mortgage industry.

Pre-implementation of FSA regulation

The Consumer Credit Act applies to unsecured as well as secured credit. Much of the Act does not apply to transactions in excess of £25,000,[235] and many lenders, including building societies, local authorities and institutions formed under the Banking Act are exempt from most of the Act's provisions.[236] In consequence, most mortgage lending already falls outside its regulatory ambit. But certain provisions of, or made under, the 1974 Act – including the Consumer Credit Act (Advertisements) Regulations 1989 (as amended) and the extortionate credit provisions[237] – currently apply to all mortgages, regardless of the status of the lender and the value of the transaction.[238]

The Consumer Credit Act and its regulations are enforced by the Director General of Fair Trading and by local authority trading standards departments. Where the 1974 Act applies, the form and content of the mortgage agreement must comply with the Act. A copy of the agreement must be provided to the borrower and a seven day 'cooling-off' period is imposed.[239] Procedure on default, termination or early settlement is controlled, and the borrower remains entitled to redeem at any time.[240]

---

[234] See, *inter alia*, Law Commission, *Land Mortgages* (WP No. 99, 1986), paras. 3.41–3.43; Law Commission, *Transfer of Land – Land Mortgages* (Law Com No. 204, 1991), para. 9.6; Bently and Howells [1989] Conv. 164 at 234.

[235] The Consumer Credit (Increase of Monetary Limits) Order 1983, Schedule, Part II, as amended by the Consumer Credit (Increase of Monetary Limits) (Amendment) Order 1998, art. 2.

[236] Consumer Credit Act 1974, s. 16, as amended; Consumer Credit (Exempt Agreements) Order 1989, as amended.

[237] Consumer Credit Act 1974, ss.137–140.

[238] *Ibid.*, ss.16 (6), 140.

[239] *Ibid.*, ss. 58, 61.

[240] For details, see Cousins, *The Law of Mortgages* (2nd ed., 2001, Sweet & Maxwell), paras. 14.01–14.08.

Any term of the mortgage that is inconsistent with these provisions is void.[241] An important recent challenge has raised the possibility that the statutory bar on the enforcement of an agreement or security that fails to comply with the prescribed requirements constitutes an infringement of lenders' rights under the ECHR.[242] The Court of Appeal has given notice to the Crown,[243] in a case involving an unsecured loan,[244] that it is considering making a declaration of incompatibility.[245] The issue is clearly of great significance to the future operation of the Consumer Credit Act, which is currently under review,[246] although it will not impact on the operation of the FSA scheme. Disclosure requirements under the FSA regime are contained within the FSA rules, and the FSMA expressly provides that breach of such rules has no effect on the validity or enforceability of any transaction.[247]

After implementation

In order to eliminate overlap and avoid double regulation, the new regime removes from the scope of the Consumer Credit Act 1974 both regulated mortgage contracts and qualifying credit promotions.[248] In consequence, where a loan is classified as a 'regulated mortgage contract',[249] or a promotion as a 'qualifying credit promotion',[250] it will be regulated under the FSA scheme alone.

The definition of 'qualifying credit' is broad enough to include promotions that relate to equitable as well as legal mortgages, to second or subsequent mortgages, and to the unsecured part of a mortgage package that combines both secured and unsecured lending.[251] When this difference in the scope of regulated mortgage contracts and that of qualifying credit promotions is added to the complexities of the Consumer Credit Act, the unfortunate result will be that there will exist the following:

---

[241] Consumer Credit Act 1974, ss. 94, 173.
[242] Human Rights Act 1998, ss. 3, 4; Sch. 1, Part I, art. 6; Part II, art. 1.
[243] As required under s. 5 of the 1998 Act.
[244] *Wilson* v. *First County Trusts* [2001] 2 WLR 302.
[245] Human Rights Act 1998, s. 4.
[246] See below.
[247] See above.
[248] FSMA 2000 (Regulated Activities) Order 2001, arts. 90 and 91, which amend the Consumer Credit Act 1974 and the Consumer Credit (Advertisements) Regulations 1989.
[249] FSMA 2000 (Regulated Activities) Order 2001, art. 61 (3) (a), as substituted by the FSMA 2000 (Regulated Activities) (Amendment) Order 2001, art. 8. See further, above.
[250] FSMA, s. 21; FSMA 2000 (Financial Promotion) Order 2001, art. 10. See above.
[251] See above.

- Loans that are regulated under the Consumer Credit Act, but any associated promotion is regulated under the FSA regime (for example, a mortgage to secure a loan of under £25,000 made by a non-exempt lender where the mortgage is an equitable or a second mortgage).

- Mortgage packages, parts of which are governed by the FSA regime and other parts by the Consumer Credit Act regime (for example, a flexible mortgage that combines a first charge on residential property with a credit card or an unsecured loan with a pre-agreed limit; an endowment mortgage that combines an interest only mortgage with an investment vehicle; an equity release product that combines a mortgage with an annuity).

- Financial promotions, parts of which are regulated by the FSA and other parts by the Consumer Credit Act.

- Loans that switch horses mid-race: both the FSA and the Treasury anticipate that there will be mortgages that fall within one regulatory regime at inception and then, because of some change, become regulated under the other. The Treasury comments in this respect do not correspond exactly with those of the FSA, but both foresee as an example the situation where the variation of an existing loan amounts effectively to the creation of a new mortgage.[252]

- Loans that are not regulated under either the FSA or the Consumer Credit Act regimes (except for extortionate credit bargain provisions of Consumer Credit Act) (examples include (i) any equitable or second or subsequent mortgage to secure a loan in excess of the Consumer Credit Act financial ceiling;[253] and (ii) any equitable or second mortgage by an exempt lender, of whatever amount).

This last category, of 'unregulated' mortgages, will continue to be subject in most cases to the Council of Mortgage Lenders' *Mortgage Code*, a voluntary code of practice established by the mortgage industry. The Mortgage Code Compliance Board maintains a register of lenders and intermediaries who fulfil the registration requirements and monitors compliance. The Council also publishes a *Statement of Practice on Handling Arrears and Possessions*. The Code is not without its problems, and is currently under review. In particular, there are no effective sanctions for non-compliance, and no mechanism that assures any form of consumer

---

[252] HM Treasury, *Regulating Mortgages* (2000, HMT), para. 41; CP98, para. 4. The difficulties relate largely to mortgages entered into before, but continuing after, the implementation of the new regime.

[253] Ironically, for certain types of mortgage the degree of consumer protection is in inverse proportion to the value of the loan.

representation.[254] There are further avenues that may prove useful in the case of an unregulated mortgage. The Unfair Terms in Consumer Contracts Regulations 1999 implement the European Directive on Unfair Terms in Consumer Contracts. The regulations allow for complaints brought by consumers to be considered by the Director General of Fair Trading (DGFT) and also empower the DGFT and other 'qualifying bodies' to seek injunctions to prevent the continued use of unfair terms in consumer contracts.[255] The *OFT Non-Status Lending Guidelines* are guidelines published by the Office of Fair Trading and apply to loans to non-status borrowers. Non-status borrowers are defined as individuals with impaired credit ratings or who might otherwise find it difficult to obtain finance on normal terms and conditions.

It is unfortunate that while devising the new FSA regime the opportunity was not taken to rationalise and unify mortgage regulation into a single, coherent and consolidated package. The Consumer Credit Act is itself currently under review by the Department of Trade and Industry.[256] The Consultation Paper identifies among its priority issues making the extortionate credit bargain provisions more effective, raising the Act's financial limits, revising the categories of exempt agreements, and simplifying the advertising regulations. This review, combined with the further consultation exercise to enlarge the scope of the FSA regime to include mortgage advice,[257] perhaps means it is yet not too late. The need for regulation is largely premised on a belief that consumers cannot without regulation understand the complexities of mortgage transactions or their rights under their mortgage contracts. Even if the FSA regime as presently proposed were to be completely successful in addressing those problems, we would still leave consumers in the position of understanding their rights but not understanding how to enforce them. A regulatory framework that distinguishes secured from unsecured lending, large loans from small ones, and certain types of lender from others, was no doubt eminently sensible at the time it was devised. But times have changed, and so have mortgages. Many of the relatively new mortgage products, which combine both types of loan, are not easily accommodated within regimes that were designed at a time when far fewer types of mortgage product existed. If we are to have mortgage regulation for the twenty-first century, should it not be mortgage regulation for twenty-first century mortgages?

---

[254] See further, Cruickshank Review (*op. cit.* above fn. 77), paras. 4.79–4.81; the Banking Ombudsman, *The Banking Code and the Mortgage Code: Suggestions for Review*, May 1999.

[255] Regulation 12. The Consumers' Association and the FSA became 'qualifying bodies' in 2000 and 2001 respectively.

[256] DTI, *Tackling Loan Sharks and More: Consultation Document on Modernising the Consumer Credit Act* (25 July 2001, DTI).

[257] The scheme initially excluded mortgage advice but, following a Treasury announcement on 12 December 2001, is to be amended to include such advice.

7

Land law and human rights

Kevin Gray

Introduction

Land law and human rights have never seemed particularly natural bedfellows. Perhaps it is because the popular notions of property and humanity appear somehow antithetical, a jarring juxtaposition of the self-regarding impulse towards personal appropriation and an other-regarding vision of the intrinsic merits of strangers. Again, land law and human rights law may have tended to look like polar extremes of jurisprudential concern precisely because, across the distance of the supposed public–private divide, the rather different resonances of their unshared terminology – the intellectual tenor of divergent legal traditions – intensified the impression that these areas were culturally and substantively quite distinct. Their lack of congruence may have appeared all the more understandable in those jurisdictions where the allocation of the primary goods of life was already largely settled and where disputes over land seldom raised fundamental issues of raw human entitlement. On this view human rights considerations were apt to penetrate the sphere of the land lawyer only in the context of aboriginal land claims or systematic ethnic displacement or gross colonial exploitation in far-flung parts of the globe. In England, by contrast, the interface between human rights discourse and the law of real property came to seem somewhat limited amidst the relative affluence of a post-war welfare state in which the oppressed and the dispossessed – Frantz Fanon's 'wretched of the earth' – were conspicuous mainly by their absence.

For these, and many other, reasons the intricate machinery of the Law of Property Act 1925 and its satellite legislation contains little which could be confused with the positive protection or reinforcement of basic concepts of human freedom, dignity and equality. The rights upheld by the 1925 legislation (and by its associated regimes of registration) are, in general, derivative or transaction-based rights rather than rights of an original character arising in spontaneous vindication of free-standing perceptions of human worth. Still less did the formative property jurisprudence propounded by an earlier generation of Victorian judges overtly endorse any intrinsic link between property and human values. For instance, the overseers of England's industrial revolution cared little for that most modern of concerns – the human right to respect for privacy.[1] The sole sense in which notions of human freedom impinged on the nineteenth-century world of real property was evidenced by the landowner's more or less unconstrained power to exploit his land as he saw fit without regard either to the needs of others[2] or to any higher conception of the irreducible rights of his fellow human beings.[3] Most famously, in *Bradford Corpn* v. *Pickles*,[4] the House of Lords allowed a landowner, even though acting maliciously, to cut off a supply of clean water that would otherwise have served the rapidly developing domestic, sanitary and industrial requirements of the city of Bradford. As Lord Macnaghten indicated,[5] the landowner might prefer 'his own interests to the public good' and might indeed be 'churlish, selfish, and grasping'. But, although his conduct might seem 'shocking to a moral philosopher', the House of Lords refused to intervene.

Yet the assumed dissociation of land law and human rights has always been one of the larger (but no less insidious) myths of the law. The law of property silently betrays a range of value judgments about the 'proper' entitlements of human and other actors.[6] These value judgments reflect a complex picture of social relationships and rankings, each casting a shadow on some extra-legal index of freedom, dignity and equality. For instance, the law of matrimonial property long bore the imprint of a dogma of marital symbiosis which ensured that, deep into the twentieth century, a substantial portion of the population lived most of their adult life in a state of legal and factual dispossession. The medieval notion of spousal unity – of husband and wife as 'one flesh' – had the effect of suspending the legal personality of the married woman and rendering her incompetent to acquire property or even to earn wages in her own

---

[1] See Gray, 'Property in thin air', [1991] CLJ 252 at 259–263.

[2] See *Tapling* v. *Jones* (1865) 11 HLC 290 at 311, 11 ER 1344 at 1353 *per* Lord Cranworth (every man has 'a right to use his own land by building on it as he thinks most to his interest').

[3] See Lord Hoffmann's recent description of human rights as 'rights which belong to individuals simply by virtue of their humanity, independently of any utilitarian calculation' (*R (Alconbury Developments Ltd and others)* v. *Secretary of State for the Environment, Transport and the Regions* [2001] 2 WLR 1389 at 1411D-E).

[4] [1895] AC 587.

[5] [1895] AC 587 at 601.

[6] See Gray and Gray, *Elements of Land Law* (3rd ed., 2001, Butterworths), pp. 95–96.

name.[7] As Lord Denning MR acidly observed some time later, 'the law regarded husband and wife as one: and the husband as that one'.[8]

The invidious discrimination practised against the married woman was reversed only slowly by the long-term effects of the Married Women's Property Acts of 1870 and 1882, but the historical process provides yet another reminder of the way in which, as Professor C.B. Macpherson pointed out,[9] the idea of property is being gradually broadened to include a 'right to a kind of society or set of power relations which will enable the individual to live a fully human life.' Indeed, in an older and more enlightened property philosophy which lies deeply embedded in Anglo-American political thought, the concept of 'property' was *always* accounted as inclusive of a person's 'life, liberty and estate'.[10] This Lockean articulation of the coalescence of property and human rights was to have energising – even revolutionary – consequences. For James Madison in 1792, just 'as a man is said to have a right to his property, he may be equally said to have a property in his rights'.[11] By that stage, of course, the American colonists, in active assertion of 'certain unalienable rights',[12] had just thrown off the yoke of British rule and, equally important, had altered the *Grundnorm* of a large part of a continent's land law.[13]

Nowadays, albeit in a rather different way, the ideology of human rights is beginning to lay an equally radical imprint on the law of land in England and Wales. Once again the process dispels any bland supposition that human rights law and land law never meet, overlap or converge. The Human Rights Act 1998 incorporates or patriates certain 'Convention rights' already enshrined for half a century in the European

7 The married woman's persona at common law was 'incorporated and consolidated into that of the husband... her *baron*, or lord' (Blackstone, *Commentaries*, Vol. I, p. 430). See Gray, 'Property in common law systems', in van Maanen and van der Walt, *Property Law on the Threshold of the 21st Century* (1996, MAKLU, Antwerp), pp. 238–240. It is remarkable that the full legal capacity of the married woman was finally recognised in England only in the Law Reform (Married Women and Tortfeasors) Act 1935.

8 *Williams & Glyn's Bank Ltd* v. *Boland* [1979] Ch 312 at 332C.

9 'Capitalism and the changing concept of property' in Kamenka and Neale, *Feudalism, Capitalism and Beyond* (1975, ANU Press, Canberra), p. 120.

10 Locke, *Two Treatises of Government* (2nd critical ed. by Laslett, 1967, Cambridge University Press), *The Second Treatise*, s. 123 (p. 368).

11 'Property' in Rutland *et al, The Papers of James Madison* (1983, University of Virginia Press, Charlottesville VA), Vol. 14, p. 266 (*National Gazette*, 27 March 1792).

12 'We hold these truths to be self-evident, that all men are created equal; that they are endowed by their Creator with certain unalienable rights; that among these are life, liberty, and the pursuit of happiness' (US Declaration of Independence (1776)).

13 After the close of the Revolutionary War the land law system of the former colonies became 'allodial' (see *Stevens* v. *City of Salisbury*, 214 A2d 775 at 778 (1965); *City of Annapolis* v. *Waterman*, 745 A2d 1000 at 1006 (Md 2000)).

Convention on Human Rights.[14] The 1998 Act requires that all primary and subordinate legislation must, so far as possible, be 'read and given effect in a way which is compatible with the Convention rights'.[15] Every 'public authority' must, moreover, act conformably with the Convention rights[16] and, given that a 'public authority' is specifically defined as inclusive of a 'court or tribunal',[17] this requirement may well mean that the Convention guarantees are broadly applicable in all litigation (whether or not between private individuals). Even if the Human Rights Act does not directly command such 'horizontal' effect,[18] it is by now inevitable that various forms of supra-national human rights protection will, in any event, infiltrate English law by more subtle or subliminal means.[19]

Amongst the Convention rights which will most distinctively affect English land law are the principle of respect for private and family life and for the integrity of the home,[20] the freedoms of peaceful assembly and association,[21] and the right to independent and impartial adjudication of one's civil rights and obligations by an appropriate tribunal.[22] Already these protective provisions threaten to render obsolete some of the time-honoured, but invasive, mechanisms of English land law which have permitted landlords, mortgagees and those in possession of land to have recourse to self-help or other arbitrary remedies.[23] But the intended focus of the present chapter is not upon these likely modifications of the English law of land. Instead our preoccupation is with the central, and

---

[14] European Convention for the Protection of Human Rights and Fundamental Freedoms (1950) (see Cmd 8969 (1953)). The 1998 Act does not derogate from any pre-existing 'right or freedom' conferred by or under any law effective in any part of the UK (Human Rights Act 1998, s. 11 (1) (a)).

[15] Human Rights Act 1998, s. 3 (1).

[16] *Ibid.*, s. 6 (1).

[17] *Ibid.*, s. 6 (3) (a).

[18] See Howell, *Land and Human Rights*, [1999] Conv. 287; 'The Human Rights Act 1998: the "horizontal effect" on Land Law', in Cooke (ed), *Modern Studies in Property Law (Vol. 1): Property 2000* (2001, Hart Publishing, Oxford), p. 149.

[19] As Lord Cooke of Thorndon observed in *Hunter* v. *Canary Wharf Ltd* [1997] AC 655 at 714A, international human rights standards 'may be taken into account in shaping the common law'. See also *Aston Cantlow and Wilmcote with Billesley PCC* v. *Wallbank* [2001] 3 All ER 393 at 404j–405a ('Our task is... to draw out the broad principles which animate the convention').

[20] European Convention for the Protection of Human Rights and Fundamental Freedoms, art. 8 (1); Human Rights Act 1998, s. 1 (1), Sch. I, Part I.

[21] European Convention for the Protection of Human Rights and Fundamental Freedoms, art. 11 (1); Human Rights Act 1998, s. 1 (1), Sch. I, Part I. Significantly the right to freedom of movement (Protocol No. 4, art. 2) is not included amongst 'the Convention rights' to which the Human Rights Act refers (see Gray and Gray, 'Civil rights, civil wrongs and quasi-public space' [1999] EHRLR 46 at 49).

[22] European Convention for the Protection of Human Rights and Fundamental Freedoms, art. 6 (1); Human Rights Act 1998, s. 1 (1), Sch. I, Part I.

[23] See Gray and Gray, (*op. cit.* above, fn. 6) pp. 286, 1263, 1295, 1404, 1417.

potentially most controversial, property-related provision of the European Convention – that which guarantees the entitlement of 'every natural or legal person...to the peaceful enjoyment of his possessions'.[24] Our concern will be with the meaning to be attributed to this provision in the context of the modern regulatory state. The Convention's property guarantee highlights an important point of convergence between land law, environmental law and human rights law and, for these reasons, promises to acquire an unprecedented significance for English land lawyers in days to come. Unfamiliar though European human rights discourse may initially appear to be, we will be increasingly required to grapple with very different ways of addressing some of the critical issues facing the land lawyers of the twenty-first century. We must also draw upon the experience of other jurisdictions which have chosen to embed the protection of property rights in constitutional or statutory form.

Property guarantees

The pivotal property provision of the European Convention on Human Rights proclaims, in Protocol No. 1, art. 1, that:

> Every natural or legal person is entitled to the peaceful enjoyment of his possessions. No one shall be deprived of his possessions except in the public interest and subject to the conditions provided for by law and by the general principles of international law.
>
> The preceding provisions shall not, however, in any way impair the right of a State to enforce such laws as it deems necessary to control the use of property in accordance with the general interest or to secure the payment of taxes or other contributions or penalties.

Despite its slightly awkward reference to 'possessions', art. 1 has been broadly understood in human rights jurisprudence as 'in substance guaranteeing the right of property'.[25] Although the protection of the Convention applies only to a person's *existing* possessions,[26] art. 1 provides important safeguards against arbitrary expropriation, distinguishing in the process between the *deprivation* of property and the mere *control of use* of property. The first, and most general, rule enunciated in

---

[24] European Convention for the Protection of Human Rights and Fundamental Freedoms, Protocol No. 1, art. 1; Human Rights Act 1998, s. 1 (1), Sch. I, Part II.

[25] *Marckx* v. *Belgium*, Series A No. 31, para. 63 (1979). See also *Sporrung and Lönnroth* v. *Sweden*, Series A No. 52, para. 57 (1982); *James* v. *United Kingdom*, Series A No. 98, para. 37 (1986); *Banér* v. *Sweden* (1989) 60 DR 128 at 138.

[26] Article 1 'does not guarantee the right to acquire possessions' (*Marckx* v. *Belgium*, Series A No. 31, para. 50 (1979)).

art. 1 comprises the principle of 'peaceful enjoyment' of possessions.[27] The second rule (contained in the second sentence of the first paragraph) places significant restraints upon deprivations of property, whilst the third rule (contained in the second paragraph) recognises the ultimate entitlement of the state to control the use of property 'in accordance with the general interest'. It is, however, a constant refrain of European Court jurisprudence that the overarching principle of 'peaceful enjoyment' of possessions qualifies, and permeates the interpretation of, the second and third rules of the article.[28]

The safeguards provided by the Convention are, in their way, mirrored across the expanse of European history during the past millennium.[29] The human right to protection from arbitrary dispossession by the state is born of a deep impulse which views lawless seizure of property as a particularly violating kind of molestation – a form of proprietary rape.[30] An instinct against arbitrary disseisin of freehold is at least as old as Magna Carta[31] and went on to animate the great eighteenth-century declarations of social and civil liberties. For Blackstone, writing in 1765, it was inconceivable that 'sacred and inviolable rights of private property' should be postponed to 'public necessity' without 'a full indemnification and equivalent for the injury thereby sustained'.[32] As Blackstone explained, in strikingly modern parlance, the state cannot act 'even for the general good of the whole community...by simply stripping the subject of his property in an arbitrary manner'. Blackstone's premise was adopted, quickly and in virtually identical terms, in the French Declaration of the Rights of Man and of the Citizen[33] and has since inspired a vast range of national and international prohibitions on the taking of property by the state except for justifiable public purposes and

---

[27] See *Sporrung and Lönnroth* v. *Sweden*, Series A No. 52, para. 61 (1982).

[28] *James* v. *United Kingdom*, Series A No. 98, para. 37 (1986); *Tre Traktörer Aktiebolag* v. *Sweden*, Series A No. 159, para. 54 (1989); *Allan Jacobsson* v. *Sweden*, Series A No. 163, para. 53 (1989); *Mellacher* v. *Austria*, Series A No. 169, para. 42 (1989); *Fredin* v. *Sweden*, Series A No. 192, para. 41 (1991); *Former King of Greece* v. *Greece* (2001) 33 EHRR 516 at 543 (para. 50).

[29] It has even been argued that the ideal of democratic government developed specifically in northwest Europe over the last 1,000 years has its roots in Anglo-Saxon and Norse concepts of 'seisin' which upheld the territorial inviolability of those in possession (see Tay, 'Law, the citizen and the state' in Kamenka *et al*, *Law and Society: The Crisis in Legal Ideals* (1978, Edward Arnold), p. 10).

[30] Compare the etymological links between 'rape' and 'rapine' (*Shorter Oxford English Dictionary* (1993, Clarendon Press), Vol. 2, p. 2477).

[31] Magna Carta 1215, arts. 39, 52 (see Holt, *Magna Carta* (2nd ed., 1992, Cambridge University Press), pp. 461, 465–466). See also *Mabo* v. *Queensland (No 1)* (1988) 166 CLR 186 at 226 *per* Deane J.

[32] *Commentaries*, Vol. 1, p. 135.

[33] 'Since property is a sacred and inviolable right, no one may be deprived thereof unless a legally established public necessity obviously requires it, and upon condition of a just and prior indemnity' (Declaration of the Rights of Man and of the Citizen 1789, art. 17).

on payment of fair value.[34] This principled approach to the institution of property accords strongly with the modern view that '[r]espect for human rights requires that certain basic rights of individuals should not be capable in any circumstances of being overridden by the majority, even if they think that the public interest so requires'.[35]

In the common law tradition this bias against uncompensated expropriation came to have the status of a strong presumptive principle in the definition of both legislative[36] and prerogatival[37] powers. The sentiment against capricious taking was to find perhaps its most famous expression in the guarantee of the Fifth Amendment of the US Constitution (authored, incidentally, by James Madison) that '[n]o person shall be...deprived of...property, without due process of law; nor shall private property be taken for public use, without just compensation'.[38] Such protection of property has, of course, no precise parallel under the unwritten constitution of the UK. But it would be wrong to suppose that, prior to the commencement of the Human Rights Act 1998, the UK never had experience of an entrenched prohibition on uncompensated appropriation. For decades the Government of Ireland Act 1920 – which ranked of course as a constitutional instrument – forbade the enactment in Northern Ireland of any law that would 'either directly or indirectly...take any property without compensation'.[39] In its time this provision generated what is now a largely forgotten cache of caselaw (emanating ultimately from the House of Lords). This caselaw has suddenly re-emerged to claim a contemporary relevance in the elaboration of the property provisions of the Human Rights Act 1998.

---

[34] See, for example, United Nations Universal Declaration of Human Rights (1948), art. 17 (2). '[T]he prohibition on the arbitrary deprivation of property expresses an essential idea which is both basic and virtually uniform in civilised legal systems' (*Newcrest Mining (WA) Ltd* v. *Commonwealth of Australia* (1997) 190 CLR 513 at 659 *per* Kirby J). The rule against such deprivation is 'fundamental' (*Malika Holdings Pty Ltd* v. *Stretton* (2001) 178 ALR 218 at 248 [121] *per* Kirby J).

[35] R (*Alconbury Developments Ltd and others*) v. *Secretary of State for the Environment, Transport and the Regions* [2001] 2 WLR 1389 at 1411D *per* Lord Hoffmann.

[36] *Western Counties Railway Co* v. *Windsor and Annapolis Railway Co* (1882) 7 App Cas 178 at 188 *per* Lord Watson; *Attorney-General* v. *De Keyser's Royal Hotel Ltd* [1920] AC 508 at 542 *per* Lord Atkinson; *Belfast Corpn* v. *O.D. Cars Ltd* [1960] AC 490 at 517–518 *per* Viscount Simonds, 523 *per* Lord Radcliffe. See also *The Queen* v. *Tener* (1985) 17 DLR (4th) 1 at 8 *per* Estey J (Supreme Court of Canada); *Newcrest Mining (WA) Ltd* v. *Commonwealth of Australia* (1997) 190 CLR 513 at 657–661 *per* Kirby J (High Court of Australia).

[37] *Burmah Oil Co Ltd* v. *Lord Advocate* [1965] AC 75 at 112–113 *per* Lord Reid, 162–163 *per* Lord Pearce, 169–170 *per* Lord Upjohn.

[38] This 'Takings Clause' is acknowledged throughout the common law world as the genesis of many other similar restraints upon expropriation by government. See, for example, s. 51 (xxxi) of the Constitution of the Commonwealth of Australia, which operates as a 'constitutional guarantee...against acquisition without just terms' (*Commonwealth of Australia* v. *State of Tasmania* (1983) 158 CLR 1 at 282 *per* Deane J). See also Allen, *The Right to Property in Commonwealth Constitutions* (2000, Cambridge University Press), pp. 36–82.

[39] Section 5 (1).

Takings and the modern regulatory state

It is universally acknowledged that the modern state retains a power of 'eminent domain' under which it may requisition land from private citizens in the interest of the public good.[40] Without such a power of compulsory acquisition the organisation of the essential infrastructure of contemporary life would prove largely impossible. Roads and railways could not be built; existing transport services could not be improved; inner-city areas could not be regenerated; water resources could not be conserved and channelled; the communications industry could not function; the list would proceed almost endlessly. But in return for the compulsory transfer of titles in land the state must pay compensation. Compulsory purchase orders lead ultimately to an award of compensation in respect of the landowner's actual loss as assessed under the Land Compensation Act 1961. The shadow of Magna Carta still falls heavily some eight centuries later.

Yet this is far from the end of the story. The pertinent difficulty is that much modern governmental activity involves, not the outright acquisition of a freehold or leasehold estate in land, but rather the imposition of substantial Community-oriented restrictions upon the *free enjoyment* of estate ownership. In such cases the landowner suffers not expropriation, but a form of 'injurious affection'.[41] We live in an age of unprecedented regulation – a feature intensified by our membership of the European Union – with the consequence that the landowner's user rights are potentially cut back by a plethora of regulatory controls which, without any divesting of his formal proprietary title, severely limit the land-owner's ability to exploit his land in precisely the way he may wish. Such constraints range from urban planning legislation to nature conservation measures; from negative controls which restrict the scope of future development[42] to positive impositions which require that the landowner cede various rights of user over his land[43] or even reinstate the land to prescribed environmental standards.[44] It is particularly significant, in this

---

[40] Eminent domain has been described as 'the proprietary aspect of sovereignty' (*Minister of State for the Army* v. *Dalziel* (1944) 68 CLR 261 at 284 *per* Rich J). See also *Clunies-Ross* v. *Commonwealth of Australia* (1984) 155 CLR 193 at 205 *per* Murphy J ('a necessary feature of government').

[41] See, for example, *Belfast Corpn* v. *O.D. Cars Ltd* [1960] AC 490 at 524–525 *per* Lord Radcliffe.

[42] See, for instance, the regime of planning control now exercised pursuant to the Town and Country Planning Act 1990 (as amended).

[43] Coercive powers are available, for instance, to initiate a 'public path creation order' over private land (see Highways Act 1980, s. 26; Countryside and Rights of Way Act 2000, s. 58 (1)). An electricity undertaker may apply for the compulsory grant of a wayleave to install an electricity line in or over land (see Electricity Act 1989, Sch. 4, para 6 (1)–(3)). Likewise a telecommunications operator may seek mandatory powers over the land of strangers in order to facilitate its operations (Telecommunications Act 1984, Sch. 2, para. 5).

[44] See, for example, Town and Country Planning Act 1990, ss. 215–219; Environmental Protection Act 1990, ss. 80–81, 81A.

context, that increasing emphasis is nowadays placed on the importance of enhanced public access to recreational land and leisure opportunities as a necessary precondition of improved community health and the promotion of 'social equity'.[45]

All such interferences with land use inevitably have an impact on the landowner. The potential use or development value of land may be dramatically limited by its inclusion in a conservation area,[46] by a change of zoning classification to exclude commercial use,[47] by its listing as a site of 'special architectural or historic interest'[48] or as a site of 'special scientific interest'[49] or by its involuntary dedication to an army of climbers and ramblers. At a stroke, the intervention of the state may curtail the possibility of profitable or convenient construction on the land, affect the intensity of permissible farming methods, or simply entail considerable personal expense for the landowner.[50] The sharp edge of regulatory control falls just as keenly on the homeowner who finds that he is not allowed to build a much-needed garage over the site of his listed outside lavatory as on the farmer who is forbidden to plough over the habitat of some protected species of animal, bird or butterfly. Moreover, such governmental interference with land use can supervene at any time – perhaps long after the date of acquisition by the current landowner – thus skewing his investment-backed expectations in respect of exploitation of the land. In the regulatory era the state and its authorised agencies have truly extensive power to intervene, on behalf of a perceived public interest, in the preservation or promotion of environmental amenity (a phrase that is wide enough to cover not merely features of urban planning and design, but also far-reaching aspects of the natural and cultural heritage).

In the present context the critical question is not about the statutory competence of relevant forms of regulation. By and large we all agree, at

---

[45] See, for example, the explicit intendment of the 'right to roam' provisions of the Countryside and Rights of Way Act 2000, as articulated in *Access to the Open Countryside in England and Wales: A Consultation Paper* (DETR, February 1998, paras. 1.8, 3.50, 3.66–7) and the *Explanatory Notes* accompanying the Countryside and Rights of Way Bill (Session 1999–2000), para. 5. Compare the legislative extension in Sweden in 1985 of free fishing rights in private waters as part of a 'public recreation policy' designed to assist in the 'important task for society . . . to make a wide range of leisure activities available to all' (see *Banér* v. *Sweden* (1989) 60 DR 128 at 132–133, 141).

[46] Planning (Listed Buildings and Conservation Areas) Act 1990, s. 69 (1), 74; Town and Country Planning Act 1990, s. 211.

[47] See Town and Country Planning Act 1990, s. 55 (2) (f); Town and Country Planning (Use Classes) Order 1987 (SI 1987/764).

[48] Planning (Listed Buildings and Conservation Areas) Act 1990, ss. 1, 7–8.

[49] Wildlife and Countryside Act 1981, s. 28 (as substituted by Countryside and Rights of Way Act 2000, s. 75(1), Sch. 9).

[50] See, for example, *Morland* v. *Secretary of State for the Environment, Transport and the Regions* (unreported, Court of Appeal, 10 December 1998) (costs of clean-up of disused quarry).

least at the level of abstract principle, that important features of environmental value require protection. The central question relates instead to the allocation of the *cost* of the environmental protection which we all profess to desire; and this cost may be measured in terms of forgone development value or lost amenity or sheer cash outlay. It remains a contingent fact of life that the promotion of environmental welfare comes at a price which must be paid either by the general community or by some subset of it. Should the individual landowner be left to bear the cost of a regulatory intervention which enures to the wider benefit of the whole community? True it is that the landowner has not been stripped of any freehold or leasehold estate in the land. Such estate ownership remains, in at least formal terms, undisturbed in his hands. But the impact of all forms of regulatory control is to delimit the scope of his user rights – of vital aspects of his proprietary sovereignty – with the result that any easy distinction between mere regulation and outright confiscation appears, in many cases, rather less than convincing.[51] And if confiscation of an estate in land for public purposes generates an unquestioned entitlement to compensation from public funds, it seems at least feasible that the impact of regulatory control should similarly constitute a compensable event.[52] The homeowner whose hopes of building a garage have been frustrated, the landowner whose garden is disfigured by an overhead power line, the farmer whose field is sterilised by the imperative of wildlife conservation – all arguably deserve some reimbursement from public funds for their uncovenanted contribution to the larger public weal. As the Court of Appeal of Nova Scotia recently observed, what is at stake is the 'policy issue of how minutely government may control land without buying it'.[53]

At this point the picture becomes pretty confused. In modern times English law has tended severely to truncate the availability of public compensation for the disadvantageous impact of land use regulation,[54] but the denial of such compensation is far from uniform. Thus, while no compensation is offered to the owner who is refused planning permission or whose house suddenly becomes a listed building or whose land is subjected to access rights under the Countryside and Rights of Way Act 2000, reimbursement from public funds is provided, haphazardly, to others. Compensation is payable, for example, in respect of the grant of

---

[51] See *Commonwealth of Australia* v. *Western Australia* (1999) 196 CLR 392 at 487–488, where Callinan J indicated that the 'real point' about regulation is that governments 'can effectively achieve the benefit of many aspects of proprietorship without actually becoming proprietors.' See also *Tahoe-Sierra Preservation Council, Inc* v. *Tahoe Regional Planning Agency*, 34 F Supp 2d 1226 at 1238 (1999).

[52] See Anderson, 'Compensation for interference with property', [1999] EHRLR 543 at 554.

[53] *Mariner Real Estate Ltd* v. *Nova Scotia (Attorney General)* (1999) 177 DLR (4th) 696 at 699 *per* Cromwell JA.

[54] See Planning and Compensation Act 1991, s. 31.

power line wayleaves to electricity undertakers[55] and cable ducting facilities to communications companies.[56] Likewise landowners can claim compensation for the compulsory creation of a public footpath or bridleway over their land.[57] Increasingly nowadays the regulatory quid pro quo merges with, and is intensified by, various semi-consensual regimes aimed at ecologically sympathetic administration of land resources. Some landowners can claim payments for taking part in 'countryside stewardship' schemes which conserve or enhance the 'natural beauty or amenity of the countryside (including its flora and fauna and geological and physiographical features) or of any features of archaeological interest there' or which promote the 'enjoyment of the countryside by the public'.[58] Farmers can be compensated for their participation in similar eco-management schemes affecting designated areas.[59] Such 'environmentally sensitive area' management schemes normally specify permissible methods of agricultural production and practices 'compatible with the environment'[60] and may also contain 'requirements as to public access'.[61]

Key questions

It is unlikely that the inconsistency surrounding compensable state intervention can survive close scrutiny under the European-derived property guarantee now incorporated in the Human Rights Act 1998. English law will, in this respect, be catapulted into the same kinds of controversy that have assailed the environmental protection laws of other

[55] Electricity Act 1989, Sch. 4, para. 7. See, for example, *R* v. *Secretary of State for Trade and Industry and Northern Electric Plc, ex parte Wolf* (2000) 79 P & CR 299 at 302–304 (power lines over garden).

[56] Telecommunications Act 1984, Sch. 2, paras. 4, 7. See, for example, *Mercury Communications Ltd* v. *London and India Dock Investments Ltd* (1994) 69 P & CR 135 at 163–169; *British Telecommunications plc* v. *Humber Bridge Board* (unreported, Chancery Division, 6 December 2000).

[57] Highways Act 1980, s. 28 (1). See, however, *Rotherwick's Executors* v. *Oxfordshire CC* [2000] 28 EG 144 at 147, where the Lands Tribunal rejected, merely on the ground that it was out of time, an exorbitant compensation claim of £1.12 million in respect of a 2 kilometre footpath created in an Oxfordshire beauty spot.

[58] See Environment Act 1995, s. 98; Countryside Stewardship Regulations 2000 (SI 2000/3048), paras. 2 (1), 3–6 (effective 5 December 2000).

[59] See Agriculture Act 1986, s. 18(1)–(4A) (as amended by Agriculture Act 1986 (Amendment) Regulations 1997 (SI 1997/1457) and Development Commission (Transfer of Functions and Miscellaneous Provisions) Order 1999 (SI 1999/416), Sch. 1). See, further, Environmentally Sensitive Areas (Stages I–IV) Designation Orders 2000 (SI 2000/3049-3052) (effective 5 December 2000); England Rural Development Programme (Enforcement) Regulations 2000 (SI 2000/3044) (effective 5 December 2000).

[60] Agriculture Act 1986, s. 18 (4) (a), (4A).

[61] *Ibid.*, s. 18 (4) (aa).

major jurisdictions in Europe, North America and the Pacific Rim. In the elaboration of the English approach to compensable takings under the First Protocol of the European Convention, it will be important to have regard to the collective guidance provided by the experience of other jurisdictions, just as it is important to observe points of continuing divergence. The remainder of this chapter is therefore concerned to pinpoint some of the key questions which bear upon the grant or denial of public compensation for the landowning citizen's involuntary contributions towards general environmental welfare.

(1) Absolutism or relativism?

In most areas of property law there exists a tension between two philosophical starting points, which may perhaps be characterised as the perspectives of the *property absolutist* and the *property relativist*. Most lay persons tend, by natural disposition, to be property absolutists – in that they believe passionately and instinctively that ownership of an estate in land confers inviolable and exclusive rights of enjoyment and exploitation.[62] By contrast the property relativist pictures property in terms, not of absolute rights, but rather of qualified entitlements based on social accommodation, community-directed obligation and notions of reasonable user.[63] The dominant modern juristic perception of property is, without much doubt, that of the relativist,[64] partly because the pressures of crowded urban coexistence have forced a fresh recognition of the heavily interdependent nature of our social and economic arrangements.[65] There remain today few

---

[62] See *Anchor Brewhouse Developments Ltd* v. *Berkley House (Docklands Developments) Ltd* (1987) 38 BLR 82 at 96, where Scott J referred to this outlook as 'a robust Victorian approach.'

[63] As one leading American commentator has said, the notion of '[a]utonomous secure rights of property' may already have given way to 'entitlements that are interconnected and relative'. Property law may come to be based 'as much on responsibilities as on rights, on human connectedness rather than on personal autonomy' (Freyfogle, 'Context and accommodation in modern property law', (1988–89) 41 Stan LR 1529 at 1530–1531). Much recent legislation in England exemplifies this approach (see, for example, Access to Neighbouring Land Act 1992; Party Wall etc Act 1996; Countryside and Rights of Way Act 2000).

[64] This perception bulked large through most of the twentieth century. See the statement of Justice Roberts in the US Supreme Court that 'neither property rights nor contract rights are absolute ... Equally fundamental with the private right is that of the public to regulate it in the common interest' (*Nebbia* v. *New York*, 291 US 502 at 523, 78 L Ed 940 at 948–949 (1934)).

[65] See, for example, *Xpress Print Pte Ltd* v. *Monocrafts Pte Ltd* [2000] 3 SLR 545 at 561H, where in the Singaporean Court of Appeal, Yong Pung How CJ recently emphasised that, consistently with the realities of the modern urban context, the law 'must ... take root in the terra firma of the principles of reciprocity and mutual respect for each other's property'. For a similar view in the USA, see *Green Party of New Jersey* v. *Hartz Mountain Industries, Inc*, 752 A2d 315 at 322 (2000) *per* O'Hern J ('At one time private property owners exercised virtually unfettered control over property. As social standards changed, the law changed to recognise the primacy of certain public interests over the rights of private property owners').

true property absolutists, although those who tend towards this view maintain that all regulatory interference with land use necessarily constitutes a compensable 'taking' of property.[66] In its most unqualified form, the absolutist approach castigates uncompensated regulation as environmental fascism and insists that, if the community wants environmental welfare, it must purchase it fairly rather than simply dump the unalleviated cost on isolated owners of real estate.

(a) Inevitability of some uncompensated intrusions

There are certainly signs that the America of President George W. Bush is drifting back towards a more absolutist view of property relationships, but relativists everywhere can still point to one pragmatic, and highly persuasive, rejoinder to the most extreme form of the absolutist argument. It simply cannot be the case that *all* regulatory subtractions from a landholder's user rights necessarily constitute compensable deprivations of 'property'. As Justice Holmes once indicated in the Supreme Court of the United States,[67] 'Government could hardly go on if, to some extent, values incident to property could not be diminished without paying for every such change in the general law'.[68] The progress of civilised society would effectively grind to a halt if every minor regulatory act of the state provoked an immediate entitlement to a carefully calculated cash indemnity for the affected landowner. Some property values, said Holmes, are 'enjoyed under an implied limitation, and must yield to the police power' (the latter phrase connoting, in the American context, a power of regulatory control exercised on behalf of the public interest).

This approach is strongly echoed in modern European human rights jurisprudence[69] and received eloquent affirmation many years ago when an urban planning control measure in Northern Ireland was challenged as an illicit 'taking' of property. Presiding over the Northern Ireland Court of Appeal, Lord MacDermott LCJ observed in *O.D. Cars Ltd* v. *Belfast Corporation*[70] that '[i]n a community ordered by law some regulation of

---

[66] Perhaps the foremost exponent of this view is Richard A. Epstein (see *Takings: Private Property and the Power of Eminent Domain* (1985, Harvard University Press).

[67] *Pennsylvania Coal Co* v. *Mahon*, 260 US 393 at 413, 67 L Ed 322 at 325 (1922).

[68] See likewise *Belfast Corpn* v. *O.D. Cars Ltd* [1960] AC 490 at 518 *per* Viscount Simonds.

[69] Environmental planning and conservation measures unquestionably fall within the ambit of the 'general interest' presumptively protected by Protocol No. 1, art. 1 (see *Allan Jacobsson* v. *Sweden*, Series A No. 163, para. 57 (1989); *Denev* v. *Sweden* (1989) 59 DR 127 at 130; *Fredin* v. *Sweden*, Series A No. 192, para. 48 (1991); *Pine Valley Developments Ltd* v. *Ireland*, Series A No. 222, para. 57 (1991)). See also *Banér* v. *Sweden* (1989) 60 DR 128 at 140, where the European Human Rights Commission implicitly endorsed the argument that '[e]veryone must be prepared to accept a certain interference in the public interest without compensation.'

[70] [1959] NI 62 at 87–88. See also *Slattery* v. *Naylor* (1888) 13 App Cas 446 at 449–450 *per* Lord Hobhouse.

private rights for the public benefit is inevitable, and constitutional restrictions of a general kind have to be read with this in mind'.[71] When the *O.D. Cars* case reached the House of Lords, Viscount Simonds added, rather sniffily, that legislative attenuation of an owner's user rights 'can be effected without a cry being raised that Magna Carta is dethroned or a sacred principle of liberty infringed'.[72] Yet the danger remains that, absent a certain level of judicial vigilance, the long reach of regulatory control may violate the cogent rule of political ethics which discountenances 'forcing some people alone to bear public burdens which, in all fairness and justice, should be borne by the public as a whole'.[73] The critical question is always whether an individual's land is being improperly 'pressed into some form of public service'.[74]

(b) A practical example

The nature of the problem is well illustrated in *O'Callaghan* v. *Commissioners of Public Works in Ireland and the Attorney General*,[75] a case whose facts exhibit (for those familiar with the television drama) a certain 'Ballykissangel' quality or flavour. Here, under powers conferred by heritage conservation legislation, a preservation order had been made by the Irish Commissioners of Public Works in respect of land situated in the vicinity of a promontory fort of early Neolithic origin. The order was precipitated by the fact that the landowner, although aware that the site comprised a listed national monument, had engaged in ploughing activities which disturbed items of archaeological interest.[76] The preservation order prohibited, without compensation, all further interference with the soil surrounding the site of the monument. The landowner later alleged that the preservation order, by preventing cultivation of his land,

---

[71] As Lord Hoffmann recently expressed the point, '[t]he give and take of civil society frequently requires that the exercise of private rights should be restricted in the general public interest' (*Grape Bay Ltd* v. *Attorney-General of Bermuda* [2000] 1 WLR 574 at 583C). See also *Wildtree Hotels Ltd* v. *Harrow LBC* [2001] 2 AC 1 at 10A–B *per* Lord Hoffmann.

[72] *Belfast Corpn* v. *O.D. Cars Ltd* [1960] AC 490 at 519. Viscount Simonds merely echoed Lord MacDermott's view ([1959] NI 62 at 87) that, on any other analysis, the power to legislate for peace, order and good government 'would be abridged to an unthinkable degree.'

[73] *Armstrong* v. *United States*, 364 US 40 at 49, 4 L Ed 2d 1554 at 1561 (1960) *per* Black J. See also *Penn Central Transportation Co* v. *New York City*, 438 US 104 at 124, 57 L Ed 2d 631 at 648 *per* Brennan J (1978); *Newcrest Mining (WA) Ltd* v. *Commonwealth of Australia* (1997) 190 CLR 513 at 639 *per* Kirby J; *Eastern Enterprises* v. *Apfel*, 524 US 498, 141 L Ed 2d 451 at 470 (1998) *per* O'Connor J; *Grape Bay Ltd* v. *Attorney-General of Bermuda* [2000] 1 WLR 574 at 583C-D *per* Lord Hoffmann.

[74] *Lucas* v. *South Carolina Coastal Council*, 505 US 1003 at 1018, 120 L Ed 2d 798 at 814 (1992) *per* Scalia J.

[75] [1985] ILRM 364, on appeal from [1983] IRLM 391.

[76] Sadly, depredation at the hands of local farmers and builders has all too often been the fate of Irish antiquities (see Weir, *Early Ireland: A Field Guide* (1980, Blackstaff Press, Belfast), pp. 99, 121, 125, 131–132, 155, 207, 219).

had sterilised the land in a manner invalidated by the property guarantees of the Irish Constitution (which are, in relevant respects, the equivalent of those contained in the European Convention on Human Rights[77]). *O'Callaghan's* case thus raised quite acutely the question whether the individual landowner should be left to bear alone the economic cost of protecting, for the public benefit, an important feature of the national cultural heritage. The Irish High Court and, on appeal, the Supreme Court nevertheless held that the facts did not disclose, in constitutional terms, any 'unjust attack' on the landowner's property rights. We shall attempt later to discern the rationale for this decision, but it becomes immediately clear how closely run are the arguments for and against mandatory public compensation for the impact of regulatory interventions. In the very words attributed by Lord Macnaghten to the grudging landowner in *Bradford Corpn* v. *Pickles*,[78] the farmer in *O'Callaghan's* case may well have taken the view that 'he ha[d] something which he [could] prevent other people enjoying unless he [was] paid for it'.[79]

(2) A viable distinction between mere regulation of use and outright expropriation of title?

It is, of course, tempting to resolve the question of compensation for state intervention by adopting a straightforward, if somewhat mechanical, rule that a mere restriction on the exercise of user rights over land, as distinct from a direct governmental acquisition of estate ownership, *never* generates any claim to compensation from public funds.[80] A bright-line rule of this sort possesses a certain pedigree. In *France Fenwick & Co Ltd* v. *The King*,[81] one of the classic cases on requisition by the state, Wright J (later Lord Wright) held that a 'mere negative prohibition, though it involves interference with an owner's enjoyment of property, does

---

[77] See *An Blascaod Mór Teoranta* v. *Commissioners of Public Works in Ireland* (High Court, 27 February 1998), *per* Budd J, confirmed without comment on appeal (*An Blascaod Mór Teoranta* v. *Minister for Arts* [2000] 1 ILRM 401 at 409).

[78] [1895] AC 587 at 600–601 (see text accompanying fns. 4 and 5 above).

[79] 'Why should he, he may think, without fee or reward, keep his land as a store-room for a commodity valued by the external community?' ([1895] AC 587 at 600 *per* Lord Macnaghten).

[80] This rule is most perfectly exemplified by the denial that restrictions on development imposed through planning control or zoning mechanisms give rise to any claim to publicly funded compensation (*Village of Euclid* v. *Ambler Realty Co*, 272 US 365 at 395–397, 71 L Ed 303 at 314 (1926) *per* Sutherland J (United States Supreme Court); *Westminster Bank Ltd* v. *Beverley BC* [1971] AC 508 at 529D-F *per* Lord Reid, 535C *per* Viscount Dilhorne; *Commonwealth of Australia* v. *State of Tasmania* (1983) 158 CLR 1 at 283 *per* Deane J; *The Queen* v. *Tener* (1985) 17 DLR (4th) 1 at 7 *per* Estey J, 23 *per* Wilson J (Supreme Court of Canada); *Grape Bay Ltd* v. *Attorney-General of Bermuda* [2000] 1 WLR 574 at 583B-C *per* Lord Hoffmann (Privy Council appeal from Bermuda).

[81] [1927] 1 KB 458 at 467.

not..., merely because it is obeyed, carry with it at common law any right to compensation'.[82] The same broad approach is indeed attempted in art. 1 of Protocol No. 1 of the European Convention, which on its face proscribes any *deprivation* of a person's property, but specifically preserves the 'right of a State to enforce such laws as it deems necessary to control the use of property in accordance with the general interest...'

(a) Eventual coalescence of regulation and expropriation

The difficulty with the purported distinction between regulation and expropriation is quite simply that it does not *work*. Every jurisdiction that has grappled with the problem of regulatory control has eventually been forced to the concession that *some* interferences with a landowner's user rights are so extreme that in substance, although not in form, they comprise a taking of land for public benefit and therefore call imperatively for compensation from public funds.[83] Excessive limitation of user rights inevitably shades into expropriation; a regulatory measure may well conceal a confiscatory act even though it leaves the formal title perfectly intact.[84] In the well-known words of Justice Holmes, 'while property may be regulated to a certain extent, if regulation goes too far it will be recognised as a taking'.[85] The force of this proposition was explicitly acknowledged by the House of Lords in *Belfast Corpn* v. *O.D. Cars Ltd*,[86] the highpoint of the Northern Ireland jurisprudence on

---

[82] See also *Northern Ireland Road Transport Board* v. *Benson* [1940] NI 133 at 145–146 *per* Andrews CJ, 172–173 *per* Murphy LJ; *Ulster Transport Authority* v. *James Brown & Sons Ltd* [1953] NI 79 at 116 *per* Lord MacDermott LCJ.

[83] See *Trade Practices Commission* v. *Tooth & Co Ltd* (1979) 142 CLR 397 at 415 *per* Stephen J (referring to the 'universality of the problem sooner or later encountered'). Nor is there much point in attempting to distinguish, for compensation purposes, between regulation which imposes merely *passive* restrictions and regulation which requires *active* performance or expenditure by the landowner. The latter form of regulation may well involve nothing more demanding than, say, the occasional lopping of trees surrounding a major electricity transmission line (see, for example, *Electricity Supply Board* v. *Gormley* [1985] IR 129 at 151–152), whilst the former may result in the loss of untold millions in development potential (see, for example, *Lucas* v. *South Carolina Coastal Council*, 505 US 1003, 120 L Ed 2d 798 (1992) and text accompanying fns. 123–128, below).

[84] See *Belfast Corpn* v. *O.D. Cars Ltd* [1960] AC 490 at 520 per Viscount Simonds. For reference in American caselaw to the 'almost imperceptible gradations' between regulation and taking, see *Stevens* v. *City of Salisbury*, 214 A2d 775 at 779 (1965); *City of Annapolis* v. *Waterman*, 745 A2d 1000 at 1015 (Md 2000). See also *Cohen* v. *City of Hartford*, 710 A2d 746 at 754 (Conn 1998).

[85] *Pennsylvania Coal Co* v. *Mahon*, 260 US 393 at 415, 67 L Ed 322 at 326 (1922). See similarly *United States* v. *General Motors Corp*, 323 US 373 at 378, 89 L Ed 311 at 318 (1944) *per* Roberts J.

[86] [1960] AC 490 at 520 *per* Viscount Simonds, 525 *per* Lord Radcliffe. In the Northern Ireland Court of Appeal Lord MacDermott LCJ had been even more obviously prepared to regard the concept of compensable taking as inclusive of 'the imposition of some restriction or prohibition or other interference with proprietary rights'. For him, there could be a taking of property 'even though the proprietary rights which are taken away do not exhaust all the attributes of ownership' ([1959] NI 62 at 87).

'takings', and is now widely confirmed throughout the common law world.[87]

The subtlety of the gradations between regulation and confiscation has also been amply recognised in European human rights law. In *Sporrung and Lönnroth* v. *Sweden*[88] the European Court of Human Rights accepted that, in pursuance of its duty to 'look behind the appearances and investigate the realities of the situation', the court must be sensitive to the possibility of 'de facto expropriation'. Thus a regulation of land use may constitute a 'de facto expropriation' if, without any formal deprivation of title, it 'affects the substance of the property' to such a degree that the measure 'can be assimilated to a deprivation of possessions'.[89] In practice there must have been some state intervention that takes away 'all meaningful use of the properties in question'.[90]

The already indistinct borderline between regulation and expropriation is then further blurred by more recent developments in European jurisprudence. In terms of Protocol No. 1, art. 1, mere interferences with land use rights fall to be considered, not as a species of 'deprivation' (which normally necessitates the payment of compensation to the landowner[91]), but as a presumptively legitimate measure of 'control' of land use (which carries no 'inherent' right to compensation[92]). The European Court of Human Rights has now clarified, however, that even this form of regulation, which includes most schemes of town planning[93] and environmental protection,[94] calls for the provision of compensation if it otherwise fails to meet the overarching standard of 'peaceful enjoyment

---

[87] See, for example, *Commonwealth of Australia* v. *State of Tasmania* (1983) 158 CLR 1 at 144 *per* Mason J; *Newcrest Mining (WA) Ltd* v. *Commonwealth of Australia* (1997) 190 CLR 513 at 639 *per* Kirby J; *Mariner Real Estate Ltd* v. *Nova Scotia (Attorney General)* (1999) 177 DLR (4th) 696 at 727 *per* Cromwell JA; *Alberta* v. *Nilsson* (1999) 246 AR 201 at 221–223 *per* Marceau J.

[88] Series A No. 52, para. 63 (1982).

[89] *Banér* v. *Sweden* (1989) 60 DR 128 at 139–140. See, likewise, *Fredin* v. *Sweden*, Series A No. 192, paras. 42–43 (1991); *Pine Valley Developments Ltd* v. *Ireland*, Series A No. 222, paras. 73–77. For an example of *de facto* expropriation, see *Papamichalopoulos* v. *Greece*, Series A No. 260-B, paras. 41–45 (1993).

[90] *Fredin* v. *Sweden*, Series A No. 192, para. 45 (1991). See, however, *Pine Valley Developments Ltd* v. *Ireland*, Series A No. 222, para. 56 (1991), where the land in dispute was held not to have been left 'without any meaningful alternative use' since its owner (a property developer), although denied planning permission, could still farm or lease the land.

[91] *James* v. *United Kingdom*, Series A No. 98, para. 54 (1986); *Lithgow* v. *United Kingdom*, Series A No. 102, para. 122 (1986); *Banér* v. *Sweden* (1989) 60 DR 128 at 142; *Holy Monasteries* v. *Greece*, Series A No. 301, para. 71 (1994); *Former King of Greece* v. *Greece* (2001) 33 EHRR 516 at 555 (para. 89).

[92] See *Banér* v. *Sweden* (1989) 60 DR 128 at 142.

[93] See *Sporrung and Lönnroth* v. *Sweden*, Series A No. 52, para. 64 (1982); *Allan Jacobsson* v. *Sweden*, Series A No. 163, paras. 54, 57 (1989).

[94] See *Banér* v. *Sweden* (1989) 60 DR 128 at 140; *Fredin* v. *Sweden*, Series A No. 192, paras. 47–48 (1991); *Matos e Silva, LDA and others* v. *Portugal* (1997) 24 EHRR 573 at 600–601 (para. 85).

of ... possessions' guaranteed by the opening sentence of art. 1.[95] There are already indications of an increased willingness to hold that the 'peaceful enjoyment' clause of art. 1 is breached by certain kinds of land use control which, even though directed towards perfectly rational regulatory aims, fail to balance fairly the interests of the individual owner and the wider community, thus leaving the landowner uncompensated for his involuntary contribution to public welfare goals. In *Matos e Silva, LDA and others* v. *Portugal*,[96] for example, the applicants' use of their land had been 'incontestably' restricted by a prolonged ban on both new construction and new farming activities. The ban had been imposed in connection with the creation of an aquacultural research station and national nature reserve for migrant birds to be sited on the applicants' portion of the Algarve coast. The Human Rights Court held that, although the intended environmental strategy 'did not lack a reasonable basis', the substantial (and uncompensated) interference with the landowners' rights had contravened the 'peaceful enjoyment' guarantee of art. 1.[97] A similar finding emerged in *Chassagnou* v. *France*,[98] where the regulatory scheme under challenge was aimed at the improved organisation of hunting and the rational management of game stocks. Under new legislation landowners were obliged to surrender to approved municipal hunting associations their exclusive hunting rights over their own lands in return for reciprocal hunting rights over the lands of other association members. In so far as the scheme extinguished, for all practical purposes, the right to prohibit entry by huntsmen belonging to the new associations (and was, of course, both futile and offensive in relation to any landowners opposed to the principle of hunting), the court held that there had been a clear derogation from the 'peaceful enjoyment of ... possessions' protected by art. 1.[99]

(b) The threshold of compensable 'regulatory taking'

The point at which regulation becomes confiscation – i.e., the threshold of a compensable 'regulatory taking' – is, of course, notoriously difficult to

[95] *Allan Jacobsson* v. *Sweden*, Series A No. 163, para. 55 (1989); *Air Canada* v. *United Kingdom*, Series A No. 316-A, para. 36 (1995); *Chassagnou* v. *France* (2000) 29 EHRR 615 at 674–675 (para. 75). The European Human Rights Commission likewise declined to rule out the possibility that a control of use may require compensation (see, for example, *Banér* v. *Sweden* (1989) 60 DR 128 at 142; *Pine Valley Developments Ltd* v. *Ireland* (1992) 14 EHRR 319 at 339 (para. 84)). See also *S* v. *France* (1990) 65 DR 250 at 262; *Former King of Greece* v. *Greece* (2001) 33 EHRR 516 at 554–555 (para. 89).
[96] (1997) 24 EHRR 573 at 599 (para. 79).
[97] (1997) 24 EHRR 573 at 601–602 (paras. 86–93).
[98] (2000) 29 EHRR 615.
[99] (2000) 29 EHRR 615 at 678–679 (paras. 82–85).

define.[100] The standard is certainly exacting. Some jurisdictions adopt the view that even an extensive diminution in the value of the affected land is not enough to establish that a 'regulatory taking' has occurred.[101] By contrast, European caselaw maintains that 'severe economic consequences' flowing from a regulatory intervention (e.g. in the form of a 'concrete economic loss' of income or land value)[102] may indicate that the 'peaceful enjoyment of...possessions' has been fatally disturbed.[103] The US Supreme Court has famously used as a benchmark the point where the landowner is 'called upon to sacrifice *all* economically beneficial uses' of his land.[104]

Although approaches to the question vary, it is clear that the state must normally commandeer at least a substantial part of the utility of privately held land before confiscatory terminology begins to seem appropriate.[105] Courts across the common law world have variously expressed the threshold of compensable taking in terms of a removal of the 'substance' or 'reality' of proprietorship[106] or the elimination of 'virtually all of the

---

[100] One commentator has described this aspect of takings jurisprudence as 'a top contender for the dubious title of "most incoherent area of American law"' (Schroeder, 'Never jam to-day: on the impossibility of takings jurisprudence', (1996) 84 Geo LJ 1531). See also *Mariner Real Estate Ltd* v. *Nova Scotia (Attorney General)* (1999) 177 DLR (4th) 696 at 716 ('no magic formula'). For an excellent guide through the morass of American takings law, see Callies (ed), *Takings: Land-Development Conditions and Regulatory Takings after Dolan and Lucas* (1996, American Bar Association).

[101] See, for example, *Mariner Real Estate Ltd* v. *Nova Scotia (Attorney General)* (1999) 177 DLR (4th) 696 at 700, 719–727 (although a decline in market value may be evidence of an elimination of 'virtually all the normal incidents of ownership').

[102] See *Banér* v. *Sweden* (1989) 60 DR 128 at 142–143. In *Matos e Silva, LDA and others* v. *Portugal* (1997) 24 EHRR 573 at 598 (para. 76), it was alleged that the profitability of the affected land had fallen by 40% during the period of the regulation.

[103] The initially awkward reference to 'peaceful enjoyment of...possessions', which lies at the core of Protocol No. 1, art. 1, may serve an important function by indicating that the threshold of compensable intervention is marked off by some sense of 'dispossession' of the landowner or of his enterprise or undertaking. It is significant that, in the old caselaw on the Government of Ireland Act 1920, the Northern Ireland courts moved slowly but surely towards reliance on the terminology of 'dispossession' (see *Northern Ireland Road Transport Board* v. *Benson* [1940] NI 133 at 157 *per* Babington LJ; *Ulster Transport Authority* v. *James Brown & Sons Ltd* [1953] NI 79 at 111, 116 *per* Lord MacDermott LCJ; *O.D. Cars Ltd* v. *Belfast Corpn* [1959] NI 62 at 82–84 *per* Lord MacDermott LCJ).

[104] *Lucas* v. *South Carolina Coastal Council*, 505 US 1003 at 1019, 120 L Ed 2d 798 at 815 (1992) *per* Scalia J (a 'categorical' taking).

[105] See, for example, *France Fenwick & Co Ltd* v. *The King* [1927] 1 KB 458 at 467, where Wright J considered the rule against arbitrary taking of a subject's property to apply only to cases 'where property is actually taken possession of, or used by, the Government, or where, by order of a competent authority, it is placed at the disposal of the Government'.

[106] For resort to this criterion in Australia, see *Bank of New South Wales* v. *Commonwealth of Australia* (1948) 76 CLR 1 at 349 *per* Dixon J; *Newcrest Mining (WA) Ltd* v. *Commonwealth of Australia* (1997) 190 CLR 513 at 633 *per* Gummow J. See also *Minister of State for the Army* v. *Dalziel* (1944) 68 CLR 261 at 286 *per* Rich J ('everything that made [the property] worth having').

aggregated incidents of ownership'.[107] Identification of the precise quantum of property which must be requisitioned by the state has proved problematical, not least in the context of environmental conservation. Has a compensable taking occurred when, for example, commercial excavation in land owned by a mining company is suddenly restricted by some regulatory initiative which incorporates the land within a national park? In *Newcrest Mining (WA) Ltd* v. *Commonwealth of Australia*[108] McHugh J opposed the provision of publicly funded compensation for the mining company on the ground that its 'property interests . . . in the land and minerals would continue as before'. The effect of the regulatory intervention was, in his view, 'merely to impinge on [the company's] rights to exploit those interests'. The majority of the High Court of Australia nevertheless believed that, in reality, there had been 'an effective sterilisation of the rights constituting the property in question',[109] thereby activating the constitutional requirement of just compensation. Kirby J thought it improper to expand a national park for public benefit 'at an economic cost to the owners of valuable property interests in sections of the park whose rights are effectively confiscated to achieve that end'.[110] When, some years earlier, a similar issue had arisen before the Supreme Court of Canada,[111] Estey J likewise adopted the criterion that, in the interests of enhancing public amenity in the relevant park lands, the landowner's assets had been so regulated as to become 'virtually useless'.[112] Other similarly directed locutions emanating from Canadian courts speak of governmental interferences with land use which are so far-reaching that they operate a 'confiscation of all reasonable private uses' of the land.[113]

(c) A residue of reasonable user rights for the landowner

Each in its slightly different way, the formulae recited above articulate the message that the denial, for regulatory purposes, of a strategically significant quantum of user rights is tantamount to a confiscation and therefore requires the provision of compensation from public funds. But to the extent that regulatory intervention has left a residue of reasonable

---

[107] *Mariner Real Estate Ltd* v. *Nova Scotia (Attorney General)* (1999) 177 DLR (4th) 696 at 717. See also *Alberta* v. *Nilsson* (1999) 246 AR 201 at 221 (restriction 'of sufficient severity to remove virtually all of the rights associated with the property holder's interest').

[108] (1997) 190 CLR 513 at 573 (Kakadu National Park).

[109] (1997) 190 CLR 513 at 635 *per* Gummow J.

[110] (1997) 190 CLR 513 at 639.

[111] See *The Queen* v. *Tener* (1985) 17 DLR (4th) 1 at 12.

[112] Canadian courts have made frequent use of this standard (see, for example, *Manitoba Fisheries Ltd* v. *The Queen* (1978) 88 DLR (3d) 462 at 473). See also *Casamiro Resource Corp* v. *British Columbia* (1991) 80 DLR (4th) 1 at 10 (private rights rendered 'meaningless').

[113] *Mariner Real Estate Ltd* v. *Nova Scotia (Attorney General)* (1999) 177 DLR (4th) 696 at 735–736 *per* Hallett JA.

user rights vested in the landowner, *no* compensable event can be claimed to have occurred. Thus, for example, in *O'Callaghan* v. *Commissioners of Public Works in Ireland and the Attorney General*[114] both the High Court and the Supreme Court declined to find that any compensable expropriation had been effected by a preservation order which prevented further ploughing of the land in question, but did not preclude its use for grazing.[115] The claim of 'sterilisation' fell somewhat flat where the sterilisation complained of related merely to the unavailability of the land 'for other more profitable purposes'.[116] Likewise in *Allan Jacobsson* v. *Sweden*[117] the European Court of Human Rights pointed out that the refusal of the applicant's request for planning permission for a second dwelling on the site of his existing home in no way prevented him from enjoying residence in the house he already occupied.[118]

The one context in which a non-exhaustive abstraction of user rights tends to be regarded as automatically compensable occurs where the relevant regulatory activity takes the form of a continuous physical invasion, or 'permanent physical occupation', of the land concerned.[119] Thus, notwithstanding the minimal impact or socially beneficial character of the intrusion, it has always been widely agreed that electricity transmission lines or pylons cannot be installed without the proffering of compensation.[120] Similarly, as evidenced by one of the classic decisions in American 'takings' law,[121] the compulsory placement of facilities for cable television reception – even though conducive to public benefit and extremely limited in scale – constitutes a physically invasive interference

---

[114] [1983] IRLM 391 at 397 *per* McWilliam J; [1985] ILRM 364 at 367 *per* O'Higgins CJ (see text accompanying fns. 75 and 76 above).

[115] 'I do not accept that all the bundle of rights constituting the plaintiff's ownership of the fort has been abolished... the plaintiff has not been deprived of all normal use of the land' ([1983] IRLM 391 at 398–399 *per* McWilliam J).

[116] [1983] IRLM 391 at 397 *per* McWilliam J. See, to like effect, *State ex rel BSW Development Group* v. *City of Dayton*, 699 NE2d 1271 at 1276 (Ohio 1998).

[117] Series A No. 163, paras. 61, 137 (1989).

[118] See, similarly, *State of Ohio, ex rel RTG Inc* v. *State of Ohio*, 753 NE2d 869 (Ohio Court of Appeals, 2001), where a takings claim by a mining company was rejected to the extent that, even following an environmentally motivated restriction of its subterranean mining rights, the company, as owner of the surface land, was able to put that land to other residential, agricultural and pastoral uses. (The company's takings claim succeeded in respect of other parcels of land in which it held not surface, but merely mining, rights.)

[119] See *Lucas* v. *South Carolina Coastal Council*, 505 US 1003 at 1015, 120 L Ed 2d 798 at 812 (1992) *per* Scalia J.

[120] *West Midlands Joint Electricity Authority* v. *Pitt* [1932] 2 KB 1 at 54 *per* Romer LJ (see also Macnaghten J at 30). See, similarly, *Robb* v. *Electricity Board for Northern Ireland* [1937] NI 103 at 117 *per* Megaw J, 123–126 *per* Andrews LJ; *Electricity Supply Board* v. *Gormley* [1985] IR 129 at 149–151 *per* Finlay CJ. In England and Wales compensation is now available under statute (see Electricity Act 1989, Sch. 4, para. 7).

[121] *Loretto* v. *Teleprompter Manhattan CATV Corp*, 458 US 419 at 441, 73 L Ed 2d 868 at 886 (1982).

with land use which must be compensated.[122] By contrast, however, it is unlikely that a casual and intermittent physical presence – such as that, say, of walkers or ramblers traversing open countryside – could properly be identified as a sufficiently direct taking of land to justify a presumptive rule of publicly funded compensation for affected landowners.

In some circumstances it may not be altogether easy to determine whether regulatory intervention has extinguished all or most reasonable private uses of land. In perhaps the most controversial of the American 'takings' cases, *Lucas* v. *South Carolina Coastal Council*,[123] state legislation intervened to frustrate the claimant's intention of building luxury beachfront homes on a notoriously unstable coastal area which he had earlier purchased for almost $1 million. A majority of the US Supreme Court pointed to the likelihood that the claimant was entitled to compensation for this regulatory imposition on the ground that, although not stripped of title, he had been deprived of all 'economically beneficial uses' of his land.[124] However, in spearheading the minority's opposition to publicly funded compensation, Justice Blackmun attached significance to the fact that the landowner, whilst enjoined from building developments, could still enjoy 'other attributes of property' such as the right to exclude strangers and alienate the land to third parties,[125] together with the right to 'picnic, swim, camp in a tent, or live on the property in a movable trailer'.[126] Much depends on whether the private uses of which the landowner must be deprived are restrictively construed as comprising only economically valuable (or 'developmental') uses or are instead more broadly related to non-commodity values inherent in the land.[127] As the majority judgment in *Lucas* demonstrates, the current American tendency is, all too predictably, to confine the 'takings' question to monetisable

---

[122] '[W]e have long considered a physical intrusion by government to be a property restriction of an unusually serious character' (458 US 419 at 426, 73 L Ed 2d 868 at 876 *per* Marshall J). See also *Penn Central Transportation Co* v. *New York City*, 438 US 104 at 124, 57 L Ed 2d 631 at 648 (1978); *Ehrlich* v. *City of Culver City*, 911 P2d 429 at 443 (Cal 1996).

[123] 505 US 1003, 120 L Ed 2d 798 (1992).

[124] 505 US 1003 at 1044, 1019, 120 L Ed 2d 798 at 815. See also *Lucas* v. *South Carolina Coastal Council*, 424 SE2d 484 at 486 (1992).

[125] For European parallels, see *Tre Traktörer Aktiebolag* v. *Sweden*, Series A No. 159, para. 55 (1989); *Matos e Silva, LDA and others* v. *Portugal* (1997) 24 EHRR 573 at 592 (para. 103).

[126] 505 US 1003 at 1044, 120 L Ed 2d 798 at 831. See, likewise, *Mariner Real Estate Ltd* v. *Nova Scotia (Attorney General)* (1999) 177 DLR (4th) 696 at 706, 728–729 ('traditional recreational uses' still available); *Steer Holdings Ltd* v. *Manitoba* [1993] 2 WWR 146 at 153; *Gazza* v. *New York State Department of Environmental Conservation*, 679 NE2d 1035 at 1041 (NY 1997); *Tahoe-Sierra Preservation Council, Inc* v. *Tahoe Regional Planning Agency*, 34 F Supp 2d 1226 at 1241, 1243 (1999).

[127] See, for example, *Lucas* v. *South Carolina Coastal Council*, 505 US 1003 at 1065, 120 L Ed 2d 798 at 844 *per* Stevens J (who proffered the example of a 'regulation arbitrarily prohibiting an owner from continuing to use her property for bird-watching or sunbathing').

aspects of land use as distinct from less tangible (and somewhat more subtle) features of human enjoyment of the resource concerned.[128]

(3) A component of social obligation inherent in rights of ownership?

The European focus on the borderline between regulation and confiscation has tended to fasten not so much on the *property* abstracted from the aggrieved landowner as on the *propriety* of the abstraction.[129] European human rights caselaw accordingly demonstrates the inescapability of some kind of value judgment as to the competing interests involved in the regulatory context. In deciding whether a particular regulatory intervention has violated the 'peaceful enjoyment' guarantee of art. 1 of Protocol No. 1, the court must determine whether a 'fair balance' has been struck between 'the demands of the general interest of the community and the requirements of the protection of the individual's fundamental rights'.[130] Ultimately, in common with the approach adopted in other jurisdictions, the European Court of Human Rights has identified the crucial issue as whether the landowner has been singled out to bear an 'individual and excessive burden' in relation to some community-directed obligation which should have been shared more widely.[131]

(a) The test of legality

It is of the essence of justice that laws should function at a certain level of generality.[132] Accordingly, it is a major premise of art. 1 of Protocol No. 1 that state intervention be 'lawful',[133] a precept which excludes any provision that operates erratically, over-selectively or in a wholly arbitrary

---

[128] See Manus, 'The blackbird whistling – the silence just after: evaluating the environmental legacy of Justice Blackmun', (2000) 85 Iowa LR 429.

[129] On this distinction, see *Loveladies Harbor, Inc* v. *United States*, 28 F3d 1171 at 1179 (Fed Cir 1994).

[130] *Sporrung and Lönnroth* v. *Sweden*, Series A No. 52, para. 69 (1982); *James* v. *United Kingdom*, Series A No. 98, para. 50 (1986); *Fredin* v. *Sweden*, Series A No. 192, para. 51 (1991); *Holy Monasteries* v. *Greece*, Series A No. 301, para. 70 (1994); *Air Canada* v. *United Kingdom*, Series A No. 316-A, para. 36 (1995); *Matos e Silva, LDA and others* v. *Portugal* (1997) 24 EHRR 573 at 592 (para. 106). See also *Former King of Greece* v. *Greece* (2001) 33 EHRR 516 at 554 (para 89). To this extent the European approach mirrors the 'weighing of private and public interests' practised by courts in the USA (see *Agins* v. *City of Tiburon*, 447 US 255 at 261, 65 L Ed 2d 106 at 112 (1980)).

[131] *Sporrung and Lönnroth* v. *Sweden*, Series A No. 52, para. 73 (1982); *James* v. *United Kingdom*, Series A No. 98, para. 50 (1986); *Håkansson and Sturesson* v. *Sweden*, Series A No. 121, para. 51 (1990).

[132] See Blackstone, *Commentaries*, Vol I, p 44; *Buckley & Others (Sinn Féin)* v. *Attorney General* [1950] IR 67 at 70 *per* Gavan Duffy P; *Liyanage* v. *The Queen* [1967] 1 AC 259 at 291 *per* Lord Pearce.

[133] See *Banér* v. *Sweden* (1989) 60 DR 128 at 141.

manner. Such randomness of application goes fundamentally to the 'legality' of the provision concerned,[134] since an excessively 'individualised' targeting of otherwise socially desirable measures tends to smack unattractively of a 'bill of attainder'.[135] Regulatory intervention which operates *ad hominem* or whose scope is unduly narrowly restricted is therefore prone to fail not only the test of 'legality', but that of 'proportionality', and, by denying equal protection under the law, is also likely to breach the anti-discrimination provision contained in art. 14 of the European Convention.[136]

Some sense of the possible response of English courts to highly specific or idiosyncratic impositions of environmental liability may now be gained from *Aston Cantlow and Wilmcote with Billesley PCC v. Wallbank*.[137] Here the Court of Appeal struck down, as inconsistent with both art. 14 and Protocol No. 1, art. 1, the liability of certain landowners to contribute towards the cost of chancel repairs in their local church.[138] This liability (of ancient canon law origin) supposedly attached to these landowners as current proprietors of former rectorial glebe land adjacent to the church in question. The Court of Appeal, although agreeing that chancel repair liability was directed towards the 'legitimate [aim] of maintaining historic buildings in the public interest', emphasised that the obligation under challenge in the *Wallbank* case had improperly 'singled out' the landowners concerned for an archaic, arbitrary and unjustifiably discriminatory form of local taxation.[139] It may well be questioned whether the nexus between the landowners in the *Wallbank* case and the object of public conservationist concern (ie the local church) was any more remote than that between the farmer in *O'Callaghan*'s case[140] and the national monument the latter *was* required to preserve. True it is that the Neolithic fort in *O'Callaghan*'s case happened to be situated on the

---

134 See *Hentrich v. France*, Series A No. 296-A, para. 42 (1994); *Aston Cantlow and Wilmcote with Billesley PCC v. Wallbank* [2001] 3 All ER 393 at 405d.

135 *An Blascaod Mór Teoranta v. Commissioners of Public Works in Ireland* (High Court, 27 February 1998), *per* Budd J (affd *An Blascaod Mór Teoranta v. Minister for Arts* [2000] 1 ILRM 401 at 409).

136 European Convention for the Protection of Human Rights and Fundamental Freedoms, art. 14; Human Rights Act 1998, s. 1 (1), Sch. I, Part I.

137 [2001] 3 All ER 393 (Morritt V-C, Robert Walker and Sedley LJ).

138 See Gray and Gray, (*op. cit.* above fn. 6) p 974. The liability in the *Wallbank* case (amounting to over £95,000) was imposed on an elderly couple who had inherited their land some 30 years earlier.

139 [2001] 3 All ER 393 at 407a–g. The court pointed out that chancel repair liability had 'long since lost its factual and legal basis' in that it was levied 'exclusively on the owners of land which has for centuries been divorced from the system of rights and responsibilities with which ecclesiatical law clothed the rectories of which the land once formed part' ([2001] 3 All ER 393 at 405h, 407a–b).

140 *O'Callaghan v. Commissioners of Public Works in Ireland and the Attorney General* [1985] ILRM 364, [1983] IRLM 391 (see text accompanying fns. 75 and 76, 114–116 above).

farmer's own land,[141] but it is precisely this element of fortuitousness which accentuates, rather than relieves, the concern that the concentration of environmental liability upon a restricted class of one may now contravene the European Convention on Human Rights.

(b) The test of proportionality

It is broadly accepted that municipal authorities enjoy 'a wide margin of appreciation' in determining both the substantive goals and the procedural mechanics of appropriate policy initiatives in the regulatory area.[142] It is therefore a cornerstone of human rights jurisprudence that art. 1 adjudications relating to 'peaceful enjoyment' inevitably entail an investigation of whether there exists 'a reasonable relationship of proportionality between the means employed and the aim sought to be realised'.[143] Any interference with land rights which fails this test of 'proportionality' in relation to its declared regulatory aim cannot be 'deemed necessary' in terms of art. 1 of Protocol No. 1 nor said to subserve the 'general interest'.[144] But amongst the factors which tend to confirm the required proportionality of ends and means are the availability of monetary compensation for the affected landowner,[145] the avoidance of any excessive delay in clarifying the extent of the regulatory imposition,[146] and the presence of any inherent risk[147] (or of foreknowledge on

---

[141] It is also true that the liability of the landowners in the *Wallbank* case derived from common law (and was only later confirmed in the Chancel Repairs Act 1932) and, again unlike that imposed in *O'Callaghan*'s case, involved a positive obligation of money payment as distinct from a negative restriction of user. But it is less than clear, on reflection, that either of these factors should render the burden of environmental guardianship less acceptable in one case than in the other.

[142] See, for example, *Sporrung and Lönnroth* v. *Sweden*, Series A No. 52, para. 69 (1982); *AGOSI* v. *United Kingdom*, Series A No. 108, para. 52 (1986); *Mellacher* v. *Austria*, Series A No. 169, para. 45 (1989); *Fredin* v. *Sweden*, Series A No. 192, para. 51 (1991).

[143] *James* v. *United Kingdom*, Series A No. 98, para. 50 (1986); *Allan Jacobsson* v. *Sweden*, Series A No. 163, para. 55 (1989). See also *Banér* v. *Sweden* (1989) 60 DR 128 at 141–142; *Mellacher* v. *Austria*, Series A No. 169, paras. 48, 57 (1989); *Fredin* v. *Sweden*, Series A No. 192, para. 51 (1991). The US Supreme Court has likewise confirmed that 'in a general sense concerns for proportionality animate the Takings Clause' (*City of Monterey* v. *Del Monte Dunes*, 526 US 687, 143 L Ed 2d 882 at 900 (1999)).

[144] *Banér* v. *Sweden* (1989) 60 DR 128 at 141.

[145] *Banér* v. *Sweden* (1989) 60 DR 128 at 142; *S* v. *France* (1990) 65 DR 250 at 262. See *Holy Monasteries* v. *Greece*, Series A No. 301, para. 71 (1994); *Matos e Silva LDA and others* v. *Portugal* (1997) 24 EHRR 573 at 593 (para. 111); *Former King of Greece* v. *Greece* (2001) 33 EHRR 516 at 555 (para. 89).

[146] See, for example, *Allan Jacobsson* v. *Sweden*, Series A No. 163, para. 60 (1989); *Matos e Silva, LDA and others* v. *Portugal* (1997) 24 EHRR 573 at 602 (para. 92).

[147] See, for example, *Fredin* v. *Sweden*, Series A No. 192, paras. 50, 54 (1991); *Pine Valley Developments Ltd* v. *Ireland*, Series A No. 222, para. 59 (1991).

the landowner's part[148]) that expectations of profitable development or exploitation might ultimately be falsified.[149] Correspondingly, any undue inflexibility[150] or over-selectiveness[151] in the operation of a regulatory imposition tends to point towards a fatal element of *disproportionality* in the measure concerned.

(c) Compensation inherent in the diffusion of regulatory benefits

In so far as factors of compensation are relevant to proportionality, it must be borne in mind that environmental regulation sometimes involves no net loss at all for the affected landholder. Where, for instance, the diffused local or public benefit of the regulation secures an 'average reciprocity of advantage' for everyone concerned,[152] a dimension of compensation can be said to be already inherent in the mechanism of regulation. The general distribution of the regulatory dividend – as evidenced, say, by an enhanced quality of life for all in the neighbourhood or by an increase in local land values or by the more effective preservation of the cultural heritage[153] – rather takes the edge off complaints of proprietary derogation.[154] Individual proprietary rights can be seen as having been

---

[148] See, for example, *Allan Jacobsson* v. *Sweden*, Series A No. 163, paras. 61, 136–137 (1989); *Fredin* v. *Sweden*, Series A No. 192, para. 54 (1991). In *O'Callaghan* v. *Commissioners of Public Works in Ireland and the Attorney General* [1985] ILRM 364 at 372, [1983] IRLM 391 at 396, 401, much significance was attached to the fact that the aggrieved landowner had been informed, prior to his purchase, of the fact that the land contained a listed national monument. See, similarly, *Loveladies Harbor, Inc* v. *United States*, 28 F3d 1171 at 1177 (Fed Cir 1994); *Alegria* v. *Keeney*, 687 A2d 1249 at 1253–1254 (RI 1997); *Brunelle* v. *Town of South Kingston*, 700 A2d 1075 at 1083 (RI 1997).

[149] Contrast the view recently adopted by the US Supreme Court that a claimant cannot be barred from compensation merely because he acquired title with knowledge of a pre-existing regulatory limitation on his rights (see *Palazzolo* v. *Rhode Island*, 121 S Ct 2448, 150 L Ed 2d 592 (2001)).

[150] *Sporrung and Lönnroth* v. *Sweden*, Series A No. 52, para. 70 (1982).

[151] *Hentrich* v. *France*, Series A No. 296-A, paras. 47–49 (1994). See also *An Blascaod Mór Teoranta* v. *Commissioners of Public Works in Ireland* (High Court, 27 February 1998), per Budd J; *Aston Cantlow and Wilmcote with Billesley PCC* v. *Wallbank* [2001] 3 All ER 393 at 405d–h.

[152] The root of this idea (classically demonstrated by zoning law) lies in the judgment delivered by Justice Holmes in *Pennsylvania Coal Co* v. *Mahon*, 260 US 393 at 415, 67 L Ed 322 at 326 (1922). See also *Re Ellis and Ruislip-Northwood UDC* [1920] 1 KB 343 at 362 per Bankes LJ, 370 per Scrutton LJ), *Agins* v. *City of Tiburon*, 447 US 255 at 262, 65 L Ed 2d 106 at 113 (1980) per Powell J; *Commonwealth of Australia* v. *State of Tasmania* (1983) 158 CLR 1 at 283 per Deane J; *Keystone Bituminous Coal Association* v. *DeBenedictis*, 480 US 470 at 491, 94 L Ed 2d 472 at 492 (1987) per Stevens J; *Lucas* v. *South Carolina Coastal Council*, 505 US 1003 at 1017–1018, 120 L Ed 2d 798 at 814 (1992) per Scalia J; *Kavanau* v. *Santa Monica Rent Control Board*, 941 P2d 851 at 865 (Cal 1997).

[153] See, for example, *Penn Central Transportation Co* v. *New York City*, 438 US 104 at 134–135, 57 L Ed 2d 631 at 655 (1978) per Brennan J.

[154] The affected landowner 'has in a sense been compensated by the public program "adjusting the benefits and burdens of economic life to promote the common good"' (see *Florida Rock Industries, Inc* v. *United States*, 18 F3d 1560 at 1570 (Fed Cir 1994), quoting *Penn Central Transportation Co* v. *New York City*, 438 US 104 at 124, 57 L Ed 2d 631 at 648 (1978)).

exchanged for improved civic rights to environmental welfare. This permutation of the law of general average helps to bridge the divergent emphases of European and common law approaches to the regulatory problem. To the extent that they can be said to promote the 'general interest' (and, thereby, indirectly the interests of the landowner himself), particular interferences with user rights more readily establish the proportionality of the provision in question.[155] Thus European tribunals have become increasingly insistent that landowners must be taken to be aware of, and implicated in, the 'general interest' which nowadays requires the regulation of land use for purposes of efficient town planning and of nature or heritage conservation.[156] Moreover, the 'margin of appreciation' principle, by focusing on the parameters of the democratic policy-making process, intensifies the sense that the individual citizen has already participated in the determination of collective environmental priorities.[157] The implicit assumption of much European caselaw is that, amidst the complex interdependencies of modern life, the landowner is obligated by a social duty to share the burdens of the 'general interest' from which he draws correlative benefits. The landowner's duty may not be absolute, but the crude principle of 'mutual benefit and burden' (with which property lawyers are indeed familiar[158]) goes some distance towards cutting back the scope of those takings which call for mandatory compensation from public funds.

(d) The net content of takings

The issue of proportionality is affected, at an even more fundamental level, by the precise impact which, in any given case, regulation has

---

[155] See, for example, *Wiesinger* v. *Austria* (1993) 16 EHRR 258 at 290 (para. 74), where the Human Rights Court rejected an art. 1 challenge to a land consolidation scheme, observing that it 'serves the interest of both the landowners concerned and the community as a whole by increasing the rentability of holdings and rationalising cultivation'.

[156] See, for example, *Fredin* v. *Sweden*, Series A No. 192, para. 48 (1991); *Pine Valley Developments Ltd* v. *Ireland*, Series A No. 222, para. 57 (1991); *Matos e Silva, LDA and others* v. *Portugal* (1997) 24 EHRR 573 at 601 (para. 88). In much the same way, US courts have held that 'legitimate state interests' are advanced by regulation directed towards providing protection from the 'ill effects of urbanization' (*Agins* v. *City of Tiburon*, 447 US 255 at 261, 65 L Ed 2d 106 at 112 (1980)) or towards enhancing the 'quality of life by preserving the character and desirable aesthetic features of a city' (*Penn Central Transportation Co* v. *New York City*, 438 US 104 at 129, 57 L Ed 2d 631 at 651 (1978)). See also, more recently, *Mayhew* v. *Town of Sunnyvale*, 964 SW2d 922 at 934–935 (Tex 1998).

[157] See, in particular, the approach adopted by the Human Rights Commission in *Banér* v. *Sweden* (1989) 60 DR 128 at 141–143. See (likewise in the context of art. 1 of Protocol No. 1) the importance recently attached by the English Court of Appeal to statutory impositions 'voted upon by a representative legislature familiar with contemporary social conditions' (*Aston Cantlow and Wilmcote with Billesley PCC* v. *Wallbank* [2001] 3 All ER 393 at 405g–h).

[158] Gray and Gray (*op. cit.* above fn. 6) pp. 1157–1159.

exerted upon the complement of rights claimed by the landowner.[159] It is in this context that, in its turn, European law may have something valuable to learn from the more highly analytical property tradition practised in the common law-based jurisdictions. Consideration of the impact of regulation requires some assessment of the degree to which the idea of 'property' comprises not merely notions of private right, but also elements of public duty. Of critical importance here is the exact scope of the community-directed obligations which define or delimit any landowner's 'bundle of rights'.[160] Uncompensated regulation of land use cannot be said to interfere with the 'peaceful enjoyment' of property if it brings about no actual *curtailment* of the landowner's existing user rights.[161] Thus, for example, regulatory interventions which simply reinforce or 'duplicate'[162] obligations already inherent in the landowner's title – which render merely more explicit a limitation on user rights which was already present[163] – do not operate any *taking* of property, let alone a *compensable* taking.[164] Where a regulatory imposition rules out some intrinsically illegitimate form of user, the rights of which the landowner may later claim to have been deprived were never, in truth, part of his

[159] It has often been said that a court 'cannot determine whether a regulation has gone "too far" unless it knows how far the regulation goes' (see *MacDonald, Sommer & Frates* v. *Yolo County*, 477 US 340 at 348, 91 L Ed 2d 285 at 294 (1986); *Lucas* v. *South Carolina Coastal Council*, 505 US 1003 at 1041, 120 L Ed 2d 798 at 829 (1992); *Mariner Real Estate Ltd* v. *Nova Scotia (Attorney General)* (1999) 177 DLR (4th) 696 at 718, 729).

[160] See *Gazza* v. *New York State Department of Environmental Conservation*, 679 NE2d 1035 at 1039 (NY 1997) ('the purchase of a "bundle of rights" necessarily includes the acquisition of a bundle of limitations').

[161] This approach is reflected pre-eminently in the stance adopted by the US Supreme Court that no compensation is payable 'if the logically antecedent inquiry into the nature of the owner's estate shows that the proscribed use interests were not part of his title to begin with' (*Lucas* v. *South Carolina Coastal Council*, 505 US 1003 at 1027, 120 L Ed 2d 798 at 820 (1992)). See also *Kim* v. *City of New York*, 659 NYS2d 145 at 147 (Ct App 1997).

[162] See *Lucas* v. *South Carolina Coastal Council*, 505 US 1003 at 1029, 120 L Ed 2d 798 at 821 (1992) *per* Scalia J.

[163] See *Kim* v. *City of New York*, 659 NYS2d 145 at 148 (Ct App 1997).

[164] There is an extensive body of American caselaw, reaching back into the nineteenth century, which denies that any compensable 'taking' can be effected by land regulations which merely suppress 'noxious' or anti-social users which are 'injurious to the community' or threaten 'public health, safety, or morals' (see *Mugler* v. *Kansas*, 123 US 623 at 665, 31 L Ed 205 at 211 (1887) *per* Harlan J; *Pennsylvania Coal Co* v. *Mahon*, 260 US 393 at 417, 67 L Ed 322 at 327 (1922) *per* Brandeis J). As Stevens J remarked in *Keystone Bituminous Coal Association* v. *DeBenedictis*, 480 US 470 at 492, 94 L Ed 2d 472 at 492–493 (1987), 'only in this way can the law give effect to the obligation expressed in the common law maxim *sic utere tuo ut non alienum laedas* [use your own property in such manner as not to injure that of another]' (see also *Munn* v. *People of Illinois*, 94 US 113, 24 L Ed 77 at 84 (1877)). For a willingness to apply similar logic in Australia, see *Trade Practices Commission* v. *Tooth & Co Ltd* (1979) 142 CLR 397 at 415 *per* Stephen J.

'bundle of rights' in the first place.[165] In such instances the regulatory control imposes no new burden; the public derives no new benefit; and there is neither need nor justification for compensation.

But to what extent does the landowner's 'bundle' consist not merely of *rights*, but also of *duties*? In the USA, for instance, the regulatory restriction of land use 'as one of the State's primary ways of preserving the public weal'[166] has long been 'treated as part of the burden of common citizenship'.[167] One of today's vital questions concerns the extent to which this 'burden of common citizenship' imports a positive obligation to promote environmental welfare.[168] In an era of increasing environmental awareness it has become much more feasible to contend that land ownership is a form of social stewardship,[169] that right and responsibility are inseparably fused,[170] and that concern for environmental integrity is, at common law, an inescapable component of real entitlement. Such perceptions gain support both from the widespread affirmation throughout Europe that property rights must ultimately promote the public interest[171] and from the insistence in European jurisprudence that 'in today's society the protection of the environment is an increasingly important consideration'.[172] But to the extent that the landowner is *already* obligated to subserve the common good by safeguarding valuable or vulnerable features of environmental amenity, regulatory controls directed towards the same end cannot be said to derogate, compensably

---

[165] See, for example, *Kim* v. *City of New York*, 659 NYS2d 145 at 147, 151 (Ct App 1997) ('plaintiffs' title never encompassed the property interest they claim has been taken'); *Gazza* v. *New York State Department of Environmental Conservation*, 679 NE2d 1035 at 1039–1040 (NY 1997); *Tahoe-Sierra Preservation Council, Inc* v. *Tahoe Regional Planning Agency*, 34 F Supp 2d 1226 at 1251 (1999).

[166] See *Keystone Bituminous Coal Association* v. *DeBenedictis*, 480 US 470 at 491, 94 L Ed 2d 472 at 492 (1987) *per* Stevens J.

[167] *Kimball Laundry Co* v. *United States*, 338 US 1 at 5, 93 L Ed 1765 at 1772 (1949) *per* Frankfurter J.

[168] It is worth bearing in mind that 'the distinction between "harm-preventing" and "benefit-conferring" regulation is often in the eye of the beholder' (*Lucas* v. *South Carolina Coastal Council*, 505 US 1003 at 1024–1025, 120 L Ed 2d 798 at 818 (1992) *per* Scalia J).

[169] See Lucy and Mitchell, 'Replacing private property: the case for stewardship' [1996] CLJ 566; McKenzie Skene, Rowan-Robinson, Paisley and Cusine, 'Stewardship: from rhetoric to reality', (1999) 3 Edin LR 151.

[170] See Gray, 'Equitable property' (1994) 47 (2) CLP 157 at 188–214.

[171] The archtypal provision is that enshrined in art. 14(2) of the German *Grundgesetz* ('Property imposes duties. Its use should also serve the welfare of the community'). Closer to home, art. 43.2.1°–2° of the Constitution of Ireland recognises that the exercise of property rights 'ought, in civil society, to be regulated by principles of social justice' and that, accordingly, the state may 'as occasion requires delimit by law the exercise of [such] rights with a view to reconciling their exercise with the exigencies of the common good'.

[172] *Fredin* v. *Sweden*, Series A No. 192, para. 48 (1991). See also *Guerra* v. *Italy* (1998) 26 EHRR 357 at 371 (para. 43) and, for a strong echo in England, *Miles* v. *Secretary of State for the Environment and the Royal Borough of Kingston upon Thames* [2000] JPL 192 at 199–202.

or otherwise, from the landowner's 'property'.[173] The community is already entitled – has always been entitled – to the benefit of a public-interest forbearance on the part of the estate owner.[174]

(e) The social limits of ownership

The definition of the social limits of ownership is, of course, controversial.[175] At stake are rival views of the political balance to be maintained between individual and community interests. In some important sense the issue highlights crucial questions about the implicit content of *citizenship*. The sixty-four thousand dollar question for the environmental lawyer of the future becomes a human rights dilemma which perhaps only the land lawyer can resolve. To what degree may the private citizen's terms of landholding be prescribed, altered or confirmed – without compensation – by the socially motivated intrusion of governmental control over land use?

This highly sensitive question is far from new. Even in the 1920s English courts, in working out the implications of early town planning legislation, were well aware of the way in which concepts of community-oriented duty could delimit the scope of compensable taking. The conflicting motivations and philosophical starting points were neatly exposed in *Re Ellis and Ruislip-Northwood UDC*,[176] where a claimant asserted a right to compensation on the ground that a local town planning scheme had prescribed a building line along a street frontage beyond which no further constructions could be erected. This prohibition deprived him of the lucrative opportunity to build a number of houses and shops on vacant land which he had purchased some time earlier. According to the Housing, Town Planning, &c, Act 1909 no compensation was payable for any injurious affection caused by town planning schemes which, 'with a view to securing the amenity of the area', prescribed the 'space about buildings' or limited the number or height or character of

---

[173] For a clear modern statement to this effect, see *Mariner Real Estate Ltd* v. *Nova Scotia (Attorney General)* (1999) 177 DLR (4th) 696 at 737 *per* Hallett JA. See also *Kim* v. *City of New York*, 659 NYS2d 145 at 152 (Ct App 1997), where a New York court denied compensation when a landowner was caused, at his own expense, to perform his common law obligation to provide lateral support for an adjacent highway. The court noted that this particular duty had been classically described as 'an obligation to the community' (see *Village of Haverstraw* v. *Eckerson*, 84 NE 578 at 580 (1908) *per* Gray J) and as a 'normal incident to the ownership of real property within the City of New York' (see *Laba* v. *Carey*, 277 NE2d 641 at 647 (1971)).

[174] Hence, as one American court has pointed out, 'the question is simply one of basic property ownership rights: within the bundle of rights which property lawyers understand to constitute property, is the right or interest at issue, as a matter of law, owned by the property owner or reserved to the state?' (*Loveladies Harbor, Inc* v. *United States*, 28 F3d 1171 at 1179 (Fed Cir 1994)).

[175] See Gray, [1991] CLJ 252.

[176] [1920] 1 KB 343.

buildings.[177] Two members of the Court of Appeal were nevertheless determined that the claimant should receive compensation from public funds for the reversal of his fortunes as a property developer. Pleading in aid the presumption that a person should not be 'deprived either of his property or of any portion of the value of his property without compensation',[178] Bankes LJ led the majority in the court to the improbable conclusion that a 'building line', as such, did not fall within the scope of the embargo on compensation. Eve J concurred and, as judges of the era so often did in relation to newfangled legislation of dubiously socialist origin, made disobliging remarks about the linguistic demerits of the legislation in hand.[179] However, in a typically robust dissent Scrutton LJ dismissed the compensation claim (together with the contrived arguments of his colleagues), observing that 'Parliament may have taken a view that a landowner in a community has duties as well as rights, and cannot claim compensation for refraining from using his land where they think that it is his duty so to refrain'.[180]

A similar concern with the delimiting effects of community-oriented perceptions of land ownership is even more readily apparent in *O'Callaghan* v. *Commissioners of Public Works in Ireland and the Attorney General*.[181] Here, in the Irish Supreme Court, O'Higgins CJ indicated that 'the common good requires that national monuments which are the prized relics of the past should be preserved as part of the history of our people'.[182] This being so, the preservation of the Neolithic fort in dispute in *O'Callaghan*'s case was 'a requirement of what should be regarded as the common duty of all citizens',[183] with the consequence that no compensation was required in respect of the restrictions imposed on the relevant landowner. Social assumptions relating to the ambit of civic responsibility thus exert a constant impact upon the definition of 'property' in land. Views will inevitably differ, however, as to the intensity of the individual citizen's obligation to contribute gratis towards the environmental welfare enjoyed by the wider community. Some may think, for example, that the uncompensated contribution to the cultural

---

[177] See Housing, Town Planning, &c, Act 1909, s. 59(2).

[178] [1920] 1 KB 343 at 361.

[179] [1920] 1 KB 343 at 372 (a 'novelty in Parliamentary nomenclature'). For evidence of similar judicial vituperation heaped on the early Rent Acts, see, for example, Megarry, *The Rent Acts* (11th ed., 1988, Stevens), Vol. 1, pp. xix–xx, 14–15.

[180] [1920] 1 KB 343 at 372. Bankes LJ had conceded that 'possibly . . . a man ought not to be allowed compensation for doing in reference to his property what, apart from compensation, he ought to do voluntarily', but thought that the claimant's position 'cannot, however, be determined by considerations such as these' ([1920] 1 KB 343 at 362).

[181] [1985] ILRM 364, [1983] IRLM 391 (see text accompanying fns. 75–76, 114–116 above).

[182] [1985] ILRM 364 at 367. On the Irish theme of preservation of heritage for the common good, see also *Webb* v. *Ireland* [1988] IR 353 at 383 *per* Finlay CJ, 390–391 per Walsh J.

[183] [1985] ILRM 364 at 368.

heritage which was forced upon the claimant in *O'Callaghan's* case went far beyond the call of duty.[184]

The contrast between restrictive and expansive interpretations of the social responsibility underlying land ownership is aptly illustrated by two relatively recent North American decisions, both of which involved the regulation of ecologically vulnerable tracts of recreational beachfront land. In *Lucas* v. *South Carolina Coastal Council*[185] the courts of the USA signalled that, as a matter of inherent obligation, owners of environmentally sensitive areas bear only an extremely attenuated duty to protect the integrity or amenity of their land.[186] The US Supreme Court ruled, by a majority, that the potential for profitable (albeit damaging) development of such areas was intrinsically limited merely by 'background principles' of property and nuisance. On this basis compensation for regulatory control could be denied to the landowner *only if* the control in question merely made explicit some restriction which 'inhere[s] in the title itself', with the result that the 'proscribed use interests' were therefore 'not part of [the owner's] title to begin with'. Beyond these parameters any regulatory legislation which wholly prohibited economically productive or beneficial land use automatically gave rise to a claim for public compensation.[187] The Supreme Court of South Carolina, to which the US Supreme Court remitted the matter in *Lucas*, subsequently confirmed that there was no common law basis in either property or nuisance on which the *Lucas* claimant's proposed development could be inhibited.[188] The outcome in *Lucas* thus reflects little sense that community-directed obligations – as, for example, in the form of an implicit duty to avoid ecological degradation or even to enhance environmental amenity – may tacitly comprise a pre-existing and constant qualification on a land-

---

[184] See, for instance, the strong dissent entered by Rehnquist J in *Penn Central Transportation Co* v. *New York City*, 438 US 104 at 140, 57 L Ed 2d 631 at 658 (1978), where a majority in the US Supreme Court found that no compensable taking had been effected by the landmark preservation of New York's Grand Central Terminal.

[185] 505 US 1003, 120 L Ed 2d 798 (1992) (see text accompanying fns. 123–128 above).

[186] See Gray and Gray, 'The idea of property in land', in Bright and Dewar, *Land Law: Themes and Perspectives* (1998, Oxford), pp. 49–51. David L. Callies has pointed to Justice Scalia's disparaging observation during argument in *Lucas* that 'I don't think wetlands regulation is something I would call one of the high concerns of public safety' (see *Preserving Paradise: Why Regulation Won't Work* (1994, University of Hawaii Press), p. 81). The reference to 'public safety' is, of course, an evocation of the revered language of Justice Brandeis in the seminal case of *Pennsylvania Coal Co* v. *Mahon*, 260 US 393 at 417, 67 L Ed 322 at 327 (1922).

[187] '[A] State, by ipse dixit, may not transform private property into public property without compensation' (505 US 1003 at 1031, 120 L Ed 2d 798 at 823).

[188] See *Lucas* v. *South Carolina Coastal Council*, 424 SE2d 484 at 486 (1992).

owner's title.[189] Significantly, the Supreme Court majority indicated that compensation could not be withheld simply on the basis that a landowner's proposed exploitation of his land was 'inconsistent with the public interest' or would 'violate a common-law maxim such as sic utere tuo ut non alienum laedas'.[190]

In *Mariner Real Estate Ltd* v. *Nova Scotia (Attorney General)*,[191] by contrast, the Court of Appeal of Nova Scotia rejected virtually identical claims for compensation even though the relevant beachfront regulation, by restricting construction on a fragile dune system, had deprived the claimants of 'virtually all economic value' in their land. Hallett JA indicated that the compensability of the regulatory intervention turned, in part, on the 'reasonableness of the development proposed for the land'. In the *Mariner Real Estate* case a government-commissioned environmental study had suggested that the claimants' proposed residential development would not be 'reasonable for the dune area', with the result (in the view of the Court of Appeal) that the province's regulatory legislation could not, in truth, be described as preventing the claimants from exercising any 'reasonable private rights of ownership' of the lots in question.[192] Absent the extinction of any 'reasonable' entitlement, the case disclosed no *de facto* expropriation which was remotely eligible for compensation. As Hallett JA pointed out, the matter was ultimately measured in terms of correlative rights and duties: there was a need for the landowners and the Province of Nova Scotia to 'recognise the rights of each other and seek a just solution that would be fair and reasonable to both'.

---

[189] See, for example, *State of Ohio, ex rel RTG Inc* v. *State of Ohio*, 753 NE2d 869 (Ohio Court of Appeals, 2001), where public compensation was successfully claimed by a mining company whose operations within a 2,000 foot radius of a well threatened to damage the aquifer which was the sole source of water for the village of Pleasant City, Ohio. In applying *Lucas*, the Court of Appeal held that the mining company had 'acted in all regards in a reasonable manner' and that the relevant regulatory restriction had imposed a restraint which was not already inherent in the company's title to the coal rights. Such outcomes demonstrate that, in the United States, the common law (as distinct from statutory or regulatory) obligations of landowners are still not far removed from the guiding spirit of *Bradford Corpn* v. *Pickles* [1895] AC 587 (see text accompanying fns. 4–5 above).

[190] 505 US 1003 at 1031, 120 L Ed 2d 798 at 822–823. See *Tahoe-Sierra Preservation Council, Inc* v. *Tahoe Regional Planning Agency*, 34 F Supp 2d 1226 at 1253–1254 (1999), where a US District Court held that inherent nuisance-based limitations on landowners did not extend to the avoidance of developments which threatened the eutrophication of Lake Tahoe and the destruction of its fish.

[191] (1999) 177 DLR (4th) 696.

[192] (1999) 177 DLR (4th) 696 at 737.

Conclusion

The seemingly improbable has occurred: an essay in a book on land law becomes simultaneously an essay on human rights and civic duties. In large part it is, of course, the imperative of environmental conservation that has caused this coalescence of discourse in respect of human and proprietary entitlements. Modern environmental debate confers a wholly unexpected prominence upon the more esoteric corners of property theory; and the inner meaning of property in land turns out to be critically dependent on the communally defined parameters of citizenship. Realty and humanity are thus closely allied in a joint battle for survival, with the consequence that proprietary rights and proprietary duties are ultimately also social rights and social duties.

The allocation of the economic cost of environmental welfare was always bound to be problematical. This chapter has attempted to illustrate some of the variables relevant to the question whether individual landowners should receive compensation for the performance of their role in furthering public environmental objectives. On such a question views will inevitably differ. Disputation in this area cuts sharply into the ideology of property, into personal perceptions of wealth, autonomy and civic responsibility. In the USA, for example, historic notions of citizenship seem to have crystallised into a deep collective distrust of all governmental regulatory activity, thereby prompting an increased insistence upon the compensation requirement of the Fifth Amendment. Decisions such as the Supreme Court's ruling in *Lucas* patently symbolise a strong judicial inclination to stem a tide of uncompensated takings from American citizens under the cover of a mere exercise of regulatory power. Yet, even in the USA, there is no unanimity of view. In an extremely powerful dissent in the Supreme Court's most recent contribution to the takings debate, Justice Stevens has pointed to the way in which the *Lucas* approach raises 'the spectre of a tremendous – and tremendously capricious – one-time transfer of wealth from society at large to those individuals who happen to hold title to large tracts of land' in environmentally sensitive locations.[193]

In the European and Canadian contexts, by contrast, notions of citizenship have tended to generate a deeper sense of individual complicity with government in the business of sensible environmental regulation. As evidenced in European human rights jurisprudence, the emerging common law of Europe seems more socially oriented – more receptive to the recognition of uncompensated community-directed restraints on property in land. A complex of historical reasons doubtless underlies the more intense perception of civic cohesion – the socialised

---

[193] *Palazzolo* v. *Rhode Island*, 121 S Ct 2448, 150 L Ed 2d 592 at 624–625 (2001).

sense of duty – which infuses so much of the caselaw on art. 1 of Protocol No. 1 of the European Convention. But even here, as we have seen, the traffic is not all one-way and there are signs of an increasing sensitivity to the argument that the regulatory activity of government may nowadays call more pressingly for compensation to be paid to affected landowners. What *is* certain is that all modern jurisdictions are actively and inevitably engaged in defining (and redefining) the social boundaries of the institution of property. The overall goal is the formulation of a new 'land ethic', replicating in perhaps more contemporary terms Aldo Leopold's noble vision of the propriety of property.[194] And, in exploring in this chapter the social ethics of land ownership, we too have been reaching out towards the elaboration of a new civic morality in the field of property relationships.[195]

Further reading

Allen, *The Right to Property in Commonwealth Constitutions* (2000, Cambridge University Press), pp. 36–82.
Anderson, 'Compensation for interference with property', [1999] EHRLR 543.
Epstein, *Takings: Private Property and the Power of Eminent Domain* (1985, Harvard University Press).
Freyfogle, 'Context and accommodation in modern property law', (1988–1989) 41 Stan LR 1529.
Gray, 'Equitable property', (1994) 47(2) CLP 157.
Gray and Gray, 'The idea of property in land' in Bright and Dewar, *Land Law: Themes and Perspectives* (1998, Oxford University Press), p. 15.
Howell, 'Land and human rights' [1999] Conv. 287.
Howell, 'The Human Rights Act 1998: the "horizontal effect" on land law' in Cooke, *Modern Studies in Property Law (Vol. 1): Property 2000* (2001, Hart Publishing), p. 149.
Lucy and Mitchell, 'Replacing private property: the case for stewardship' [1996] CLJ 566.
McKenzie Skene, Rowan-Robinson, Paisley and Cusine, 'Stewardship: from rhetoric to reality' (1999) 3 Edin LR 151.
Michelman, 'Property, utility and fairness: comments on the ethical foundations of "just compensation" law', (1966–1967) 80 Harv LR 1165.

---

[194] See 'The land ethic', in Leopold, *A Sand County Almanac* (1987, New York and Oxford (first published 1949)).
[195] See Gray and Gray [1999] EHRLR 46 at 102.

Index